For Marilyn Lynch
with best wishes,

[signature]

5/91

THE FIRST
UNIVERSAL NATION

Also by Ben J. Wattenberg

THE FIRST
UNIVERSAL NATION

*Leading Indicators and Ideas
about the Surge of America
in the 1990s*

Ben J. Wattenberg

THE FREE PRESS
A Division of Macmillan, Inc.
NEW YORK

Collier Macmillan Canada
TORONTO

Maxwell Macmillan International
NEW YORK   OXFORD   SINGAPORE   SYDNEY

The Free Press
A Division of Macmillan, Inc.
866 Third Avenue, New York, N. Y. 10022

Collier Macmillan Canada, Inc.
1200 Eglinton Avenue East
Suite 200
Don Mills, Ontario M3C 3N1

Printed in the United States of America

printing number

2   3   4   5   6   7   8   9   10

Library of Congress Cataloging-in-Publication Data

Wattenberg, Ben J.
    The first universal nation: leading indicators and ideas about
the surge of America in the 1990s / Ben J. Wattenberg.
        p.   cm.
    ISBN 0-02-934001-2
    1. United States—Population.   2. Population forecasting—United
States.   3. United States—Economic conditions—1945-   4. Economic
forecasting—United States.   I. Title
    HB3505.W28   1991
304.6'0973—dc20   90-3803
                                                                CIP

To my father and my late mother
Judah and Rachel Wattenberg
who immigrated to America in the early 1920s
and to the nation which received them

Contents

Introduction:
Origins and Architecture

In the 1960s, the 1970s, and the 1980s, I wrote books that came to be known, at least to me, as "census books," or "decade books."

The first one, *This U.S.A.* (in collaboration with Richard M. Scammon) was indeed a book that dealt with social demographic data and the decennial census process.

Now, it takes time for decennial census data to be processed and published, and it takes time to write a book. As the years go on, much of the data get somewhat stale; fresher data—often from Census Bureau sample reports,—become available. So, *This U.S.A.*, published in 1965, included much material that had come out after the 1960 census was taken.

My 1974 census book, *The Real America*, expanded the franchise. I had become involved in national politics (as a speech-writer for President Johnson), and I had coauthored (with Scammon) *The Real Majority*, a book about politics and public opinion. A broader man, I tried in the *The Real America* to marry the hard data of the census with softer data about attitudes and politics.

The eighties book was entitled *The Good News Is the Bad News Is Wrong*, which doesn't even sound much like a census book. I had become affiliated with the American Enterprise Institute. Again my horizons had broadened. The *Good News* book had a lot in it about economics and "the quality of life," about how media shape the reality of our time, and about American foreign policy

In the early eighties, my professional life changed. I began writing a weekly syndicated newspaper column. I thought it would be easy. It is not. It means coming up with 52 ideas each year. I take it seriously. I try to write about topics that are related to the news, in a way that also has staying power in a general sense.

The columns are about everything I have dealt with in my books, plus some other areas I have become interested in, like global demographics (I did a book in 1987 entitled *The Birth Dearth*), the spread of American entertainment, and the relationship of everything to American commerce.

Toward the end of the eighties I was approached by Erwin Glikes, publisher of The Free Press, to do a collection of columns. Sounds great, I said to myself. Why not? The work is already done; pick the best ones and slap a cover on it.

That's not what happened. Not even close. As I look back upon it now, I obviously wanted to write another in the "census book" series, although those books had long since gone way beyond social demographics.

After all, I began to realize, the 1990 census would soon be coming out. With the current advanced state of data-gathering in the field of sample surveys, there was no reason to wait years for data that was essentially already available. The key points that the 1990 census will reveal were already well known on the day the census was taken (April 1, 1990), which was while I was still writing.

I wanted to do a book that explained what I thought about America and the world as we entered the 1990s, what I thought was coming at us, and what I thought we ought to do. Pieces of it were already written, in some of the columns. As I reviewed the columns, I came to realize that I had been forming a central, if skeletal, theme about what was going on. As the world shook, first sort of slowly in the mid- to later 1980s and then with a rush in the miracle year of 1989, flesh went onto the skeleton. More went on as the turbulence of 1990 unfolded, from Lithuania, to Iraq, to what was always called a "looming" recession. Hardly thinking about it, I was writing many new columns with that theme, and this book, in mind.

Fortuitously, in 1989 I signed on to write a series of monthly articles for the "Tomorrow" section of *U.S. News and World Report*. Many of those pieces fit into the general theme and are so designated here.

As authors do, I got excited by the idea. How could I put all these forming pieces into a coherent work, one of my decennial book series, but substantively broader and designed to take advantage of my new and peculiar circumstance as a columnist at a time of remarkable change?

Glikes and I talked again. I set down the theme in whole (see Chapter One). I wrote 60 interstitial mini-essays, some not so mini-, with many new thoughts that hadn't, or wouldn't, fit into the column format. I realized that readers might have some difficulty understanding what I was about unless they knew a bit about me, what I had done, and who I had worked with. So there is some memoir here.

Then, I remembered what I have always believed; that we can't get a good fix on what we're up to without statistics for guidance. The pages of fresh indicators here are selected to tell some stories, I hope painlessly. All told, there are more than 100 data sets. Many have cells more current than the 1990 census.

In all, the great majority of the material here was written either directly for this volume, or with it clearly in mind.

What you see before you is an unusual book. It is an irregular piece of goods—theme, memoir, data, reportage, futurism, analysis, policy. That's a lot, but after all, you will find out in these pages that I am a paleoliberal, a supply-side infrastructuralist, a neomanifest destinarian, a numbers nut, a pro-natalist redistributionist capitalist, and still a hawk. Perhaps it takes many formats to deal with that.

Some of this book is about the American future. Alas, there has been some monumentally foolish stuff written under the flag of futurism.

There have been those straight-line extrapolatory projections—so uncannily accurate that they explain why we ran out of oil in the 1980s.

There is a futurism keyed to "new machines." Surely you've noticed all those Americans who commute to work these days with their strap-on helicopters.

There are those who will tell you to keep your eye on certain people, the influentials, who will shape our time. That's why you knew in 1979 that an anti-communist former Hollywood movie actor and a young Soviet agricultural bureaucrat would be the leading players of the eighties, and end up linking arms in Red Square. That's also why you knew in mid-1988 that in 1991 you may witness a Quayle-Yeltsin summit.

Some prognosticators will even tell you about events to come, but of course we didn't know about AIDS, perestroika, or Eastern Europe before they were upon us.

It's not only machines, people, resources, and events that we don't know much about. We may not even sense many of the trends that must already be operating.

Consider: In the late fifties, no one predicted the sixties, that is, the sort of near-radical social and cultural changes that were to come.

In the late sixties, there was no common view that the seventies would yield the economic turbulence that would travel under the disagreeable banner of "stagflation."

In the late seventies, did anyone say that some of the most important ideas of the eighties, debated by intellectuals around the world, would be called "Reaganomics," "Reaganism," and the "Reagan Doctrine?"

But I suggest here that we do at least know *something* about the short- to intermediate-term future, say, the next decade. What we do know, or what we can know in part, is best understood by the word *terrain*. That knowable terrain, I sense, is composed of at least three interrelated parts.

First, we should be aware that *some things we've been told are wrong.* (For example, despite the hoopla to the contrary, the high school dropout rate is at an all-time low.) Accordingly, we should quickly subtract from our sense of the future all those conditions, trends, and developments that have not happened but that we have been *told* have happened. Let us scrub our brains and start afresh.

Second, we need to know *those trends, conditions, and developments that have already happened and are quite likely to stay in place.* (There are more than two million black college graduates, 1600 percent more than in 1950. The black middle class is not likely to go away, no matter how much we dwell on black poverty and family decomposition.)

Third, we must consider those conditions *that are not yet in place but that are likely to be in place shortly.* Without getting into simplistic straight-line projections, there are things headed at us that are nearly inexorable. (A unified Germany will be the largest, richest country in Europe and will almost surely be losing population the most rapidly.)

"Not happened," "already happened," "likely to happen"—through these prisms we can usefully look at the terrain of the 1990s. Insofar as there is a methodological base to this book, that's it. We should have a sense of the lay of the land, of the terrain upon which the unknowable events, trends, machines, and personalities will act. We can expect the unexpected, but when it comes, we ought to know the territory.

Understanding some of the terrain of the nineties can make the transition easier for those in the public policy community and those in commerce, to name just two groups with interests in trying to understand the dim topography of the decade to come. In any event, terrain-watching is an interesting speculation for all who just like to think about the nature of our circumstance.

Knowing all that, we can—ho, ho, ho—easily agree on what we ought to do. The only problems that will remain are personal.

August 1990
Washington, D.C.

The Case Is Made, in Context

1

Thesis: America at the Beginning of the Middle

There is every indication that the world as known is coming apart and reassembling itself in a new way.

The process, and the sometimes addled perception of the process, did not begin with the sensational season of 1989.

By the mid-1980s, the Japanese were emerging as a monumental new financial superpower. They did everything right and they would shape the new world—at least that's what many American businessmen were saying as they gathered at their skull sessions in hostelries across the Sunbelt.

Then, as the plans and procedures for the European Common Market of 1992 became clear, that too was heralded as the dawn of a new time. Wow! A single trading bloc compromising about a third of a billion prosperous consumers!

And what about those "four tigers" of the Pacific Rim—South Korea, Taiwan, Singapore, and Hong Kong? Their economies kept on booming. Mightn't they be the model of the future?

Indeed, these were all powerful changes, and going on at so many spots on the planet. The new world, we were told, would be "multipolar," not "bipolar."

What about the United States? Tsk tsk. America, it was said, was in decline. The 1990s would show that America was not competitive. (After all, what could you expect? Our children were ill-educated clucks.) The

7

end of the twentieth century would be the end of the American Century. The United States of America, victim of "imperial over-stretch," would no longer be "Number One," whatever that meant.

For the record, I believed then that the claim that America was in decline was mostly bunk. For reasons that will be explained, I thought that America, even with its problems, would be getting more influential as the decades rolled on, and as the world changed.

In any event, it was against that background that the whirling events of 1989 and 1990 spun out.

The communist regimes of Eastern Europe were overthrown. The walls came down. New governments, democratic ones, were formed. A kind of personal liberty emerged in the Soviet Union, even as the Soviet economy teetered on the edge of collapse, even as the glue that held together the actual union of Soviet republics became thinner and thinner.

There was related serious talk not only of "EC '92" but of a "Grand Europe," stretching from the United Kingdom to (at least) the edge of the USSR (wherever that might turn out to be.) A half a billion people! Perhaps in political union!

In Japan, something else happened: the allegedly invulnerable economy shuddered; stock prices tumbled, the yen declined.

And perhaps most important, rather suddenly, the values of political democracy and/or market economics, ideas which had been gaining force throughout the 1980s, erupted in just about every available corner of the world, including Nicaragua, Haiti, Albania, Mongolia, and South Africa.

And relentlessly, beneath that whirlwind, perhaps indeed driving it, a communications grid was being put in place across the face of the earth, and in the skies above it. (In 1980, there were about zero consumer video cassette recorders in the world. In 1990, there were 250 million. By the year 2000, how many? Who knows? A half a billion? A billion?)

What will happen in and to the United States as, and after, this reconfiguration takes place?

Economist Walter Mead of the University of California at Santa Barbara says that a united Germany "could push the United States out of Europe, and into inglorious isolation in the western hemisphere." Yale professor Paul Kennedy says he was right all along, America must now manage its relative decline gracefully.

Europeans have joined in. Jacques Attali, the new head of the European Bank for Reconstruction and Development writes that "America has become Japan's granary, like Poland was for Flanders in the seventeenth century." (Flanders? Poland? The *what* century?) An article in *The Washington Post* says "European leaders such as former French Prime Minister Jacques Chirac and German Chancellor Helmut Kohl now speak openly about a future dominated totally by Europe and the Asian Pacific Countries."

All that, I believe, is wrong. America is not in decline. Not only that, in my judgment we are not even going to just remain Number One, as we have been in so many ways since the end of World War II.

I think the remarkable things that have been happening around the world, politically to be sure, but also economically, militarily, demographically, and culturally—particularly culturally—have been extremely positive for America.

For five hundred years, America has been the biggest story in the world, page one above the fold. That story isn't over; my sense is that we're just getting to the best part. I believe that despite some formidable problems (crime and drugs certainly qualify; so might quotas), we will be better off at home during the nineties, and more influential around the world.

The United States of America, in more ways than one, is becoming the first universal nation. We are universalizing at home; Americans now come from everywhere. And the American way of life—for good and for ill, although mostly for good—is the pervasive, persuasive, universal model for activity all over the world. Isn't that what the number one nation is supposed to be about?

I think that the United States is becoming the most influential nation in history. There were no television sets and no VCRs to purvey Athenian or Roman or Victorian values into every village in the world.

(In the spring of 1990 West Germans debated about the specifics of new military arrangements in Europe. The Green party, as might be imagined, had a forthright view of matters. American troops, they announced, should leave Germany. Who needs them now? But, the Greens added, that demand for Ami withdrawal does not include the personnel assigned to the American Forces Network (AFN) based in Frankfurt. Oh, no. AFN is a radio service for American servicemen overseas, broadcast in English, with heavy doses of rock music. But, said the Greens, so many Germans had listened to AFN for so long, that it had become a part of "the German cultural heritage." Those particular Americans should please stick around. What a strange incident. Hadn't they heard that America was in decline?)

(In Indonesia, a few months earlier, an American social scientist, burly and wholly bald, visited a remote village. He felt quite proud of himself for seeking out sociology in the raw, in its most primitive environs. He walked down the street. Soon, a band of children began following him, Pied Piper fashion. They were chanting "Kojak, Kojak!" Hadn't those kids heard America was in decline?)

In the late Spring of 1990, there was an Elvis look-alike contest in Moscow.

America has many problems. One of them concerns nomenclature.

The word "super power" is no good anymore. It came about when there were two, and there aren't two now. We need a word with no plural connotations and one that describes a nation one notch up from a super-power. I wrote a column announcing a contest to come up with the elusive word. Among the best answers that surfaced were: hyper-power, magna-power, maxi-power, mega-power, multi-power, omni-power, semper power, solo power, supra-power, ultra-power and uni-power. (What word won? Why? You will find out at the end of this chapter.)

Such, at least, is the general theme here. The whole thing is breaking loose. What you see on the back of the American dollar bill is what we're getting, "Novus ordo seclorum," that is, "a new order of the ages." It's American.

To make such a case, several things should be demonstrable: that America is doing better at home, that America is doing better around the world, that America is doing well compared to potential competitors.

Let's look at the terrain. Following the schematic laid down earlier, let's look at what's not happened, at what has happened, and at what's likely to happen. Through such lenses, how do we stand?

Here are some general thoughts. *Elaborations, elucidations, examples, tangential bites and back-up data are to be found in the chapters that follow.*

Let us look at America first. What about this first universal nation idea? It's happening before our eyes.

In the fifty years prior to 1965, about 11 million immigrants, legal and illegal, came to the United States. About 75 percent of those were of white European ancestry.

But in the quarter-century since 1965 about 14 million immigrants have come to the U.S.—27 percent more in half the time. And about 85 percent of these are *not* of white European ancestry. Americans, for the first time, can be accurately said to come from "everywhere."

So, the process that earlier brought us Einstein, DiMaggio, Colin Powell (mother from Jamaica), Cuomo, Salk, Bob Hope, Fauci, Brzezinski, and many Kennedys has now been reinvigorated. Among the recent new Americans are Drs. Charles Y. C. Pak and Fu-kuen Lin, researchers who have made headway toward cures or treatments for osteoporosis and anemia.

Higher intermarriage rates among most American ethnic, religious and racial groups (including Asians and Hispanics but not blacks) are creating what English poet John Masefield said about Americans, that they are "a wondrous race."

This new universalizing of America, while not without its problems, should be very good for us. It can help tilt the balance of global commercial power in our favor. It can also tilt the related balance of geopolitical, technological, and demographic power in our favor. It can accelerate a process already very much in motion—the Americanization of world culture. That may turn out to be the most important aspect of it.

A part of all this has to do with raw numbers. Numbers still count; not for everything, but for plenty. In the decades to come, all of our major competitors—in Japan and Europe—will have domestic populations, markets, and labor forces which will be either non-growing or actually diminishing, and aging rapidly. That will happen, almost inexorably, mostly because of earlier very low birth and fertility rates, rates that are still running about 25 percent below what is required to merely "replace" a population. Even if birth rates were to go up in those nations (and there is no serious sign yet that they are going up) it would take a long, long time to produce new adults in the labor force. A generation.

Immigration is the only way out of such intermediate-term demographic stasis. But it is culturally and politically very diffucult for the European countries or Japan to take in more immigrants. They are not pluralist nations.

We are. Because we deal with immigration, and because it now seems likely that we will deal with it more wisely in the years to come, we can grow, and we will.

And, suddenly, it's not just immigration that is a positive demographic indicator for the United States. Fertility has gone up, not enormously, but not trivially either. America is still at a "below replacement" fertility rate, but only barely.

Accordingly, relative to our major competitors, we will be more influential, not less.

This disparity of growth-for-us and no-growth-for-them will yield further capital inflows to the one place in the world that meets all the criteria for an investor's dream: a large, stable, democratic, capitalist, growing market. That's us, and only us. A recent paper by demographer-economist Jean-Claude Chenais, head of the demography and sociology department at the Institut National d'Études Demographiques in Paris, notes that ". . . the investment rate depends directly, in the long term, on the population growth rate. Keynes and Kuznets clearly demonstrated this in their day; since then it has been demonstrated statistically by various econometric tests."

As discussed in greater detail later, we can help shape our own destiny, wisely, by increasing legal immigration. We should also change some of the criteria by which we accept immigrants—moving toward a somewhat more skill-oriented system rather than the largely nepotistic one we have now. Another immigration change should deal with an odd situation: it is now typically much more difficult for an immigrant to come to the United States from European nations than from Hispanic or Asian nations. We need a level playing field. This can be accomplished without cutting back existing immigration streams.

The Congress should act. Over the history of this republic, what the Congress has legislated about immigration has been among the most important things it has done. You can depend on this: when the history books come to be written, if this (1989–90) Congress, or the next one, acts seriously and generously about immigration, that will end up as far more important than whatever it does about the deficit, clean air, or the defence budget, probably more important than the three of them put together. Nations are only people.

When *The Birth Dearth* was published in 1987, the American fertility rate had been mired well below replacement level for seventeen consecutive years. And all the informed discussion was about how the Congress would cut back immigration, at best capping it where it was then. Now, fertility is up and it looks as if legal immigration will be legislated upward.

What a difference! Under the earlier conditions, according to the "most likely" (current levels extended) Census Bureau projections, America would have had a population of 301 million by the year 2030. And the country would be approaching demographic decline.

But projections based on the new level of fertility and the likely new level of legal immigration show that the swing by the year 2030 would run to about an additional 45 million people. (And America would still be growing moderately.)

It is said by some that earlier immigration was good for America but that now the situation is different. My word-processing program has a neat key labelled "Reveal Codes." Press that key on that thought and the code revealed is that too many Hispanics are coming in and they are not pulling their fair share of the sled.

That is plain wrong. Hispanics born in the United States or who have been here ten or more years have already reached all-U.S. levels in occupation, education, income, and *language proficiency*.

Talk to manufacurers on the West Coast and in Texas and one hears the same story over and over again: Hispanics are upwardly mobile, motivated, responsible workers, with a strong sense of traditional family values. The CEO of a Southern California aerospace company tells of corporate family picnics where Mexican-American workers bring their children over to new aircraft and proudly say, "Your daddy built that plane!"

The statistical portrait of Hispanics today is probably not much different relatively from that of Italians or Poles in the early part of this century.

One of the reasons offered for tough times for America in the nineties is that our new young entrants into the labor force will be dopes.

I do not propose to offer a vigorous defense of the American educational establishment. It does not deserve it. But that is not the same thing as saying our young people won't be able to compete with those hard-driving nerds from Japan, Germany, and England.

The high school dropout rate in America is at an all-time low. Yes it is. Data presented later shows that clearly. Illiteracy is also at an all-time low. College enrollment, which was scheduled to go down for demographic reasons, has gone up. Corporations spend an estimated $40 billion a year to educate their workers. Our educational statistics don't even bother to count what goes on in our 8,000 proprietary trade and professional schools. American young people understand that we have many diverse entry points to education in this country, and they use them.

The business end of a modern educational system is at the university level. That's where the engineers, doctors, biologists, chemists, and managers come from. A recent study by scholars in Asia ranked the top twelve universities in the world. Eight of the twelve were American. It is estimated that if the calculation were to be made for the top fifty universities, two-thirds to three-quarters would also be in America.

There is even a sort of proof of that. Students, like other humans, vote with their feet. More than 360,000 foreign students are in American universities, many of them in science and graduate business programs. Only about 60,000 Americans are studying in foreign schools, and many of them are there in an undergraduate "year abroad" program, mostly to learn a language and how to read a menu.

Anyway, how come dumb Americans keep coming up with all those inventions and innovations that the Japanese allegedly steal? Why are American scientists winning a greater percentage of Nobel prizes in science and medicine than ever before? (In the 1980s, the American share was 62 percent!) What about our teen-age computer-hacker whiz kids? Are they all going to jail for virus implantation?

Trashing our kids—is kiddism. Another aspect of kiddism concerns who the kids are, the circumstance of their birth, and their sex. It's bad, we are told: More than 85 percent of the new entrants to the labor force will be female or minority, so very many are growing up in poverty, and way too many are the products of teenage out-of-wedlock unions.

Wrong. Why are women on that list? Talk about sexism. Does anyone in this day and age not know that women are productive workers? Women are doing well, very well, in the labor force. They are moving into better jobs, to better levels of employment, and with higher pay ratios relative to men—with a speed that must surprise even the most vigorous feminists (when they are not publicly complaining in order to keep the heat on). Why do we think the next generation of working women will be less proficient than this one?

The black community is clearly a troubled one. But blacks, too, have made enormous headway. The blacks involved in the Labor Day altercation at Virginia Beach in 1989 were primarily college students. By one count there were an estimated 100,000 involved in that one situation, almost as many as the total number of black college students in 1950. There has been a geometric progression in the total number of black college graduates in America. There were about 125,000 in 1950, double that in 1960, double that in 1970, double that in 1980, double that in 1990, to a total of more than two million.

The proportion of out-of-wedlock births is much higher in the black community than in the white, about 60 percent versus about 15 percent. But, for what consolation it may be worth, the black rate has been stable recently while the white rate has been soaring. (The illegitimacy rate is also very high in some Western European nations; the Swedish rate is almost as high as the American black rate.) Moreover, out-of-wedlock birth, while no piece of cake, indeed frequently a tragedy, is often quite different from its image: two-thirds of out-of-wedlock births are not to teen-agers, a quarter take place among unmarried couples who are living together in a stable union, half of the mothers end up married within 5 years and 70 percent within 15 years.

With all that, poor and near-poor kids are our number one domestic problem. And it's crazy. In the richest nation in the world, almost a fifth of the children live beneath the poverty line at any given moment, and a third of them will live beneath the poverty line at some period before their 18th birthday. Now, along with many others, I believe the so-called "official" poverty line itself is statistically distorted. I think it overstates the situation. But overstated or not, way too many of our children are living with too little. That hurts us all, short-term and long-term.

There is a way to make most low-income children into not-low-income children: money. *Let their parents keep more of the money they've earned, bypassing the welfare bureaucracy.* This is the idea behind the enhanced Earned Income Tax Credit (EITC) that was working its way through the Congress in 1990. As explained later, "Earned Income Tax Credit" is a hokum label for "a children's allowance for low-income parents who work."

It's about time we had a children's allowance. Every other modern democracy does. Financially, the new plan doesn't do the whole job. Yet. The amount of monies going to low-income people, for their children, ought to be increased. The eligibility threshhold ought to be raised, in order to accommodate much of the middle class. That could yield, finally, a pro-natal economic policy in this country. We ought to make it easier for young people—if they want to have children—to be able to have children.

Sooner or later, that would probably mean a modest increase in the general tax rate, which can, however, be made "revenue neutral." In effect, such a change in the tax code would moderately redistribute wealth from those without children at home and to those who are rearing children. The country will not go wrong by diverting resources to its children.

As will be shown, Americans are richer than ever, when measured by per capita, family, or household income, not even counting non-cash income which should be counted. The standard of living has gone up. Poverty is down.

The rubrics of what-has-not-happened, what-has-happened, and what-is-likely-to-happen are also useful tools in looking at American government.

What has not happened is gridlock, although that is the fashionable buzz word. The heart of the gridlock, we are told, is the deficit, that intractable, dirty old deficit, that nasty deficit the Republicans won't eliminate by raising taxes, that rotten deficit the Democrats won't eliminate by cutting spending, that malign deficit that accounts for most everything wrong in America from looming recession to too little money for the homeless, that evasive deficit that can be solved in a hundred ways except of course by growing out of it, because everyone knows that won't work.

But, although one is not supposed to say it, it looks suspiciously as if we're sort of growing out of it. The deficit as a proportion of the Gross National Product is going down, already halved from 1982 to 1989, from roughly 6 percent to roughly 3 percent *and slowly shrinking*. It is even shrinking if the Social Security surpluses are not included in the calculations.

Remember the numbers one-two-three. The U.S. Government will spend 1.23 trillion dollars per year, according to the Fiscal Year 1991 budget submitted by the president. That is gridlock to some who see a pressing need for more education spending, more spending on drug interdiction, more aid to the homeless. That is the view that enspirits the cover of *Time* magazine with a portrait of George Washington with a live tear running down his cheek, and a headline that bleats, "Is Government Dead?

Unwilling to Lead, Politicians Are Letting America Slip into Paralysis."

One point two three trillion dollars per year ain't chopped liver, nor pork rinds. It provides for the world's most costly and far-flung military, for the largest amount of domestic social spending in our history (yes, in constant dollars and measured per capita, yes, despite the vaunted Reagan cuts.)

Now, there is a political party in the United States that profoundly believes that one point two three trillion dollars is roughly enough for the time being, and that greater prosperity will come about by inciting the private economy, rather than the public economy. One can legitimately argue about it.

But the standard-bearer of that party, George Herbert Walker Bush, won the persidential election in 1988. What seems like gridlock is in fact a deeply held and sometimes deeply disguised Republican political philosophy. Not-spending is very popular, but not totally popular. So Republicans get it both ways when they not-spend and then rhetorically accommodate the gridlockists, saying, gee we'd like to help out, but we're broke and, as you know, the system is gridlocked. Easy for those Republicans to say, but we're too smart to be gulled. The system is responsive to them that won the election, and it's not in bad shape.

There is other progress, of a different sort, to report—half-domestic half-global. The eighties saw the excision of a malign word in the democratic lexicon. Because that happened the nineties will be better, for America and for others.

The word is "inexorable." Recall that through the 1970s there was a near-ritual sentence in the public dialogue: "The growth of the welfare state is inexorable." Liberals gloated about it, conservatives grumbled about it, but almost everyone believed it. The welfare state (it was believed) had so many constituencies that it could not be stopped.

Now, I am no knee-jerk critic of government spending. On Mondays, Wednesdays, and Fridays I'm even sort of for it, less so than at an earlier time, but still for it. We need environmental spending, federal health research, highway spending, monetary aid to the poor.

It's the "inexorable" part that makes me think bad thoughts. The power and glory of democratic nations is that the people believe that they control their own destiny. That means that the growth in government services can be halted, indeed reversed. We are the sovereigns.

Reagan and Thatcher, in the eighties, tested that principle. It lives. We have learned that if we want to, we can at least slow down the spending machine. We did. Now we can decide what to do next, in fact pick and choose how to go about it with a clear head. Most everything is on the table, which is as it should be in a democratic society.

In the late 1970s, Irving Kristol, my colleague at the American Enterprise Institute, was asked what was coming at us. His answer was simple and prophetic: "a conservative welfare state."

We got it, and it's been pretty good for us. George Bush, in fact, even more than Ronald Reagan, is the exemplar of the model, mixing kinder-and-gentler with meaner-and-tougher. A philosophy of governance that combines mush, markets, and military is not bad for an advanced modern industrial democracy. It certainly will not put us at a disadvantage in the competition among nations.

At home, we are strong and getting stronger.

What about the global situation? How does America look now?

We won the Cold War. It didn't just end. We won it because we stayed strong, because we rallied our allies, and because we were right. We ought to understand that and say it. It was probably the most titanic ideological struggle in the history of this planet, surely the most expensive, and we won it. No more of that pantywaist stuff about how one day it just ended.

The whole world will gain a great deal from the end of the Cold War. America may well gain disproportionately. The most obvious fact of the changed global circumstance concerns military power, one of the key topics scholars used to talk about at length in the "Number One" discussions.

There is a great discussion today in America about whether there will be a real "peace dividend." There will be. There already have been several.

As Senator Daniel P. Moynihan points out, the peace dividend is peace. That's the most important.

Beyond that, because of recent events, after forty-five years of trying, the United States has become the most powerful military force on earth. Try as we might, for the moment at least, we could not disarm fast enough to become weaker than the Soviet Union. Those guys are in the process of losing a war to Lithuania. Indeed, it is hard today to even visualize the future correct name for our once-potential adversary. "Soviet *Union*" is a phrase which may become an oxymoron.

If the United States were being described today on a theater marquee, one appropriate billing might read "Now, Finally, The Most Powerful Military Force In The World." What a strange way to describe a nation in decline.

Here is another phrase that I believe accurately describes America's current global status: "the most culturally potent nation in the history of the world."

We like to torture ourselves in America. We say: "Isn't it terrible, Americans invented the video cassette recorder, but the Japanese developed it, and now all over the world, there are Japanese VCRs." True as far as it goes. The hardware is indeed Japanese. *And the software is American.*

The tapes being fed into the quarter of a billion VCRs around the world typically show American movies, and, if you'll excuse the expression, American music. If you're in the superpower, super-culture business, it's better to own the software than the hardware. The Japanese, in short, have mass-produced and mass-marketed a machine to disseminate American popular culture. There is one proper American response to such a sequence of developments: Thank you, Japan-san.

Beyond that, there are three daily American newspapers in circulation around the world (the *International Herald Tribune, USA Today,* and the *Wall Street Journal*), three weekly American newsmagazines in circulation around the world (*Time, Newsweek,* and *U.S. News & World Report*), and a universal monthly (the *Reader's Digest*). By my lights, Ted Turner is a strange duck, but hand him this: the Cable News Network, his idea, is revolutionary. The CNN signal is now brought down almost everywhere, not only in Moscow and Managua, but in Hanoi as well, at the request of the North Vietnamese.

And, of course, for the first time since the Tower of Babel there is something approaching a universal language. It is American, or if you prefer the more traditional word, English. In Eastern Europe today, schools are abandoning the mandatory study of Russian as a second language. The Czech ambassador to the United States was asked what was the most important thing America could do for Czechoslovakia. She did not ask for money, or trade, or debt relief. "Send us English teachers," she said.

These, too, are odd developments for a nation in decline.

The domestic and international situations come together in American foreign policy.

Americans have the opportunity to be the most important player in the shaping of the new world. For decades, our foreign policy had a neat, clean, and worthy bumper sticker to guide us: "Anti-communism." That foreign policy theme, because of our victory in the Cold War, has been diminished. We need a new bumper sticker: "Waging Democracy."

It can be a less expensive policy than anti-communism, but no less important, and perhaps more difficult to accomplish. But if we are successful, we can pass along to our children a safer world that is user-friendly to the values we hold dear.

As part of that policy we ought to remind ourselves (after the euphoria wears off) that democracy comes in many forms and faces. American-style democracy, a way of life as well as a political system, is different from European-style democracy, or Japanese-style democracy. If, twenty years from now, the global model of democratic governance is, say, Swedish-style—did we get all we could have gotten from our Cold War victory?

There will be a contest for the culture in the years to come, a friendly and constructive contest, but a contest nonetheless. We ought to use all the tools in our kit to non-coercively wage democracy, American-style. These tools include immigration, the draw of our universities, our entertainment monopoly, tourism, our global business establishment, our military, our immensely appealing market philosophy, and the spreading English language, all this in the service of our unique and much-emulated opportunity society. Our doctrine ought to be "neo-manifest destinarianism."

Does it all matter? What difference does it make if America remains Number One, whether we become even more influential than before?

It matters to Americans. We have a history that has been both isolationist and profoundly internationalist. There is a missionary tradition. Since colonial times Americans have wanted to cast a global shadow. John Winthrop said America would be "a city upon a hill. . . . The eyes of all the people are upon us." Later, President Andrew Jackson said America is "a country manifestly called by the almighty to a destiny." In a different way, we still are, as will be discussed.

———————

Are the American people up to such a role? Let's talk politics. As voters, Americans in recent decades have passed the test of intelligence.

They have refused to vote for "the stupid party." That's what Democrats called the Republicans during the 1960s and it wasn't a bad appellation. The Republicans opposed civil rights legislation and dragged their heels on moving into the modern era, from environmentalism to health care to health research. The Democrats were the unstupid party of progress.

I am a Democrat. I write the following words with sadness. My party stands hoisted on its own phrase. Tens of millions of Americans who proudly voted for the fairly-liberal party of Roosevelt, Truman, Kennedy, and Johnson will not vote for the very-liberal party of George McGovern, Teddy Kennedy, Jimmy Carter, Michael Dukakis, and Jesse Jackson. (I put Walter Mondale in a separate category.)

The voters believe the very-liberal Democrats have gone overboard on social permissiveness, economic giveaways, racial quotas, and international weakness. The voters believe the very-liberal Democrats have been trashing America and traditional American values. Voters sense these policies and attitudes are stupid and wrong, and they will not vote for a presidential candidate who they believe comes from the wrong end of the stupid party.

The voters have demonstrated that they behave rationally and in their own best interests. Now it is the turn of the Democrats to show the same attributes. When they start behaving un-stupidly they will start getting votes. Americans believe in political redemption.

There may be signs of a major change on the most prominent of the divisive issues within the Democratic Party. Democrats today are internationalists again. President Bush, they say, doesn't have "The Vision Thing." They do, they say. They want to help Eastern Europe and let freedom ring on a big brass bell labelled "America." That's what they say; it may take a while to remember the music, but there is some hope. It might turn out to be something like neo-manifest destinarianism.

In examining this idea of "Who's Number One," we must take a look at how America stacks up when compared to specific other countries and other areas.

It is said that it will be revealed in the nineties that the United States will lose the trade wars, that foreigners will buy up America, and that the United States will not be competitive in world markets. The bookkeepers and the bean-counters have decided that's the way to measure who's Number One.

It's silly. Look: there is every indication that our children will be better off than we were, that American per capita GNP will continue to climb. Now, suppose the Japanese per capita income goes up by 3 percent per year, and ours goes up by 2 percent per year. Big deal. Eventually, under the iron laws of compound income, the Japanese might have a higher standard of living than Americans. So what? We'll be richer, they'll be richer, our joint accretion of riches will make each other richer still— that's what free trade does. (For now, though, and for the foreseeable intermediate future, Americans still have the highest standard of living in the world. Isn't that strange for a country allegedly in decline for many years now?)

Should Japan become richer per capita than us—someday—that will not make Japan the number one country in the world. Not long ago, Kuwait had the highest per capita income. They were not number one. The Japanese live on a small island, defended by the United States, speaking a language few others know, lacking natural resources. Let us ask M. Attali: Did Poland defend Flanders? Was Flemish the international language? Did Flanders have the largest GNP in the world? Japan has about

125 million people, about half the U.S. total. Japan has the most rapidly aging population in the world. It has below-replacement fertility (1.57 children per woman), a rate that still seems to be declining, despite exhortations by the Japanese government imploring their people to do their duty. Japan will not likely grow and most probably will lose population. In xenophobic Japan it is difficult to suggest, let alone predict, any new large immigration flow.

The Japanese are feared by many of their neighbors, who look to America as the global stabilizing force. Notwithstanding many truly remarkable economic and technological achievements, notwithstanding great wealth fairly earned, Japan still has an archaic agricultural sector, a pre-modern retail sector, crushing housing costs, and an undernourished consumer sector. They are not in the running for global superpower.

The Europeans, a greater grander Europe, free and free-market from the Atlantic to the Soviet border, have a better chance to challenge America as the prime influence in the world. But they, too—as we shall see—will fall way short.

Anyway: What if they gave a trade war and no one came? It may be that the concept of trade wars is long gone. Perhaps it never existed. What exactly happens if we lose it? We've been allegedly losing, that is, we've been running trade deficits, and yet we have had full employment, a rising standard of living, higher incomes and less poverty. We get quality goods that foreigners are nice enough to produce for us at relatively low prices, and they are then considerate enough to "finance our deficit" as well. In any event, there are experts who maintain that if we ever properly valued the exports of the service sector, we'd already be in a net surplus trade position.

It is said, for one example, beware, beware, the Japanese are coming on strong in pharmaceuticals. One more American industry will be under threat. Hah! Someone must explain very carefully to me how the American consumer will be hurt if the Japanese come up with a drug to cure cancer.

The same people who keep repeating, "The world is interdependent" keep forgetting that the world is interdependent. The human condition is advanced, uh, when the human condition is advanced. When a U.S. drug company came up with a drug to treat ulcers, the human condition was moved forward—almost everywhere. Those drugs were quickly sold overseas and Frenchmen could deal more effectively with their ulcers. If a Japanese drug cures cancer, mankind gains, not just the Japanese.

So let's make one thing clear. That America is getting better does not preclude the idea that the whole world is also getting better. It is. In part, that is coming about due to the spread of American ideas. And in part, American ideas and prosperity are fed by what's going on elsewhere. It is not zero sum, nor close to it. It should also be noted, that in a burgeoning and successful world, the world leader may well tend to burgeon and succeed faster than the rest of the gang.

And one other thing to state clearly. America has some severe problems. What we also have is a remarkable record of dealing with our problems, perhaps sometimes even through the zany crisis-mongering we inflict upon ourselves. I don't see serious evidence that we've lost the ability to self-correct.

How can the world be doing so well, with all those big global crises allegedly coming at us, all of us, everywhere? The big ones aren't.

It is said that the great issue of the nineties will be the environment. That may well come to pass. And should it happen, it will show just how remarkable is this age we live in.

Free and active people need crisis. It puts meaning in their lives. A war is a clear and galvanizing example, despite its ugliness and futility. Sometimes, the crisis is less immediate, or less real, but no less galvanizing: a crisis about poverty, even when poverty is diminishing, or about illiteracy, even as it too is diminishing.

The crisis about the environment belongs in the lesser category. It is a crisis generated by material success. It is a crisis that is diminishing. It is a crisis that has not been very harmful. When money is spent, the crisis diminishes. Read all about it.

We can indeed spend a lot of money, probably usefully, on the crisis-that-isn't-quite-a-crisis. From those expenditures we get less pollution and a sense of dealing with the best possible apocalyptic crisis remaining, the one we get when the world is peaceful and the economy is humming.

The "population explosion" has been the catastrophic handmaiden of environmentalists. Sooo many people, causing sooo much despoliation, and sooo much poverty. Arguable. A revisionist school of thought, call it "supply-side demographics," makes the point that people produce as well as consume, that culture causes poverty and wealth, that population growth is, in itself, neutral. A landmark recent study by the National Academy of Sciences confirms this view of how the world works. These issues will be discussed here.

What is not arguable is that even if population growth is a monumental problem, there is a clear light at the end of a medium-sized tunnel. The population explosion, it is rather apparent, will be a phenomenon of the last half of the twentieth century and the first half of the twenty-first century.

Fertility rates in the less developed countries are tumbling. The Mexican total fertility rate has fallen from 6.8 children per woman to 3.6 children in the last twenty-five years; that's 68 percent of the way to a replacement level of 2.1. The total fertility rate for all the less developed countries has fallen from 6 to 3.9 children per woman in just one generation.

World population will grow—probably from the current 5 billion to about 10 or 11 billion. And at that point, sometimes in the latter half of the next century, we will likely be faced with a new catastrophe. Call it the population erosion.

Will Americans be competitive in this new world? You bet. Toqueville, still the best observer of the American scene, talked of "American exceptionalism." Americans, he said, are very different from the peoples in the other democracies. Particularly, he noted, they are more individualistic. Now, trans-national polls measure this.

Tom Smith, a sociologist at the National Opinion Research Center, has studied the surveys. He says America is an "opportunity society" while Western Europe and Japan are "security societies." Americans are much more likely to view their work as self-defining and meaningful; they gain a sense of accomplishment from it. Europeans and Japanese are more likely to view their jobs as a paycheck and no more.

If the nature of the contest is competition, it is hard to believe that individualism in an opportunity society will not provide major payoffs.

It is not an accident that America holds the technological lead in aircraft, airlines, pharmaceuticals, computers, biotechnology, plastics, synthetic fibers, telecommunications equipment, and petroleum exploration, to only begin a very long list.

Talk to the cab-drivers in Washington, D.C. They come from Africa, Latin America, the Moslem lands, India, and Asia. Ask them how America is different not only from their homelands, but from other nations. One word comes up, almost monotonously: "opportunity."

If American business was fat and lazy a decade ago, that is true no longer. In the 1980s about half of major American corporations had reported significant sharpening (downsizing) of their operations. The era of "lean and mean" had begun. Exports climbed, powerfully albeit irregularly.

Now, American business leaves something to be desired. Businessmen, like everyone else, like to get government subsidies and protection, even if they know better than most that in the long term it's best to keep the government at bay. They preach "markets," but it is sometimes a thin preachment. Yet, compared to other industrial societies, our trade is so free, our government so un-intrusive, our commerce so open—that, despite our normal human tropism to free goodies, we benefit enormously.

The number one nation does not have to have the lead in everything. We don't. It should have the lead in lots of things. We do.

In late 1989, the global computer business was beginning to go through one more in a series of wrenching changes that are common to explosive new industries. It was said that new softwear would become the driving force of the industry. Softwear development demands speed and innovation, perfect for what has been called "garage start-ups." Said one industry expert: "We've got more garages with smart people than anyone else. We really thrive on anarchy."

We are the first universal nation. "First" as in the first one, "first" as in "number one." And "universal" within our borders and globally.

In America, we now come from everywhere, becoming one people, getting along pretty well with each other, and vastly enriched by our pluralism. We are a large nation, and growing. We have the world's highest standard of living, and diminishing poverty. We cope with periodic, but infrequent, recessions.

We have the best universities, and the best researchers. We are the largest exporters, the largest importers, and yet we are the most economically independent major nation. We are the strongest military power. More so than most modern nations, we retain a strong core of traditional values.

Around the world, people tap their feet to American music, watch American movies and television, follow American fashions, are enthralled with American culture, speak American, emulate American economic and political ideas. We even export political consultants, briefcases chock-full of 30-second commercials. All this influence is increasing exponentially as the American-driven communications grid spreads everywhere. It should not be taken lightly; it already won the Cold War for us.

Well now, we must still deal with choosing a winner for the contest to replace the word "super-power." Recall the list of best entries: hyper-power, magna-power, maxi-power, mega-power, multi-power, omni-power, semper power, solo power, supra-power, ultra-power, uni-power.

How interesting. Almost all the good entries had Latin or Greek prefixes. When we think of "number one" the first thoughts always go to Greece and Rome, powers that shook, and shook up, the world more than 2,000 years ago. Here we are still drawing on their language, which reflects their culture.

But does anyone recall the merchandise trade balance of the Holy Roman Empire? And if we could accurately compute it, how much would it matter?

Could it be that we have been gulled in the "number one" debate? The terms have been set by the ABC Gang, the Apocalyptic Bean Counters. Who appointed accountants, economists, or business lobbyists to tell us about which are the great civilizations? Who appointed a British-born economistic historian of commerce, still wounded by England's fall?

Is the prize of being number one really going to be conferred on the basis of which nation sells the most semi-conductors, or which foreign investors own some office buildings in New York? Be serious. It's culture that counts.

Would we judge the Romans by how many chariot wheels they sold outside of Rome versus how many potatoes they brought into Rome?

The winner of the contest, as you should have guessed, although it took me a while to figure out, is "omni-power," submitted by a number of readers, but first by Ken J. Flamily of Maitland, Florida, and Greg Ritchie of Satellite Beach, Florida.

Of course. "Omni-", as in "universal."

In 1942, when the Royal Air Force finally beat off the Luftwaffe in the skies of England, Winston Churchill took to the airwaves, cautioned Englishmen against overconfidence, but told them which way the wind was blowing. "This is not the beginning of the end," he said, "but it is the end of the beginning."

That was a half-century ago. We have moved on. Led by Americans, the free nations have vanquished totalitarians of right and left.

We are now at the beginning of the middle. It could well be the best time. Churchill said that if we got through the current mess, we would find the "broad sunlit uplands." Not mountaintops, mind you; the prime minister was too smart to think about utopian mountaintops for flawed humans. The uplands were as good as we'd get, but they'd be broad so lots of people could fit, and they'd be sunlit, which is a nice bonus.

We got it. You'll see that terrain in the nineties, in America, and in an ever-growing portion of the world. Americans, the new universal people, will fare very well in such a world. After all, we invented, and still own, the sunlight factory.

2

Background

To judge and weigh a work in the realm of public affairs, the reader ought to have some advance sense of the writer. Why does he do what he does? What experiences influence his thinking? Whom does he admire, and why?

Teddy White Remembered

I am in great personal debt to author Theodore H. White, who died the other day.

In 1960, Teddy followed candidates John Kennedy and Richard Nixon across the country. The result was *The Making of the President, 1960*, a marvelous, ground-breaking book, the first of a famous series. White viewed the presidential race as personal dramatic combat, and he had the narrative flair to make it sing. He told about secret meetings and inside campaign strategies, what it was like on the press plane and how the candidates rose to great heights.

And then, smack in the middle of the book came what was, for me, a stunner: a whole chapter about—of all things!—the 1960 census. White broke away from the hurly-burly of the political conventions to talk about the voters the candidates were trying to seduce, and he looked at them through the lens of statistics.

He took the census numbers and limned a national portrait. There was great population growth from 1950 to 1960, and yet the data showed that both core cities and rural areas were losing population. White artfully mixed the numbers with people; he recalled a Minnesota farmer delegate rising at a causus saying, "Two miles from Dalton, we have 17 vacant farms. We can't afford to lose our small farms." Sound familiar?

White told of the growth of suburbs, and noticed that the suburban split-levels used oil or natural gas for fuel, not coal. OPEC later taught us what that meant. White used census numbers to show that Americans were less likely than earlier to work for themselves, noticed the rise of chain stores, and wrote, "From Massachusetts to Wisconsin, one could see the boarded-up windows of the little groceries and butcher shops wiped out by the spread of the supermarkets."

He used the data to describe the political impact of the move of blacks from South to North, and wrote about a Chicago railroad station where "Negroes . . . step off the train, blinking in the station lights, some dressed in their best go-to-meeting clothes, others dressed in tattered work clothes, with all their possessions wrapped in a cloth sack." He noted black progress in the North and the social friction brought about by black migration.

And in 1960, the year when John Kennedy's Catholicism became a national political issue, White delved into the tangled religious and ethnic demographics of this most pluralist nation on earth.

The book came out in 1961. That chapter inflamed my mind. Imagine! Using numbers to explain people, without boring readers! I was 28, trying to set up a small publishing firm in New York. I ran into my partner's office and said, "Let's get someone to do a book explaining census trends in human terms—maybe a novelist!" My partner said, "Dumb idea."

The partnership soon ended. I became a free-lance writer. I decided to write that book. I ultimately teamed up with Richard Scammon, then director of the Census Bureau, to do it. The result was a book called *This U.S.A.* and subtitled "An Unexpected Family Portrait of 194,067,296 Americans Drawn from the Census."

Later, Scammon and I wrote *The Real Majority*, which linked election results and attitudinal trends to the demographics that White had illuminated in that chapter. Since then, I've written other books on the same general theme—data and people, watching trends change over time.

And, of course, American political activity has moved dramatically in the direction White pointed to: There are now more than 50 active pollsters and high-tech firms that will sell a candidate psycho-demographic data down to the city-block level. Some of it has gotten out of hand but, on balance, it's good that politicians have a better sense of who the voters are.

As for me, Theodore White pretty much set me on the course of a big piece of my life's work. I told him this story once, and he was pleased.
May 22, 1986

> *Forewarned: trends change. The one about little merchants being driven out of business that White wrote about—has changed. Americans are now somewhat more likely to "work for themselves" than when White reported the trends that showed up in the 1960 census. One reason is that those "little groceries and butcher shops wiped out by supermarkets" have been statistically replaced by little franchise operations (fast foods, donuts, brake linings) and by small specialty shops (video stores, fat men's clothing) and by lots of freelance consultants and programmers. Joseph Schumpeter described capitalism as "creative destruction." It's still an operative phrase.*
>
> *One additional word about Dick Scammon, whose name will appear again in these pages. He was my collaborator on two books and has been my colleague and friend for a quarter of a century. He is an expert in the field of elections, perhaps, over the years, America's leading psephologist. (Look it up.) He has offered me several words of advice, several dozen times: "Wash your hands in the data."*

I met Senator Henry M. ("Scoop") Jackson in 1971 as he prepared to run for the presidency. I was particularly attracted to his views on foreign policy.

I had already worked in the White House for President Johnson, in a Senate campaign in 1970 in Minnesota for former Vice President Hubert M. Humphrey, and in a House of Representatives campaign in 1964 for Congressman Donald J. Irwin (D-Conn.).

I was on Scoop's paid presidential campaign staff in 1972 and worked unpaid in his 1976 presidential race. We stayed in close political touch during those campaigns and thereafter, often on matters relating to the Coalition for a Democratic Majority, a Democratic factional group of which I was chairman. I delivered one of his eulogies in 1983.

Scoop

Senator Henry M. "Scoop" Jackson was, by far, the most decent, and most professional, and most idealistic man I have known in American political life. In a unique way, these traits intertwined to create an American legislative giant whose legacy here and around the world may well surpass that of many who held our presidency—which is the job he trained for and deserved.

He was so un-pompous it was almost laughable. "Carrying-your-own-bag" would become a symbol in 1976, with presidential candidates photographed leaving a plane carrying their own garment sack—a way of saying here's a man who would not be an "imperial" president. Well, Scoop not only really carried his own bag, but I remember times in the 1972 presidential campaign, coming off little chartered planes late at night, with no press in attendance, when staff aides had to be quick and tough to physically prevent him from carrying their bags as well as his own.

He was so un-phony, it could be politically painful. He was a religious man. It was pointed out to him that it would be helpful to allude to that in his campaign speeches. No, he said, that was private. He never took a dime for a speech. The money went quietly to a scholarship fund.

In the 1976 campaign he was advised to borrow money personally to keep the campaign alive; it was what other candidates were doing when federal matching funds were snarled by a legal battle. Jackson refused. It was likely that the money would be repaid, but not certain. Jackson wouldn't do it even though it meant dooming his chance for the presidency. "I'm not a wealthy man," he said. "I've got a wife and young children. Suppose something happens to me? I'm not going to risk their future by going into debt."

He cared deeply about his staff and their problems. More than one of them regarded him as a father.

There are many decent men in the world, but Henry Jackson's personal decency had a political dimension. It ended up writ large on the international scene.

Those who didn't know him, or where he came from, called him a "cold warrior" and a "hawk" and thought him obsessed with weaponry.

He was, in fact, an idealist. Jackson was obsessed all right—about indecency. He had fought fascists—the Silver Shirts—back when he was a young prosecutor in Washington state in the late 1930s. He was with the American forces that liberated Buchenwald. He loathed totalitarianism—of right and left—because it was indecent. He was not surprised that the Soviets were capable of shooting down a civilian airliner.

And so it came to pass that this man who some thought cared mostly about military hardware—became the father of the human rights movement.

There are arguments pro and arguments con, about the specific efficacy of the Jackson amendment, which stipulated that America would not grant trade benefits to nations that did not allow free emigration.

But when all is said and done, when all the charges and countercharges are set aside, two facts remain. Several hundred thousand people—Jews and non-Jews—were able to emigrate from the Soviet Union because of the Jackson amendment. And the United States went on record as saying human rights mattered to us. We were prepared to reward those who were moving toward human rights and punish those who would not.

In 1975 I visited Andrei Sakharov at his dacha outside of Moscow. The Jackson amendment was as controversial then, as now. I asked him what he thought about it. "Jackson knows how to make things happen," he said. "He is our champion."

The bedrock premise of the Jackson amendment has energized much of American foreign policy ever since—for the better. We Americans said, finally: We care about decency.

Scoop cared enough about what his politics meant—to become a consummate professional politician. He raised plenty of money, and raised it early. He campaigned for Democrats all over the country, including those whose politics did not always appeal to him. He knew that you couldn't get help unless you gave help.

He was elected to the Senate in 1952 with 56 percent of the vote. That was too close. In the next five elections he averaged 72 percent of the vote. One year he got 82 percent. He rather liked that one.

Jackson's decency drove his idealism. His professionalism bolstered his idealism. He ended up at a unique spot in the firmament of American and global politics. He was a liberal on domestic affairs: That was the decent thing. And he was the man who understood that we had to be strong if we were to promote the values of decency around the world.

It is the tragedy of recent American politics that such a position combining domestic and international decency—which is at the essence of what most Americans believe—has had such a difficult time finding a home in Scoop's party, let alone the other party.

The battle is not over, however. Millions of people still believe in what Scoop believed. They call themselves Jackson Democrats.

September 2, 1983

Henry Jackson died in 1983. Seven years have gone by. The Soviets have executed a U-turn. Another man named Jackson is talked about as president, and his views are not close to Scoop's. It's been said that "the Jackson wing" of the party is now a feather. Perhaps.

Yet, most of the foreign policy and defense leaders of the Democratic Party happen to reflect Jackson's view of the world. Senator Sam Nunn is now the chairman of the Senate Armed Services Committee. Congressman Les Aspin is chairman of the House Armed Services Committee. Congressman Dante Fascell is chairman of House Foreign Affairs Committee. An Oklahoma senator and an Oklahoma congressman, David Boren and David McCurdy, chair the Intelligence subcommittees. To one degree or another, I believe they would all be proud to be called Jackson Democrats. The speaker of the House is Tom Folcy, a protégé of Scoop's.

There are lots of others, although not nearly as many as I'd like. On many issues even the leaders mentioned above are not so influential as I wish they were, because the party they lead has become too dovish for my taste and for its own good. Still, there is a lot of Scoop around the Democratic Party.

For reasons explained later in this volume, I believe that the next Democratic president will come from the Scoop Jackson tradition. Why? Because even with all the change, perhaps especially because of all the change, Scoop's ideas were right: You don't get peace, freedom, or stability without strength. Voters know that, and they won't elect a presidential candidate who doesn't know that.

(And by the way, a great deal of the Reagan foreign policy was set in motion by people who were Jackson Democrats.)

―――――――

The first full speech I ever wrote for anyone, including myself, was for President Johnson.

In the summer of 1966, I had been asked to come down to the White House and have lunch with Bill Moyers. We ate in the White House Mess. National Security Council Director Walt Rostow stopped by the table and said he was reading This U.S.A. *Vice President Humphrey stopped by and said he was reading it, too. I was flying! Then Moyers said he wanted me to meet someone. I followed him through labyrinthine corridors and up a small elevator.*

Moyers knocked on a door; we entered a bedroom; and there were Henry Ford, in a business suit, and President Johnson, in blue pajamas, just finishing up lunch. Gulp! I was 33 years old; I had never worked in Washington before. Moyers (my age) had already been on the cover of Time *as "The Young Man Next to the President." Ford was Ford. And LBJ . . .*

I am not normally tongue-tied. More than that: normally I am a loquacious buttinsky. After Ford left, Johnson talked at me for 15 minutes or so. My part of the conversation, at least until I was coaxed out of it, was a series of affirmative grunts.

I was offered a job for "a few months" to serve as an LBJ speechwriter. I started in August of 1966 and stayed until just about the end of Johnson's term. I never did leave Washington, at least I haven't left yet. Nor did I ever quite get the hang of arguing with LBJ. Once— only once—I got a call from him, on a Saturday morning, at home, in my bedroom. After the conversation had proceeded for a while I heard my six-year-old daughter Sarah scamper down the stairs bellowing, "Mommy, Mommy, Daddy's on the phone with Mr. Yes Sir."

Memos to the President were a different matter. LBJ aides were encouraged to speak their minds, and I did.

Johnson was an internationalist on foreign policy. He was a sensible activist on domestic policy. After the mugging of Vietnam policy by liberals and the trashing of Great Society domestic policy by conservatives, it is heavy lifting defending his views and policies. But when I've had a drink or sit down to write a column, I often do that, as will be noted in many places later in this volume.

Of course, this is not to say Johnson's policies were all wonderful or that they are immune from criticisms. I have problems with some of the Great Society programs. We all have been rethinking Vietnam for almost two decades now. But some of the attacks have been mindless, like Caro's and Goodwin's.

Sculptor Chisels Johnson

In this month's *Atlantic Monthly*, author Robert Caro wraps up his long and thinly documented tale of Lyndon Johnson's 1930s relationship with Alice Glass in this way:

"(It) was ended only by the Vietnam War, which Alice considered one of history's horrors. . . . she told friends that she had burned love letters that Johnson had written to her—because she didn't want her granddaughter to know she had ever been associated with the man she considered responsible for Vietnam."

Now, as it happens, in the LBJ Library in Austin there repose half a dozen letters from Alice Glass to Lyndon Johnson written after Johnson left the presidency. The letters are warmly supportive of LBJ. One of them, dated May 22, 1971, says, "Many people in the country love you, including me, and want to hear your voice." Another, dated April 26, 1971, compares LBJ to Churchill and ends saying, "There is nothing in the books to say you can't be President twice. Get in the ring."

Of course, it is easy to find credibility-shattering items in any magazine excerpt, and it will surely be even easier to find more such items in the massive, just-published 882-page parent work of Caro's, *The Years of Lyndon Johnson: The Path to Power.*

But Caro is asking for it. He apparently believes that he is writing more than biography. He thinks he is in the history-sculpting business: research is his chisel. Quoted in *Newsweek* talking about his book, Caro says: "I often wonder what would have happened if during the Roman Empire—not 200 years *after,* but about the time of the second or third of the insane emperors—someone had written a thoroughly documented book that told ancient Rome: 'The emperors are nuts.' Would history have been the same?"

Caro apparently thinks not. He has spent seven years on his Johnson study (two more volumes are to come). So far Caro has proven to his own satisfaction some stunning charges: that Lyndon Johnson was ambitious, that his alliances shifted and that he didn't always say the same thing in the same way to different people, that he understood that money was useful in politics, that he had—in the old phrase—a roving eye for the ladies.

Although ambition, money, sex and political duplicity are not rare commodities in Washington, Caro is apparently shocked by it all. He weaves his shock into a central thesis: that Lyndon Johnson was a thoroughly unprincipled hustler who would become a cause of national grief.

As Caro puts it, Johnson lacked "any consistent ideology or principle, in fact lacked any moral foundation whatsoever—(he had) a willingness to march with any ally who would help his personal advancement."

This is an old charge about Johnson. In the mid-1960s, I was a speech-writer on the LBJ White House staff. Truth be told, those of us on that staff spent a lot of time trying to counter the idea that LBJ was just such an amoral "wheeler-dealer."

As a young man, fresh to Washington in those days, I was astonished by the charge. Seeing it now in print again 15 years later, I am amazed even more. For there is a central dilemma that such an analysis must face up to. How did it happen that such an unprincipled man did so many principled things *against* his own best interests?

After all, if a politician is concerned only about his own advancement, one can assume that he doesn't take on unpopular causes.

Now—whether one agrees with what he did or not—Lyndon Johnson took on the two most unpopular causes in recent American political history: civil rights during a time of racial turbulence and a nasty, brutal war in Vietnam.

Johnson was not a stupid man; he knew these were difficult causes, he knew they would cause him deep personal and political trouble. He was right. He was reviled as a traitor in parts of his native Southland for his liberal views on race. Polls in early 1968 showed him losing political support because of his outspoken support of civil rights measures.

On Vietnam, he gave out medals of honor posthumously and presented them to grieving widows, saw his sons-in-law off to combat and was savaged by old friends who wanted to know how many kids he killed today.

Now, Caro may be able to square this circle. To do so, however, he must soon answer one question: if LBJ was such an amoral brute, why did he act so idealistically for so long after it could possibly yield him any profit?

November 30, 1982

Shrinking LBJ

About Richard Goodwin's new book, *Remembering America* (Little, Brown): You may buy it, you may enjoy it, but don't you believe it.

Goodwin's book is subtitled, "A Voice from the Sixties." He had a unique perch from which to view the socio-cultural politics of that time. He was a speechwriter and policy aide to Presidents Kennedy and Johnson, and to presidential candidates Sen. Robert Kennedy and Sen. Eugene McCarthy.

Intertwined with rich personal history and anecdote, supported by trend-trumpeting, a theme emerges: 1) Once upon a time there was a great moment in a great country (the early '60s in America)—embodied by President John Kennedy. 2) When Kennedy was killed, the gargantuan spirit of Lyndon Johnson—"the good Lyndon," that is—enhanced the '60s-Kennedy impulse. 3) Alas, the passion of the good Lyndon was soon destroyed by "the crazy Lyndon." It was, according to Dr. Sigmund Goodwin (after consulting colleagues) "a textbook case of paranoid disintegration." 4) Johnson's "uncontrollable compulsions" played a major role in escalating the war in Vietnam. 5) That war drove a nail in the heart of progress in America, even causing blacks to riot. 6) We've never recovered.

Johnson cuckoo? His instability yielding war? No progress since? Fie!

Admittedly, I speak in part as a Johnson partisan. After Goodwin had departed, I was a Johnson speechwriter. LBJ did not seem gaga to me. Nor did he to long-term Johnson associates. Was LBJ eccentric and extravagant? You bet. Unpredictable? Sure, on small things, on personal things. Privately, usually for dramatic effect, he exaggerated and embellished, sometimes inaccurately. But Johnson's eccentricities did not affect serious national policy, which is the implication of Goodwin's diagnosis.

If verified, Goodwin's Syndrome will make medical annals. A most peculiar desease: LBJ's symptoms manifested themselves only in foreign policy, never on domestic issues. Indeed, the period of which Goodwin writes, 1964—65, was when Johnson was being feted as a miracle man, a legislative genius, the promulgator of the Great Society.

Johnson, says Goodwin, got guidance about Vietnam from a handful of advisers. Odd: All were appointed by President Kennedy. All favored escalation. Were they going mad, too? And what about John Kennedy? Goodwin admits he doesn't know whether Kennedy would have escalated. If he had, would he have been loony, too?

Goodwin has taken a major geopolitical argument and trivialized it into one man's problem. That switch is nothing less than substance abuse.

Goodwin thinks Johnson was paranoid, first, because he thought that Kennedy loyalists hated LBJ and wanted a Kennedy restoration, and, second, because he thought communists were trying to take over the world.

Curiously, Goodwin's book itself provides plenty of instances of the first charge. And about communists: Today the observation is made that Gorbachev is unique among Soviet leaders. Why? Because (perhaps) he is the first not to publicly stress communist global domination.

What about the death of the Great Society? When liberals today denounce Reagan, they point to the JFK-LBJ 1960s as a time when good things really happened. When conservatives denounce liberalism, they always go back to the '60s when the bad things began. Most every line of American socioeconomic statistics verifies that both teams are right. Like it or not, the '60s set into motion an ongoing advancement of funds for the poor, for minorities, for health, education, the environment, etc. The Great Society lives.

Goodwin, a very good speechwriter, loved alliterative triads; he favored peace, progress, prosperity. His book can be described in that manner: interesting, ill-informed, irresponsible.

September 1, 1988

In the 1988 presidential campaign, Governor Michael Dukakis, the Democratic nominee, was accused of being "a liberal" (see page 333). He finally bit half the bullet. He acknowledged that he was "a liberal

*in the tradition of Franklin Roosevelt, Harry Truman, and John
Kennedy"—and sometimes he added a fourth name, Lyndon Johnson
This is progress. Johnson had been reviled by many in his own party
for many years. The Johnson Restoration is only beginning.*

*As that Restoration proceeds, it will be noted that LBJ's foreign
policy was very much of a piece with the overall American strategy
pursued by the eight U.S. Presidents who served following World
War II, and that the strategy was backed solidly by the American
people. Some big problems emerged in the course of pursuing the
strategy. Vietnam was one of them. On balance, however, it may
well have been the most successful, concerted, and sustained foreign
policy in history. It preserved and extended freedom.*

*There is another restoration I'd like to see: Hubert Humphrey's. I
worked for him in his 1970 senatorial campaign in Minnesota. I'd
go out with him in the evenings to hear him speak at rallies. Frequently,
I went out as sort of a neoconservative and came back a sort of liberal.
Humphrey's was a very special brand of the L-word faith.*

Has Hubert Humphrey Come of Age?

This month will mark 21 years—the traditional age of majority—since
Hubert Humphrey was nominated at the 1968 Chicago Democratic Convention. The ensuing street riot split the Democrats like a cleaver slamming
into an overripe melon.

With the world changing, it is a good time to revisit Humphrey, and a
good time to reconsider Humphreyism—an often-misunderstood political
philosophy. It may be that Humphreyism, too, has reached political majority, more in tune with new times than old, worth re-consideration by
Democrats trying to put the melon together.

I had the fine fortune to work as Humphrey's speechwriter in his 1970
campaign for the U.S. Senate. I learned what others learned earlier: that
he was incandescent, a gifted speaker and a political genius.

When Gary Hart ran for president, he said that if elected he and his
team would not be "a bunch of little Hubert Humphreys."

No doubt. Humphrey was a sophisticated public man with a graduate
degree in political science. He never was, as sometimes described, a reflexive
let's-throw-Washington-money-at-the-problem politician.

To see how Humphrey and his "ism" would fit the present moment,
consider this formulation: He was an anti-communist, capitalist, federalist,
flag-waving, dedicated liberal.

Humphrey's early battles were as mayor of Minneapolis, where he successfully fought organized crime and Communist-run unions. As a former

mayor, he knew that Washington couldn't do it all. His father was a local merchant: Humphrey always boosted small-businessmen. Today that's called entrepreneurialism.

In 1970, Humphrey had a shtick to wind up his stump speeches. He would recite the Pledge of Allegiance with soaring interstitial commentary explaining the patriotic grandeur of certain words like "indivisible," "under God" and "the republic for which it stands." (Just try targeting Humphrey about the Pledge in a presidential contest!)

Cornball? You bet. Humphrey's staff would murmur, "Here it comes again"—and then notice that people in the audience soon had tears in their eyes. So did some of the staff.

And he was a liberal. He cared about the old, the ill, the poor and the children. He was a blood brother to the trade-union movement, the key activist in the civil rights fights, a leader for arms control.

He was the preeminent liberal consensus-seeker. But sometimes a man's strength can also be seen as his weakness. Humphrey was so spectacular as a politician that he could spread his wings very wide in a search to bring Americans together. Some interpreted that as his tragic flaw: a lack of toughness stemming from the attempt to be all things to all men. That aspect of Humphrey is arguable, and it's a long argument.

But his root ideas look better and better. Time and tides change; what might not have been quite ripe or right then, may be riper and righter now. What wasn't destined to simultaneously handle Brezhnev and the domestic loony left, could offer a useful answer now.

If and as the Soviet threat really diminishes, one split in the Democratic party may diminish along with it. Hawks and doves may have less to fight about. As and if that happens, the political zodiac may move into Hubert's alignment.

What a time for Humphreyism! He was rampantly pro-freedom—and the world is now on a democracy binge. He knew the evil of communism and the role of sensible arms control—and now we must understand both. He was pro-market and pro-labor; that too is a formula we'd be wise to learn. He knew how to be simultaneously pro-flag, tough on crime and pro-civil liberties; Democrats may still need lessons. He synthesized pro-civil rights and anti-quotas—now the struggle to find synthesis may again fracture the party he loved.

It's such good stuff for the Democrats, they'd be wise to re-grab it before George Bush steals it. He's already trying.

August 2, 1989

Hubert Humphrey was one of my heroes; Bill Baroody, Sr., was another. Humphrey was a liberal. Baroody (before I knew him) was

issues director for the Barry Goldwater presidential campaign in 1964.
This may sound inconsistent but, for reasons that will crop up
periodically in this book, I don't think it is.

Tanks Are Welcome

As I listened to George Bush's first speech to Congress, and as I have
listened to some conservatives ponder its meaning, I remember one man:
the late William J. Baroody Sr.

From 1954 until his death in 1980, Baroody was the guiding spirit of
the American Enterprise Institute (AEI), a Washington "think tank." He
was a man of intellectual bent, gracious and charming, and an operator.

I got to know Baroody in the late 1970s, when I became an AEI fellow
(I am still one). It was a time when liberal views were in firm command
of the American agenda. Liberals had the ideas, everyone knew that. Conservatives (and Republicans) were seen in the media to be businessmen or
icky nerds, without creative thoughts in the realm of public policy.

Baroody believed that ideas other than the dominant liberal ones should
be heard. He tried to make this happen by establishing a new kind of
think tank. It would be an institution that would generate good ideas formu-
lated by good minds, such ideas to be weighed in fair competition with
other ideas, and to be broadly publicized.

By 1980 or so, Baroody's labors took off and flew. Among the scholars
at AEI at that time were Robert Bork, Jeane Kirkpatrick, Irving Kristol,
Michael Novak, Antonin Scalia and Herbert Stein, to name just a few.

Suddenly, non-liberal ideas were bubbling through the intellectual marketplace. (I do not call them "conservative" ideas. Many of them weren't,
although many of their promulgators have since been labeled that way.)

What were the ideas at issue? One was "deregulation"—much of which
has been enacted into law. Another was "mediating structures"—which
became known as "voluntarism" and then "a thousand points of light."
There was "anticommunist insurgency," which freed Afghanistan. There
was "supply-side economics." There were others.

Were the ideas "new"? Most public policy ideas aren't, and these surely
had earlier roots. What was very new was that the non-liberal side of the
spectrum was being heard from. The medly of American ideas was no
longer just Johnny One Note humming old liberal tunes: it included a
clash of cymbals.

Baroody's new-style think tank helped set the new terms of intellectual
trade. Since then, think tanks have multiplied, flourished and evolved.
There are now such institutions across the ideological spectrum, deeply
involved in the policy dialogue. An American innovation, think tanks are
now forming in other nations.

Those ideas were brought center stage by Ronald Reagan. The Republicans became known as the "party of ideas."

Which brings us to George Bush's speech. It was more like later-Lyndon Johnson than vintage-Ronald Reagan. (And I admire Johnson and many of his basic ideas.) At its core was a laundry list of "programs" needing more funding to get more kindness and gentleness. It was the address of a manager, not an idea merchant.

So conservatives, and non-liberals, are wondering, Will Bush let the Republicans drift back into their gray managerial mode? Will his accomplishment be only to achieve an exalted civil service rank, say, GS-100? Is the excitement gone? Or is something else happening, a consolidation and sorting-out of the Reagan Revolution, still with idea content, pausing now only for digestion? Will there be a second round of non-liberal ideas?

We shall see; Bush's laundry list lecture is not his last word. My sense is that Bush will prove to be much more ideological than he now seems. The intellectual revolution Bill Baroody helped form has not yet run its course.

February 16, 1989

In college in the 1950s, I knew a girl who grew up in a small town in New Hampshire. She told me that Herman Wouk's Marjorie Morningstar *was really about what it's like to be growing up in New Hampshire. She said that the fact that the book was set mostly in Manhattan was irrelevant. I was astonished; I knew the book was about Jews in New York City. Upon reflection, she was right. Wouk's books have a long reach in both human and political terms.*

I have admired Wouk's work since I first read Aurora Dawn *and* City Boy *in the late 1940s. I met Wouk when one of his sons was working on the 1972 Scoop Jackson presidential campaign. Over the years, I have found him to be a man of rare dignity.*

My attempt to put Wouk's writing in a political setting (which follows) was attacked by Jonathan Yardley, the book editor of the Washington Post. *Yardley wrote:*

Marjorie Morningstar, *which I had quite foolishly imagined to be about a young woman's longing for romance and theatrical glamor, emerges under the Wattenberg microscope as a depiction of "the shallowness of Bohemian values against the solidity of traditional middle-class values." . . . Wattenberg seems to have gone hunting for right-wing bear in Wouk's forests. Thus he was able to find just what he wanted in* The Caine Mutiny, *a book that the last time I read it struck me not as about politics—the thought never crossed my mind—but as about human nature and the strange directions it can take when men are too isolated and too much at risk*

That the thought that The Caine Mutiny *was about politics "never crossed" the mind of the book review editor of the* Washington Post *tells a lot about what happened to liberal thinking in recent decades. One big idea of* Caine *deals with the linchpin political question of our time: what happens if free nations aren't strong and assertive?*

What Herman Wouk Sees

We normally think of Herman Wouk as one of America's premier story-tellers, on top of the best-seller lists with books like *The Caine Mutiny, Marjorie Morningstar, The Winds of War*—and now, *Inside, Outside.*

He is indeed a great yarn spinner and with a rich comic flair. He was once a gag writer for comedian Fred Allen. But Wouk is much more than that. In the world of the arts, he was probably the first proponent of a view that in politics these days is called "neo-conservatism."

Thus the point of *The Caine Mutiny* was that liberal scorn of the military is wrongheaded—even when the military was personified in the worst light. And the Caine's skipper, Captain Queeg, psychotic and unbalanced, was indeed the military at its worst. Still Wouk reminded us, it is the military that defends our liberty in a harsh world.

In *Marjorie Morningstar*, Wouk dealt with the shallowness of Bohemian-ism versus the solidity of traditional middle-class values. The book was written when Ronald Reagan was still a resident of the sin city called Hollywood, and when Jerry Falwell was just out of high school.

The Winds of War—and its sequel, *War and Remembrance*—are about World War II. They are deeply patriotic books. Wouk knows that America is the good guy in history.

Traditional values, strong defense, an America on the right side of history, and yet, with all that, a liberal, non-rigid, pluralist outlook on life—the very stuff of the neo-conservative creed.

Wouk's new novel, *Inside, Outside*, touches all of these themes, and others. It is a wonderful personal tale of growing up in New York City in an immigrant Jewish household. Now, this is a field that has been pretty well plowed by a small army of Jewish novelists who, to say the least, are far from neo-conservatism: Philip Roth, Joseph Heller, Bruce Jay Friedman, to name only a few.

These writers have chosen to accentuate what they see as the vulgarity and vapidity of the Jewish experience in America, often, it seems, as a metaphor for what's wrong with America itself. Roth's vulgar *Portnoy's Complaint* is probably the best-known model of the Everything-Is-Ugly school of literature. In a sense, Portnoy is only a latter-day Jewish version of Sinclair Lewis's Babbit, who represents the ultimate put-down of American middle-class values.

But that's not for Herman Wouk. His book is suffused with love. It is not a love with blinders on; there is pettiness, materialism, raunchiness. But there is also the richness and lyricism of the Orthodox Jewish experience, the feeling of Jews for the State of Israel, the gratitude of persecuted Jewish immigrants for the freedom found in what was called the "Goldeneh Medinah," the State of Gold, otherwise known as America, the Beautiful.

Wouk is devilish as he deals with his literary adversaries in the Portnoy Gang. The central character in the book is cast in the role of a lawyer who halfheartedly defends the premier Portnoy author. Wouk deftly slices the author's head off with a blade so fine that the body still moves, still acting for all intents and purposes like a moral man.

But *Inside, Outside* is more than a book about Jewish life, or American life, or life in Israel, or the theatrical world, or political ideology, or a book that settles some literary scores. Wouk goes back to his early works, the small novels *City Boy* and *Aurora Dawn*, to create a universal story of a young boy, and young man, growing up, always wondering—even as he approaches age 60—what he's going to be when he grows up. He keeps finding out—a little bit at a time—in Herman Wouk's masterful new book.

April 25, 1985

What Will They Run on the Front Page?

I was 6 years old, living in the Bronx, when World War II broke out in 1939. During the years after that I used to look at the war maps in the newspapers and ask my father to explain the headlines: "Germans Advance on Kharkov," "Corregidor Surrenders," "Americans Land in Sicily." In August 1945, at a summer bungalow colony, I ran from cottage to cottage yelling, "They've harnessed the atom, they've harnessed the atom."

During those years, I remember asking my father, "What will there be to read in the newspapers after the war is over?" I couldn't think of anything worthy of the front page except the Dodgers, the Yankees and the Giants. And if they put sports there, what could they put in the sports section?

As it turned out, there was a good half-century worth of big front-page story to come: "The Soviets vs. the West."

Only now that there is a possibility of that big story winding down is it apparent how all-pervasive it was. It dealt with arms, the balance of power, military alliances, the money needed to produce the arms, and what the money might be spent for if it didn't have to go for arms.

But it went much beyond that. What were our motives for foreign aid to poor countries? One big reason was to keep them from becoming "fertile breeding grounds for communism" and to keep them on "our side."

That East-West big story permeated the whole of intellectual life as well. The goal was to "be free," to "stay free" and to "help others be free." After all, human liberty had come under serious threat around the world from the communist totalitarians. Just prior to that, from the time of the ascent of Adolf Hitler in Germany in 1933, liberty had been under serious threat from fascist totalitarians.

How potent was the issue? Well, it is now 1989. Suppose we assume that a person must be at least 14 years old before he or she has a sense of the issues of the day. That means that no one under 70 has been seriously involved in a world where the primary focus has not been on totalitarianism.

The big argument raged over decades: Was the threat exaggerated? Weren't we somewhat guilty, too? Why was everything East-West?

Free vs. non-free: It was the ultimate issue. It brought people into public life who in other times would have been poets or playwrights. Rest assured, they wouldn't have been involved if the issue were international trade.

Ironically, the central question of our time may turn out to be whether we will be able to acknowledge that such an all-pervasive issue is not always the central question of every time. Is it really the normal order of being for humans to be constantly concerned over such a titanic and meaningful cause? Perhaps everything since 1933 is not the way the world works.

Suppose the Soviets unwind. Suppose the Soviet Union remains militarily strong, and non-democratic, and poor—all likely, in my judgment. But suppose, too, they come to be correctly seen as a non-expansionist power and one that is highly unlikely to pose a nuclear threat.

I can visualize what the key issue of the geopolitical transition period will be, assuming there is such a transition. Now that the advent of a less confrontational world is possible, the agenda seems obvious, if difficult: Keep the pressure on, remain militarily strong so that the process can continue. That transition could happen in a year or two; more likely it could take a decade. This must be the central focus of the Bush administration. It dwarfs deficits, drugs, the environment.

It is the hope of our time. But I still can't figure out what could come after that. What will they run on the front page?

January 26, 1989

I was born in 1933. My late mother told me that when she was pregnant with me she marched in demonstrations chanting "We want Hitler with a rope around his neck." An uncle I never met was shot by Stalin's thugs in a Moscow courtroom in the early 1950s.

The American People

3

The Changing Face of America, and Why It Matters

*W*hat *is the lay of the land for the 1990s? We begin by trying to gain a sense of who we are as seen through an ethnic, racial, and religious prism.*

From that perspective, the American terrain has changed in ways both stark and evolutionary. The changes, I believe, are monumental facts of our time, with global implications.

We are a unique nation, getting more not less unique, benefiting more than ever from our uniqueness.

Several things seem to be happening simultaneously.

We have become accustomed to the miraculous success stories of, say, the Irish and the Jews. But recently, the rich fruits of other previous immigrations are ripened suddenly in a most public way: Scalia, Cuomo, Muskie, Iacocca, Giamatti, Dukakis.

Moreover, it is also clear (at least to me) that there has been enormous, if variegated, progress among the groups that are over-represented in the alleged American "underclass," Hispanics and blacks.

At the same time, now, new healthy rootstock is being planted in America from parts of the world from which only few Americans had come before. Until 1960, about 80 percent of American immigration had come from Europe; since 1960, about 80 percent come from places other than Europe. They are predominantly Hispanics, Asians, Moslems, and Caribbean and African blacks.

We are becoming what we had professed to be, the first universal nation, and we're very successful at it.

It is very much in the American interest—commercial, geopolitical, demographic, and ideological—to encourage this tendency toward diversity. We ought to encourage it, even if it itches a little. It's one big reason America is, and will be, the omni-power.

Indicators: *Ethnicity*

A. The composition of the U.S. population is slowly changing; Hispanics and Asians are growing proportionately most rapidly.

Projected Population Shifts

Percent of Population		
	1990	2080
Hispanic	8%	19%
Black	12%	16%
White (non-Hispanic)	77%	55%
Asian and other	3%	11%

B. People of white European ancestry (most of the U.S.) tend to think that immigrants from their own groups have been most beneficial to the U.S.

Q. Has the arrival of the following religious, racial, or ethnic groups been a good thing or a bad thing for the United States?

Group	Good Thing	Bad Thing
English	66%	6%
Irish	62%	7%
Jews	59%	9%
Germans	57%	11%
Italians	56%	10%
Poles	53%	12%
Japanese	47%	18%
Blacks	46%	16%
Chinese	44%	19%
Mexicans	25%	34%
Koreans	24%	30%
Vietnamese	20%	38%
Puerto Ricans	17%	30%
Haitians	10%	39%
Cubans	9%	59%

Source notes are on page 391.

C. The smaller the group, the higher the intermarriage rates; intermarriage is much more prevalent than in the recent past; interracial marriages are much rarer than interethnic.

Exogamy Rates (the Percentage of People from a Specified Group Marrying Outside of that Group)

Group	Male	Female
White	1.1%	0.9%
Black	4.6%	2.1%
Other*	17.6%	26.2%
Hispanic	15.5%	19.1%
Jewish	37%	25%
Protestant	18% (total)	
Catholic	40% (total)	

Rate by Age	Under 25	65+
English	44%	38%
Irish	64%	45%
Italian	77%	34%
Polish	82%	43%
Swedish	90%	78%

* Other—primarily Asian-Americans

D. American fertility rates range from very low European-style to rather high Third-World-style.

Total Fertility Rates by Region, State, Race, and Ethnicity in 1980

Classification	TFR (Children Per Woman)
Total U.S.	1.84
Cuban	1.29
Massachusetts	1.45
Jews	1.5
New York	1.63
White	1.75
California	1.90
Black	2.23
Puerto Rican	2.46
Hispanic	2.53
Mexican	2.95
Utah	3.22
Mormon	4.0

Symbol for the World

Covered with glitz, television, fireworks and celebrities, it may be hard to discern why the Liberty Lady is so important these days.

Let's go back a bit. At about the time the Statue of Liberty was unveiled 100 years ago, the patterns of American immigration were changing rather dramatically—just as they are changing dramatically now.

Prior to the 1880s, it would have been fair to characterize the American population in roughly this way: white people who originally came from the countries of northwestern Europe and black people who originally came from Africa as slaves. The white people, be it further noted, came from countries that typically had had at least some democratic experience.

Then, suddenly—at about the time the statue arrived—new kinds of immigrants began pouring into America: Italians, Jews from eastern Europe, Poles, Slavs, Ukrainians. They were people from countries with little or no democratic tradition.

There was great consternation in the United States. Wise men worried whether these swarthy, unwashed primitives could ever learn to be Americans in the way WASPs were.

Well, of course, they and their children, and their grandchildren, managed well enough: Lee Iacocca, George Gershwin and Edmund Muskie come immediately to mind.

And so, a message was sent from these new-style, ethnic immigrants who arrived in America sailing beneath the shadow of the Statue of Liberty. The message was this: Democracy in America could work for people other than just northwestern Europeans with democratic backgrounds.

Today, something similar is happening on the immigration front. Most American immigrants these days are not coming from Europe—not northwest Europe or southern Europe or eastern Europe.

Most new immigrants today are from Latin America, and from Asia, and some from the Moslem lands. From everywhere. They no longer typically arrive in a harbor with a colossal statue. These day they come into airports, but they are immigrants just the same. And once again, it's working: How many times have you seen on television the story of the little Vietnamese girl who came here speaking no English and became the high school class valedictorian?

So now a new message is going out. Democracy in America can work not just for all kinds of Europeans—even those without democratic traditions—but for everyone.

Well—democracy can work for everyone who comes to America. That is an interesting, indeed heart-rending domestic story. But it has become transmuted into a foreign policy story as well, perhaps the most important one in the world today. For once you say democracy works for everyone in America—Europeans, Africans, Latins and Asians—there is a corollary question that begins to form. Might democracy work for everyone, everywhere—not just in America?

Remember, the Statue of Liberty faces outward to the world. Its message may be universal. If Filipinos can be democrats in America, why not in the Philippines? If Nicaraguans can be democrats in the United States, why not in Nicaragua? How about Cuba? Haiti? Poland? South Korea? Hungary? Russia?

This is the nature of the global struggle today. Is the symbolism of the Statue of Liberty ours, or everyone's?

July 3, 1986

It's All Greek to Us

A few words about ethnicity. True to my own ethnic heritage I offer hoary advice: Keep your eye on the bagel, not on the hole.

There has been much attention paid to the ethnic/racial importance of Jesse Jackson's candidacy. He is the first black to be a serious presidential player. I don't like the substance of Jackson's politics, but no one can take anything away from his dynamic candidacy, and its symbolic and positive contribution to American democracy.

The attention paid to Jackson's achievement, however, has tended to downplay something else that is at work, and quite remarkable.

Gov. Michael Dukakis of Massachusetts will be the Democratic nominee for president this year. Right now he is solidly ahead of George Bush in the polls. His parents were Greek immigrants. If elected president, he'll be the first "ethnic American" to live in the White House, at least by my definition.

I offer my own definition because experts have not been able to agree on one. In fact the *Harvard Encyclopedia of American Ethnic Groups* offers 14 different criteria that may define ethnicity, including "geographical origin," "language or dialect," "food preferences," and "shared traditions, values and symbols."

Of course, one can make the case that all Americans except native American Indians are ethnics. But that makes "ethnic" a near-meaningless word. It's not. In the everyday political argot, it has real meaning.

So look at it my way: The early settlers in America were people from northwestern Europe—England, Scotland, Wales, Ireland, Holland, Germany. I declare all the rest as "ethnics," including blacks, who also came here early, but typically in slavery, and many of whom fill in the ethnic blank on census forms as "Afro-American." By such a reasonable definition, John Kennedy, of Irish descent, would not qualify as ethnic. In any event, both of his parents and all four of his grandparents were born in America.

Michael Dukakis is a genuine ethnic.

Just a year or so ago it was said that many voters, particularly in the South, wouldn't vote for a man named "Dukakis." Well, well. Today Dukakis is leading Bush in the polls in some Southern states. Moreover, other stories are coming in. One voter was recently quoted this way: "My father came over from Italy; Dukakis' father came from Greece. I like that."

There are 1,555,340 people of Italian ancestry in the South alone. The total Greek-ancestry population is 954,856. We also have Azerbaijanis, Bosnian Muslims, Carpatho-Rusyns, and Frisians. The Harvard volume counts at least 106 ethnic groups—not a bad coalition if a candidate could put it together. Suddenly, strangely, it seems as if Bush is being penalized because he comes from an elite WASP family (born, as one wag puts it, with a silver foot in his mouth).

Things are changing in America. The first Italian-American is on the Supreme Court. Blacks are making headway in politics. Asian-Americans will likely dominate the next generation of Nobel Prize winners in the sciences. Jews don't even bother to complain that there is no Jew in the so-called Supreme Court "Jewish seat." We might have a Greek-American in the White House. If we don't, it may be because he is perceived as too liberal, but not because of his ethnic heritage.

These days pundits wonder about how the next decade will be character-ized. We've been told that the '50s were "silent," the '60s "revolutionary," the '70s "self-actualizing," and the '80s "greedy." We ought to look at it differently. Forget the adjectives and look at what's happening. Maybe the '90s will be known as the Decade of the Ethnics.

June 30, 1988

Finalmente!

There have been 106 Supreme Court Justices appointed in all American history.

There are almost 20 million Italian-Americans. Until the nomination of Antonin Scalia, none—zero—had been on the U.S. Supreme Court.

Scalia is a Republican and a conservative. New York's Gov. Mario Cuomo, the most prominent Italian-American politician, is a Democrat and a (perceived) liberal. I asked Cuomo what he thought of the appointment.

"Finalmente!" he said, which roughly translates to: "It's about time."

"My first reaction," said Cuomo, "was a visceral burst of pride. It showed the upward mobility of Italian-Americans. It's a magnificent moment. July Fourth is coming up. I just visited Ellis Island where my immigrant mother landed. And now we have a Supreme Court Justice who says, 'My friends call me Nino.'"

"My second reaction was also positive," said Cuomo. "Here's a bright, thoughtful lawyer, a professor of law, with reverence for the law, picked for the highest court, a man eminently qualified. He's a good lawyer. We'll wait for the confirmation hearings, but I think he'll be a fine judge."

Washington is a conspiratorial town, sometimes absurdly so. I asked Cuomo about the Washington rumor that one reason Scalia was appointed was to harm Cuomo, a possible Democratic presidential nominee. Scalia, so the rumor went, would keep Italo-Americans in the Republican Party— so that Cuomo couldn't steal them for Democrats.

"Anyone who thinks that is dumb and stupid," said Cuomo. "Elevating and honoring a decent and brilliant Italian-American helps me and other Italian-Americans. It doesn't hurt us. If they wanted to hurt me or other Italians, they'd be grandstanding Mafia material."

Cuomo is not the only Italian-American happy over the Scalia appointment. There is a feeling among many that a Supreme Court slot is the best remedy for the Mafia and criminal stereotype that has long plagued the Italo-American community. Lee Iacocca—executive—that's one fine thing in an upwardly mobile ethnic group. A. Bartlett Giamatti—former president of Yale—that's another. But a justice of the Supreme Court! One of only nine high priests protecting the majesty of the law. That's the best!

"To Italian-Americans," says Jack Valenti, president of the Motion Picture Association, "it's a root-stirring appointment, aimed like a lance at the distorted media image of ordinary Italians."

Scalia is not only a wise, warm and qualified judge, but a man who runs against the grain of the Italian-American stereotype in more than one way. His parents died recently: His mother was a school teacher; his father a professor of romance languages at Brooklyn College, who used to correct his son's English grammar even after he became a judge. Still, Scalia grew up on the sidewalks of Queens, N.Y., and knows the taste of big-city, ethnic America in a way that most other justices don't.

As Cuomo says, "Finalmente." Historically, the Supreme Court has always been behind the curve of American demography. It was 1916 before a Jew (Louis Brandeis) was appointed. It was 1967 before a black (Thurgood Marshall) was picked. It was 1981 before a woman (Sandra Day O'Connor) was chosen. And now, 1986, an Italian-American. It's a step in the right direction. But there is a long way to go. We will be a better country, with a better high court, when the pool from which justices will be chosen will include people of Polish-American, Slavic-American, Asian-American, Hispanic-American and Arab-American heritage.

I am not for quotas, but we are moving past the time when it can be said that there are no minority candidates of real excellence (like Scalia). As it stands now, despite the recent progress, one must still ask whether the Supreme Court is an institution that reflects the full flavor of America. Is it a body that cries and breathes and bleeds in tune with the rest of this variegated country? Or is it mostly composed of stuffy elites, of whatever political ideology? The sooner it becomes more of the former and less of the latter, the better it will be.

June 26, 1986

Wedded to Intermarriage

When Andrew Cuomo, son of New York's Governor Mario Cuomo, recently married Kerry Kennedy, daughter of the late Senator Robert Kennedy, it was hailed as the remarkable coming-together of two political dynasties. It was. Moreover, one assumes, it was also the marriage of two young people in love.

Beyond all that was unique and beyond all that was universal, the marriage was also a symbol of a profoundly important American situation that has reached true majority status only in recent decades. Barely noticed nowadays, the Melting Pot has happened. Americans of European ancestry are becoming one people. Arguably, the same process is going on among most non-European Americans, although at a lesser incidence.

In the langauge of scholars who study the field, the Cuomo-Kennedy union was "exogamous"—that is, it was an "intermarriage." Mr. Cuomo is of Italian ancestry. His wife is of mixed Irish ancestry.

Today, intermarriage between whites of European ancestry is the rule. That was not true in earlier generations. Among Italian Americans (IA) born in America prior to 1920, almost two-thirds (63 percent) married other IAs. But of IAs born after 1950 (like Andrew Cuomo), only about a fifth (22 percent) marry other IAs.

Similar patterns of prevalent intermarriage now exist among Irish Americans, Polish Americans and English Americans. The overall figure is about 75 percent. (The data comes from the 1980 Census, as analysed by Professor Richard Alba of the State University of New York.)

Another way of looking at the identity of Americans is through the prism of "mixed ancestry." Just 8 percent of all IAs born prior to 1920 were of "mixed ancestry." Of IAs born after 1960, the rate is 70 percent.

The Census Bureau doesn't keep statistics about religion, but estimates show that almost half of new marriages involving Jews now include non-Jewish partners, compared to less than 10 percent in 1950s.

Now, intermarriage has been an issue about as passionate, and sometimes poisonous, as has existed in American life. But whatever the opinions, intermarriage is now a massive fact. We are witnessing the birth of *genus Americanus*, and we're never going to be the same.

The impact is powerful. In the old days, newly arrived white ethnic and religious groups faced scorn. Alba writes that Italian immigrants "became a focus for explicitly racist thinking and stereotypes," perceived as "swarthy" people with "low foreheads," and that the derogatory anti-Italian epithet "guinea" referred originally "to slaves from the Western coast of Africa."

Much of that, not all, has vanished. It's a lot harder to countenance the rejection of other peoples when your in-laws and grandchildren are them, and even harder when, in the next generation, you are too.

It is unlikely that Joseph P. Kennedy, the "founding father" of the American Kennedy clan, envisioned having granddaughters married to people named Cuomo (Italian), Schlossberg (Jewish) and Schwarzenegger (Austrian). But who's going to argue, particularly with Schwarzenegger?

These trends of European assimilation are relevant to Americans of non-European ancestry. We are hearing a great deal about increased tensions, focusing on Hispanics, Asians and blacks. Most of the evidence is anecdotal, with little effort to compare what is happening now with earlier times.

But the marriage data points toward more amity rather than more hostility. Intermarriage trends among Hispanic Americans and Asian Americans are similar to European ones, but at a lower level. Almost a third of Hispanic Americans intermarry today; the earlier generational figures were half that. About the same proportions hold true for Asian Americans.

The black rates are significantly different, but the direction again is the same: 4 percent of those born after 1950 have intermarried, compared to about a half of one percent born prior to 1920.

From intermarriage and immigration, from inside and out, speedily in some realms and slowly in others, America is becoming a universal nation.
June 20, 1990

All the attitudinal evidence available shows that Americans are indeed more tolerant than in earlier times. The incidence of "hate crimes," much discussed, is not measurable over time. It is not a new phenomenon, only newly measured.

The De-otherization of America

There is an "other" explosion going on in the United States. Have you ever met an "other"? Maybe, indeed, you are an "other."

Until now that's how 8.5 million Americans were described in the regularly issued U.S. Census population estimates. "Others" (whole name,

"Other Races") were those Americans who were described by what they were not. They were not "white," "black" or "of Hispanic origin."

In short, they were either "Asians and Pacific Islanders" (API) or "American Indians, Eskimos or Aleuts" (AIEA). Striking a blow for semi-clarity, the Census Bureau has wisely de-otherized their population estimates (previously, only the decennial census categorized others by their otherness.) Now, APIs are counted as APIs and AIEAs as AIEAs in estimates as well as decennials.

The big news from the just-issued estimates concerns the APIs, who shall be called here Asian-Americans, because that's where most of the APIs come from. (Anyway, where are Pacific Islands like the Marianas and the Marshalls—in The Bronx?)

In 1980 there were 3.8 million Asian-Americans. By 1988, there were 6.5 million. That's an increase of 70 percent! In eight years! It's twice the rate of increase of Hispanics (34 percent) and vastly greater than the increase of AIEAs (19 percent), blacks (13 percent) or whites (6 percent).

About two-thirds of the growth of Asian-Americans came from immigration, and the greatest number of Asian immigrants were from the Philippines, South Korea, China (including Taiwan), India, Vietnam, Cambodia and Laos. Newer immigrant streams are also now coming from Thailand and even arch-competitor Japan. (Why are Japanese coming here if everything is allegedly so great over there and allegedly so terrible over here?)

Today, Asians make up almost 3 percent of the U.S. population. In 20 years the figure will be about 5 percent.

The Asian influx represents the last step in the universalizing of America. In substantial numbers and proportions, Americans can now be said to come from everywhere. No other nation, ever, could have made that claim.

It will stand us in good stead as the years roll on. Nineteen of the forty newly announced 1990 Westinghouse Scholars are Asian-Americans. The Westinghouse awards are based on the most prestigious high-school-level science competition in the United States, if not the world. Not a bad contribution from immigrants to a nation (ours) that allegedly is going to need all the help it can get to compete in the world. And not a bad boost to some lazy American kids who may need intellectual shock treatment to understand that the days of academic coasting are over.

But that's already a cliche; Asian-American scientists, engineers and doctors. It's going to go far beyond that. The largest and richest new markets in the world will be coming from Asia in the years to come.

Japan is already a global economic powerhouse. South Korea and Taiwan are experiencing explosive economic growth. Malaysia and Thailand are not much behind. India didn't quite make it in this century, but the economic portents are clear: It will be a commercial giant in the next century. And then there is China. If China takes off (and there are signs that it might), we're talking about an additional one billion middle-class consumers, which is more than a little.

There are those who say that the next century will be called "the Pacific Century," or "the Asian Century." That is supposed to be a threat to continued American global hegemony. But, hold on, we are a Pacific nation. In fact, we are the only Pacific nation that has substantial numbers of people from all the other Pacific and Asian nations. We may turn out to be the common denominator nation in the Pacific-Asian world, thereby extending Pax Americana for a long time to come.

March 7, 1990

Chu, Wu, Hor—and Harvard

Does Harvard discriminate against admitting potential Nobel Prize winners? My recent reading offers a roundabout answer: probably so.

Consider first a recent *New York Times Magazine* article, "In the Trenches of Science." It deals with a historic breakthrough in superconductivity—the hottest topic in science today. Superconductivity is also believed to be the next big arena in the global "competitiveness" race; America has big stakes riding on the outcome.

The big new discovery in superconductivity was made by an American physicist at the University of Houston named Ching-Wu Chu, a man who was born in China, came to graduate school in the United States in 1962 and has been here ever since. Chu is in the race to get a Nobel Prize for superconductivity research.

The *Times* piece mentions Chu's colleague at Houston, Pei-Herng Hor, and notes that Chu has expanded his team to include a group of University of Alabama scientists headed by one of his former students, Maw-Kuen Wu. Times writer James Gleick describes a phone conversation where Chu is "using one of the increasingly common languages of American physics, scientific Chinese, every fourth word an English technical term."

Against this backdrop, consider a recent article by John Bunzel and Jeffrey Au in *The Public Interest* magazine, "Diversity or Discrimination? Asian-Americans in College." Bunzel and Au examine the possibility that there is anti-Asian discrimination at elite American universities. They look specifically at data from Harvard, Princeton, Stanford and Brown.

At Brown, the most recent data show that 20 percent of all applicants are admitted but only 14 percent of Asian-Americans; that is, the Asian-American admission rate is only 70 percent of the overall rate. The ratios are similar at the other schools. More disturbing is that the ratios declined through the first part of the 1980s, the latest time for which statistics are available.

A committee at Brown investigated and said their inquiry "reinforces the idea that there exists an unwritten quota for Asian-Americans at Brown." Committees at Princeton and Stanford reported that those schools are not guilty of anything at all, but don't explain apparently discriminatory data. Mighty Harvard did not allow the release of any official documents, but Bunzel and Au cite some damning statistics: Caucasians offered admission to Harvard had average Scholastic Aptitude Test scores of 1,355, while Asian-Americans had an average of 1,467. Thus, at Harvard, an Asian-American had to be 112 points better in order to have the same chance of admittance as whites. Would younger versions of Chu, Wu or Hor make the cut at Harvard?

Bunzel and Au examine some other possible reasons for the apparent discrimination against Asian-American students: charges that they engage in less extra-curricular activity, that they have different personality characteristics, that they are over-concentrated in the fields of science. The available evidence shows none of these excuses are valid.

The real problem with Asian-Americans is that they do too well. Why? A study of high school students by Stanford professor Sanford Dornbusch led the professor to this comment: "My bottom line is there's no question the Asians are working a heck of a lot harder."

The bottom line of this tale is that our best students are having difficulty getting to our best universities. This is not only unfair, but it could theoretically harm our national ability to compete successfully. Luckily, if that happens, it will probably only be true for a while. Sooner or later, what are now our best universities won't be best anymore because they won't have the best students. Too bad. It would be less than a national tragedy if Nobel Prizes were to go to the University of Houston instead of to Harvard.

September 3, 1987

Worrying Jews

Jews tend to worry a lot, and for good reason. In one way or another, on several continents, they have felt the sting of persecution for 2,000 years. And so, when things go badly, many Jews start looking over their shoulder.

It has not been a happy time for worried Jews in America. In late 1985, Jonathan Pollard, an American Jew, was caught spying for Israel. In the spring of 1986, the "insider" trading scandals broke on Wall Street. Most of the accused were Jews. Then came the Iran arms affair. The American government knew what it was doing, but the Israelis provided much of the intelligence. Just when Pollard was sentenced to life in prison—the Israelis promoted two of his "handlers."

So there has been a troubled air in the Jewish community. The scandals linked up uncomfortably with some old anti-Semitic stereotypes: The Wall Streeters could be seen as those unscrupulous Jewish financiers. The Pollard case raised the old question of "dual loyalty"; Pollard was loyal to Israel, not America.

A group of American Jewish leaders went to Israel to tell the Israelis how wrong they were. Some Israelis countered that the nervousness displayed by American Jews betrayed their own exile mentality, and, even in America, Jews couldn't really feel safe.

But one critical item was missing. There didn't seem to be any increase in anti-Semitism in America. The public argument about dual loyalty, for example, was essentially speculation about what other people would say. But "they" didn't say it.

There is, I think, a reason for the missing rise in anti-Semitism. This: There is not much anti-Semitism in America.

In 1982 a Roper poll gave respondents a list of different races, religions and nationalities. The respondents were asked whether they thought it was a good thing or a bad thing for America that the various groups had come here. The results showed the English in first place, the Irish in second place and the Jews in third place—with 12 other groups strung out behind. (See page 47.)

Such results are astonishing to any student of Jewish history. It would be unfathomable to get such findings in the European countries, either in the old days or even now. Jews were and in some cases still are considered aliens. Such a result would have been most unlikely in America even a few decades ago, when Jews were denied admission to many colleges or businesses. But every additudinal index shows that anti-Semitism is losing ground in America.

This doesn't mean it's gone. A variety of forms of discrimination lingers on. (But the same can be said of prejudice against most other groups as well: not only blacks, Hispanics and Asian-Americans, but Italians and Poles, as well.)

Why is there so little anti-Semitism in America? First, we are a pluralist nation: everyone is a minority of some kind. That makes serious persecution a dangerous game in most cases.

Second, a sort of philo-Semitism has grown up in America to serve as a counterbalance to anti-Semitism. The late Sen. Henry Jackson had many Jewish supporters during his runs for the presidency in the 1970s. He once told me, "as I travel around I'm always amazed. The same Jews who are supporting me are also likely to be the head of United Way, on the board of local hospitals, active in community support for the arts, the most respected doctors."

Jews, indeed, have been both successful in American society and given much back to it. That seems to go a long way toward combating negative stereotypes.

So when incidents like Pollard, Iranscam and financial skulduggery surface, they are surfacing in a reservoir of comparative good will. And soon they are forgotten, and life goes on as before in a nation that has, in its way, opened up not only for Jews, but for so many peoples from all over the world.

April 9, 1987

The Opportunity Age

A great national tragedy, a quick and brutal snapshot in time, sometimes offers us an especially clear lens through which to see ourselves.

Nineteen years ago three astronauts were killed in a terrible accident in their capsule on the ground. They were authentic American heroes: Virgil Grissom, Roger Chaffee and Edward White. They precisely fit the mold of what we then thought American heroes were: white Anglo-Saxon males. That went without comment.

Last week we experienced another American tragedy: the fireball that blew up the space shuttle Challenger. The second snapshot shows how we have changed. Seven Americans were killed, but it happened in a different nation.

Three of the seven victims were, again, white Anglo-Saxon males. Two of them were pilots, one was an engineer.

Of the remaining four, one was an MIT physicist originally from South Carolina—a black man. Another had a doctorate in electrical engineering—she was a Jewish woman. A third was a former Air Force test pilot—a Japanese-American. The fourth was a history teacher from New Hampshire, a woman with two children, who years ago had complained that only men got to go to space.

It wasn't an accident that the three astronaut heroes we mourned in 1967 were all white men, and it wasn't an accident that a majority weren't in 1986. In the mid-'60s who could have said seriously that most of the crew of a space vehicle would be black, Asian, Jewish and/or female? And in the mid-'80s who would seriously imagine a shuttle crew of seven white men?

We have entered a new time in American life, and I am not talking about the Space Age. It is the Opportunity Age.

In some very direct way, there was a black man in space in the 1980s because of the civil rights movement of the 1950s and 1960s. Barriers against women came crashing down awhile later. It is a not-unrelated phenomenon that in many technological fields young Asian-Americans are now the outstanding students in America's most prestigious universities. It is not unrelated that at just about the time when our perceptive political scientists were worrying that American Jews could only be successful in behind-the-scenes politics—Jews began running for high elected offices, often from areas with only few Jews. Running—and winning. In the 1960s would you have believed Jewish senators from Nebraska, New Hampshire and Nevada? Conservatives all?

The list could go on. Italian-Americans are a growing force in business, the arts, politics and the academy. Hispanics—from Mexico, Cuba, South America and the Caribbean—may be only a half-step behind, if that.

What intuition doesn't tell you, the census figures do. Our immigrants used to be 80 percent from Europe; now they are 20 percent from Europe. One day soon there will be American astronauts whose parents were born in India, the Philippines, Ecuador and Nigeria.

It would be disingenuous to say that NASA officials picked their astronauts randomly. They didn't. They wanted a cross-section of American excellence. There were politics, public relations and poetry involved in their choices. NASA needs public support. To its credit it knows that the public supports as never before the idea that, in this country, in this day, everyone participates.

It doesn't happen to be the easiest way to run a society. It causes some bumps and bruises and dislocations. The sound you hear is the breaking of tradition.

But it's the way we are, and nobody's been this way before.

February 6, 1986

Tomorrow: Hispanics

The words are so often spoken together that they have almost become one—blacksandhispanics—especially when the context is a discussion of who is not making it in America. While there has been a great deal of highly publicized and often sophisticated analysis of the status of blacks, less attention has been paid to Hispanics.

But beneath the surface of some gloomy data, the evidence shows that Hispanics will be another immigrant group that made its way up the ladder.

The rapidly growing Hispanic community in the United States now numbers about 20 million, of whom 62 percent are of Mexican origin, 13 percent Puerto Rican, 12 percent Central and South American, and 5 percent Cuban. In general, the data show that Cubans have fared the best while Puerto Ricans have had the most difficult adjustment.

A key to understanding Hispanics' apparent lack of statistical progress is

Indicators: *Hispanics*

Source notes are on page 391.

A. The number of Hispanic-Americans has grown rapidly, at more than three times the rate of the rest of America.

Number of Hispanics, 1950–90

Year	Number (in Millions)
1950	4.0
1960	6.9
1970	9.1
1980	14.6
1985	16.9
1988	19.4
1989	20.4
1990	20.9

B. Hispanic status improves with longer residence in the U.S.

Reading Scores (Out of a Possible 500) and Hourly Wages of U.S. Hispanic Population, Age 21–25, by Years in U.S.

Years in U.S.	Score	Hourly Wage
0 to 5 years	156	$4.83
6 to 10 years	180	$5.61
More than 10 years	270	$6.49
Native born of Hispanic descent	270	$6.19
All U.S.	282	$6.20

C. Hispanics are moving up the occupational ladder.

Percent of Hispanics in White Collar Occupations

Year	Percent
1980	35%
1982	37%
1984	37%
1986	39%
1988	40%

D. Although there have been only relatively small changes in income ratio . . .

1. Ratio of Hispanic to U.S. Total Personal Income

Year	Family Income Ratio	Per Capita Income Ratio
1973	.72	.59
1977	.71	.61
1981	.73	.63
1984	.71	.62
1987	.66	.62
1988	.68	.61

D. (Cont.) . . . . many economic analysts believe that real Hispanic income gains have been masked by the recent arrival of substantial numbers of new Hispanic immigrants.

2. U.S. Hispanic Population

Year	Percent of Mexicans that are: Emigrés	Percent of Hispanics that are: Mexican	Emigrés
1970	18%	50%	20%
1980	26%	59%	29%
1988	33%	62%	34%

that 36 percent of them are immigrants to the United States and half of those arrived within the last 10 years. Historically, new immigrants usually have difficulty starting out. Accordingly, the statistical status of their entire group is artificially depressed. But when the data for Hispanics are adjusted to reflect the difference in nativity and duration of residence, a different portrait emerges.

For example, Census Bureau data show that Hispanic immigrants in the United States for more than five years have a poverty rate half that of more recent immigrants. And while 1987 Hispanic family income was only 63 percent that of whites, young Hispanics—who are much more likely to be American-born—had almost the same earnings as young whites. Also, American-born Hispanics are twice as likely to hold white-collar jobs as are recent Hispanic immigrants.

A recent examination of the 1985 National Assessment of Educational Progress, by Professor Francisco Rivera-Batiz of Rutgers University, found further evidence that the longer Hispanics have been in the United States, the more money they make. (See chart, page 60.)

Not surprisingly, the data can be interpreted in different ways in the public policy debate. Rafael Valdivieso of the Hispanic Policy Development Project stresses that, notwithstanding individual progress, Hispanics as a group still lag far behind whites; they are far more likely to drop out of high school and to live in female-headed households. He concludes that Hispanics need massive government and private help.

Linda Chavez, former staff director of the U.S. Commission on Civil Rights and a former official in the Reagan White House, believes the current data is essentially heartening. Chavez, who is writing a book on Hispanics entitled "Tipping the Melting Pot," suggests that stressing bad news is the worst thing for Latinos because it "inculcates the idea that they are permanently and structurally disadvantaged, which corrodes self-esteem, and can be self-fulfilling." Indeed, it might be wise to stop thinking of Latinos as Americans who are down and out, and look instead to models of earlier upwardly mobile immigrant groups, who struggled and made it.

September 25, 1989

Turning the Kerner on Racism

Has the Kerner Commission report of 1968 been repudiated?

It's an important question. Ideas have consequences. The Kerner study, which came after black riots, shaped the thinking of a generation. If Kerner was flawed, the thinking that grew from it may be flawed.

Kerner's central statement was that America "is moving forward two societies, one black, one white—separate and unequal." Why? The answer was clear said Kerner: "white racism." The results of racism were also clear to Kerner: Conditions for blacks were dreadful, apparently deteriorating, and would worsen unless the federal government acted massively.

Comes now a new study, by the National Research Council: "A Common Destiny: Blacks and American Society."

The NRC report does not seek to discredit Kerner, or even deal with it directly. Yet, consider the summary of NRC by the director of the study, Professor Gerald Jaynes of Yale: "Although better by a wide margin than it was in 1940, by nearly all objective measures, the status of blacks relative to whites has stagnated or regressed since the early 1970s."

So: NRC says there was great progress in the good old days of the civil rights movement—until the early 1970s. But Kerner, which came out in those good old days, said things were terrible, and likely to get worse.

Which is right? NRC's statement of no relative progress for blacks since the early 1970s is arguable; I think black progress has continued. But NRC's conclusion that progress was made in the '60s is correct. It is supported by mountains of data.

Kerner was not only off-base factually. It sent out harmful messages to blacks and Americans generally. By concentrating on racism and government, Kerner shortchanged the argument now called "the culture of poverty," which stresses internal problems of the black community.

Some NRC scholars (by no means all) understand that Kerner was misguided. Professor Glen Loury of Harvard, an NRC panelist, states: "By saying that implacable white racism brought about poor conditions, Kerner posed the situation as a white problem, not a black problem. That is a harmful notion for blacks."

Loury, who is black, is right. Efforts to root out racial discrimination must continue. But the doors of opportunity are open. Loury believes blacks are better served by focusing on open doors rather than blaming their situation on racism.

Professor Nathan Glazer of Harvard, another NRC panel member, says: "The Kerner Commission taught us to concentrate on the undoable or the unimportant."

Glazer believes Kerner's stress on racism led to stressing civil rights enforcement as the major tool of black advancement. That led to disruptive fights about school busing, reverse discrimination and quotas. Glazer believes that was a wrong turn because major legislative battles had already been won. Education should have been emphasized: The payoff is surer and less polarizing.

Another sad Kerner legacy is a paradox: that the tool of big government doesn't work—and that only the tool of big government can possibly work. Wrong twice.

In the 1960s America mounted a major governmental effort to help minorities. Social and welfare spending went up by 89 percent in real dollars. Black poverty was cut almost in half. Along came Kerner and said things don't get better even when the government spends. Conservatives whooped. When early-vintage Reaganites said, "we're throwing money down a rathole," the unstated subtext was "and Kerner proves it."

But Kerner also said only vast amounts of government dollars could solve the problem. As with the racism idea, that de-emphasized individual effort.

Dr. Bernard Gifford, NRC member and vice president of Apple Computer, says that dwelling on either of the grand arguments, racism or government, "can cripple those who are trying to make change one day at a time." Gifford, a black, says Kerner was not scholarship, but "a political period piece that delayed serious intellectual thought about the real pathologies in the black community."

Correct: Kerner was politics, not sociology.

August 23, 1989

Atten-chun! Blacks in the Military

There is a fascinating article—mixing sociology, race and politics—in May's edition of the *Atlantic* magazine. The piece is "Success Story: Blacks in the Army," by Dr. Charles C. Moskos, a Northwestern University sociologist who specializes in race relations in the U.S. military.

To begin, Moskos believes this: The U.S. military is the most successfully integrated institution in America.

Consider: There are 400,000 blacks in the U.S. armed forces. That's almost 20 percent of the entire force, while blacks make up only about 12 percent of the total population. In the Army, which Moskos has studied with particular care, 30 percent of the personnel are black.

Blacks, says Moskos, do pretty well in the Army. About 30 percent of the Army's non-commissioned officers are now black. That's almost 100,000 black sergeants!

It doesn't stop with NCOs: Fully 10 percent of the Army's officers are black, and the rate is rising. One in five of the Army's new ROTC graduate officers are black. The proportion of blacks in the incoming West Point class has gone up tenfold in one generation. Of the active generals in the Army today, 7 percent are black. More are on the way.

Moskos is not foolish enough to say everything is all racially wonderful. He notes reflections in the military of an American society where blacks are poorer and less educated than whites. He sees the reflections, too, of a society that has still not fully conquered discrimination. But he says this: "Today one is more likely to hear racial jokes in a faculty club than in an officers' club. And in an officers' club, one will surely see more blacks."

Moskos points to another heartening fact: Each year about 5,000 black officers and NCOs reach the young military retirement age and return to civilian work. This number will be growing as the decades roll on. These are productive, disciplined people. They have been bossed by whites. And they have bossed whites. In the years to come, one may expect that these veterans will play a large role in making integration more successful in the rest of America.

Moskos also has a political point. He notes that black elected leaders are out of touch with this large group of upwardly mobile blacks—and the feeling is mutual.

The elected blacks (says Moskos) are almost invariably very liberal; not so the military blacks among whom, for example, some substantial Reagan support exists, as well as support for moderate to conservative Democrats. Most elected blacks favor preferential treatment for blacks; blacks in the military are often dubious and draw pride from having made it on their own. And there is foreign and defense policy. Recall that Jesse Jackson has called for a 25 percent cut in defense spending and that the Congressional Black Caucus always leads the parade for less defense spending.

Here's what Moskos says about the black elected liberal leadership: "Most of them are uninterested in, even alienated from, the long-term goals of American foreign policy. . . . When foreign-policy issues are raised by black leaders, the discussion generally involves racist features of U.S. behavior overseas, especially in Africa and the Caribbean."

When the Congressional Black Caucus issued a formal condemnation of the U.S. invasion of Grenada, Moskos reports the reaction of one black general was, "Why can't they support us just this once?"

Very interesting. Now, I have a question. There are 400,000 blacks now in service. Many more are going into the military each year, and many are coming out with military retirement pay. Add to that all the spouses and growing families. Question: Isn't it possible that there may be a growing and potent pro-defense, pro-moderate, black political constituency out there? Is it possible that politicians—black and white, of both parties—are ignoring something big that has already happened?

May 15, 1986

In August 1989, President Bush appointed General Colin Powell, who is black, to be as chairman of the Joint Chiefs of Staff, the highest rank in the military.

Don't Lebanonize America

President Bush is being urged to be a good fellow and go along with the proposed Civil Rights Act of 1990. It is said that it is good for America, good for blacks, and good for Republicans.

It's bad for America. It's probably bad for most blacks. It is political quicksand for Republicans.

Proponents say the bill does not mandate hiring quotas. OK. So stipulated. But will it encourage actions that lead to the effect of quotas?

Yes. That's why the Supreme Court acted last year to define what procedures are appropriate to outlaw discrimination without yielding reverse discrimination.

The American business community may often be praised for many saintly characteristics. Courage is not one of them. The proposed law says that if hiring doesn't yield what quotas would yield, the burden of proof is on the corporation to show why not.

That foreordains that most corporations will respond anatomically. Short on spine, institutionally gutless, always covering their asses, they will prefold their hands. Rather than face a lawsuit, punitive damages and bad publicity, they will supinely hire to ensure proportionality, a polite word for quotas.

This harms America. Affirmative action makes sense, in law and in life. But some specific legal aspects of affirmative-action-via-goals-and-time-tables tend to push behavior based on group proportionality rather than individual merit.

If there was ever a justification for such pressure, it is gone. When the Civil Rights Act of 1964 was originally passed, about 15 percent of Americans were of non-white, non-European origin. More than two-thirds of these were blacks. Today, due to healthy immigration, almost 25 percent of the population is non-white, non-European. The percentage is slowly rising. Only about half are blacks.

Won't the new law push proportionality for Hispanics? Asians? Moslems? Caribbean blacks? The newly free from Eastern Europe? Do we want a society where the goodies are divided on group identity rather than on merit and content of character? There is a model for such a proportionalized country: Lebanon.

Proportionality, quotas, preference—call it what you will—is harming blacks. Writing in the New York Times Magazine, Professor Shelby Steele argues that preferential treatment "nurtures a victim-focused identity in blacks and sends us [Steele is black] the message that there is more power in our past suffering than in our present achievement."

The power to "exploit" suffering, says Steele, is insubstantial and diverts energy from the power that comes when blacks take "responsibility for their own . . . development." He says racial preferences reinforce America's oldest myth, "that whites are superior . . . that blacks are inferior . . . they have the effect of stigmatizing the already stigmatized."

That is why the politics of proportionality yields no good to Republicans. It fosters racial antagonism. Republican moderates look at the black vote, 90 percent Democratic, and muse, "If we wink at quotas, we'd get some of that vote, and we'd be elected to everything forever."

Wrong. The polls show that almost half the blacks—just those that might vote Republican—disapprove of preferential treatment. And 90 percent of whites disapprove. Anyone who thinks those voters "have no place to go" didn't follow politics in the 1960s and the rise of then-racist George Wallace.

The principal race issue then was about discrimination. Those favoring it were wrong and in a minority. Today the principal race issue is about unfair proportionality. Those upset by it are right and in a majority.

America's political strength is nothing if not flexible. If, in the negotiations with Congress to come, Bush does not represent those anti-quota views vigorously, those views will find other outlets, perhaps unpleasant ones.

That's happening in Louisiana today. David Duke, a swinish ex-Klansman, a registered Republican, is running for the U.S. Senate using quotas as his lance, splitting the Republican party, setting race against race.

Re-creating the politics of racial conflict is no good for Republicans. Or for America. Or for blacks.

May 23, 1990

The quota issue, if not wisely settled, could be the most serious social problem we have in the 1990s. By setting group against group, it could turn the idea of a universal nation into a bitter charade. I don't believe it will happen. Americans are too smart to accept a theory, however well-meaning, that could destroy the village in order to save it.

The fight will occur on the post-Brennan Court. In Justice Brennan's last big victory (a July 1990 Federal Communications Commission case) the court broke astonishing new ground. Congress can now blithely pass laws that discriminate racially, if a mere "important governmental objective" is served. (Could a nasty Congress legislate re-segregation?)

Also in July of 1990 every Democratic Senator, 100% of them, collapsing under pressure from the civil rights lobby, voted to pass the Civil Rights Act of 1990, described above.

Indicators: *Blacks*

A. The black high school drop-out rate has fallen, and perhaps plateaued.

Percentage of 18–19-Year-Olds That Have Dropped Out of High School

	18–19 Year Olds	
Year	Black	White
1970	31%	14%
1975	25%	15%
1980	21%	15%
1985	17%	14%
1988	18%	14%

(see Education Indicator B for 25–29 rates)

B. More Americans are going to college; blacks have made great advances.

Percentage of All 18–24-Year-Olds Enrolled in College

Year	Black	White	Total
1967	13%	27%	26%
1970	16%	27%	26%
1975	21%	27%	26%
1980	19%	26%	26%
1985	20%	29%	28%
1988	21%	31%	30%

C. The number of black college graduates has about doubled each decade since 1950.

Number of Blacks Completing Four Years of College or More

Year	Number (in Thousands)
1950	150
1960	281
1970	457
1980	1,108
1985	1,645
1990 (est.)	2,100

D. The ratio of black to white income, both family and per capita, has not changed much recently.

Ratio of Black to White Personal Income

	Family Income	Per Capita
Year	Ratio	Ratio
1967	.59	.54
1970	.61	.56
1975	.62	.59
1980	.58	.58
1985	.58	.59
1988	.57	.60

E. A large majority of Americans reject the notion of preferential treatment on the basis of race, gender, or minority status. This aversion to preferential treatment has been in place for more than a decade.

Q. Some people say that to make up for past discrimination, women and minorities should be given preferential treatment in getting jobs and places in college. Others say that ability, as determined by test scores, should be the main consideration. Which point of view comes closer to how you feel on the subject?

Year	Give Preference	Ability
1977	10%	83%
1980	10%	83%
1984	10%	84%
1989	10%	84%

Source notes are on page 392.

So: The court said the Congress may legislate racial preferences. The Senate said it was afraid not to.

Quotas are passionate stuff. Many blacks, egged on by activist leaders, say the anti-quota position is racist. Many other Americans, blacks and whites, believe that merit is a powerful ingredient in the glue that holds America together.

My sense is that the new Supreme Court will do away with quotas. It will be a bitter pill for some blacks. When Brennan retired, I speedily wrote a column urging President Bush to nominate Judge Clarence Thomas, who is former Chairman of the Equal Employment Opportunity Commission, a vigorous opponent of quotas, and black. When the anti-quotas decisions come, I reasoned, domestic tranquility will be served if blacks see that those decisions are based on reason, not race.

(Appointing Thomas would not be quota hiring. Because he might de-fuse racial animosity, he would be best qualified.)

Alas for President Bush, he moved even more speedily to nominate Judge David Souter, and consequently ended up acting with neither my advice nor consent. Worse, I had to kill the column.

Does Less Prejudice Equal More Prejudice?

You will be pleased to know—probably—that 98 percent of white Americans would have no problem if blacks moved in next door, that 88 percent would have no problem if their 6-year-old child brought home a black friend, that 95 percent would have no problem having a black boss, that 89 percent would have no problem going to a black doctor.

Golly, it's nice to live in such an open-minded country! And it must be so, because it's in a poll from *U.S.A. Today*, and polls never lie.

On the other hand, you will—probably—be discomfited to know that the same survey shows that 60 percent of blacks believe that they encounter racial prejudice either "daily" (9 percent), "frequently" (13 percent) or "sometimes" (38 percent).

A further break-out of the poll shows that well-to-do blacks are much more likely to feel discriminated against than are poorer blacks. Thus, 66 percent of blacks earning over $50,000 feel they have been viewed as a criminal just because they are black; 79 percent report they receive prejudiced treatment while shopping.

It's a mystery. All those unprejudiced whites, and all those blacks being discriminated against. Who's doing it? The other person. Of the white respondents, 60 percent say they are less prejudiced than "the average person," and only 3 percent say they are more prejudiced.

To add to the confusion, the poll shows solid majorities of whites and solid pluralities of blacks believing that opportunities for blacks have improved in the past 10 years and will continue to improve in the next 10.

What's happening? There is progress. If the poll were taken a couple of decades ago it would not have dealt with upper-income blacks. There weren't many. But the *U.S.A. Today* story on the poll quotes a black female engineer saying that store clerks "often ignore you. . . . So one day I put on my mink coat, my Gucci bag and my diamond ring and walked into the store"—and then service improved. Exaggerated? Sure, but that's not your standard exaggerated anecdote from yesteryear.

And there is even evidence of a form of almost perverse progress revealed by the fact that upper-income blacks feel discriminated against. That is likely coming about because as blacks move up the income ladder, there is more integration and contact with whites.

There is also a form of attitudinal progress shown when white respondents are fearful to suggest, even to a pollster pledging confidentiality, that he or she may act in a prejudiced way.

Further, there may well be acts that appear racist to blacks, but not to whites. On a recent "Nightline" program following ABC's special "Black in White America," a black ABC reporter noted bitterly that even when a black had achieved status, it was hard to successfully hail a cab. The cab drivers just whizzed on by.

But is it racist when a black cab driver passes by a potential black fare? (They do.) It is surely a prejudiced act. But we can assume that a black cab driver is not acting out of race hatred. Something else is at work.

Cab drivers, blacks and whites, know that the violent crime rate among blacks is proportionally five times greater than among whites. The cab drivers, of both races, are often nervous about picking up blacks because they are fearful of becoming a crime statistic. Is that racism?

And so, complexity and paradox. Blacks are making headway—and finding discrimination. Whites are becoming less prejudiced as time goes on—but reacting understandably to real fears.

September 20, 1989

Black Families: Actuality and Anomaly

An important debate is beginning. Bill Moyers' fine program on CBS has crystallized concern about the very high rate of female-headed black families in America. The concern is proper: It is the No. 1 problem for blacks.

Unfortunately, as the dialogue unfolds, a caricature of the problem may be emerging: It is said that morality in the inner city breaks down, welfare offers incentives to have babies, teenage black girls get pregnant, black teenage boys drop out of school and can't get jobs, ever-more babies are born into poverty and with no male role model, teenage fathers remain dead-ended, the cycle of welfare, sexual irresponsibility and crime is continued, and blacks destroy themselves.

There is some tragic truth to all that, but there are complicating facts and questions that are not often considered. It is important to try first to unscramble the curious pattern of black birthrates.

Item: Contrary to perception, the black birthrate in America has come down dramatically in recent years for all income groups. Remarkably, even the illegitimate birthrate for blacks has come down somewhat. Question: If welfare creates a bonus for poor blacks to have babies—why have these birthrates gone down?

Item: Because marital birthrates have fallen so sharply, the proportion of black babies born out of wedlock has soared—to a devastating 56 percent. Questions: How can this happen when there is more sex education about birth control in the schools? Is it simply sexual irresponsibility? But then why is the overall black birthrate, legitimate and illegitimate, falling?

On the topic of irresponsibility, other anomalies emerge.

Item: The black rate of abortion is twice as high as the white rate. Questions: Does this indicate sexual irresponsibility regarding conception, or sexual responsibility regarding termination of pregnancy, or the lack of the right kind of sex education which would encourage abstinence and discourage abortion—or all of the above?

Item: Most black teenage mothers with out-of-wedlock children end up getting married. An Urban Institute study showed that about three-quarters of such mothers are married by age 24. Question: Is it really a never-ending cycle of matriarchy if most of these children end up in married households, at least for part of their lives?

Item: More black children are living in female-headed households because their parents have been divorced or separated than because their parents were never married. Questions: Are we ignoring a big part of the problem by concentrating only on the out-of-wedlock syndrome? But is it "irresponsible" for blacks to get divorced? How about for whites?

What about education and employment?

Item: The black high school dropout rate has gone way down. Five out of six young blacks graduate from high school. A million young blacks are now in college. Questions: Isn't it likely that these young blacks will make out all right? Or, conversely, why hasn't more schooling taught more responsibility?

Item: Black teenage unemployment rates are very high, but they are somewhat misleading. The rates don't even deal with the majority of black teenagers—who are in school. Moreover, the rates don't predict the future.

Black unemployment rates shrink dramatically as individuals get older—down below 10 percent by age 35. Question: Are jobs the real long-term problem?

What does it add up to? It is a convoluted situation, perhaps not as bad as popularly described, but bad enough.

January 30, 1986

Tomorrow: Black Progress

Recent data about the condition of blacks suggest that while they are making progress, including some catching up with whites, as a group they are far behind and are plagued with social problems.

With progress in medicine and health-care coverage, black health has improved. Life expectancy at birth climbed for blacks by 5.6 years to 69.7 from 1970 to 1987. Infant mortality improved from 1970 to 1986, falling from 32.6 deaths per thousand to 18.

Education reform may be paying off. The dropout rate is at a historic low. From 1980 to 1988, the rate of young blacks completing high school rose from 75 percent to 80 percent. The white rate stayed at 87 percent. The number of blacks who completed college climbed from 1.1 million in 1980, 4.5 percent of all graduates, to an estimated 2.1 million in 1990, 6.3 percent of the total. However, the rate of increase of black male high-school graduates entering college has now stalled. Still, blacks are moving into better jobs. About half are now in the higher-salaried categories (white-collar and precision crafts), compared with 70 percent of whites. And the number of black elected officials climbed from 1,469 in 1970 to 7,226 in 1989.

Growing influence, better health, education, and jobs should pay off in income. That hasn't happened. Both black and white income has gone up since the early-1980s recession, but black income is still mired at about 57 percent to 59 percent of whites' income. The reasons seem to be social. Since 1980, the rate of black children living "with mother only" has climbed from 45 percent to 52 percent. (It was 22 percent in 1960.) The white rate is 16 percent. Female-headed households (FHH) have lower household incomes, particularly among blacks. Black married couples have 77 percent of the income of comparable whites, black FHH's 57 percent. There are other massive social problems. More than 300,000 blacks are in prison—47 percent of total inmates, although blacks are 12 percent of the population. And blacks are much more likely than whites to be on hard drugs. As long as so many blacks stay outside the social mainstream, their aggregate income can't improve much relative to whites' income.

There is controversy about the causes of black disadvantage. Is it the fault of discrimination and changing economic patterns (external causes) or the "culture of poverty" (internal causes)? Laws and programs can be wisely directed at things like the elimination of job discrimination or the provision of health and education benefits. Yet it is doubtful that laws can change individual behavior such as criminality, drug abuse and out-of-wedlock pregnancy. Moreover, there are scant available resources or public support for programs aimed at massive social transformation. If the statistics are to move upward, behavior will have to change.

There may be evidence that change is beginning. Out-of-wedlock birth rates have plateaued for blacks. Black violent-crime rates were falling before the crack epidemic hit. Now, although too high, drug abuse is falling for both races. And today there is a model of a successful black middle class that can motivate and assist the personal upward mobility of blacks.

January 22, 1990

Adam Smith said that each nation should capitalize on its "comparative advantage." Immigration is the comparative advantage of the first universal nation.

The best arguments for immigration are names. Add these: Toscanini, Kissinger, Javits, I. M. Pei, Robin McNeil, Navratilova, John Kenneth Galbraith, Edward Teller, Oppenheimer, Paul Orrefice (chairman of Dow Chemical), Roberto Goizuta (chairman of Coca-Cola), Adolfo (Cuban), de la Renta (Dominican).

If you believe that America will have problems concerning "competitiveness" in the years to come, if you believe that we are ill-educated and undermotivated, if you believe there will be a labor shortage or a customer shortage in the nineties, if you believe we are short of engineers, physicists, nurses, tile setters, maids, nannies, and busboys—consider the immigration fix.

If you believe we face a problem in funding Social Security liabilities because we are an aging society—consider the immigration fix.

If you believe, as most Americans do somewhat inchoately, that America has some sort of mission (beyond prosperity) in this world, if you believe that global influence has some relationship to population size (Belgium won't be a superpower, no matter what), if you believe that American influence will diminish if it is a slow-growth player in a high-growth world—consider the immigration fix.

Some facts: only immigration provides a society with "instant adults" to deal with labor shortages; increased fertility doesn't provide worker bees until several decades go by. Immigrants are likely to be young workers; they not only relieve a labor shortage, but put a quick dent *in any potential "customer shortage" (for example, they need houses). A typical extra young immigrant worker will add about $3,000 per year to the Social Security trust fund; that cuts the deficit now; in the future the now-young immigrant worker will be a middle-aged American, and helping to pay the spiralling pension and health costs of the then-elderly baby-boomers. Immigrants are often educated at another nation's expense; if we are selective in our choosing procedure they are also (typically) ambitious and patriotic.*

I believe in "designer immigration." In early 1990, my American Enterprise Institute colleague, Karl Zinsmeister, and I published a study regarding American immigration policy. It included specific proposals. Get tougher on illegal immigration. Raise legal immigration from 600,000 to about 850–900,000. Raise the number of immigrants who come in via skills criteria from about 50,000 to about 300,000, using a point system that gives a bonus to young people. Cut back on non-immediate family preference immigrants (brothers, sisters, uncles, aunts). Award 150,000 "Liberty Visas" per year for 10 years to the newly liberated people of Eastern Europe and the USSR. Award 75,000 visas, based on skills criteria, to other nations that have been systematically shortchanged in recent decades (primarily, but by no means entirely Western European).

All this should not yield any decrease in Asian, Hispanic, or other so-called Third World immigration; indeed, it might well increase it.

The economic and environmental arguments against immigration are thin: that immigrants take jobs away from Americans, that America is overpopulated, overpolluted, and running out of resources—and that more immigrants exacerbate these conditions. Less thin are the arguments of those who think, but rarely say, that the racial and ethnic balance is tipping and America will no longer be a country of white European ancestry.

Most serious economists do not believe that immigrants eat up American jobs. Immigrants, of course, do "consume" jobs. But they also "create" jobs. Working immigrants buy food, clothing, and books. That activity yields demand, and demand yields jobs.

Is the world running out of resources? No, but if it were, slower population growth would only mean that we would all hit "empty" a few years earlier. Is America overcrowded? More than a third of its counties are losing population. Is America overpolluted? Pollution is lower than it was two decades ago, even though population, and immigration, have climbed. (See Chapters 7 and 8.) And, environmentalists, please take note: immigration does not increase global population; it only shifts it around.

Indicators: *Immigration*

A. The number of new immigrants to the United States has been steadily rising since World War II . . .

1. Number of Immigrants

Period	Immigrants (in Millions)	
1901–10	8.8	
1911–20	5.7	
1921–30	4.1	
1931–40	0.5	Counting
1941–50	1.0	Estimated
1951–60	2.5	Illegals
1961–70	3.3	3.8
1971–80	4.5	6.0
1981–90	5.8*	7.8

* See note.

A. (Cont.) . . . but the proportion of immigrants to the total population is lower than in some earlier times.

2. Rate of Immigration

Period	Rate (Per 1000 in U.S.)	
1901–10	10.4	
1911–20	5.7	
1921–30	3.5	
1931–40	0.4	Counting
1941–50	0.7	Estimated
1951–60	1.5	Illegals
1961–70	1.7	2.1
1971–80	2.1	2.8
1981–90	2.5*	3.3

* See note.

B. Americans, including Hispanics, do not favor increased immigration.

Q. Should immigration be kept at its present level, increased, or decreased?

	Total	Hispanic
Kept same	35%	36%
Increased	7%	25%
Decreased	49%	31%

C. Most immigrants are admitted on the basis of family relationships.

Percent of Immigrants Admitted by Occupational or Skill Preference

Year	Occupational or Skill Preferences	Including Families
1970	5.1%	9%
1980	3.9%	8.4%
1989	3.7%	8.6%

D. The European/Canadian immigration stream has diminished.

Immigrants from Europe and Canada

Period	Percent from Europe & Canada
1901–10	94%
1911–20	88%
1921–30	82%
1931–40	86%
1941–50	77%
1951–60	68%
1961–70	46%
1971–80	22%
1981–88	14%

E. According to the previous "most likely" population projection, the U.S. population begins to level off by about the middle of the 2020s, and subsequently falls. An increase in fertility or immigration substantially changes that projection.*

U.S. Population Projections (in Millions)

Year	Previous "Most Likely" Projection	Previous Immigration, 2.0 TFR	Previous TFR, 800,000 Immigration	Current Estimated "Most Likely"
1990	251	251	251	251
2000	268	272	272	276
2010	283	292	291	300
2020	294	312	307	325
2030	301	328	318	346
2040	302	340	324	364
2050	300	350	327	379
2080	292	356	333	402

* See note.

The "composition" argument is more troubling. It is true that the proportion of "white-European" immigrants is diminishing and that many Americans are worried that the complexion, and the essence, of the nation will change. (When I give speeches on demographics, to serious and educated audiences, I am frequently asked: ". . . but aren't the wrong people having the babies? Aren't the wrong people immigrating?")

This feeling can be ameliorated (although never eliminated) by some history lessons and by some changes in the immigration code.

Let's remember that immigration has never been popular. One gets the feeling that when the folks on the Mayflower went out to Plymouth Rock to watch the next boats come in, they muttered to one another, "There goes the neighborhood." Americans were once afraid of Irish, Italian, and Jewish immigration. Now the public generally says isn't it wonderful that they came here.

If the immigration code were changed to restore equity to European candidates, that could help counter the "composition" argument.

But there is no going back. A threshold was passed, probably with the passage of the 1965 immigration law. America is becoming the world's first universal nation. That universalizing will not be a painless process, but I believe on balance it is going to be very good for us.

We should proceed with increased immigration cautiously and moderately. No one knows with any precision how the future will play out. But we should proceed. It is a new part of our manifest destiny.

Chang Backhands Immigration Cliche

There was both a tennis lesson and a public policy lesson on display the other day in Paris.

When Joe Chang came to America from Taiwan in 1966 there were people who generically disapproved of his move because they believed the stereotype that, "Immigrants take jobs from Americans." That was dubious economics then and dubious economics now. But today we have an additional fact to consider in the debate about immigration: Twenty-three years after Joe came to America his son, Michael, dealt that immigration stereotype a zap. Michael took a job away from a foreigner.

The poor foreigner who was dejobbed was a young Swede named Stefan Edberg; he lost the job of holding aloft the winner's cup of the French Open tennis tournament. The winner, Michael Chang, has specifically paid America back for the job his father generically probably never took from anyone. Michael is the first American male to win a Grand Slam tournament in five years and the first to win the French Open in 34 years.

Michael Chang, 17 years old, has zapped a few other stereotypes in his short life. In California, some people will tell you that the reason so many Asian-Americans excel in high school and take up so many precious slots in the best colleges is that they're all grinds, that all they ever do is study and that they're not interested in athletics. Chang is interested in athletics. And further contra-stereotype, he got his high school diploma via a correspondence course, he grew up in Minnesota not California, and he is a devout Christian.

There have been other Asian-Americans in the news recently. A man named Fu-keun Lin discovered the genetic secret that led to a drug that may do away with kidney dialysis, and may go a long way toward dealing with anemia. (Whose job did he steal?) In Dallas a few months ago, Dr. Charles Y. C. Pak announced that his research team has devised a new treatment for osteoporosis that reverses bone loss. (Job thief!) The top American candidate for the Nobel prize in the field of super-conductivity is a man at the University of Houston named Ching-Wu Chu. (If super-conductivity becomes an American domain it will create, not eliminate, American jobs.)

But let us not fall victim to any new stereotypes. All Asian-Americans are not tennis phenoms nor researchers who will enable elderly women to stand up straight and kidney patients to lead normal lives. Asian-Americans come from many diverse places—Taiwan, China, Japan, the Philippines and India to name a few—and are from many different backgrounds. There are Asian-Americans on welfare, in teen-age gangs and in dead-end jobs. There are Asian-Americans, too, at just about every other spot on the socio-economic spectrum. The sociology tells us, not surprisingly, that the more education an Asian-American has, the better that person does. (That does not include a 17-year-old correspondence-school graduate who snaps a backhand like a crackling buggy whip.)

There is a moral to this tale, simple but not simplistic. Productive immigrants are productive. They produce science for all of us and American victories for us tennis nut chauvinists.

There is a public policy aspect to that moral: We ought to take in immigrants with productive skills.

As a general rule we don't. Our immigration policy today is geared almost exclusively to taking in people by the criterion of family relationship. Only about 4 percent of our legal immigrants come in on the basis of skills (9 percent counting their families).

The criterion of family preference is important and beneficial. It should never be abandoned. But the near-total reliance upon it in our immigration code is foolhardy. It keeps out many people who would be most helpful to us. (Michael Chang's father is a chemist who, in 1966, was just the sort who was able to come to America under a skills criterion.) And today, in a bizarre twist of fate and bureaucracy, that immigration law is keeping out skilled East Europeans who seek to emigrate here from communist nations.

June 15, 1989

> *Tennis as metaphor:*
> *Seven of the top twenty tennis players in 1989 in the world were American. Of these seven, five were immigrants or the children of immigrants or minorities. The two best American players, then and now, are named Ivan and Martina. Both were born in Czechoslovakia. Michael Chang is in the group. So is Andre Agassi, whose father was the national boxing coach for the shah of Iran (try putting that on a census form). Zina Garrison is a brilliant black player.*
> *That leaves Pam Shriver and that model of American civility and decorum, John McEnroe.*
> *Five out of seven. Might this be a portrait of the future?*

Catch 23 for European Immigrants

America now has a refugee policy that goes something like this: "When you can't get out, you can come in—but when you can get out, you can't come in."

It is a bizarre policy, yet grounded in some reality. It is a policy that is wrong and dumb. We can have a policy, Congress willing, that is right and smart.

The current situation is rooted in the starkly changed circumstances in the Soviet Union and some of the Eastern European nations. The communists, it used to be said, were primitive barbarians. Their nations were prisons; people couldn't leave. Shame!

But today, in that economic basket case called Poland, emigration is allowed. Hungary today has an open border. The Soviet Union is letting out many Jews, Armenians and Pentecostal Christians, and the numbers are expected to mount.

Now that many can leave, what has been the response from the West? Several words come to mind: Inchoate. Weird. Amoral.

America has laws concerning refugees. Until recently, people from the Soviet Union and Eastern Europe were almost automatically granted refugee status by the United States. But the legal definition of "refugee" concerns a "well-founded fear of persecution." So what happens when a nation like Poland becomes less nasty to its citizens? The legal presumption of persecution falls away.

Accordingly, when liberalization began in the East, American policy was changed from blanket approval to a "case-by-case" approach. The case-by-case procedure takes more time, money and personnel—and it was applied to what quickly became a flood of applications for refuge. Naturally enough, in a Kafkaesque sense that is, the U.S. Immigration and Naturalization Service stopped interviewing potential refugees from Poland. The backlog was too big, they said. Nice policy: "Case by case, but, by the way, we're not accepting cases."

The Bush administration will soon be allocating an extra 22,500 refugee slots. The numbers are far too small. A real solution lies in the realm of "immigrants" not "refugees." Immigrants at least don't face the Catch-22 question of "persecution."

American immigration patterns have changed. It used to be that about 80 percent of our immigrants were whites of European ancestry. Today, 80 percent are not.

The growth of Asian, Hispanic, Moslem and black immigration has been generally healthy for the United States. But it has not been publicly applauded. People are saying America will literally change complexion—and they are not pleased.

There are anomalies in the current immigration law that allow us a golden opportunity to do several good things at once. Almost all of our immigrants today come in on the basis of family preference criteria. Because of the recent non-European makeup of our immigration, it is very difficult for Europeans to emigrate to the United States; they have no close relatives here. It is also very difficult for people to come to America on the basis of what skills are needed in the United States.

We need a new legal immigration policy that will provide a more level playing field for all. It should allow more slots for Europeans and more slots for skill-based immigration. By raising the annual total, this can be done, and done *without cutting back on existing immigration sources*. We now take in about 650,000 legal immigrants per year. We should move toward 1 million.

Establishing a new stream of immigrants—European, skilled and legal—would help unfree people be free. It would take some of the current racial and ethnic hostility out of American attitudes toward immigration. It would help us deal with labor and customer shortages that America will face in the 1990s. It would help America grow and prosper.

June 22, 1989

*It isn't only engineers and nurses we want and need. What's wrong
with busboys, and people to tend the lawns, and housekeepers and
nannies? America is a middle-class, and an upper-middle-class, society.
Many American households have two working adults in them. Is
there something wrong with being able to hire a nanny without breaking
an immigration law?*

*Who loses when a housekeeper or nanny comes to America? The
working mother gets the day care and house care she needs. The
emigre nanny or housekeeper gets a better job at a higher standard
of living than she likely could have had in her home country; that's
why she emigrated. She may well send some money back home,
which is the best form of targeted foreign aid because it doesn't go
through foreign bureaucrats who sometimes divert it to Swiss banks.*

*There might be an argument against this kind of emigration on
the grounds that it sets up an aristocratic class structure in the United
States. But it won't. We know that—from the history of tens of millions
of previous immigrants. That nanny is going to get married. She
will have children. The children will be electricians. And their children
will be electrical engineers, or even insurance agents.*

Lucky US

Americans are pretty smug these days as the Fourth of July approaches.
The world seems to be picking up on some of our big ideas. Democracy
and free market economics are sweeping the board.

Are we really a light unto the nations, a model for mankind? If so,
why? It's not just because we're so swell, with such fine principles. We
tend to forget another factor in our success: unique circumstance. Call it
luck. And if luck is involved, maybe we're not as much of a universal
model as we like to think.

At a dinner party, a visiting Soviet intellectual, in the United States for
the first time, was asked: What do you think about America?

The thing that astonished him most was how many ethnic, racial and
religious groups there were here, and how well they got along. It was
due to democracy, he said, and that was one reason Russia needs more
of it.

Interesting. He knew about our real racial, religious and ethnic tensions.
But he also knew what life was like in another demographically diverse
super-power—the U.S.S.R., a place where internecine hostility is an ancient
art. Over the years, it has manifested itself in slaughter, pogroms, purposeful
famine and forced relocations. Today Armenians hate Azerbijanis, Uzbeks
hate Meskhetians, anti-semitism is potent, and a good portion of the people

who are not Russians despise Russians. These include Balts, Georgians, and many millions of Ukrainians.

Surely, if the Soviet Union ever survived a transition to democracy there would be less hate. Political brokerage can solve many disputes. But it's not only a lack of freedom that is plaguing the Soviet Union. Lenin called the Soviet Union "a prison of nations." Those are indeed real nations over there; they have contiguous land areas typically populated by people of common ethnic, racial or linguistic backgrounds.

And nationality indigestion is not only a Soviet problem. Remember the Kurds and Tibetans. In the democratic world, remember the Basques, Corsicans, Quebecois, and the situation in Northern Ireland.

What about the American circumstance? Our people came from many places, but they were not organized as nations. Suppose when the English began coming to America in the 17th century, they all decided to come only to New England, to all stay there, and not allow anyone else in. Suppose the Germans did the same in Pennsylvania. Under this scenario New York becomes all Jewish, Texas all Hispanic, California all Japanese, and Nevada all Basque. Illinois? All Polish. Michigan? Only Arabs. Georgia? Exclusively African-American.

We'd have one state with 50 million Germans, one with 30 million blacks, one with 12 million Mexicans and one with 4 million Swedes. Our history books might tell the tales of wars involving Iranians, Czechs and Bangladeshi, let alone Frisians, Hutterites, Wends and Manx—all right here in America. And foreigners wouldn't be coming over to tell us how well we get along with each other.

But, instead, we got all mixed up. Call it geographical pluralism. So we usually (not always) got along. Did we get this enormous gift because we were smart or because we were unique? We were smart because our constitution allowed us to move freely. Americans didn't need passports to take advantage of the Homestead Act.

But we also had a unique situation. America was believed to be a "virgin" continent. It wasn't. Indians lived here. But they were few in number and powerless. So we behaved as if the land were unpopulated, gobbled it up, and scrambled most of our eggs together.

Because we were usually (not always) at peace with each other, our principles could flourish. Most of the rest of the world has a different sort of history.

Smart? Yes. Unique? Yes. Those are two reasons we can celebrate the Fourth of July together, one nation, indivisible.

June 26, 1989

4

What's Happening to Us, Mostly for the Better

W ith some merit, children and families have become our new crisis issue. It is an overstated, exaggerated crisis, to be sure, but that doesn't mean it isn't very important. Today's kids are tomorrow's adults. They represent a large piece of the terrain to come.

Kids and families moved center stage because the problem is real, and first liberals and then conservatives had different but convergent interests in the topic.

Liberals will tell you that it is a scandal that so many of our children live below the poverty line. It is indeed a scandal in a nation as rich as ours.

But in recent years it has been almost impossible to have a good crisis unless it could be related in some manner to "competitiveness" and "American decline," issues that resonate solidly with conservative and commercial types.

Go to the annual meeting of a trade association these days and you will find out that we won't be competitive in the nineties because our children are ill-educated, illiterate, undermotivated, lazy, drug-addicted slobs. It is explained that the new entrants to the labor force in the nineties will be blacks, Hispanics, and women. (Some women are sometimes counted twice, as minorities and as females.) It is further explained that so many of these new entrants come from broken homes, or from out-of-wedlock births, or live in poverty.

Businessmen, properly, are concerned about the terrain of the future. How, we are asked, will we ever be able to compete with the Japanese with that kind of a work force? How indeed? Let's back up and look at the terrain.

Indicators: *Health*

A. Infant mortality has decreased sharply.

Infant Mortality (per 1,000 Live Births)

Year	Total	Black
1950	29	44
1960	26	44
1970	20	33
1980	13	21
1987	10.1	18
1989	9.7	na

B. Americans are living longer than ever.

Average Life Expectancy

Year	Life Expectancy at Birth	Life Expectancy at Age 45
1950	68.2 years	na
1960	69.7 years	29.4 years
1970	70.8 "	30.2 "
1975	72.6 "	31.4 "
1980	73.7 "	32.1 "
1985	74.7 "	32.7 "
1987	74.9 "	33.0 "
1988	74.9 "	na

C. Health care costs continue to rise.

National Health Care Expenditures as a Percentage of GNP

Year	% of GNP
1960	5.3%
1965	5.9%
1970	7.3%
1975	8.3%
1980	9.1%
1985	10.5%
1986	10.6%
1987	10.8%
1988	11.1%
1990	12% (est.)
2000	15% (est.)

D. Even in the poorest countries, people are better fed than in earlier years.

Caloric Intake in Low Income Developing Countries

Year	Daily Caloric Supply as a Percentage of Requirement
1960	87%
1970	90%
1983	102%
1986	104%

E. There has been a sharp increase in the rate of out-of-wedlock births.

Births to Unmarried Women as a Percentage of All Births

Year	Percentage of White Births	Percentage of Black Births
1970	6%	38%
1980	11%	55%
1986	16%	61%
1987	17%	62%

F. Teenage births rose and then fell as a percentage of all U.S. births, although birthrates for unmarried teenage women have soared.

Births to Teenage Mothers by Marital Status Per 1000 Women

Year	Mother Married (1000)	Mother Unmarried (1000)	Total as a Percentage of All U.S. Births
1950	365	59	12%
1960	502	91	14%
1970	456	200	18%
1980	290	272	16%
1987	170	302	12%

Source notes are on page 393.

Infant Mortality Reality

It is interesting to check out the facts behind what is being peddled as a new crisis—infant mortality. The *Washington Post* headlined, "War on Infant Mortality Seen Lagging." The *New York Times* put it on page 1 above the fold on a Sunday: "Decline Slowing for Death Rate of U.S. Infants." Post columnist Haynes Johnson wrote about it under the heading "The Weaker America." A task force of the Southern Governors' Association has issued a report; so has the Children's Defense Fund. The *Times* followed up with an editorial entitled, "On the Death of Poor Babies."

Now, infant mortality is a serious matter: we're talking about real babies. If conditions were getting worse, if conditions were not getting better—that would indeed be an important story. But, when you dig into it, that's not the situation.

Visualize a ski slope. From the top of the mountain, the course drops steeply. Then, following a sharp plunge, the downhill path continues, but the angle of descent is somewhat less sharp as the ski lodge comes into sight. Finally, the course flattens out so you can take your skis off.

The first two legs of that ski course—a steep drop changing to a steady drop—accurately describe the recent pattern of infant mortality rates in America. From the mid-1960s to the late 1970s, the rate dropped from 24 deaths per 1,000 births to 14. That is a decrease of 42 percent in a dozen years. It represents one of the great untold American success stories, and one, by the way, that affected both whites and blacks.

Since 1977, the rate has continued down—from 14 to 11 deaths per 1,000 in 1983. That's a somewhat slower rate of descent to be sure, but it's still clear and potent progress.

Why the slowdown in the rate of decline? There are two schools of thought about it. One: As the infant mortality rate goes down toward zero, further progress gets harder and harder to achieve. After all, we'll never get to zero. That's not the way the world works; some infants will always die, and we're already down to about one infant death per 100 births. There's only so much that medicine can do.

This flattening-out phenomenon is already apparent among many other advanced nations that have experienced sharp drops in infant mortality. Incidentally, contrary to some of the scaremongers, U.S. rates are not generally higher than those of other industrial nations. Actually, we are about in the middle of a tight range of rates: lower than Belgium, about the same as England, Italy and West Germany, and higher than Sweden and the Netherlands.

The second school of thought maintains that the slowdown in the drop of rates reflects the cutbacks in funding for women-and-children programs by the Reagan administration. Now, a good case can be made that the Reaganauts have been too quick in slicing some of these expenditures. Such cuts may indeed have some effect on infant mortality rates in future years. But arguing against this, at least for the moment, is the generally unreported fact that the slowdown started in the late 1970s. That, of course, was several years before Reagan came to Washington.

Now, all this is interesting in terms of social science and medical science. It is surely worthy of continuing investigation.

What it is not, however, is a scandal or a crisis or anything close to it. The numbers—as always—are being massaged and distorted for political purposes. If activists want to keep the programs intact, activists will maintain that babies are dying because of program cuts. The media will reflect these charges.

But that's not really what's going on. At its root, what it's all about, is good news at a somewhat slower rate.

April 4, 1985

As shown in the Indicators section (page 82), the infant mortality rate has continued to fall.

Families: N. Rockwell Re-visited

Because "family policy" is now one of the key issues, it might be useful to understand just how complex the situation really is. Here are some facts that are rarely thought about:

Consider the case of mothers who bear out-of-wedlock children. It's a real problem. But one of the best-kept demographic secrets is that the great majority of mothers of out-of-wedlock children end up getting married!

Arthur Norton of the Population Division of the Bureau of the Census says: "Mothers of children born out of wedlock end up with a marriage rate only slightly lower than the population as a whole, which is about 90 percent." In other words, many of those "illegitimate" children end up in whole families, at least for a while. That means that those children are likely to have more stability and permanence in their lives than we generally think.

Or consider the alleged disaster of "latchkey" children. Those are the kids whose parents are still working when the kids return home from school to an empty and allegedly lonely residence. Sad. Truly sad in some cases. Except that a study recently presented to the American Psychological Association reports that the children of working mothers scored higher on IQ tests, had better communication skills, scored higher in math and reading, and were more self-reliant than children whose mothers did not work!

Indicators: *Family*

A. Since the baby boom, American fertility has fallen sharply, plateaued, and now may be rising somewhat.

Total Fertility Rates (Expressed as Children Born Per Woman)

Year	Fertility Rate
1950	3.0 children
1955	3.5
1960	3.6
1965	2.9
1970	2.5
1975	1.8
1980	1.8
1986	1.8
1987	1.9
1988	1.9 (est.)
1989	2.00 (est.)
Mar. 1989–Mar. 1990	2.00 (est.)

B. The total number of births has gone up recently, primarily as a consequence of the "echo effect" of the baby boom.

Total Number of Births (in Thousands)

Year	Total
1950	3,632
1960	4,258
1965	3,760
1970	3,731
1975	3,144
1980	3,612
1985	3,761
1987	3,809
1988	3,913 (est.)
1989	4,021 (est.)

Source notes are on page 393.

C. The divorce rate seems to have peaked and dropped slightly, but the marriage rate has not picked up . . .

1. Divorces (per 1,000 Married Women Aged 15 and Over) vs. Marriages (per 1,000 Unmarried Women Aged 15–44)

Year	Divorce Rate	Marriage Rate
1950	10	166
1960	9	148
1970	15	140
1980	23	102
1985	22	94
1988	21	92

C. (Cont.) . . . as women are getting married later.

2. Median Age of Women at First Marriage

Year	Age
1963	20.3 years
1970	20.6 "
1980	21.8 "
1986	23.3 "
1987	23.6 "

D. The steady trend of more women wanting to work seems to have reversed.

Q. If you were free to do either, would you prefer to have a job outside the home, or would you prefer to stay home and take care of a house and family?

	Women's Responses	
Year	Prefer to Stay at Home	Prefer to Have a Job
1974	60%	35%
1980	51%	46%
1985	45%	51%
1989	51%	42%

Mind you, it's still nice to have mom at home when a child returns from school, but apparently when that's not the case, the child can do quite nicely, thank you.

Or think about divorce. It's a real problem. It's true that about half of all first marriages will end in divorce. But what is not generally mentioned is that the divorce rate has stopped rising and about 9 out of 10 divorced Americans get remarried. That's not exactly the portrait of a nation that's given up on marriage.

Moreover, it may well be that the only thing worse than a very high divorce rate would be a very low divorce rate, as in many Third World countries. After all, a divorce is usually the joint and voluntary action of a husband and wife who have decided their lives together have become miserable. Typically, they both know in advance that it will be a rocky passage for them if they split. But still, as the numbers have shown us, the two partners become ex-partners. After a while, most of them get new partners. Some of them even live happily ever after. And some don't, but may try yet again.

It's not Norman Rockwell's America to be sure. But then again, there were a lot of very unhappy marriages in those days, where people didn't have a chance at a second chance.

It's also said we're spending too little money and time on our children. Well, spending on schooling per child has risen by 50 percent just since 1970, after discounting inflation. Infant mortality—alleged to be rising—has been cut in half in the last 15 years. Isn't that helping our children?

Or think about this. It's said that the "extended family" is breaking down. But polls show that more than half of all Americans "spend a special evening with relatives at least several times a month." Other research confirms that "kinship ties" remain very important, and makes the point that the much-revered extended family of the "good old days" was—in large measure—a myth.

Or forget the past for a moment: a recent poll showed that a husband and children were included in the lifestyle of choice for 94 percent of American women. The writ of the family has been extended.

September 18, 1986

Family Hour

This year's big topic will be the difficulties of women, children, working women and family.

ABC-TV did a big special called "After the Sexual Revolution" showing some career women exulting in their new found executive power, and some executive women crying and smearing their mascara because they hadn't married and hadn't borne children.

Phil Donahue gave us five hours of "The Human Animal" on NBC-TV. Some of it was very good and some of it approached the absurd, i.e., a concluding interview with Dr. Benjamin Spock telling us that the only way to save the family was through arms control.

In the *New York Review*, Andrew Hacker reviews nine books and three court decisions before presenting his own remedy: Be proud of spinsterhood.

In *Commentary*, Professor Michael Levin attacks day care plans on the theory that a young mother's place is in the home, and it only takes some knowledge of genetics to understand that.

Congress is acting: Legislation for unpaid maternal leave is moving through the system.

And of course there's America's grandad himself, Ronald Reagan, crowing that his new tax bill is pro-family because it increases the deduction for children (of course it increases it for everyone else, too).

Whew! Why?

Because America has real family problems. The divorce rate is high. The illegitimacy rate has risen sharply.

Accordingly, the rate of female-headed families has skyrocketed, and many of them live in poverty. Beyond all this, and intertwined with it, is the plight of working women who are confronted by the "supermom" model that asks some women to be wives, mothers, lovers and executive vice-presidents, not necessarily in that order.

It is facts like these that get writers, legislators and television producers to wring their hands about the erosion of the family.

Is there any good news on the family front? Yes, of three kinds.

First, American attitudes toward family and children remain extremely positive. In fact, the polls show that Americans feel that family and children are the most important aspect of their lives. A Roper Poll taken for Virginia Slims shows that about 90 percent of American women want a life that involves marriage and children, with 63 percent wanting a career in addition.

The second piece of good news is that people are paying attention to the bad news. Some of it is silly, as when Donahue incants the statistic that only 5 percent of Americans live in the "traditional" husband-wife, two children, husband-only-earner family. Phil, what about young people who just got married, or couples with one child or three, or couples whose children have grown up?—are they all non-traditional?

Still a blizzard of authentic bad news about the family has reached the ears of Americans and their legislators.

And that leads to the third part of the good news. Americans respond. That is the standard way American society acts: Attract attention by media gloom-mongering, raise it to agenda level and start dealing with it, publicly and personally.

This one will be difficult on the public front. Pro-choice and pro-life activists have opposite views on how to handle one aspect of the family situation, abortion.

On the other hand, bigger tax deductions for children, child allowances, expanded day care (particularly on the work site), maternal leave and flextime are some of the issues around which a fairly broad public consensus may well be formed.

On the personal side, a new generation of women is sifting out what makes sense in the women's movement and what doesn't. Maybe some women will decide not to go for executive v.p.

As these sorts of things are shaped and refined, things will begin to change for the better, publicly and personally.

August 21, 1986

Kids Say the Smartest Things

We have heard the bad news about children. There have been a series of well-publicized suicides and suicide pacts. Television has focused in on child abuse. Social scientists tell us that high divorce rates yield a very high rise in female-headed households which, in turn, yield a very high rate of children in poverty. Beyond that, we have heard all about rotten schools, drug abuse, children bearing children (teenage pregnancy). Interesting: All the news comes to us courtesy of adults.

Comes now another view: what the kids think about it. Rather surprisingly, over the years there has been very little public opinion polling of children. What there was dealt mostly with what cereals and candy children ate, and what television shows the children watched.

This kid gap has been remedied by a major new poll, the first comprehensive survey to ask youngsters how they see the world around them. The poll was taken by the Roper Organization, commissioned by the American Chicle Group and asked questions of 1,000 youngsters aged 8 to 17.

The results are full-bodied and complex—and quite different from the view of crisis often presented.

Consider a child's-eye view of his or her "family and home life." Given a choice between "happy" and "not too happy," 90 percent reported they are happy. Asked if they are happy or not too happy about "the amount of love your parent(s) show you," 93 percent say happy. Now, these are discriminating children; do not think they are wildly happy about everything. Only 62 percent say they are happy about "how well you get along with your brother(s) or sister(s)."

There is complexity, too, about family life, particularly about how children view working mothers. Kids say they think kids are likely to get into more trouble if the mother works. They also think the children of working mothers are more independent than other kids. On balance, however, by 59 percent to 34 percent, children prefer that their mother have a job out of home.

What about those terrible schools? This may sound surprising, but most American children "like school"—77 percent. When asked to grade their schools in the same way most schools grade them, by letters from A to D, 29 percent gave their school an A and 49 percent gave them a B. The aspect of school that children liked the least should not come as a surprise: "cafeteria food."

Now, don't get them wrong: American youngsters do feel that there are big problems among our youngsters. The Roper pollsters asked the teenage part of the sample about what's going on. More than half the teenagers observed "a lot" of smoking (52 percent), drinking (37 percent), sexual activity (30 percent), crime (19 percent), drug abuse (19 percent), marijuana (23 percent), teenage pregnancy (13 percent), crack/cocaine use (6 percent).

What to do about it? It turns out, according to the survey, that less than half of our schools offer sex education or classes on drug and alcohol abuse. But an overwhelming majority of students in those schools (almost 4-to-1) think such classes are good.

One general sense suffuses the survey results: optimism. Fully 80 percent of the youngsters say they plan to go to college. (Only about 45 percent of their parents attended.) Many of them (69 percent) already know what they want to do when they grow up. Far and away, the field of "medical/ health care" is in first place.

It's a time when we adults are once again embarked on a small orgy of self-flagellation, partly because we think our kids are in trouble, what with suicides, abuse, dope, poverty, latchkey kids and bad schools. But our kids apparently think differently. When asked what makes them "feel good"— 95 percent responded "being an American." Here's a question some pollsters should ask: "Who knows best about kids?"

March 26, 1987

Tomorrow: Out-of-Wedlock Births

The high rate of children born out of wedlock is often seen as a near disaster: A black teenage phenomenon locking mother and child into a never ending cycle of welfare. But the latest data indicate that picture has probably been overdrawn.

Much attention has been paid to the fact that black out-of-wedlock birth rates are roughly four times higher than those for whites. But, according to the National Center for Health Statistics (NCHS), since 1970 the white rate has increased by 67 percent while the black rate has declined by 15 percent. And there has been little notice of what happens to out-of-wedlock mothers, both black and white, after their children are born. According to a new study by Larry Bumpass and James Sweet of the University of Wisconsin, almost half marry within five years, and nearly 70 percent marry within 15 years. Those numbers dilute the notion that an out-of-wedlock birth is a one-way ticket to the underclass. Census data show that marriage is the best boost out of poverty for a female-headed household.

In addition, almost a fourth of out-of-wedlock births occur among unmarried couples who live together. The children from such unions are likely to be in a better economic situation than those in a female-headed household. The most recent NCHS data also reveal that out-of-wedlock birth is not mostly a teenage problem; two-thirds of such births occur among women who are over 20.

The demographic factors driving up the out-of-wedlock birth rate include later marriages, more divorces and more cohabitation. Half of all those getting married today have lived together. There have been attitudinal and behavioral changes, too. While the America of yesteryear was far from virginal, sexual activity has significantly increased, and the AIDS crisis apparently has not changed behavior dramatically. There is also less stigma to an out-of-wedlock birth than there was in the days when a child born outside marriage was described as "illegitimate" or even "bastard." A third of young unmarried women in a 1987–88 survey said it was "all right" to have a child while unmarried.

Surely the damage caused by out-of-wedlock birth can be both immeasurable and deeply personal. But Frank Furstenberg, Jr., a sociologist at the University of Pennsylvania, describes it as a "disadvantage" but not necessarily a "disaster." He has tracked a sample of black women who bore children conceived before marriage or born out of wedlock when the mothers were teenagers in the mid-1960s. In 1987, 71 percent had graduated from high school, 68 percent were employed, 71 percent were not on welfare and family size was relatively small. In continuing studies, Furstenberg is finding a similar pattern in the next generation. Most have gone on to graduate from high school, and they have not had out-of-wedlock children of their own.

Demography is not always destiny. Out-of-wedlock mothers and their children should not be seen as automatic born losers. They haven't necessarily been so in the past, and there is no reason to expect that they will be in the future.

July 3, 1989

Indicators: *Education*

A. Foreign students are coming to America in increasing numbers. At lower levels, more Americans are studying abroad.

Foreign Students Studying at American Universities; American Students Abroad

Year	Foreign Students in U.S.	American Students Abroad
1959	48,486	na
1961	58,086	6,600
1969	134,959	17,571
1979	286,343	20,836
1987–8	356,190	62,341
1988–9	366,354	na

B. The high school dropout rate has fallen, while the rate of college graduates is at a record high.

Educational Status, Persons 25–29

Year	High School Dropouts	4+ Years of College
1940	62%	6%
1950	50%	8%
1960	39%	11%
1970	25%	16%
1980	15.5%	22.1%
1987	14.0%	22.0%
1988	14.1%	22.7%

C. Public sector spending on education has increased.

Education Spending Per Student in Public Elementary Schools and Public Teacher Salaries (1989 Dollars)

Year	Per Student	Per Teacher
1959–60	$1,536	$21,208
1969–70	$2,521	$27,491
1979–80	$3,648	$23,604
1988–9	$4,598	$29,629

D. Class size has diminished.

Grades K–12 Pupil:Teacher Ratios

Year	Pupils:Teacher
1955	26.9
1965	24.7
1975	20.4
1985	17.9
1990	17.2 (proj.)

E. Although lower than earlier, Scholastic Aptitude Test scores are somewhat higher than in 1980.

Average SAT Scores

Year	Score (1600 Max)
1959–60	975
1964–5	969
1970	948
1975	906
1980	890
1982	893
1984	897
1986	906
1989	903

F. American 13-year-olds fare poorly in math and science.

Educational Progress in Science and Math for Age 13: 1988

Country	Math Mean	Science Mean
Korea	567.8	549.9
Quebec (French)	543	513.4
Quebec (English)	535.8	515.3
Ontario (English)	516.1	514.7
Spain	511.7	503.9
United Kingdom	509.9	519.5
Ireland	504.3	469.3
Ontario (French)	481.5	468.3
United States	473.9	478.5

Source notes are on page 393.

91

Are You an Illiterate?

Prepare for another crisis: functional illiteracy. It's on "Nightline."
It's high on the op-ed pages. Jonathan Kozol has written a book
about it entitled *Illiterate America.* Kozol's alarmist tract is best summed
up on the volume's jacket: "One out of every three adult Americans
cannot read this book." I urge that the remaining two out of three—
don't bother.

It's not that the lack of reading skills among some adults isn't a
problem in America; indeed it is. But Kozol's analysis is so exaggerated,
illogical and politicized that it is useless. (He says we purposefully
mal-educated the oppressed, and they must now be mobilized to
express their rage.)

Unfortunately, Kozol is not merely one radical educator. In an
overblown way he echoes some seminal silliness in the broader
education establishment, including, in some respects, the conservative
parts of it.

Thus, Kozol attacks Census Bureau data that maintain that 99
percent of adult Americans can read and write. Kozol disagrees. Using
a variety of studies, he says 60 million adults are either "functional
illiterates" or "marginal illiterates." Much of his data come from
government studies, including ones from the Department of Education
and the National Institute of Education. These days, conservatives
like to trumpet such crisis numbers to prove education is in bad
shape because of prior liberal policies.

The thing is preposterous—left and right. We are being victimized,
not for the first time, by "definition inflation." What is a "functional"
or "marginal" illiterate, anyway? Kozol says that functional illiterates
can't read a menu, can't read traffic signs, can't use a phone book.

How do you measure it? Kozol says to look at whether a person
"has *master(ed)* the objectives of specific grades in *excellent* and
successful schools." Remember that definition.

Here's the snapper: Kozol tells us that functional and marginal
illiterates can read and write only at fifth- and ninth-grade levels,
respectively. Huh? A 15-year-old student who has mastered the work
in an excellent school is marginally illiterate? How many such 15-
year-olds do you know who can't read "french fries" on a menu?
Elsewhere Kozol says that if you can't understand an insurance policy
or a tax form, even you may be an illiterate. (Me, too.) In short,
the numbers are vastly over-inflated. They are described, even by
the government workers who generate them, as "junk."

Nor are the numbers growing. How could they be? However one measures adult illiteracy, it is much more prevalent among the elderly than among younger adults. That's because in the past many kids used to drop out of school at an early age. In recent years, to our credit, youngsters have been staying in school much longer. Accordingly, as old people die off and young people mature, the illiteracy rate declines, at least by any absolute standard.

Is there a problem? Yes. Actually, two problems. Kozol and others correctly note that we need greater literacy these days: learning to program a computer requires more reading skill than learning to plow a field. Secondly, some of our children are not getting as good an education as they should. Why? Because schools followed advice offered earlier by Kozol and others — less discipline, relaxed curriculum standards.

What's the solution? Surely not the revolutionary one Kozol suggests. He wants a $10 billion-a-year program whose goal is "civil disobedience" to denounce "imperial injustice" imposed by "dynastic power." (That's us.)

Isn't there a more sensible posture? Let's acknowledge that we've made some real headway; that we've made some dumb mistakes; that we've got to set up tough standards in our schools; that we ought to help re-educate adults who want help; that this is a problem where governments can help. And then go to work on it, without America-bashing.

June 13, 1985

The best way I know to get kids to read better is to give them paperback books about topics that interest them and that they select themselves, books about sports, adventure, whatever. That was the premise of an organization called Reading Is FUNdamental (RIF) on whose board I once served. The project was headed by the late Mrs. Robert MacNamara.

I got into RIF because, in early 1968, there was a plan afoot in the White House to make "reading" LBJ's cause in his second term, in the way that the "March of Dimes" (to cure polio) was Franklin Roosevelt's cause. Now reading is Barbara Bush's cause, and it is a good one.

P.S. By some earlier definitions Abraham Lincoln and Gen. David Sarnoff (former chairman of RCA) would have been labelled "functional illiterates" (not enough years of formal schooling).

Dropouts Drop In

It is no secret that the American education system has been under attack in recent years. The secretary of education has just come out with a report describing the sort of tough high schools we need. And education seems to be the favorite bogyman issue of just about every presidential candidate this year; if only we had better education, we are told, we'd be more "competitive" in the world. In this general context of the trashing of American education, it has been noted that the high school dropout rate has been rising and is intolerably high. Conditions for blacks have been singled out for particular crisis-mongering. The president of the American Association of Community and Junior Colleges recently spoke of "the horrible high school dropout rate."

I do not propose to announce that American education is without problems. There are very real problems. However, looking at just one part of the issue—that high school dropout rate that is supposedly high and going higher—it just is not so. In fact, there has been solid progress. And, further, there is reason to believe that the progress has caused some of the problems— yet one more manifestation of the ever-present Law of Unintended Side Effects.

A new Census Bureau report on educational attainment has the latest data. It shows that the dropout rate is not high, and it is not climbing; in fact, it has steadily declined for decades and is now at an all-time-low plateau. Moreover, the data for blacks are quite encouraging.

The best statistical way to measure a true, relatively current, dropout rate is to look at young adults age 25–29 and see how many have finished high school. This picks up those teenagers who may have left school for a while but then returned to get a degree either in a regular high school or via a high school graduate equivalency, the General Education Development degree.

The census data show that back in 1970 just 75 percent of young Americans of all races had taken their education at least as far as a completed high school education. By 1975 the rate had climbed to 83 percent. And in 1985—the new data—the rate is 86 percent.

The rate for blacks climbed much more sharply and is actually beginning to approach parity with whites. The black high school completion rate was only 56 percent in 1970. It went up to 68 percent in 1975. In 1980 it was up further to 77 percent. And in 1985 it was 81 percent, closing in on the white-only rate of 87 percent.

(Data for Hispanics only go back to 1974. In that year 53 percent graduated from high school. The 1985 data show a 61 percent completion rate— very low, behind both whites and blacks, but a solid gain nonetheless.)

For confirmation, the Census measurements of enrollment of 18- and 19-year-olds show the same general trends, although at somewhat lower levels.

In a very important way, these data are both encouraging and remarkable. Uniquely among the nations, America is attempting to provide every youngster with a high school education. That is not the case in the more elite education systems in Europe and Japan.

Like most human advances, however, this one is not without second-order problems. When you try to educate everyone, you bring into schools many young people who in earlier years would have dropped out. Some of them are emotionally stunted. Some are behavior cases who are disorderly or violent. This can make it harder to keep discipline in a classroom; it can force a lowering of the general level of instruction, making school less interesting and less challenging to brighter students. Ironically, higher enrollment levels can harm quality.

So, the candidates and the secretary of education are right to stress that we have an education problem. We do. But it is also in order to note that a good part of that problem stems from a success story.

January 14, 1988

Tomorrow: Is Education as Bad as Ever?

To sense "the education problem" in the United States, it is useful to see what it is not. Suppose one had surveyed the education scene in 1970. What changes needed to be made? Here is a plausible partial list: Reduce the high-school dropout rate, particularly for minorities. Increase the participation rate in college and preprimary school. Spend more money on schooling. Reduce classroom size. Raise test scores, particularly for minorities.

To one degree or another, all that has happened. Yet rhetoric about the dreadful state of education, on these very items, is still much the same. The truth is that in some areas the nation is making progress. But glaring problems remain.

The country is doing well quantitatively. There has never been a nation that has put such a large proportion of its young people into college. "Great," grumbles Chester Finn of Vanderbilt University's Educational Excellence Network, "and in college all that most of them are getting is the high-school education they missed. In the average case, the product stinks." He cites recent test results showing only 6 percent of 11th graders get solidly good marks on mathematics-proficiency tests. Only a third can identify the half-century in which the Civil War took place.

A qualitative comparison of American students with foreign students is not a happy exercise. A recent study by the Educational Testing Service ranked 13-year-old students. Americans were dead last in mathematics and near the bottom in science.

There are caveats. However low the test levels may be, the trend lines on test scores have gone up in the last few years, albeit slowly and from a low level. Some of the international comparisons have also been challenged as skewed. The United States sends a greater proportion of young people through high school than other nations, so some tests compare most of our young people with the best of their young people.

That does not apply to the ETS study, which sampled students of predropout age. Still, being charitable, the fact that American kids do not learn science by age 13 does not mean that they will not ever learn it. Maybe they will learn what they need when they need it.

In fact, American education has a helter-skelter quality. That is not all bad. For example, the nation's true high-school dropout rate is very low, because many young people who drop out go back to school later on.

Business people complain that too many young people do not know enough. So businesses set up training programs. American business spends $40 billion a year on education. It is too bad—wasteful—that much of this education is not accomplished in school, but it is accomplished somehow, somewhere, sometime.

America also has a booming "proprietary" educational sector. There are about 8,000 private trade and professional schools, training young people in television repair, electronics, computers, plumbing, cosmetology, X-ray. The students learn what they have to learn when they have to learn it.

At the college level, the much awaited drop in enrollments (because of the aging of the baby-boom babies) never happened. Why not? Adults are going to college, many of them part time. They learn what they want to learn when they want to learn it.

There is little doubt that excellent college education is available. Why else do so many foreign students come to study in the U.S.? Almost a million foreigners get degrees here yearly.

Even most education bashers acknowledge the quality of the best part of the American university system. And the open culture yields creative and innovative students. The Japanese are now trying to recruit young American scientists to work in Japan.

Is America really turning out a generation of noncompetitive clucks? Probably not. Where the system has missed, America's bootstrap culture often takes over. Still, there is something to Finn's stern assessment. Much more can be done. America can be open and still teach kids math and science. A high-school graduate should write coherently.

The nation needs better teachers. Their salaries have gone up some in recent years but typically not enough to draw in top-flight talent.

Albert Shanker, president of the American Federation of Teachers, thinks the old-fashioned school is not working any more. He says the country needs customized schools teaching kids at the rate they can absorb, using not only teachers but businessmen, paraprofessionals, parents, older students and a "merit badge" approach. Finn says the old-fashioned schools can still work if we keep standards and discipline tough. Both are right: Tougher schools for those who can use them, different schools for those who can't.

The discipline situation is not good. Almost half (44 percent) of the teachers say that student "disruptive behavior" has increased in the past five years. By the time they become seniors, 6 out of 10 students have tried drugs.

Teachers lay much blame on parents. They say the major cause of students' difficulties in school is "children left on their own after school—single-parent families." The teachers are right; parents have to help.

Who's going to change the system? George Bush says he is going to be the "education President." But the federal government only accounts for 6 percent of public-school expenditures. The states are the biggest source of education dollars.

America needs "education governors." Many have taken up the challenge. Schooling is getting better. At least the public thinks so. In 1973, 58 percent of the public had a "great deal" or "quite a lot" of confidence in our schools. By 1981, that rate had plunged to 42 percent. Today, the rate has come halfway back, to 50 percent. Halfway home—and still a long road awinding.

March 20, 1989

Playing Academic Football

Quick, ritual response: Why isn't America competitive in the global commercial marketplace? Answer—everyone knows—because our education system is so bad.

Second question: To be competitive, what's the most important part of the education system? Answer: Higher education—colleges and universities—that's where the scientists, engineers and managers come from.

Third question: What nation has the best colleges and universities? Answer: America.

A survey of scholars from East Asia—where everyone is so energetic and perfect, especially those Japanese—ranked the world's universities. Eight of the top 12 were in uncompetitive America—Harvard, Stanford, University of California (Berkeley), MIT, Yale, Cornell, Michigan and Princeton.

In the forthcoming book, *The University: An Owners Manual* (W. W. Norton), Professor (and former dean) Henry Rosovsky of Harvard says it's no accident, and if 50 schools were ranked, America would still have two-thirds to three-quarters of the best. (He says Columbia, Chicago, UCLA, CalTech and Wisconsin can be quickly added to the list.) Why? American universities, says Rosovsky, are better mostly because they are more competitive.

Let me offer an analogy: American universities are good for the same reason that American college football is good—they have, uh, changed the rules.

Foreign universities don't scour the world for the best educators, throwing money and perks at them. Tut, tut. Very ungentlemanly. But American universities, perhaps inspired by their aggressive football recruiters, or by their assertive national culture, do just that. Top scholars are wooed as if they were high school quarterbacks.

By contrast, Rosovsky notes, in many foreign universities professors must have attended the school they teach in. The result is often an inbred, uninspired faculty.

It's not only scholars who are in play. American universities compete for the best students, for public attention, and for funds.

Rosovsky supports the much-criticized American tenure system. Most foreign schools award tenure based on seniority. In America, tenure is granted only after tough peer review, inside and outside the university. "At Harvard," says Rosovsky, "We ask . . . who is the best person in the world to fill a particular vacancy, and then we try to convince that scholar to join our ranks. . . ." This process, he says, is common in top U.S. schools.

Foreign schools usually operate in lock step with a ministry of education; professors often act like civil servants. Frequently the administration is elected—yes, elected—by the faculty, staff and students. Elections yield politics. Academic politics in Holland yields excruciating attention to the egalitarian comfort of the electors. Education, research—and excellence—are subsidiary items.

But in America, the university president—like the coach—can be fired. So can deans, provosts and chairmen. That provides accountability.

Rosovsky also stresses regional competition. In many foreign lands the best school is in the capital; outlanders need not compete. But here it's football all over again. In Massachusetts, North Carolina, Wisconsin, Michigan and California, people want to wave their forefinger and say they're No. 1. (Administrators like it too. When a professor becomes famous, the university can raise more money. It's like winning a bowl game.)

There are caveats: Rosovsky says he is talking about the best 50 research institutions, with about 10 percent of our students. Even there, it should be noted further, the research is often better than the teaching. And, perhaps especially there, while the quality in the hard sciences is top-flight, the ideology in the humanities (by my lights) is often naively super-liberal. Still, we're No. 1.

America's big education problem is not in the university. It is in the public elementary and secondary schools. What don't they have that our universities have? Competition. Maybe the folks who run those schools ought to go to classes taught by football coaches.

January 10, 1990

Winning Drug Wars, Past and Present

The strategy that favors the legalization of cocaine and other narcotics is describable in two words: "declare defeat." That is ironic. The American drug situation is horrific. But, past and present, it may be better described by different, strange-sounding words: "slow victory."

Our collective memory is short. We forget: We have had success in drug wars. Because we are assailed with images of drug horror, we ignore a central idea: We're probably going to do well in this drug war, too.

There was a massive cocaine addiction epidemic in America earlier this century. By 1910, cocaine had been used, legally, in patent medicines, ointments, sprays and beverages like Coca-Cola. It was used as a hay fever remedy. (The guillotine is also a cure for a head cold.) The epidemic struck everywhere: among working men and women, little old ladies, teen-agers, minorities.

Society responded: pure food and drug laws, illegalization, import prohibition, media campaigns, public education. Drug war! And by the 1930s cocaine was about wiped out.

Something similar happened with heroin and LSD during the 1960s. There was an explosion of use, and then a tapering off.

Today it is crack cocaine. It is a menace. Researchers don't yet know its full costs. They do know that plenty of users will die, that some will make misjudgments so severe that others will perish, and that many surviving users may be permanently scarred.

Will the drug crisis continue? History offers a clue. "Wars" on drugs tend to work because people ultimately respond to grim circumstances.

Dr. David Musto of Yale examined the earlier cocaine epidemic in his book *The American Disease: Origins of Narcotics Control.* He writes that the primary cause of "the practical disappearance of cocaine . . . was disillusionment with the initial claims for a new drug and shock at its effects on the lives of individuals and their families."

We can sense a logical cycle at work, then and now: Some people fry their brains on narcotics. Because there is a drug war, many dealers are killed and put in prison.

All this is publicized by the media, by drug war education campaigns and, most importantly, by personal witness. Users and dealers have friends, neighbors and siblings. They see the drug horror and vow not to participate. Many succeed. This process may begin in the middle class, but it filters down everywhere.

It's already happening. Data from the National Institute on Drug Abuse shows that the number of cocaine users dropped from 12 million to 8 million from 1985 to 1988. Total use of illicit drugs is down from 37 million to 28 million.

The data regarding crack cocaine is newer and less precise. Still, studies by the Institute for Social Research at the University of Michigan show a decline of annual crack use among high school seniors from 4 percent to 3.1 percent from 1987 to 1988.

Attitudes have changed dramatically. The rate of people who believe cocaine use presents a "great risk to health" climbed from 54 percent in 1985 to 71 percent in 1988.

Other indicators have not yet turned around. Deaths and emergency treatment of drug abusers are growing, lending credence to the idea that no progress is being made. But many experts, including Musto, believe that reflects a reaping of the whirlwind of earlier crack addiction, which increased the universe of risk. By these lights, the recesisonal trends will arrive in years to come.

Musto has treated addicts—he is a physician, psychiatrist and medical historian—and believes we are on the down slope of the cycle of tragedy. The crack disaster, he judges, will set in concrete negative attitudes toward drugs.

Legalization is surrender. Yes, say the legalizers, the drug situation is terrible. Yes, they say, legalization would probably hook innocent new users. But, they moan, what's going on now is so bad that we'd better learn to unhappily live with it.

It is a faint-hearted formula. It's a war that has been waged fairly success- fully in the past. We may now have started to win the new war. Why surrender?

September 27, 1988

Crime Up? Crime Down?

It is a truism that "there is more violent crime." But is it true? No one knows. And therein is a message.

There are two standard data series to measure crime. Both come from the U.S. Department of Justice. Both showed a sharp increase in violent crime in the 1970s. Both showed decline in the early 1980s. But from that point forward, they diverge. One trend says "up." The other trend says "down," or at least "a plateau at a lower level than earlier recorded."

Curiously, both may be right.

The Uniform Crime Reports, or UCR, prepared by the FBI, look at crime as seen from the eyes of the police, that is, "crimes reported to law enforcement." By that perspective violent crime went up by 23 percent from 1984 to 1989.

The National Crime Surveys, or NCS, published by the Bureau of Justice Statistics, are based on a large sample of special Census Bureau interviews. That data shows crime seen not from the perspective of a police blotter, but from the recall of a victim. This "victimization" rate fell about 15 percent from the early 1980s to the mid-1980s and roughly stayed at that level through 1989.

What's going on? What theories fit what parts of what trends? With what caveats? Here are some:

Demographic theory. Violent crime, it's said, is related to how many young males there are in a society. As the baby boomers reached their teen-age years in the 1960s, the crime wave began. As the number of teen-agers declined in the early 1980s, violent crime declined.

Crack cocaine theory. The crack epidemic hit in the mid-'80s and that, it's said, pushed up the UCR rates. However, many experts believe crack is overstated as a cause of crime. Moreover, much crack-related crime is dealer-on-dealer, which typically exempts law-abiding citizens (except when hit by a stray bullet).

Further, recent observations from the National Institute on Drug Abuse indicate that the crack wave has crested. It's trench warfare, but America may be winning the drug war.

Reagan-was-a-rat theory. There were allegedly fewer social services in the 1980s, allegedly an increase in the underclass, which allegedly led to more crime, particularly among blacks and Hispanics, who are both perpetrators and, alas, victims.

Better police work theory. The police have more resources, are better qualified and are concentrating on drug work. This increases arrests and reported crimes, raising the UCR. But that doesn't mean that there are more victims, only more apprehensions.

More arrests also yield more prisoners, yielding more incapacitation of potential criminals. There are 400,000 more prisoners today than in 1980. At an estimated 5 to 10 crimes per criminal per year, that means 2 million to 4 million crimes don't occur, keeping victimization down.

Further, the criminal justice system is tougher: A serious offender is twice as likely to go to prison today than in 1970–80. Increased deterrence also allegedly keeps victimization down. America may also be winning the trench warfare against crime.

Joseph Bessette, the retiring acting director of the Bureau of Justice

Indicators: *Crime and Drugs*

A. The number of prisoners has more than tripled since the mid-1950s, passing the half-million mark.

Sentenced Prisoners in State and Federal Institutions

Year	Total
1955	185,780
1965	210,895
1975	240,953
1985	465,236
1986	503,069
1988	584,382
1989	653,886

B. After a decline, reported crime rates have gone up since the mid-1980s . . .

1. Index of Crimes Reported to Police, 1980–1988

Year	Rate per 100,000 Inhabitants
1980	5,950
1982	5,604
1984	5,031
1986	5,480
1988	5,664
1989	5,816 (est.)

B. (Cont.) . . . as have arrest rates, although arrests had dropped for a longer period of time.

2. Total Arrests by Race, 1980–88

Year	Rate per 100,000 Inhabitants		
	Total	White	Black
1980	2,707	738	974
1982	2,831	682	923
1984	2,186	604	776
1986	1,914	473	631
1988	2,567	654	858

C. Criminal *victimization* rates (as opposed to "crimes reported to police") declined fairly steadily in the eighties for the population as a whole. At the end of the decade, however, there was some increase in violent crime directed at blacks.

Victimization, 1973–88 (per 1000)

Year	Total Personal	Total Violent	Violent, Blacks	Home
1973	124	33	42	218
1975	129	33	43	237
1980	116	33	40	227
1981	120	35	50	226
1982	117	34	44	208
1983	108	31	41	190
1984	103	31	41	179
1985	99	30	38	174
1986	96	28	33	170
1987	96	29	40	171
1988	100	30	40	170
1989	101	29	na	166

D. Drug use among students went up and is now falling.

Percentage of High School Seniors Who Have Ever Tried Illicit Drugs

Class	Cocaine	Crack	Any Illicit Drug
1975	9.0%	na	55%
1978	12.9%	na	64%
1980	15.7%	na	65%
1981	16.5%	na	66%
1982	16.0%	na	64%
1983	16.2%	na	63%
1984	16.1%	na	62%
1985	17.3%	na	61%
1986	16.9%	na	58%
1987	15.2%	5.6%	57%
1988	12.1%	4.8%	54%

Source notes are on page 394.

Statistics, carefully says this: "The reported UCR increase may well be reflecting the fact that more professional police forces, using microcomputers, more attuned to proper reporting, are more accurately picking up crime rates that existed earlier but weren't fully reported. That is consistent with NCS data which show no significant increase in violent crime in the last few years."

In short, we may be seeing a statistical increase, not a crime increase.

Which data is right? The most revealing fact is that no one is certain. When one compares that with the perception of a new crime wave, a thought emerges: It's probably not happening. If it were happening, as it did indeed happen in the '60s and '70s, the case would be clear.

If anyone thinks that's ground for complacency, forget it. The American violent crime rate is still the highest in the world. There is still plenty to do about a high crime rate that isn't getting worse, but not getting too much better either.

July 7, 1990

Marrying Later, Not Never

The results of a famous study about drastically low marriage rates for white female college graduates is under sharp challenge in a paper now being prepared by U.S. Census demographer Jeanne Moorman.

Moorman's study says that marriage rates for college women are not falling, but in fact rising, and will ultimately reach 96 percent. The paper will be presented to the Population Association of America.

The original study by Dr. Neil Bennett and Patricia Craig of Yale and Dr. David Bloom of Harvard caused a sensation: a cover story in *Newsweek*, a cover story in *People*, featured coverage in the *New York Times* and elsewhere.

The Bennett-Craig-Bloom work spread gloom among many women. The study maintained that if a woman college graduate wasn't married by age 25, she had only a 50 percent chance of ever marrying.

At age 30, the B-C-B paper said, the rate shrunk down to 20 percent.

By age 35, it was maintained that the rate fell all the way to 5 percent.

And at age 40, it declined so low that, in a much-quoted sentence in *Newsweek*, "Forty-year-olds are more likely to be killed by a terrorist," than to get married.

Moorman's results are at striking variance with the B-C-B projections. At age 25, for example, the Moorman data show an 85 percent chance of marriage, compared to B-C-B's 50 percent.

At age 30 the Moorman data shows a 65 percent chance of marriage, compared to 20 percent in the earlier survey.

At age 35 the comparatives are particularly stunning: 5 percent in B-C-B and 40 percent in Moorman!

The projected marriage rates for women over 40 also show stark differences between the two sets of data. Moorman's figures show a 22 percent chance of marriage for college women at age 40, and a 10 percent chance for ages over 45. Those numbers are well beyond terrorist probabilities.

All the data concerns first marriages only.

Because the number of unmarried women declines as women age and marry, the likelihood that a given woman will ever marry goes up over time, yielding Moorman's 96 percent projection, which is slightly higher than in earlier decades.

At the root of the wide variance in the two sets of figures is a difference of opinion about rarified statistical projection techniques.

Moorman maintains the earlier B-C-B statistical procedures "don't fit the current circumstances for women who are postponing but not eliminating marriage because of more education and more career opportunities." The data in her paper came from a special report from the 1980 census, projected forward on the basis of the most recent standard life-table models.

On the other hand, Bennett sticks solidly by his team's work: "The model we employed is a well-tested and time-proven technique for projecting marriage rates."

Because both studies are based on projections of future behavior, there can be no definitive answer as to which analysis is correct. To this writer, judging intuitively, the Moorman results may be somewhat overstated but, as the future unfolds, will prove to be much closer to the truth than the B-C-B study. To believe otherwise, recall, means that 19 out of 20 never-married women aged 35 will never marry.

In any event, the new report is likely to cause as much of a stir as the earlier one. That study provided fuel for those who maintained that the woman's movement had failed because it had the effect of denying marriage and family to working women. To some extent, the Moorman study under-cuts that idea.

What is not dealt with in either study, however, is child-bearing. A recent census report showed that American women were averaging only 1.8 children, a figure well below that needed to replace a society over time.

Later marriage, as indicated in the Moorman paper, could serve to encourage such lower birth rates, following the old demographic dictum "fertility delayed is fertility denied."

August 27, 1986

Moorman was right. B-C-B were wrong. Their final published paper, published in the American Journal of Sociology, *abandoned their earlier methodology. Note to never-married women over 30: It's not as bad as you've been told. Relax. A little.*

The Yuppie Disease

NBC recently ran an interesting television special called "The Baby Business." The program began on a troubling note. Infertility, said NBC, was becoming a major national problem. Correspondent Maria Shriver asked: "Is this surge in infertility the yuppie disease of the '80s: the curse of the career woman?"

Despite the fact that it is a real problem of intense concern to many, despite the fact that NBC left a different impression, the real answer—although complicated and qualified—is probably "no."

Most scientists and researchers believe that there has been a moderate increase in infertility. But recent medical advances cancel out much of, or more than, the reported increase.

The reasons and arithmetic: The older a woman gets, the less likely she is to be fertile. Data from the National Center for Health Statistics show only 2 percent of couples trying to have children are infertile in their teens, 10 percent in their 20s, rising to 14 percent between ages 30–34. The big jump occurs at about age 35: The rate for couples aged 35 to 39 is 25 percent and rises to 27 percent at ages 40 to 44. (This includes couples wanting a first child and those seeking more than one child.)

Now, recently, people have been getting married later and are likely to try to start having a family later in life. In this sense there is not much infertility as such, but only an increase in older women trying to get pregnant, at an age when it is harder to do so.

Another factor: Young people are likely to have more sex partners before marriage than in earlier times. This increases the risk of sexually transmitted diseases, which can be a cause of infertility. Still, the vast majority of women have not contracted any such disease, a large majority of women who have had such diseases remain fertile, and a little more than half of those who have developed problems can still get pregnant, typically by in vitro fertilization.

So: Sadly related to age and disease, there has indeed been some increase in infertility. How much is debated. It is hard to measure and harder to judge; refined statistics don't exist. One set of NCHS data show that about 2.3 percent of all couples were childless and infertile in 1965, and 5.8 percent in 1982. Most of the rise occurred before 1976.

That can be seen as an increase of 150 percent. But the increase is from a very small base. Such numbers, while representing real human tragedy, do not seem to most experts to be of a magnitude to bolster the

idea of a Yuppie Curse. Moreover, infertility for couples seeking more
than one child is believed to have gone down.

In any event, there is countervailing activity. From a different perspective,
Dr. William Andrews of Norfolk, Va., a past president of the American
Fertility Society, makes this overall estimate: of 100 couples, about 80
can get pregnant within a year. Another 10 percent can get pregnant by
trying for another year. The remaining 10 percent have a fertility problem.
Of those, about half can be successfully treated in an uncomplicated way.
The remaining half need more sophisticated treatment and, of these, about
half will be able to conceive and half won't.

That means that 97.5 percent of all couples who are willing to do everything possible to conceive—can conceive. There has been a medical breakthrough in fertility enhancement. Andrews estimates that 20 years ago
only about 50 percent of the problem cases could be helped. Now it is
75 percent. Ten years from now it hopefully will be 85 percent. (And
progress could be quicker and greater if the National Institutes of Health
rescinded their foolhardy policy of not funding any in vitro research.)

In all, Andrews believes that, on balance, fertility enhancement has
been greater than the rise in infertility.

That means that while it may be more difficult for some, women today
who want to get pregnant have a somewhat better chance of success than
did women in their mothers' generation.

April 16, 1987

Making Motherhood Issues

I have uncovered the way to separate people who understand American
politics from those who don't. Those who don't understand our politics
use the word "impossible."

Consider: A book of mine has recently been published called *The Birth
Dearth* (Pharos Books). Its theme is elemental: People in the United States
and the whole modern Western world are having children at well below
the rates necessary to keep a population from declining over an extended
period of time. I think that such very low fertility rates can harm us economically, geopolitically and personally. I recommend in the book that action
be taken, some of it governmental, to make it financially easier for young
couples to have children. Among the ideas I discuss are higher standard
tax exemptions for children, child allowances, paid maternity leave, day
care and forgiving some repayment of college loans for those who are
having children.

Some of my critics have said low birth rates are not really a problem and Wattenberg is a dolt. Fair enough; it's a complicated and controversial issue. If dolts want to call me a dolt, I can live with it; after all, I'm not one of those thin-skinned authors.

It is another sort of criticism that bothers me. Yes, some critics say, there is a problem; yes, it would be good to do something about it; but—ah—it's too expensive, the Congress will never vote for it, it's impossible.

I ask you to forget the merits of the argument; forget whether pro-natal government policies are needed. Concentrate on that word "impossible" as used by the nay-sayers. What does it say? That even if we recognize a problem, we free people can't act to deal with it. Distilled, it is a view that says democracy doesn't work. But it does. And people who say it doesn't, or can't, don't understand the situation.

Consider: Back in the 1930s, the idea of a Social Security system was raised. Pensions for the elderly would be a good idea, the nay-sayers might have said, but it's too expensive, the Congress won't fund it, the voters won't want to pay the taxes for it—it's politically impossible. Today—surprise!—we spend over $200 billion a year on Social Security, and congresspersons go into tantrums if it is suggested that benefit increases should go up less quickly. What happened? Voters were alerted to a real problem—elderly poverty—and responded in a decent way.

Turn the hands of the clock ahead to the early 1960s. Rachel Carson writes a book called *Silent Spring*. She maintains that our environment is being poisoned. It is clear that, over time, it will cost many hundreds of billions of public and private dollars to clean up. What would the nay-sayers think about that? Good idea, but too costly, the Congress will never approve it, it's impossible. But today politicians fall all over themselves to spend more to do environmental good things. Why? The environment has become, as they say, a motherhood issue.

Or take an issue seen to be on the conservative side of the spectrum: national defense. After World War II, America disarmed. But the Soviets were on the move. Geopolitical thinkers said that the shattered forces of democracy would have to be led by the United States. The costs would be enormous. What would the nay-sayers say? Important idea, but too costly, the Congress won't approve, impossible. Today we spend $300 billion a year for national defense. We don't spend it because we like to but because we perceive that we must do it.

So: Don't say impossible. The record is clear. Democratic peoples do what they think it is necessary to do.

Now an idea is surfacing, and not just in my book to be sure, to make motherhood a motherhood issue. It may not happen, but if it doesn't, it won't be because it can't happen.

July 23, 1987

Tomorrow: Children's Allowances

In recent American history, social engineering has been the work of liberals who favor big government. The young brain-trusters of Franklin Roosevelt's New Deal brought forth Social Security, and in later years the architects of Lyndon Johnson's Great Society passed the medicare health-insurance program. Now, conservatives are getting into the act in a way that could change family life in the United States.

The effort in Congress to pass child care legislation is the current case in point. What began as a push for a federal program to provide aid to day-care centers, and to parents who use them, could emerge as a bipartisan change in the tax code to give a full-fledged children's allowance to poor and middle-class families. The idea of a family allowance has been the longtime dream of many American liberal social engineers. Every modern industrial nation except the United States has such a program. A rough consensus to change that seems to be forming in Washington.

The shift began with the Democrat's day-care proposal, the Act for Better Child Care Services. The Bush administration countered with a proposal for a tax credit for families with children under 4 years old, regardless of whether or not the mother is working. In earlier days, conservatives like Bush would have criticized that as redistributing wealth. Bush's move toward the tax code reflects both his "kinder and gentler" theme and conservative opposition to another big government program. The ante was upped by liberal Representative Thomas Downey (D-N.Y.), who proposes raising the individual tax rate for those with incomes over $149,500 and using most of the money to give more help per child to poor and lower-middle-class families, and to children of all ages.

The tax code is often viewed as arcane, but creative politicians like Senator Daniel P. Moynihan (D-N.Y.) know that it is the most potent way to make large-scale policy changes. Unlike regular federal programs that must be funded annually and are vulnerable to political shifts, programs with a base in the tax code are more difficult to change.

That is one reason why Social Security, which disburses $223 billion each year and has changed the economics of being old in America, is politically "untouchable." A similar example is the mortgage-interest deduction, which has helped shape the American middle class and last year cost the Treasury $35 billion.

The conservatives see a move toward social engineering as a way to advance their pro-family agenda. Gary Bauer, former adviser to Ronald Reagan, now president of the Family Research Council in Washington, is an example of the shift in thinking. He too favors a big tax-credit plan for children, but one that is available to the middle class and applies to nonworking mothers. Bauer's concern over the erosion of family values outweighs his fear of more big government. Besides, the conservatives know that using the tax code keeps bureaucrats out of the action.

So far, the dollar figures under consideration are modest. But if the principle of a children's allowance moves forward over the years, as seems likely, Congress could expand it by raising the proposed tax credit per child and the income qualification ceiling. Also, the plan could be made "revenue neutral." Everyone would pay a slightly higher general tax rate, but parents with children would get more back.

Since the time of Franklin Roosevelt, a driving idea of American government has been to redistribute wealth from rich to poor. Politically, that idea is more difficult to sell today because it is regarded as too liberal. But as education and moral values are perceived to be failing, as drug abuse is sensed to be increasing, as poor children remain a massive problem, pro-family sentiment in America is growing. That is the attitudinal Archimedian lever that George Bush, and conservatives, and liberals, are using to push forward a new, but not antithetical, kind of redistribution: to the child-rearing from the empty nesters.

May 22, 1989

Money: The Root of Much Progress

Money is making a comeback. America's No. 1 problem is low-income kids. Luckily, our government has figured out how to make low-income kids into not-low-income kids: with money. If we're even luckier, money will also start helping middle-class kids.

It sounds easy. Money is wonderful. Even economists know that: they say it's fungible, which means you can do damn near anything with it. For a low-income child, money can buy better food, clothing and housing, day care, books, eyeglasses.

Yet, foolishly, money has gotten a bad name in the policy-and-politics community.

It's said that liberals want to "throw money at problems." That's neither true nor bad. What liberals have too often done is "throw programs at problems."

Conservatives also have a problem with government money; they don't usually like to spend it, except on defense.

But money has just won big in Washington. Money is so wonderful that it has united two energetic congressmen—one liberal, one conservative, Tom Downey (D-N.Y.) and Tom Petri (R-Wis.)

Their cause is helping children and families who need help. Their vehicle is called the "Earned Income Tax Credit" (EITC). It should be called "a children's allowance for low-income parents who work." It's not called that because, as Downey says, "children's allowance sounds too European."

True. The European democracies, indeed, every modern democracy—except America—has a children's allowance. That's one reason poor kids are our most devastating problem, but not theirs.

Downey and Petri were instrumental in placing a much expanded EITC in recent House legislation. Because liberals love kids more than programs, because conservatives love families more than they hate spending, because George Bush was one architect of the approach, it will become law.

The EITC is a simple tax device. Its biggest effect, achieved by jiggling the W-2 exemption form, is to lower taxes at the point of paycheck, yielding a pay raise.

An EITC is in the tax code now, but it tops out at about $900 per year per family, with the benefit reaching its maximum at $7,000 to $11,000 of annual income and phasing out at $22,000.

The new EITC moves into greener and conceptually fresh territory. The 7–11–22 parameters remain the same, but much more money is provided—up to $2,220. It establishes an age principle; a family with a child under 6 gets up to $430 per year.

And it establishes a "per kid" principle, the nub of a children's allowance. The government will take progressively less money (taxes) from low income taxpayers, depending on whether they have one, two or three children.

The EITC has clean lines. Unlike welfare, there are no bureaucrats involved. Recipients spend the money according to their own priorities, not the government's. It rewards a man for staying with his family, not leaving it. It is only available to people who work, diminishing fears of "baby-farming" or enhancing dependency. Unlike day care legislation, it doesn't distinguish between mothers who pay for care and those who don't, allowing both to help their families as they see fit.

Low-income children correlate with crime, drugs, and poor education. Typically, the EITC moves kids out of low-income neighborhoods by letting parents keep the money they've earned.

There are two problems: It's not enough money, and it doesn't cover enough people. The $2,220 is better than a sharp stick in the eye, but at the maximum benefit a low-income working family of five still only ends up with $13,000. Not enough.

And it doesn't deal with the middle class. Young adults complain these days about how difficult it is to have a family. There are student loans to pay, housing is expensive, wives must work to make ends meet.

If the income ceiling were to be raised, the per kid and age criteria of the EITC would provide help to middle classniks who want children.

That's called pro-natalism, and we're likely to get some. Not many politicians will vote against kids, mom, family and the middle class.
October 11, 1989

> *When there is a social problem that is serious and can be alleviated by raw money, throw money at the problem. (Most social problems aren't so easy).*
>
> *The Congress and the President are expected to do that in the fall of 1990.*

———————

About "values," this can be said, with surety: everything is true and so is its opposite.

Many Americans, probably most Americans, almost surely most conservatives, believe that "eroding values" are America's number one problem. A number of reasons for that view are touched upon in this section: crime, drugs, out-of-wedlock births, female-headed households.

However, there is an equally long list of howevers. Americans are more religious, by far, than any other modern nation. Americans are more patriotic. (See data, page 116.) Family is still, by far, our bedrock belief.

In the early 1970s, the late Whitney Young, President of the Urban League, set up an appointment to meet with Scammon and me. It was a long discussion and covered a lot of ground. Young asked what we thought of the plausibility of a black man trying to become Vice President of the United States. On a Republican ticket. (Good idea, we said.)

He reminisced about Martin Luther King: "Martin always told me, Whitney, never forget that blacks are religious, patriotic and materialistic."

I believe that is still true, for blacks, and for the rest of the country.

Middletown Won't Budge

I've just returned from a fascinating week in the Sociology Capital of the World—Muncie, Ind., more-or-less midway between Indianapolis and Dayton, Ohio. Muncie, as it turns out, is the most studied, most researched community in the world. For half a century now it's been sending us messages that we too often ignore.

It all began in the mid-1920s when Robert and Helen Lynd, seeking typicality in America, arrived in Muncie to conduct a study of religion.

They quickly realized that to study religion you also had to study the whole community. And so, after several years of intensive study, "Middletown" came out, using the then-new disciplines of sociology and cultural anthropology. The Lynds, indeed, studied the folks of Muncie under a clinical microscope as if they were a tribe in New Guinea—with love but dispassion.

"Middletown" was a blockbuster. The Lynds saw Muncie as a place of traditional American values, a booster culture going through a struggle between the dominant business class and a weaker working class. All this was played against a backdrop of what the Lynds saw as a harmful time of sweeping, modernizing social change.

Of course, H. L. Mencken saw "Middletown" as proof that America was really "Moronia" inhabited by the "booboisie." The people in Muncie first liked the study, then denounced it.

"Middletown" was published in 1929. The Depression began in the same year. Robert Lynd returned to Muncie in the mid-1930s to write "Middletown in Transition." By then, Lynd was quite a left-wing radical. He came back to Muncie looking for evidence that under the lash of the Depression, the heartland was become fascist. He found no such thing. He found distress, to be sure, but not much change in values, either political or social. Life went on.

Then, in the mid-1970s, another team of sociologists arrived in Muncie, headed by Dr. Theodore Caplow of the University of Virginia. Again, as in the '30s, it would be logical to expect change: We had just lived through Vietnam, riots, Watergate, women's liberation, stagflation, inflation, drugs, crime, coming out of the closet, the greening of America and Future Shock.

But what Caplow's team found—and document in their fascinating new book "Middletown's Families"—was continuity, not change. Muncie's values—regarding the family, religion, work and even politics and sex—were not much different in the mid-1970s from what they had been in the '20s or the '30s. Moreover, Caplow maintains that the data from Muncie is generally representative of America.

In the late '70s and early '80s, film-maker Peter Davis came to Muncie with several cinema teams to begin the shooting of the "Middletown" television series, essentially a set of vignettes, which is just concluding a run on PBS stations. At the same time, Davis was shuttling back and forth to Hamilton, Ohio, a couple of hours down the road, doing research on another Midwestern community. That led to Davis' new book "Hometown." His conclusion is similar to Caplow's: Life in America hasn't changed all that much.

And now the big recession has hit Muncie—hard. Its key facilities are automotive-related: a Chevy plant, Warner Gear and Delco. The unemployment rate in "typical" Muncie is now third-highest in the nation, a very untypical 18.5 percent. People back in the wicked East are speculating about whether there is a chance that America is now heading into another depression. We see and hear stories of despair and desperation on our nightly news shows.

My week in Muncie to do a wrap-up on the PBS series tells me that Caplow and Davis are still right and the networks and the pundits, as usual, are crisis-mongering. Keep your eye on continuity, not change.

It's not that there is no distress. There is plenty. Mayor Alan Wilson says the recession is putting a severe strain on social services.

State Rep. Hurley Goodall is a black and a former firefighter. His electoral district has just about all of Muncie's blacks and yet is 3-to-1 white. Rep. Goodall says that, indeed, the situation is serious; there are middle-class people, black and white, who have never before been unemployed, and who are now. Goodall's big concern is that it may take a while after the jobless go back to work until they are confident enough to start buying again, priming the pump of the economy.

But, Howard Snider, who owns the Shakey's pizza parlor, says trade is picking up—and this was before the story of his little business in crisis aired on PBS. A shoe-store owner downtown says you have to work a little harder these days, but people are still buying shoes, especially top-of-the-line brands. Meanwhile, Muncie's own Ball Corporation is having one more very good year, and is planning expansion. There's little talk about depression, and if there is a grass-roots movement for a nuclear freeze in Muncie, no one bothered to mention it to me.

Muncie remains a place for family, religion, patriotism and optimism. It's a place where the tribes have fun by watching young people throw balls through hoops. It has its share of crime, corruption, and avarice.

Well, you might say, all that's not news: news is when man bites dog. I think I disagree. After all we've been through in 50 years—boom, depression, war, prosperity, dissent, inflation, culture shock and future shock—if dog still bites man, then no news is big news.

April 26, 1982

The May 1990 unemployment rate in Muncie was 5.0 percent. If a recession comes to Muncie again, that rate will surely go up, but due to much recent industrial diversification, it will not come close to approaching the horrific levels of 1982.

Mapxxxthorpe

CINCINNATI—The words about Robert Mapplethorpe's exhibit of photographs here are harder to handle than the pictures. The legal process must judge the pictures not the words. Accordingly, that process will end up giving a gold star of martyrdom to the thumb-in-your-eye parts of the arts community who have been appropriately crying "censorship."

Roughly—very roughly—the published words describing some of the photos are these: "an arm up a rectum," "a finger in a penis," "a man urinating in another man's mouth," "a man's nipple pierced by a pin" and "a bullwhip handle in a rectum."

The words are true, and tough, but in the end misleading. They bring one to the show prepared to say, "If a conservative city like Cincinnati feels this repugnant show violates community standards on obscenity, then, as the law says, the exhibition may be closed down."

But it's the wrong show and the wrong city for such a judgment.

There are 175 photographs in the exhibit. About 165 are full-sized works. They are displayed, museum-like, along the walls of the Contemporary Arts Center here. The great majority are portraits or pictures of flowers. If you get off on flowers, particularly their reproductive organs (pistils and stamens), you will be moved.

Also on the walls are a few photos of penises in various hues and sizes, and two men in leather jackets, rapt, and wrapped in chains.

Beyond that, still on the walls, are two pictures of naked young children. One is of a boy, and not very different from what is found in family photo albums, almost a baby picture. The other is of a seated girl, perhaps five years old, whose dress has crept upward, revealing, as the phrase has it, "that she is not wearing underwear."

The most repugnant photos, the so-called "portfolio X"—finger-in-penis, arm-in-rectum, urination-in-mouth, etc.—are small, appearing almost as snapshots. They are displayed separately in a glass-covered case (designed by the artist before his death from AIDS-related causes.)

A Supreme Court justice has said, "I may not be able to define obscenity, but I know it when I see it." The Mapplethorpe exhibit shows that the same statement can be made about non-obscenity.

Portfolio X shows a tawdry and disgusting lifestyle in which the photographer participated in the late 1970s (the bullwhip handle is in his body, the pierced nipple is his). It may not be art, but the pictures are anatomy and anthropology. The same pictures, dealing with the practices of a primitive tribe, would yield no obscenity trial. Nor is there danger of corruption or easy acceptance of alternative sexual proclivities. I can't envision a buying panic of bullwhips after this show hits town.

Another root of the indictment concerns not the nature of the pictures, but the nature of Cincinnati, typically described as a straight-laced and conservative city. Do Mapplethorpe's photographs violate community standards?

The answer is there to see when you leave the gallery. Fountain Square in downtown Cincinnati is gleaming in the spring brightness; the architecture is modern and post-modern. It yells at you: "You've got it wrong; this is no provincial backwater." Indeed, the Queen City has a long history of support for cultural endeavors.

If America is going to argue about censorship, Cincinnatians want to be in it. They say, wisely: When in doubt, don't censor. A Cincinnati Post poll shows that, by about 3-to-2, they say keep the exhibit open. Other survey research shows Cincinnati is attitudinally similar to the rest of America.

It's true that Cincinnati has cleaned out the porn shops and nudie shows; it's also true that a full menu is available just across the river in Newport, Ky.

This is the paradox of normality. Americans condemn pornography. But on Saturday nights, good ol' boys, often accompanied by their wives, can occasionally be found in their pick-up trucks at the rural, XXX-rated, drive-in theater.

And then in church on Sunday morning.

April 25, 1990

Don't censor the Mapplethorpes, or the piss Christs, or the naked woman performing live, covered with chocolate, or the other naked woman who does things with yams. And don't fund them with tax dollars.

Is baseball a traditional value? Be serious.

Is Baseball Snoreball?

If what follows sounds like sour grapes, designed to ruin your World Series season, well, maybe that's what it is.

As a boy and a teen-ager, I rooted for the Brooklyn Dodgers, and at no small sacrifice. I lived in the Bronx, home of the repugnant Yankees. All my friends mindlessly rooted for those pin-striped poobahs.

I knew all the averages, followed all the games, worshipped all the players. (When I was 8, I wanted to be Pistol Pete Reiser.)

Indicators: *Values*

A. Percent affiliated with churches or religious organizations

Country	Percent
U.S.	57%
Northern Ireland	51%
Holland	35%
Rep. of Ireland	31%
Britain	22%
Spain	15%
W. Germany	13%
Norway	10%
Belgium	9%
Sweden	9%
Italy	7%
France	4%
Denmark	4%

B. Percent that are very or quite proud of their country

Country	Percent
U.S.	96%
Ireland	91%
Britain	86%
Spain	83%
Italy	80%
France	76%
Japan	62%
W. Germany	59%

C. Black and white feelings about the U.S.: 1986

	Blacks	Whites
Very proud to be American	90%	89%

D. If a man and woman have sex relations before marriage, do you think it is always wrong, almost always wrong, wrong only sometimes, or not wrong at all?

Year	Always/Almost Always Wrong
1972	46%
1975	42%
1978	40%
1982	37%
1985	36%
1989	35%

E. Item cited most frequently as the biggest problem with which public schools must deal

Year	"Discipline"	"Drugs"
1970	18%	11%
1972	23%	—
1974	23%	13%
1976	22%	11%
1978	25%	13%
1980	26%	14%
1982	27%	20%
1984	27%	18%
1986	24%	28%
1988	19%	32%
1989	19%	34%

Source notes are on page 394.

F. Are you satisfied or dissatisfied with the way things are going in:

	The U.S.		Your Personal Life	
Year	Satisfied	Dissatisfied	Satisfied	Dissatisfied
1979	19%	77%	79%	19%
1981	27%	67%	81%	17%
1983	35%	59%	77%	20%
1985	51%	46%	82%	17%
1986	58%	38%	84%	14%
1987	45%	49%	83%	15%
1988	56%	40%	87%	12%

1989: How optimistic or pessimistic are you about life in the year 2000?

The U.S.		Your Personal Life	
Optimistic	Pessimistic	Optimistic	Pessimistic
71%	23%	82%	10%

Then they took my team from Brooklyn—Hodges, Reese, Snider, Furillo—and plopped it, cold turkey, into Los Angeles.

As a young man, I came to Washington, D.C., which then had a bad baseball team called the Senators. With my young children, I went to the Senators games, knew most of the averages, followed most of the games, admired many of the players—monumental Frank Howard, semi-monumental Mike Epstein ("Super Jew," he was called) and un-monumental Ed Brinkman who looked like a skinny water rat. The manager was the maxi-monumental Ted Williams.

One day the team disappeared and re-surfaced in Arlington, Texas, which I learned was between Dallas and Fort Worth.

That was 18 years ago. To this day the capital city of the United States—one of the most affluent and fastest growing areas in the nation, a community zonked on spectator sports (the Redskins)—does not have a major-league baseball franchise.

Let me tell you something about not having a baseball team. It's OK. It's fine. You can live without it real easy.

It's sort of a dumb and boring sport. Some of our finest columnists and intellectuals have been trying to tell us otherwise as they wax sagely about the true meaning and poetry of baseball generally, and too often about the Chicago Cubs particularly.

Baseball is the soul of America, we have been told. You can't really understand the nature of America if you don't understand baseball. Oh, the finesse and drama of a pitcher's duel! Oh, the geometric purity of the diamond in the church of baseball!

It's got zero to do with the soul of America. Did America not have a soul before Abner Doubleday didn't invent baseball in Cooperstown, N.Y., in 1839? Did Benjamin Franklin play baseball? Did Tocqueville know from baseball when he explained America? Did Tom Jefferson worry about hitting the curveball? Did Joltin' Jim Madison know the sound of horsehide meeting hickory? Did George Washington have a good move to first?

And don't get me going about a pitchers' duel. I was graciously invited to a major-league game the other week, and saw a major-league pitchers' duel. Snoreball. Three hours and no one hit more than a double.

The better games aren't much better. Eighteen men in shrunken knickers. At any moment almost half of them are sitting on a bench yelling "Way to go, Bubba." Seven of the nine men in the field are doing zip for 99 percent of the time. The total action time in a nine-inning game must be about three minutes. Watch the highlights on the evening news.

In football, all 22 men on the field are playing at the same time. In basketball everyone is playing all the time. That's roughly true in soccer, too. If you must watch a game played with a stick, watch lacrosse or tennis, where athletes at least work up a sweat. Baseball is team golf.

The lure of baseball comes from journalism, fable and statistics. When you don't know that your shortstop can make .300 this year if he hits .320 for the rest of the season, when you don't know that your team is Cinderella coming from nowhere, when you don't know that the young left-hander with the fastball is in the manager's doghouse, and is about to face Mighty Casey in front of 60,000 fans—baseball is snoreball squared.

So have a nice time watching the playoffs and the Series. Call me when they expand the leagues and there's a team in my town.

October 4, 1988

George Will has written a very interesting book about baseball, entitled Men at Work. *But what does it tell you when the book is better than the game?*

5

Income and Programs

How are we doing? Some of the broadest and best indicators come from the realm of income and wealth.

Several key questions in this area have animated recent public policy arguments. These include: Has there been a redistribution of income from poor to rich, from the needy to the greedy? Is poverty growing? Is the middle class eroding? Have "the programs" worked?

Loosely connected is another question: What should the government's role be in building a burgeoning economy?

The answers, I think, yield one view of the terrain of the nineties, and it is not the picture that we normally hear about. There are things that are not happening that we have been told are happening.

There will be a middle class in the nineties. It's been growing, it is growing now, and it will probably keep on growing. Whether or not there has been a redistribution from poor to rich is a tricky statistical question. If there has been, it has been overstated. Poverty is slowly shrinking.

Viewed broadly, our recent experiments in political economy each sort of work. At least for a while. The conservative welfare state, alluded to earlier, seems to be working pretty well now. Of course, so too did the LBJ-style liberal welfare state. That leads one toward a position that it is America that works well. Typically, when things do get out of joint, both our economics and our politics change sufficiently to make the boo-boo better.

Anyone who doesn't sense that it is our market system, in both economics *and politics, that is driving this success does not have a clue as to what is going on.*

Having paid ritual and realistic obeisance to the private market system, we shouldn't neglect the role of the public sector as a tool of economic vigor. There is a policy, or at least a point of view, that lets public sector liberals participate in making the pie grow, not just in carving it up. Call it "supply-side infrastructuralism."

Indicators: *Income/Programs*

A. Family income, after a long plateau, has resumed climbing . . .

1. Cash Income of Families in Constant 1988 Dollars

Year	Median Income	CPI-U-X1*
1967	$28,098	$25,853
1970	$30,084	$28,263
1975	$30,167	$28,878
1980	$30,182	$30,219
1982	$28,727	$28,997
1985	$30,493	$30,493
1988	$32,191	$32,191

A. (Cont.) . . . while per capita income has gone up steadily.

2. Cash Income Per Capita in Constant 1988 Dollars

Year	Median Income	CPI-U-X1
1967	$ 8,727	$ 8,030
1970	$ 9,687	$ 9,100
1975	$10,594	$10,142
1980	$11,180	$11,193
1982	$11,009	$11,112
1985	$12,108	$12,108
1988	$13,123	$13,123

C. Americans are the most prosperous people in the world.

Table of International Comparisons (1989–90)

Country	Per Capita PPP*
United States	$17,615
Canada	$16,335
Switzerland	$15,403
Luxembourg	$15,247
W. Germany	$14,730
France	$13,961
Kuwait	$13,843
Sweden	$13,780
Iceland	$13,324
Japan	$13,135
United Kingdom	$12,270
Saudi Arabia	$ 8,320
South Korea	$ 4,832
Mexico	$ 4,624
China (PRC)	$ 2,124
India	$ 1,053

* PPP—Estimated Purchasing Power Parities (see note)

B. Domestic social welfare spending reached a plateau during the Reagan years, as a percentage of Gross National Product, but rose per capita.

1. Social Welfare Expenditures

Year	Social Welfare Spending as a Percent of GNP
1950	8.2%
1960	10.3%
1970	14.7%
1975	19%
1980	18.5%
1985	18.6%
1987	18.8%

2. Per Capita Social Welfare Spending

Per Capita Spending (in Constant 1987 Dollars)	
1950	$698
1960	$1,039
1965	$1,316
1970	$1,952
1975	$2,684
1980	$2,956
1985	$3,251
1987	$3,364

Source notes are on page 394.

Charles Murray Is Half Right

Charles Murray has written a book that public policy analysts—and politicians—are talking about. It's called *Losing Ground,* and that is precisely
its theme: That poor people in America have been losing ground since
the mid-1960s.

Murray, a Fellow at the Manhattan Institute for Policy Research, says
it's no accident. The poor are worse off, he believes, because of our vastly
expanded social-welfare programs. The programs were well-meaning, but
counterproductive. What are Murray's solutions? His most publicized one
says we should dump the programs—an idea that excites conservatives,
who like the idea that cutting the domestic budget is now on the front
burner.

It is a strange book. It is carefully argued and interestingly written. It is
dead wrong in much of its factual base, and dead wrong in many of its
policy prescriptions. And yet, there is a solid core of redeeming thought
worth pondering.

Thus, one key predicate of Murray's argument is that since the early
1970s there are greater rates of poor people in America. That is not only
wrong, it is even wrong according to data Murray casually mentions in
his own book.

The "net" poverty rate—that is the poverty rate including "non-cash"
items like food stamps—was down to 6 percent in 1979. But the rate was
nearly 30 percent back in 1950 (Murray's estimate). It was 22 percent in
1960, and 12 percent in 1970. That's a decrease, not an increase, and a
portion of the decrease is surely ascribable to "the programs."

There is more. Murray says he is writing about "Americal Social Policy
1950–1980." But he quickly narrows his focus—almost to absurdity.

First, he says, let's not count the elderly, that's a separate story. So it
is. Net poverty for the elderly in Murray's time frame went down from
about 40 percent to about 4 percent. But this decline happened largely
due to what Murray condemns, namely, American social policy—which
includes Social Security increases, and the advent of Medicare and Supplemental Security Income.

Next, Murray says, let's not count white people. In a dazzling fast shuffle,
Murray contends that we ought to judge poverty results by what has happened
to blacks. But why? Whites make up about 70 percent of the poor people.
And net poverty for whites has gone way down.

The selective winnowing continues: Murray points out that things haven't
been going too badly for blacks who are age 25 or older—unemployment
is actually lower than it used to be.

So what is he talking about? He's talking about young blacks. But to draw a portrait of American social policy from blacks aged 16–24 is odd. They make up about 2 percent of the U.S. population. Even there the picture is mixed. After all, the number of young blacks in college went up by 883 percent from 1950 to 1980!

Still, surely, there are massive problems among some young blacks these days. Murray focuses on the key ones: high crime, poor education and out-of-wedlock birth.

He notes, correctly, that some liberal ideas ended up hurting more than helping. A soft attitude about crime made some ghetto neighborhoods into places of terror. A soft attitude about discipline in school, coupled with quotas, undermines minority students who want to work hard. Easy welfare standards can encourage out-of-wedlock births.

But, curiously, most of these problems were not caused by the big-spending social-welfare programs. The soft judicial approach to crime was not a liberal big money "program." It came from something quite different: a liberal "attitude." So too with educational permissiveness and quotas. Welfare spending is different. But even there, remember that the controversial "man in the house" rules were originally changed by court challenges, not by legislated money programs.

Where does this leave us? There are fewer poor than there used to be in America. That's to the good, and probably partly due to expanded programs. There are some counterproductive programs. They ought to be re-examined.

Most important, there are some philosophies that should be re-examined, as Murray suggests. Educational permissiveness, quotas, criminal coddling, welfare laxness have hurt poor people most. It is in those philosophical areas—but not about the big-spending programs—where Murray is on target.

January 8, 1984

> *In the spring of 1985, I was a panelist (along with Charles Murray) at a session of the LBJ School in Austin. The topic was "What Worked? What Failed? Why?" Here is a transcript excerpt of my presentation. (Murray is now a colleague of mine at the American Enterprise Institute.)*

What Worked? What Failed? Why?

Ben Wattenberg: If you take the broad picture from 1959 to 1984, you are talking about a drop in poverty from 22 percent to 8 or 9 percent. That's a drop of two-thirds. That is not a failure. It would seem to me that would be characterized as a partial success. It leaves twenty million people in poverty; that's a lot of people in poverty. I personally think the government has a role and a duty to try to get those people out of poverty.

Why did this happen? It seems to be fairly elemental: it happened because the government threw money at problems. If you give poor people money or the equivalent of money, and then you try to measure it, you are going to find that fewer people are poor.

The idea that throwing money at problems helps solve them is not an exceptional idea. Conservatives, and some people like myself who don't even regard themselves as conservatives, although some other people do, think that you can solve some of America's defense dilemmas, for example, by spending more money on defense. Scientists who want to go to space—to the moon, to Mars—say, "If you give us more money, we can do it." And they're right. Accordingly, it seems to me that in the public policy community, we ought to understand that if we throw money at problems, it helps.

It also causes, as Mr. Murray has pointed out, second-order problems—dependency is surely one of them—and now is a very good time to be dealing with those problems because we are very short of money in Washington. It's a good time to see what worked and what didn't work and try to save some money here, and tinker with the system there, to make it work better.

Now, what failed?

It seems to me that the failure was an intellectual and political one, by those Great Society liberals who neglected to dissociate themselves from subsequent ideas labeled "liberal," but which were ideas that sidetracked liberal energy and power. Let me explain what I mean.

Most of the public perception about dismay with American liberalism does not stem from the Great Society era or programs. Around 1970 or so, American liberalism really split into two camps. Handy labels for it are the Great Society versus the New Politics. The personalities associated with them are Lyndon Johnson, certainly, as the exemplar of the Great Society, and perhaps George McGovern as the exemplar of the New Politics. But it's much too simple to talk about personalities; they were a set of ideas.

Despite what you just heard from Mr. Murray about educational permissiveness and criminal permissiveness, there was no Soft-on-Crime Act of 1968. There was no Permissive Curriculum Act of 1967. There were no Great Society laws mandating busing or quotas. There were no Great Society laws that were entitled the Let's Be Vindictive to Business Acts. There were no Great Society laws that called for no, low, or slow economic growth. And there was certainly nothing in the Great Society or in Lyndon Johnson's tradition that said we ought to beat up on defense and diminish America's assertive role in the world.

These notions, however, attached themselves to the idea of American liberalism after the Great Society. They did so, as Mr. Murray pointed out, via the courts, via the regulators, via the guideline writers, via the congressional staff, but not by Great Society law and usually not even by post–Great Society law. Unfortunately, too many Great Society liberals failed to draw distinctions. And so, when the new ideas and the Great Society programs mixed and muddled together, people said, "Well, we don't like liberalism anymore."

Lyndon Johnson and the great Congresses of that era legislated what people in their heart wanted—civil rights, helping poor people, health, education—you have heard the list. The New Politics agenda, on the other hand, dealt with ideas that people didn't really want, or it pushed good ideas to far-out extremes.

If we are interested in pursuing the road of liberalism, it seems to me that we ought to go back to the point in time where that road was sidetracked into unsupported territory.

It's true that President Reagan won elections by campaigning against Big Government. It's true when you look at the public-opinion polls that people say, "No, we don't like the Great Society." On the other hand, when you look at those same public-opinion polls and you ask people about civil rights, education, medicine, and the environment, people say, "Oh, we're all for those kinds of programs," which, of course, are the essence of the Great Society program.

And you have one other keystone political fact about public opinion in the United States, which it seems to me should give us great optimism in the future. In the first debate in 1984 between Ronald Reagan and Walter Mondale, Ronald Reagan presented himself as the man who saved your safety net. Now, Ronald Reagan is a man who for twenty-five years campaigned against weaving almost every strand in that safety net. But it is an understatement to say he is a very smart politician.

So he understands, the country understands, the public-opinion polls surely reveal, that this is a country that wants and needs a safety net. When we go back to where that road went in the wrong direction and figure out how to go forward on the original direction set by the people in this room, I think we will continue to make a greater society.

April 19, 1985

Re-boomeranging Poverty

It is just 25 years since the publication of *The Other America*, Michael Harrington's seminal book on poverty in America. Looking back, one can sense both the power and the paradox of the volume. It's followed a circular path. It exaggerated a problem. Its exaggeration helped form a movement—

the "war on poverty"—that set some remedies in motion. Its continued exaggeration, by author and movement, led to a boomerang bashing of its cause. And now—full circle—it's time to resuscitate the idea, responsibly, and move ahead.

Harrington's 1962 book said that about a third of Americans were poor, that little was being done for them, that they were "immune from progress," that they were "invisible" to the affluent eye.

It was overstated. The rate of poverty from 1949 to 1964 dropped from 33 percent to 18 percent. During the 1950s, social welfare expenditures climbed by 52 percent. (Actually, in an appendix, Harrington said the poverty rate was 20–25 percent, not a third.) This is not statistical nitpicking. There was plenty of poverty, but it was clearly decreasing.

Harrington's book crystallized what was in the air, a willingness to further help the poor. When Lyndon Johnson became president, "war on poverty" was declared. Soon, enormous new sums were allocated. There were "cash" programs, such as additional Social Security, Supplemental Security Income and welfare. There were "non-cash" programs such as food stamps, rent supplements, Medicaid, job training and education grants.

In some important ways, the "war on poverty" has been successful. In 1959, the poverty rate for the elderly was 35 percent. In 1986 it was 12 percent, or somewhere between 3 percent and 8 percent if you count in (properly) the "non-cash" benefits. Poverty among married-couple families has declined from 19 percent in 1959 to 7 percent in 1986, or 5 percent, counting "non-cash."

Yet, while poverty was diminishing, Harrington and the poverty warriors neither acknowledged nor saluted progress. They apparently thought poor-mouthing would keep the heat on America's conscience. The strategy boom-eranged. It let Ronald Reagan and conservatives agree that poverty warfare wasn't working, highlight those parts that were legitimately flawed, and make an easy case that a war on poverty was "throwing money down a rat hole."

Well, that was then. Now is now. It's clear today that the parts of the poverty puzzle that were dealt with successfully were the easiest to handle. More cash worked for most of the elderly. Some programs and, mostly, a healthy economy worked for most of those in poverty who had a solid family.

Now, because of rising divorce and out-of-wedlock births, the biggest part of the poverty population is composed of "female-headed households." that sounds neat and statistical. It shouldn't. We're talking mostly about poor kids. It's our No. 1 social problem. More than a fifth of American kids are now in poverty! One-third of our children will be in poverty at some point before their 18th birthday!

Indicators: *Poverty/Pensions*

A. After rising during the recession of the early eighties, the poverty rate has been coming down.

Percentage of People Below the Poverty Line

Year Only	Cash	Noncash Included	CPI-U-X1*
1959	22.4%	*	na
1969	12.1%	*	na
1979	11.7%	8.9%	10.5%
1980	13.0%	10.2%	11.5%
1983	15.2%	12.8%	13.5%
1985	14.0%	11.5%	12.3%
1987	13.4%	11.0%	11.9%
1988	13.1%	na	11.6%

* See notes.

B. The percentage of elderly people (65 and over) in poverty has declined dramatically.

Percentage of Elderly Poor

Year	Cash Only	Noncash Included*	CPI-U-X1
1959	35.2%	*	na
1969	25.3%	*	na
1979	15.2%	8.7%	13%
1983	13.8%	8.1%	10.7%
1985	12.6%	6.7%	9.5%
1987	12.5%	6.4%	9.8%
1988	12.0%	na	9.6%

* See notes.

C. Baby boomers will be the most financially secure retirees in history.

Percentage of Persons Aged 65 and Older Receiving Benefits from or Eligible for

Year	Social Security	Pensions*
1976	89%	31%
1980	90%	34%
1984	91%	38%
1986	91%	40%
2010–20	97%	71%

* See note.

D. Private pensions are growing rapidly.

Retirement Benefit Payments (in Billions of Constant 1988 dollars)

Year	Social Security	Pensions All*	Private
1950	$ 3.2	$ 6.7	$ 1.8
1955	$ 16.5	$ 10.6	$ 3.1
1960	$ 32.8	$ 19.3	$ 6.9
1965	$ 46.8	$ 32.4	$ 12.2
1970	$ 57.6	$ 53.5	$ 22.4
1975	$ 87.2	$ 82.6	$ 32.6
1980	$107.0	$107.0	$ 45.2
1985	$139.7	$160.2	$ 86.7
1988	$148.2	$220.0	$137.2

Source notes are on page 395.

E. The poverty rate for female-headed families is about six times higher than for two-parent families.

Characteristics of Families with Children under 18

Year	Percentage of Two-Parent Families	Two-Parent Family Poverty Rate	Percentage of Female-Headed Families	Female-Headed Family Poverty Rate
1959	89%	NA	9%	60%
1969	87%	NA	11%	45%
1974	83%	6%	16%	44%
1979	79%	6%	19%	40%
1987	75%	8%	21%	46%
1988	75%	7%	21%	45%
1988 (counting non-cash income)	NA	6%	NA	35%

This is crazy. The poor kids didn't create their condition. We do not serve anyone's cause by bringing up a generation of economically scarred children. Moreover, the current situation makes it less attractive for young couples to have children, yielding other problems that come with very low fertility rates.

Can we help? Sure. Start by saying that the way poor kids become non-poor kids is by getting money. By changing the tax code, this can be done in a manner pleasing to liberals, conservatives, pro-family activists, feminists and pro-natalists. Such a plan could yield one more partial victory in our ongoing, semi-successful war on poverty, one more dent in the overstated, but real, problem of the poor people who inhabit Harrington's other America.

October 8, 1987

Do not doubt that "non-cash income" is real income.

I was asked to talk at the Philadelphia branch of the Federal Reserve Bank. It is, among other things, a great big money-processing plant. In one huge room, there is a swirling blizzard of green. Green money comes in from local banks. Sophisticated electronic machinery sorts it, counts it, bales it, and when the green money is cruddy, shreds it.

In an adjacent smaller room, there are other flashing colors including brown and purple. The same process is performed on non-traditional money, food stamps. Poor people buy food with food stamps. Their merchants deposit them in a bank, just as they would with cash. The local banks send them to the Federal Reserve for a cash credit.

It seems as if everyone counts food stamps as money except the people who want to make a point that poverty is going up. Urged on by liberals, the U.S. Congress legislated programs to reduce poverty. Then liberals almost invariably argued that we should not count the fruits of their legislation in calculating the poverty rates, lest it show poverty declining too much, even if it showed that their nostrums work. Old axiom: liberals forming a firing squad assemble in a circle.

Tomorrow: Counting the Poor

The received wisdom of our time is that little progress has been made in recent years in reducing poverty, raising middle-income earnings, or narrowing the gap between rich and poor. From that perspective, it is an easy pessimistic glide to say that it will be very difficult to make headway in those areas in the future. But last week's Census Bureau report on income and poverty suggests more significant progress and has fueled a growing debate over the best way for the government to measure income.

It is an article of the gloom-mongers' creed that poverty has not declined significantly even though the U.S. economy is now in its seventh consecutive year of growth. In apparent confirmation, the new census report shows that in 1988, the poverty rate dropped from 13.4 percent to 13.1 percent, a decline the Census Bureau categorizes as "statistically insignificant." Fair enough. But a steady series of small-to-medium "insignificant" changes all in the same direction can indicate real change. And that is just what has been happening since 1983, a year of recession and high unemployment in which the poverty rate reached 15.2 percent. During the last five years, the number of poor people has declined by 2.1 percentage points or 14 percent, a drop that Census Bureau economist Gordon Green says is "significant indeed."

This year's report contained several newer measurements that also show poverty numbers in a more favorable light. For the first time, the bureau published an alternative measure that uses a different consumer-price-index deflator to calculate the poverty line. It is considered by most economists to more accurately reflect housing costs and would lower the poverty rate to 11.6 percent. If some noncash benefits, such as food stamps and medicaid, were added in, the rate would decline even further to 10.5 percent. Combining both, which makes statistical sense, yields a single-digit poverty rate of about 9%.

Another measure in controversy is family income. There is a pervasive notion that it plateaued in the early 1970s and that middle-income Americans have made no real economic progress since, a case made prominent by Prof. Frank Levy, author of *Dollars and Dreams: The Changing American Income Distribution.*

Indeed, according to the traditional census data, family income was up a minuscule 0.3 percent between 1973 and 1988. But when the alternative measurements are applied to that same period, they show a slow-to-moderate 7.5 percent real increase in family income, as well as a robust 28 percent rise in per capita income. (The no-progress notion was never true for per capita income, which rose by 19 percent under the original formula.) Levy agrees that the new measurements offer a better way to track income, but he still says that family-income growth in recent decades, if no longer to be seen as flat, has been sluggish compared with the upward movement of the 1950s and 1960s.

Last week's report also dealt with the much publicized "income inequality" trend that in the last two decades has appeared more pronounced, with richer people getting a somewhat larger "share" of national income and poorer people getting somewhat less. The data series used to support this

trend, however, counts only cash income and does not correct for different tax rates of the various income groups. The new report includes an alternative calculation for taxes and noncash income. Not surprisingly, it shows the gap between rich and poor is narrower than has been officially reported.
October 30, 1989

Throwing Money Works

Conservatives like to say "You can't solve problems by throwing money at them."

This is usually wrong, dead wrong—and this is just the right moment to demonstrate that it is wrong. Fifty years ago—on Aug. 14, 1935 to be precise—President Franklin Roosevelt signed the Social Security Act into law. The act provided that some elderly Americans would begin to receive old-age pensions in 1940. Soon, life insurance coverage was added to Social Security. In 1956, disability insurance was added. And in 1965—Medicare.

Today the Social Security system is the essence of what is called the "safety net," most particularly for the elderly. Last year alone, $125 billion was disbursed in Social Security pensions. In 1940 only 1 percent of elderly Americans were covered. In 1950, still only 20 percent of those over 65 received Social Security. Today just about all the elderly are covered. Back in 1940, the average benefit for a couple was $35 a month. Today it is $775 per month. Even when you discount for inflation, that is three times as much. (The maximum benefit is now $1,100). Just since 1960, the after-inflation average monthly payment went up by almost 80 percent—four times as fast as the real wage rate.

All that doesn't include another $45 billion spent for the elderly in Medicare payments.

In addition, it should be noted that most Social Security recipients receive much more money than they ever put into the program. A person retiring today at age 65 will recoup the amount of all his contributions to the system within 22 months.

In short, we've thrown a lot of money at a problem.

The problem was "elderly poverty," and make no mistake about it, that was a massive problem before the advent of Social Security. In 1935, according to one estimate, almost two-thirds (65 percent) of the elderly were living at standards below what today we call "the poverty line."

Of course, that was during the Depression. But as recently as 1960, the census showed the elderly poverty rate at 35 percent.

Those numbers signified great misery. It wasn't that long ago that old people in America worried about going to what was called "the poorhouse."

Almost as distressing was the idea of having to live off of one's middle-aged children—typically at a time when those middle-aged children were strapped themselves, trying to support their own kids through school. It was a corrosive human situation.

Social Security has gone a long way toward solving that age-old problem. Middle-aged children no longer feel constrained to give money to their parents. They give it to the government. The government gives it to their parents. Accordingly, parents and children can go on loving each other while, respectively, they denounce the government for benefits that are too low or taxes that are too high. Social Security is the ultimate pro-family program.

Today, the poverty rate for the elderly in America is not the 65 percent of 1935 or the 35 percent of 1960 but about 5 percent when you count in all benefits.

So—America has pretty well remedied elderly poverty by doing what conservatives said doesn't work—throwing money at a problem.

August 15, 1985

Did family income hit a long and harmful plateau from the early seventies to the mid-eighties? That question is at the root of different perceptions about what has happened in America the last few decades.

Tables on page 121 do seem to show that family income did flatten out. But there are unstated factors in that critical number that much dilute its message. These include: (a) a generally accepted view that the Consumer Price Index was miscalculated for housing costs (the revised census series is found adjacent to the straight family income numbers and shows a steady increase); (b) the tremendous growth of the so-called underground, and unreported, economy, due to increased illegal immigration, increased self-employment, higher tax rates due to "bracket creep," more government programs based on low incomes, and more criminal activity; (c) more noncash income, including middle-class benefits such as health insurance and pension plans; and (d) changing family structure, particularly the increase in smaller families and female-headed families, partially mitigated by an increase in two-earner households.

Many, probably most, serious economists do not buy the notion that there has been no growth in family income in America for roughly fifteen years. If you are old enough to remember 1970, you may test that proposition in a personal way. Are there more cars on the road today? Are more young people in college today? Do more people

Indicators: *Spending*

A. Although economists and social scientists debate the actual meanings of income statistics, the evidence from actual spending patterns points upward.

1. Recreation Expenditures as a Percent of Total Personal Consumption

Year	Percent
1945	5.1%
1950	5.8%
1955	5.5%
1960	5.5%
1965	6.0%
1970	6.7%
1975	6.9%
1980	6.6%
1985	7.1%
1988	7.6%
1989	7.7%

2. Percent of Households Owning Cars

Year	Percent
1954	73%
1962	77%
1969	79%
1977	85%
1983	87%
1988	90%

3. Air Conditioning Ownership Rates

Year	Percent of Households with Air Conditioning
1960	12%
1970	36%
1975	49%
1980	57%
1985	63%
1987	66%

4. Travel to and from the United States in the 1980s (in Millions)

Year	Americans Abroad	Foreigners to U.S.
1980	22.4	22.5
1981	22.9	23.1
1982	23.1	21.9
1983	24.9	21.7
1984	34.4	26.9
1985	35.3	25.7
1986	37.7	26.3
1987	40.0	29.7
1988	41.2	34.2

Source notes are on page 395.

5. Professional Sports Attendance (in Thousands)

Year	Baseball	Football	Basketball
1975	30,373	10,769	7,591
1980	43,746	14,092	10,697
1985	47,742	14,058	11,491
1989	55,910	14,311	18,446

6. Percent of Households with Selected Electronic Devices

Year	Computer	Answering Machine	CD Player	Color TV	Cable TV
1980	—	—	—	83%	20%
1983	7%	3%	—	90%	37%
1985	13%	5%	1%	91%	49%
1990	23%	31%	19%	96%	60%

own air-conditioning units today? Are people more likely to travel overseas? Do people get the benefits of new medical technology? Are people more likely to eat out? Do you own a VCR? Do you get cable televison? Don't all those goods and services cost money?

Some indicators showing evidence of increased income are displayed throughout this book, and particularly on the preceding page.

Vanishing Upward

There has been a great hullabaloo recently about an idea called "the vanishing middle class." Simply put, the argument goes roughly like this: There are more rich people than before and the rich are getting even richer— and there are more poor people and the poor are getting even poorer.

Therefore, it is said that the middle class is vanishing, shrinking, disappearing, squeezed or stagnating. You may choose your own adjective because no expert has ever come up with a definition of "middle class" that other experts will agree upon.

For that matter, no experts seem to have ever agreed upon a definition of what "rich" is, either. It's been counted as a family income of about $40,000 or $50,000 or $100,000 or even much more. It has also been measured by accrued wealth rather than annual income.

Interestingly, the only definition where there is any agreement at all concerns poor people. There is an "official" poverty line and the Census Bureau each year duly records how many Americans are poor, after adjusting for inflation. The current level for a family of four is $11,000 per year ($10,989 to be precise). Below that, and you are officially poor. That figure includes only cash income.

Moreover, for the past seven years, the Census Bureau has also developed nine different statistical series that measure "non-cash" income for poor people. These non-cash items include things of true value like food stamps, rent supplements, Medicaid and Medicare. Remarkably, the non-cash disbursements involve about two-thirds of all government help to poor people!

What does all this have to do with the middle class that is allegedly vanishing, shrinking, disappearing, squeezed or stagnating?

This: Within the last month, the Census Bureau has issued two poverty reports. One measured how many people fell below the cash-only poverty threshold. The second measured how many people are below the poverty threshold if you count in the value of the non-cash items.

The verdict of the two poverty reports is clear and consistent: In the two years since the end of the big double-dip recession and the fall of unemployment rates in 1983, poverty has come down. Measured at the official level, the drop has been from 15.3 percent in 1983 to 14 percent in 1985. When the non-cash items are counted in, there has been a similar sort of drop in all nine ways of measuring it. Of the nine choices, the one I think makes the most sense shows a two-year drop from 10.6 percent to 9.3 percent.

Question: If there are fewer people in poverty, what does that tell us about the idea that the middle class is vanishing, shrinking or disappearing?

Answer: If it's happening, it's good! Why?

Well, if there are fewer people in poverty, where could they have gone? Only up.

Most likely, they made their way into the lower rungs of the middle class. And if the middle class is statistically shrinking (as is maintained), where could they possibly have gone? Only up—to the upper class.

That's good—not bad.

In fact, there used to be a much-used phrase to describe this process: "upward mobility." It defined American life. It's a phrase we should start using again. It's still what's happening.

October 16, 1986

Flash! Government Does Job

Brace yourself. Despite much political rhetoric to the contrary, there is at least one major realm where the U.S. government is doing what it is supposed to do!

For the last half-century the government—as expressed through its laws— has tried to lessen poverty and reduce inequality between the rich and the poor. Is it doing so? A ground-breaking new income report by the Census Bureau says yes. But does that mean that all the talk about how greed, the underclass, family breakup and loss of good jobs are ripping apart the American economic fabric is just malarkey? Not quite. For a full answer to that, we have to wait.

What, at this late date, could be "ground-breaking" about income data? Well, until now there has been at least one big problem. It only counted cash. That wasn't so bad some decades ago; most personal income was in cash. But more recently, income has tended to come to Americans in other ways.

For example, the great majority of people now get a medical benefit plan from their employers. In 1986, the year covered by the Census report, those insurance plans paid out $90 billion in medical costs. But that money was never counted by the Census as "cash income" to the beneficiaries.

These days, elderly Americans receive Medicare benefits that pay much of their health bills. Children get school lunches at subsidized low prices. Poor people now get "non-cash" benefits: food stamps, Medicaid and rent subsidies. None of this has been counted as income. Why not? After all, food stamps buy groceries as well as cash does. On the richer side, capital gains transactions were not counted as income either.

Beyond all that, tax rates changed, and federal cash programs like Social Security and welfare grew rapidly.

What does income now look like in a given year if all these variables are counted in? That's what the new report, "Measuring the Effect of Benefits and Taxes on Income and Poverty: 1986," tries to deal with.

Easiest to observe is that there is less poverty than commonly assumed. The "official" rate for 1986 was 13.6 percent—about one in seven Americans. The "adjusted" rate—counting non-cash income—is 10.3 percent, about one in 10. (The black rate drops even more, from 31 to 24 percent.)

Inequality is also substantially lessened when all money is counted. As officially measured, the poorest fifth of American households gets only 3.8 percent of aggregate income. But under the adjusted, and more accurate, formula they get 4.9 percent. (That is an increase of 29 percent.)

Is the government responsible for this upgrading? Yes. Without government money transfers, the poverty rate would be 21 percent—40 percent for blacks. Without government money, the poorest fifth would only get 1.1 percent of the income pie.

Heartening. Whether you like the idea or not, at least the government seems to be doing what it set out to do.

Still, the report covers only one year (1986). But what is the trend over time? Poverty is surely down; few non-cash programs for the poor even existed 25 years ago.

But what about inequality? This report only tells us that it's less than the previous cash-only view reveals and that the government makes it so. It doesn't state whether this adjusted figure is better or worse than a comparable figure would have been earlier. The Census Bureau now plans to compute such a data series going back several decades.

That should be fascinating. The money-only data since the mid-'70s has shown more, not less, inequality. That has lent credence to the idea that the economic fabric is rending, that our current situation is more heartless, less kind, less gentle than in earlier times. The new method of calculating income suggests that a full study may well reveal that there is less to that than meets the eye.

January 5, 1989

Hidden Wealth

Two studies about wealth in America recently made the front pages. There were several reasons for the publicity.

The first was that we don't have much data about wealth. About income—how much we make—we have plenty of statistics. But regarding wealth—

that is, net worth in terms of real estate, savings accounts, stocks, money-market funds and IRAs — the statistical armory is thinly stocked.

The second reason was that both studies revealed the rich are very much richer than the not-rich. (Flash: The rich are ripping us off!) These reports are interesting and useful, but, I think, misleading.

The first study, by the Census Bureau, was straightforward and scholarly. It showed that the median amount of wealth per household was $32,677. It showed that well-to-do people (those earning more than $4,000 per month) had about 25 times as much wealth as the lowest-income class (those earning less than $900 a month). Moreover, net worth for whites was about 10 times that for blacks.

The second report was based on data from the Federal Reserve Board, as massaged by "The Democratic Staff" of Congress's Joint Economic Committee (JEC). The Dem-Staff report trained its sights on the "super-rich," that is, the wealthiest one half of one percent of all households. In 1983, these "supers" had average wealth of almost $9 million dollars per household!

The Dem-Staffs went further. They looked at a similar survey from 1963 and showed that the super-rich were getting richer much faster than the rest of us. The supers now own 35 percent of all wealth, compared to 25 percent in 1963. Off with their heads!

The Dem-Staffs do their work for Congressman David Obey, chairman of the JEC. The report was the occasion for an Obey press release denouncing Ronald Reagan's tax policies. (Surprise!) Well, are the rich really that much wealthier than the non-rich? Are they really getting richer compared to others? Or is something wrong with these studies?

It is clear that wealth disparities are greater than income disparities. That is logical. The old saw has it that it takes money to make money. Wealth is accrued and compounds over time. That makes the differences in accumulated wealth comparatively greater than the differences of any one year's income.

What's amiss? The value of private pension plans and Social Security were not counted. And it is in the realm of pensions that the middle class has made its biggest gains in recent years.

Consider Social Security. One scholarly estimate of the future discounted value of benefits to recipients amounts to $4.6 trillion. Trillions! That's $53,000 per household—much greater than the entire net worth of the typical American household. And the real value of Social Security has more than doubled in recent years.

(It's true that pensions are not the same as other wealth. But you have to pay money to own them, you get money from them when you retire, and if you want to get an annuity to match them, it will cost you plenty.)

Indicators: *Housing/Infrastructure*

A. Houses are getting bigger . . .

1. Floor Areas of New Privately Owned One Family Houses

Year	Average Floor Area (Square Feet)
1955	1,170
1970	1,500
1980	1,740
1985	1,785
1987	1,905

A. (Cont.) . . . and the percentage of homeowners has remained almost constant.

2. Homeowner Rates (Percent Owning Home of Own)

Year	Percent
1973	64%
1976	65%
1980	66%
1983	65%
1987	64%
1989	64%

B. The relative cost of housing increased, and moderated.

Percent of Personal Consumption Expenditures Spent on Housing

Year	Percent
1950	11.3%
1960	14.8%
1970	14.7%
1975	16.7%
1980	16.0%
1985	15.3%
1987	15.5%
1988	15.5%
1989	15.4%

C. Federal investment expenditures on infrastructure have gone down in the past half century, as a percentage of gross national product.

Federal Outlays for Major Nondefense Physical Capital Investment

Year	Percent of GNP	
	Direct Spending	Grants to State/Local
1940	2.1%	0.5%
1950	0.5%	0.2%
1960	0.4%	0.7%
1970	0.3%	0.7%
1980	0.3%	0.8%
1990	0.3% (est.)	0.5%

Source notes are on page 396.

These numbers change the rich and non-rich equation. That $53,000 almost triples the wealth of a typical American, but it's peanuts to the $9-million-dollar super-rich household.

The numbers for private pension plans are similar. They amounted to $200 million in 1970—and $1.5 trillion last year. This too redistributes the wealth numbers from the super-rich to the middle class. A study by Robert Friedland of the Employee Benefit Research Institute shows that the very-rich don't usually have big pensions. When they age, they live off their own massive wealth.

So maybe we need some new wealth surveys. Let's count all wealth next time.

August 7, 1986

Sewing Up the Safety Net

The standard of American health care is probably the best in the world. Why? Because it's mostly private rather than governmental, because our doctors are well-trained and well-rewarded, because we have devoted great resources to develop new technologies, medicines and procedures.

However, our private system has one central flaw. It is not available to everyone. Because our health care is so good, it is expensive. Most Americans only feel safe because their medical bills are paid through group health insurance provided by their employer. The government steps in only when there are typically no employers: Medicare for the elderly and Medicaid for people in deep poverty.

About 85 percent of Americans are covered. But what about the rest— the 15 percent who aren't insured? That's 37 million people. If they get ill, they can be in trouble. They seek a charity ward or just forego treatment. There is a hole in our social safety net.

Sen. Edward Kennedy has long been a champion of a broader, safer safety net. But in the past his remedy involved a greater governmental role. Opponents characterized it as "socialized medicine." He never could get it enacted into law.

Now Kennedy has come up with a new way to skin the cat, or about two-thirds of it anyway. Twenty-four million of those 37 million uninsured are in families where a member works full-time. But their employers, unlike most, don't provide group health coverage. Individual coverage is often prohibitively expensive. So Kennedy's new bill mandates that employers of these uninsured workers provide group insurance.

The approach goes with the flow of the new political and budgetary circumstance. It adds to the private, not the public, part of the medical system; there is no big-spending government program. Kennedy takes a non-ideological view of his shift from a public to a private plan. He says, "This can do the job. Let's get the job done."

The Kennedy proposal has other advantages: No one need stay on welfare just to get medical benefits. It takes a big step toward offering catastrophic health insurance for all. It should also have some allure for conservatives: They complain that an increase in the minimum wage ratchets up everyone else's wages in order to retain existing wage intervals. The Kennedy plan is a "benefit," not a "wage" and would not generally have that effect.

Still, most conservatives oppose it. They don't want government mandates. It could slightly increase unemployment. And they recite their mantra: "There is no free lunch." In lunch terms, they are correct. Most of the costs are borne by the businesses involved, so costs will be passed along to the consumer.

But the question at issue, central to the debate about the Safety Net State, is not whether we should provide entitlements, but which entitlements. Should we guarantee vacations overseas? Memberships in country clubs? No.

The Safety Net State offers goods and services that the society has come to see as necessities and not merely desires. Why? For reasons of humanitarianism and self-interest. It is humanitarian to say we won't let people go hungry. It is also selfish: We don't like the sight of skeletal beggars. So we have welfare programs and food stamp programs. Thus: As a society, relatively recently, we have come to believe that adequate nourishment is a human desire that is also a social necessity.

Health care is now crossing that desire-necessity threshold. The issue is not free lunch, but minimum lunch. There is too much that modern medicine can offer these days. Can we accept the idea that someone with curable cancer will not be able to afford the cure?

Kennedy's bill is not perfect. It ought to be closely scrutinized in some of its important details. But its direction is sound. It goes a long way to stitching up a big hole in the safety net.

July 2, 1987

Uncle Sam: Cathedral Builder

Do not be deluded by the hum coming from Washington that seems to be about spending cuts, tax cuts, regulation, money supply, inflation, investment and that wonderful catch-all phrase "supply-side economics."

All the noise is really about cathedrals. There are medieval cathedrals— and modern ones.

During the years from 1050 to 1300 (roughly) there was an explosion of technology in Europe. In his book *The Medieval Machine*, the French writer Jean Gimpel calls that period "the first industrial revolution." Productivity soared. Invention and innovation flourished.

That was when eyeglasses and mechanical clocks arrived. It was when men learned the right way to harness a horse to get maximum power in front of their plows. It was when water mills and windmills effectively began to thresh grain, to treat cloth, to tan leather and to super-heat coal in order to melt iron.

And it was a time when proud societies expressed their pride by building the great, soaring cathedrals that even today attract throngs of Japanese cameras with tourists attached. The cathedrals, of course, had a religious function. But they were also civic structures; cities competed to build the biggest and the best. The cathedral in Strasbourg is as tall as a 40-story skyscraper.

Then, rather suddenly, it all stopped. Science was attacked by the church. Mysticism flourished. Witches were burned at the stake. The currency was devalued. Inflation ballooned. Europe was visited by famine. Disruption raged. Armies marched. Finally, the Black Death of bubonic plague arrived and killed proportionately more people in more places than any modern horrific nuclear scenario is likely to produce. (About one-third to one-half of the exposed Europeans perished.)

During this time of chaos, the rate of "new starts" on cathedrals plummeted. This was not just a coincidence, Gimpel indicates. Cathedrals soar only when men's minds are bold and free. Bold people compete to build the highest, the best, the biggest. When they do, their spirit is infectious and their societies as a whole gain. Water mills and cathedrals create each other.

But periodically, says Gimpel, great societies flounder, lose faith in their dream, turn inward, stop building their cathedrals, decay and worry themselves near to death. It took Europe 150 years to get back on track.

There is a big argument going on in America today about our own cathedrals.

One school of thought—and Gimpel subscribes to it—holds that America has stopped building its cathedrals and that our age of greatness has passed. Gimpel says it is important to note that in 1971 the Congress voted to abort the SST, which was to be "the fastest."

Other, more recent examples of retrenchment come quickly to mind: Intellectuals assail nuclear power in a classic spasm of anti-technology. We are told that "America is no longer the world's policeman." We are told that we have entered "an era of limits." Our automobile industry is decimated. Inflation eats away at our spirit.

New power sources, global responsibility, big cars on fast roads—in Gimpel's terms, those would be some of our cathedrals. He says we've stopped being bold enough to extend our spires to the sky. That's the tip-off: other forms of subtle decay must follow. Can liberty survive without spirit?

Another school of thought, of course, holds a very different view. Our cathedrals, they say, should be wrapped around a phrase called "quality of life." Bigger isn't better, they maintain. But insofar as we can measure these things, that "small is beautiful" idea suffered a monumental defeat with Ronald Reagan's election.

Reagan's team wants America to build cathedrals again. Like Gimpel, they are worried that we have indeed stopped, but, unlike Gimpel, they think that we can reverse this trend. They want a "can-do" America that produces oil, gas, coal and nuclear power, an America that has military superiority, fast cars and broad highways, an America that can make the case for liberty.

The Reagan economic plan that we hear so much about is an attempt to address the idea that government has been obstructing the "can-do" idea in America. There is more than a little truth to that. Over-regulation stifles. Over-taxation can destroy incentive. Over-spending by government takes away money from private productive ventures.

Only high-spirited people build modern equivalents of cathedrals and water mills, the Reagan economists say. If you can charge them up, get them excited again, get them to roll dice with nature again, you not only get great achievements but you keep a society off the slippery slope of self-indulgence. Liberty survives.

Cuts in taxes, spending, money supply and regulation are only instruments in this quest. It would be nice to get the numbers to add up; indeed, if they do not, the enterprise may self-destruct. But it's all much more important than massaging tax rates, and the smartest of the Reagan folks know that. They don't want to find out what form of plague the 21st century will visit upon decaying democracies.

Well and good. That's the right idea. But there are some points that should be raised. Maybe the Reaganauts are over-reacting. Maybe we haven't really stopped building cathedrals. The space shuttle is a cathedral. We've just broken the frontier of biogenetics. We are curing diseases that have scourged mankind. The new skyline in Houston is bold and energetic.

Our biggest cathedral, of course, is that we Americans brought alive the concept of human freedom for common folk—and that idea, although threatened, is still alive on this earth. So maybe, just maybe, we don't have to worry that much about it all.

Better safe than sorry, you say? I agree—and let's get to it. But one of the problems may be Reagan's own philosophy of greatness. It apparently leaves little room for the government. Reagan, sometimes doctrinairely, says government is a hurdle in the way of greatness. Indeed, these days it often is.

But our man on the moon was sent there by the government. Atomic power was created by our government. The cancer cures we're beginning to see were stimulated by government-funded research. Our rivers were made navigable by the government. Ironically, the great American symbol of achievement that kept Reagan in the political spotlight in the 1976 presidential primaries was built by our government: the Panama Canal. And when you come to think of it, the soaring cathedrals of Europe were not built by private entrepreneurs but by churches, kings, dukes, communities and, yes, by governments.

As the president recuperates from his wound, he might do well to ponder one point: Government is neutral. It can do dumb things and restrict human spunk. It can also do great things, when well-directed. For a few more years, he might remember, he's the director.

April 13, 1981

The Environment

6

The Nice Crisis

T he previous part of this volume dealt mostly with people-sized dimensions: ethnicity, race, family, children, money, Italians, Asian-Americans, blacks, Jews. Our focus now begins to broaden to examine what we might expect of the national and global terrain of the nineties.

We begin with the environment and demography, topics which are related, but not so closely as we have been led to believe.

Futurists wisely enjoy playing around with demographics. A great deal is indeed known about the population of the future. After all, so many of the people who will be alive in the future have already been born. And every twelve months, each of the survivors becomes one year older.

But futurism and environmentalism is a far less exact combination. There is inherently much less known about the environment, and beyond that, it is a relatively new area of study. Further, some aspects of the situation can change fairly quickly because of our own actions, for example, new fuel standards for automobiles.

The mixture, the mishmash, really, of combining environmentalism and demographics is the pits for terrain-watchers. It is too often a politicized endeavor, frequently yielding a brew of exaggeration and embellishment.

We begin our scrutiny of the terrain by looking, once again, at some things that are not so, these in the environmental realm.

Indicators: *Environment*

A. **By almost any measure available, our air is getting cleaner.**

Pollutants Emitted Annually (in Millions of Metric Tons)

Year	Lead*	Carbon Monoxide	Ozone Pollutants	Nitrogen Oxide	Sulfur Dioxide	Total Suspended Particulates
1978	128	82	24	21	25	9
1980	71	77	22	20	23	8
1982	54	69	20	20	21	7
1985	9	65	20	20	21	7
1987	8	61	20	20	20	7

* In thousands of metric tons.

B. **Federal spending on the environment dipped slightly in the early eighties, but has risen somewhat.**

Federal Expenditures on the Environment and Natural Resources

Year	As a Percentage of GNP	As a Percentage of the Federal Budget	In Millions of 1989 Dollars
1961	0.34%	1.8%	$ 7,378
1970	0.31%	1.6%	$ 9,795
1975	0.48%	2.2%	$16,931
1980	0.52%	2.4%	$20,854
1985	0.34%	1.4%	$15,393
1987	0.30%	1.3%	$14,586
1989	0.31%	1.4%	$16,182
1990 (est.)	0.32%	1.5%	$17,499

C. **Environmental cleanup has become a multi-billion-dollar business.**

Manufacturers' Pollution Abatement and Control Expenditures

Year	Total (in Billions of Constant 1989 Dollars)
1961	$ 1.2
1965	$ 2.4
1970	$ 8.1
1975	$14.9
1980	$13.8
1985	$10.4
1988	$10.5
1989	$11.0
1990	$11.3 (est.)
1991	$11.8 (est.)
1992	$12.5 (est.)

D. **Population assistance funding declined since peaking in the mid-1980s.**

U.S. Agency for International Development Population Assistance

Year	Total (in Millions of Constant 1989 Dollars)
1965–7	$ 40
1968	$124
1971	$294
1975	$253
1980	$278
1985	$334
1988	$238
1989	$239
1990	$252 (proj.)

Source notes are on page 396.

Lamm's Mega-travesty

The approach of adjacent zeroes on the calendar seems to have a devastating and depressing effect on the human mind. Toward the end of the last century, the European intelligentsia shuddered as the well-publicized countdown to the year 1900 proceeded. Decadence was in fashion, and it was said that progress had hit a dead end.

That happened with only two zeroes to confront. Now we have three zeroes to face, and the apocalyptic millenarians are already out in force, slapping their tambourines. Consider the interesting case of Richard Lamm, the governor of Colorado and author of *Mega-Traumas*, subtitled "America at the Year 2000." It is a book that spells out Lamm's current concerns in the words of memos to a fictional president at the coming turn of the century.

Lamm's claim to fame is that he worries a lot. His nickname is "Gov. Gloom," and he believes we are running out of energy, running out of food, running out of jobs, running out of minerals. He says we have too much crime, debt, health care, doctors and lawyers. We have too many dead-end jobs, illegitimate children, people speaking Spanish, old people and, mostly, too many immigrants—which is the topic of another new book by Lamm, *The Immigration Time Bomb*.

Lamm's metaphors go beyond bombs. Mankind, he says, "is a cancer on the earth," or alternatively, "a locust on the land." Lamm says that the biggest problem we malignant insects have is that we won't face up to the grim facts. That is an odd approach from a man who broods about an energy crisis during an energy glut, a food crisis during a food glut, a mineral crisis when mineral prices have fallen, rising unemployment when unemployment is dropping, a shrinking gross national product while GNP grows, exponential population growth while fertility rates are declining almost everywhere.

Further, Lamm frets about exploding bilingualism and an "American Quebec"—when bilingual education programs are being dismantled. He believes that more health care has tended to make us less healthy—despite the fact that adult life expectancy is going up at the fastest rate in our history.

To give Gov. Gloom his due, his catalog of horrors includes a few that are worthy of attention. The official Social Security projections are probably too optimistic, and benefits will have to be stretched out. And Lamm does say that not all of his dreadful scenarios are likely to occur. Indeed, the purpose of his harum-scarum alarums is to let us act now to head off disaster.

But, ultimately, Lamm, Lammism and all the little Lammniks who will try to scare us about the impending millennium—will not help us as we go from here to there. That is so because of the iron rule of public activity: Wrong premises yield bad policy.

Thus: Living in his tiny Darwinian zero-sum world, Lamm has become petrified of immigration. His premise is that immigrants use up resources, cause crime, engender separatism and steal jobs from Americans. His remedies go beyond the sensible call to crack down on illegal immigration. Lamm wants a big cut in legal immigration. Yet most serious scholars doubt that his immigration policies would have much bearing on crime, unemployment or resources—and scoff at the idea of separatism. But the result of his scare-mongering could yield intellectualoid justification for an ugly anti-Hispanic campaign. Faulty premise, faulty policy, harmful result.

A thousand years ago, as the millenium approached in medieval Europe, crowds were whipped into a frenzy by religious zealots who proclaimed that when three adjacent zeroes popped up on the calendar the world would end. It didn't. In fact, life goes on, and a thousand years later there are still zealots saying the same thing.

September 23, 1986

Carter's Globaloney

Jimmy Carter is worried.

Speaking to the Global Tomorrow Coalition in Washington last week, he said he was worried that the world is running out of resources and that Americans don't seem to understand that we live in an era of limits, even though he had mentioned it several times while he was president.

He is worried, he said, because our government is not paying attention to the "Global 2000" report that he commissioned while president, and upon which he based his remarks. He did not seem to be worried that leading experts in a wide variety of disciplines have denounced that report as "globaloney."

He is worried, he said, because world leaders do not typically show the political courage of the Japanese emperor who said a few years ago that, because of pollution, he never saw butterflies around the Imperial Palace anymore. Because of his political courage, the Japanese launched an aggressive air-quality program. And so, courageously, the emperor was able to say later that the butterflies had returned.

He is worried, he said, that petroleum-based fertilizers that he used to sell from Carter's Warehouse in Plains, Ga., for $40 a ton, now sells for

$125 a ton. This indicates that resource shortage was causing higher prices. But he was also worried, he said, that the farmers who bought the fertilizer were unable to charge more for their crops. He did not mention that low prices for crops indicate surplus, not shortage.

He was very worried, he said, about the effects of the OPEC oil price increases. He did not mention the oil glut or the decreases in oil prices.

He was very worried that world population is growing very fast—90 million more mouths to feed next year, he said. He did not mention that birth rates have sunk to negative levels in most of the developed countries and are dropping rapidly in less-developed countries.

He is worried, he said, that weak political leaders would not recognize, or did not understand, that dwindling resources cause conflict. In the Middle East and Central America, he said, one big cause of escalating violence is the shortage of water and arable land. It is tragic, he said, that world leaders still think that it is primarily political rivalry or communism which causes our international problems. (He did not say what caused human conflict in earlier times.)

He is very worried that deserts will expand, that carbon dioxide is melting the polar icecaps, that tropical forests are shrinking, although he did not mention that these gloomy projections are under sharp professional challenge. He said that the first thing we need to deal with all this is a federal coordinating unit within our government.

He is worried that people don't understand that our "progress in computer modeling of complex problems" is not being used to solve the world's problems. He did not mention that the most famous of those computer models—sponsored by the Club of Rome some few years ago—was ultimately shown to be dead wrong, so much so that it was disowned by the Club of Rome itself.

He is worried, he said, that people think that he is a prophet of doom because he salutes the "Global 2000" report whose conclusion (in its words) was that "if present trends continue, the world in 2000 will be more crowded, more polluted, less stable ecologically and more vulnerable to disruption . . . the world's people on earth will be poorer . . . life for most people on earth will be more precarious. . . ." That's not doom, he said. It was, in Carter's words, "an expression of confidence and hope," because all this could be avoided if only we would improve our long-term planning.

He is worried, he said, because rich nations like America consume so much. (That is an idea which has escaped most Americans.) We are, he said, only one-sixteenth of the world's people, but demand one-fourth of the world's resources, "at the expense of others who are becoming increasingly aware of their relative deprivation."

He did not mention that this zero-sum theory of economics went out with feudalism. Nor did he mention that it leads by logical extension to the idea that it would be better for the rest of the world if America cut our share of use of world resources, making us poorer. Of course, this would engender a global depression and destroy the entire international trading economy, the success of which is the best hope that poor countries will escape poverty.

If you think Jimmy Carter is worried stiff—what about me? I am petrified. The presidency is supposed to be the best education in the world. Mr. Carter was president for four years and still doesn't understand how the world works.

June 7, 1983

Tomorrow: Environmental Activism

Spurred by the massive oil spill in Alaska's Prince William Sound, fed by media coverage and pushed by activists, the environmental wars are escalating again. The images coming from Alaska are strong and politically potent: Pristine blue water suddenly covered with a black slick, pitiful sea otters struggling to escape the sludge and volunteers using toothbrushes to scrub oil-caked birds. There is at least one apparent, delicious villain: An irresponsible oil company. Some environmentalists have called the Valdez spill "an American Chernobyl." The immediate environmentalist demand: ban oil exploration in the Arctic National Wildlife Reserve (ANWR).

Last week it was oil spills. Before that is was pesticides, apples, ozone and the greenhouse effect. A second environmental spasm has arrived, and it raises a central political question: Is exaggeration good for your health? The standard political answer is, "Yes; that's the only way things get done." But exaggeration may not be the best method. It can inflict its own costs.

Make no mistake about it: There are real concerns. Most scientists believe there will be some global warming from "greenhouse gases," although its effects are not clear. Most scientists also believe there have been some significant changes in the ozone layer that can cause some harm to some human beings.

There has also been real progress. New air-quality data from the Environmental Protection Agency show that the enormous investments in clean air have been paying off. The EPA also says some forms of water pollution are down significantly. And studies by the U.S. Fish and Wildlife Service indicate that populations of many game species in North America, such as deer, have increased.

World Watch Institute's "State of the World" report, by Lester Brown, claims we face a land and food crisis. But scholars at Resources for the Future have rebutted much of that. Specifically, per capita food consumption has increased and should continue to rise. Further, an alleged "alarming" drop in world grain acreage isn't due to land deterioration but to a U.S. decision to take acreage out of production because of surpluses. And, contrary to the fears expressed by many, the National Academy of Sciences states that there is no significant evidence that pesticides increase the risk of cancer.

Some environmentalists say that population growth equals pollution growth. But a 1986 study by the National Academy of Sciences says that population growth is only a minor player in pollution and poverty. According to the NAS, it's not how many people there are, but how they behave. In any case, population trends are changing dramatically as less developed countries modernize. Demographic momentum will probably double the current world population, but population stability will be the story of the mid-to-late 21st century.

And there has been exaggeration. Because of environmental stress, says Carl Sagan, America is "moving toward underdeveloped-nation status." The "State of the World" volume speaks of "the collapse of social and political institutions." Brown lauds China's coercive one-child-only policy and says governments everywhere ought to limit families to two children.

But is exaggeration necessary to get action? Look at the last environmental burst in the late 1960s and 1970s. We were regaled with ecological news, some valid and important, but some hyped. We were told we were running out of resources, particularly oil. (Now, there is an oil glut). We were also told we were a profligate people, addicted to something called "the single-family-home ethic." We were told that an ice age was coming and that we should close a dam to save a snail darter. "GNP" was said to stand for "gross national pollution."

This environmental crisis-mongering helped make some good things happen. Clean-air and clean-water standards were established. Fuel standards were set. Toxic wastes came under some control.

It is the received wisdom that this spasm of activity was an unmitigated social good. But was it? Perhaps the best example that it wasn't is the unfulfilled promise of the U.S. nuclear-power industry. We were told the nuclear plants would explode, or melt down, or irradiate us. But nuclear is probably the safest major energy technology. Moreover, in a time of heightened concern about global warming, it is an energy technology that yields no warming greenhouse gases.

No nuclear plant has been ordered in the past decade. This happened mostly because the bumper-sticker politics of "No Nukes" helped shape nuclear policy in America. Today, even as the environmentalists complain about global warming, they also try to stop two new nuclear plants from starting up. The power not generated by Seabrook (N.H.) and Shoreham (N.Y.) will sooner or later have to be generated by fossil fuels yielding greenhouse gases.

There is a further downside to runaway rhetoric. The public ultimately catches on. When building an oil pipeline depends on caribou mating habits, something happens politically. A potent equation starts working: Environmental exaggeration makes an easy political target. Liberals, remember and beware: Excesses by various cause movements helped elect Ronald Reagan.

Crisis-generated remedies are in the air again, especially in the wake of the "Exxon Valdez" spill. Environmentalists say that since ANWR is one of the last pure breeding grounds for the porcupine caribou, and one of the last pure spots left on earth, no oil exploration should be allowed. Their pressure has delayed a pro-exploration bill. But we need oil. Hamstringing domestic production makes us vulnerable to foreign suppliers. Moreover, spill damage has often been exaggerated. While Alaska's cold waters may pose a special problem, an NAS report indicates that the ecological harm is generally transitory.

Activist pressure and overblown rhetoric will continue to mount on this and other issues. Last week, a judge who set an unusually high $1 million bail for the former captain of the oil tanker compared the Valdez disaster to the atomic bombing of Hiroshima.

Will we go overboard again or look to more sensible initiatives? Tighter spill-cleanup and safety standards for tankers are a good place to start. The current wave of activism need not yield irresponsible results. We can learn from the overzealousness of the past and do it right this time.

April 17, 1989

More Oil Spill Residue

The television news producer and his wife entered the nice New York restaurant. She checked her lynx coat.

The maître d' ushered the couple to a quiet corner table.

"What a day!" said the producer. "That oil spill we're covering is incredible. It's tragic." The producer's wife agreed. "It's a catastrophe," she said. "It just gets worse and worse."

A waiter came over and presented menus. "Let's have the duck," the producer's wife said. The producer nodded absently.

"Those poor sea otters," said the producer. "Just think, scrubbing them with a toothbrush to clean off the oil."

His wife said, "It's tragic." She thought: I have to get my fur coat cleaned and stored for the summer.

"Just think of those poor little birds caked with oil," the producer said as he pulled a leg off the duck on the table.

"What's so tragic," the producer went on, "is that it happened in a pristine area." The woman concurred: "Terrible," she said. "So pristine. Hardly anyone lives there."

The producer chewed on the duck's wing and said, "It's too bad. It will be two or three years until all those people who don't use the beaches and don't see the coastline, won't use it again, or won't see it again. Why couldn't it have happened on Cape Cod, or Miami Beach? Why did it have to happen where it was pristine?"

"And those poor fishermen," said the news producer's wife. "They're going to have a hard time making a living if the Japanese don't buy Alaskan salmon for sushi."

"It's almost as bad as being fired," said the producer, slicing into the body of the duck. He thought suddenly of Joe and Judy and Henry and Mel and Sarah, who had just been terminated from his network in a cost-cutting program.

"It's all the fault of Exxon," the producer's wife said. "Right," said the producer, "they'll have to pay those fishermen. They're liable. They ought to pay through the nose, those greedy rats."

"They will," said the producer's wife, "and that captain ought to be hanged."

The couple left the restaurant and got into their air-conditioned Lamborghini Countach equipped with power windows, power steering, power brakes, and power seats, getting 6 miles per gallon. "Damn oil companies," said the producer as the car roared off into the night. "We ought to go to windmill power."

The couple entered their apartment building and took the elevator up to the penthouse floor. "Or solar power," said the wife as they entered their air-conditioned apartment. She turned on the twelve-bulb chandelier in the vestibule.

Their dog barked and wagged his tail. "What we really need is more energy conservation," said the producer. "We're destroying the earth, eating too much, using too much land." He gritted his teeth in anger as he fed ground beef to the dog.

"It's really sad," said the wife as she took off the pelts of once-trapped lynx, "and so cruel."

"It's a sad day," the producer said.

And that's what he was thinking later that night as he read his leather-bound Thoreau and savored his bedtime snack of venison ragout.

April 13, 1983

Taking Ehrlich Seriously

I met Dr. Paul Ehrlich in 1970, the year of the first Earth Day, when we appeared together on the Johnny Carson program. Our dog-and-pony show, offering two views about population, was preceded by slob-comic Buddy Hackett.

Twenty Earth Years later, after reading Ehrlich's new book, that long-ago Carson episode seems an apt metaphor for what's both right and wrong with environmentalism. The good part is that serious issues are discussed before a mass public. The bad part is that it's hard to be serious in such a setting.

Ehrlich is important in both the positive and negative aspects. He is an astonishingly successful popularizer; as much as anyone he has introduced Americans to environmental demographics. And he is hard to take seriously.

Ehrlich exploded on the scene with his 1968 book, *The Population Bomb*. It said that the American people were a "cancer on the planet," and that we would have to consider putting contraceptive chemicals in the water supply to control population.

He said that the world would soon see famines because of overpopulation, that longevity would diminish, that India was a dead duck, and that more people would cause more wars.

Twenty years later: no famines caused by overpopulation and caloric intake in the poor nations is up; longevity is way up, India is flourishing, and peace is breaking out everywhere.

So, what does Ehrlich say about it in his new book, *The Population Explosion*, co-authored with Anne Ehrlich? That he was right all along and that population growth will cause ecological apocalypse soon.

Can you take seriously a man who describes recent demographic trends as a "slight slackening in the human population growth rate"? In two decades, fertility rates have plummeted among the poor from 6.0 children per woman to 3.9—60 percent of the way to replacement level. Developed-world birth rates fell by more than 20 percent, far below replacement for the first time ever.

Can you take seriously a member of the National Academy of Sciences who chooses to ignore the landmark 1986 NAS study on population, which refutes almost all of his claims, especially the tarnished one that we're running out of nonrenewable resources?

Take him seriously? Despite his self-diminished credibility, you must. Many environmental issues, if not all environmentalists, are serious. Global warming may prove to be one such.

And take him seriously because influential people do, and many of his proposals would yield malign effects. Ehrlich says the solution is less affluence. Americans are too rich, he says, which will be news to most voters. He writes: "Any more stuff in the world should not go to the likes of us." ". . . The world can't afford more Americans." "Rich nations will now have to pay for their greed."

So, Ehrlich wants to reduce per capita income, reduce Social Security by having the elderly work longer, vastly increase foreign aid, and double the price of gasoline. He says Americans will have to give up some "personal freedoms," like choosing how many children to have.

He says he knows how to do it: by setting up a mass movement. It sounds grandiose, but Ehrlichite environmentalists already have already influenced masses.

Believe me. I write and speak about demographics. (My recent book, *The Birth Dearth*, quotes Ehrlich attacking me, and vice versa.)

After speeches, women come up to me and say: "I wanted to have another child, but I was made to feel guilty that I would pollute the world, so I didn't, and I'm very sad about it."

Take him seriously. The most chilling words in Ehrlich's book are the jacket blurbs. Senator Tim Wirth, D-Colo., says, "This superb, closely reasoned, and fact-filled book should do much to clear the way for badly needed political action." Senator Al Gore, D-Tenn., says, "The time for action is due, and past due. The Ehrlichs have written the prescription. . . ."

These senators, who are two of the brightest, write not only blurbs, but laws, which affect us all.

April 18, 1990

Thanks, Environmentalists

Do not doubt, not for a moment, that environmentalism is the hottest game in town, sweeping all before it, in hallowed groves of academe, in holy places of religious thought, in legislative bazaars, on entertainment soundstages, and in the sacred temple of the free press.

It's a great crisis all right, and what it all shows is just how very healthy modern society is.

At a recent conference, Charles Alexander said, "As the science editor at *Time*, I would freely admit that on this issue we have crossed the boundary from news reporting to advocacy." (Surprise.)

A full-page advertisement by the Jewish Theological Seminary (J.T.S.) at the time of the Jewish New Year headlined "WHAT ARE WE DOING?" quoted Psalm 104 counterpoised against the horror of modern despoliation. Some examples: "You make the grass grow for the cattle and herbage for man's labor, that he may get food out of the earth" (toxic pesticides).

"There is the sea, vast and wide, with its creatures beyond number, living things small and great" (oil spills).

So, the JTS has divined that the divine will is anti-modern-agronomy, and anti-marine-transportation-of-petroleum-products. (Does that mean God is for rotted crops and expensive energy?)

A leading Washington private school canceled the release of helium balloons during its Halloween program. The balloons might ultimately come down in the Potomac and harm marine life. (You should see what happens to marine life when it is broiled, squirted with lemon, and eaten.)

Television is never far behind a trendy trend. In the year to come we will be able to tune out environmental specials, enviornmental kiddie shows, and trillionaress Barbra Streisand co-hosting a two-hour Earth Day program entitled "A Practical Guide to How You Can Save the Planet." (Probably by putting the second Rolls on blocks.)

The president and Congress are seeking new standards for pesticides in a rhetorical atmosphere that one public health worker calls "anti-science."

All this proves not pollution, but health.

Modern people crave crisis; it is a tropism not unlike a green plant bending toward the sun. Sometimes the crisis is potent and immediate— like war. When such crises are not available, catastrophes of lesser magnitude come to the surface. Such is the case with the environment.

The environmental crisis, remember, is a crisis engendered by people living better. If you're going to have a crisis, that's the place to start.

Next, in terms of what has been measured by the Environmental Protection Agency, the environment is healthier than it used to be by far. Pollution has diminished in fairly direct proportion to the amount of money spent to diminish it. That's not something that can be said for every crisis.

Moreover, near as can be figured, environmental pollution has not been very harmful. Elizabeth Whalen, of the American Council of Science and Health, says that of the 1 million annual preventable deaths in America, most are due to smoking and alcohol. Those due to pesticides or chemicals in the food supply, she says, account (by the best scientific estimate) for zero. And, she says, air pollution as a general cause of illness or death "provides an extremely minor or hypothetical contribution."

And finally, despite all that, there isn't much of a down side to paying some attention to the panic-mongers. It's probably even good for us if we don't go overboard. (It's certainly good for whales and elephants.)

A few hundred billion dollars for environmental spending won't hurt us much. We're rich. At worst, it will make things somewhat nicer for the aesthetically minded, and somewhat tighter for the poor.

Environmentalism is the nice crisis. It's the one that a civilization arrives at when there is no war, when the totalitarian threat is shriveling, when the economy is doing pretty well.

Environmentalism is the residual crisis. So, thanks environmentalists. Thanks for a crisis that is never-ending, never provable or disprovable, perennially partially conquerable, and psychologically necessary when there is no other game in town.

November 1, 1989

7

Supply-Side Demography

*In the summer of 1984, I was a member of the United States delegation
to the United Nations Population Conference in Mexico City. My stay in
Mexico City was fascinating. We worked 16-hour days in the eye of a
whirlwind.*

*The actual United States policy paper was, as described here, moderate
and generally progressive. But a preliminary draft, prepared at the National
Security Council, before most of the delegation was either appointed or
consulted, was starkly overstated. Shrewdly, the population/environment
lobby attacked (and sometimes still attacks) the unapproved draft, not the
official United States paper.*

*The final United Nations document approved in Mexico City reflects
some thinking that I worked on, stressing that great economic progress was
made in the Third World during the population explosion, and that Third
World birth rates are coming down rather remarkably.*

*Another item, that free market economies grow faster than command
economies and hence reduce fertility faster, was deemed very controversial
by the communist nations and was much diluted in the final United Nations
document. (You remember communist nations, don't you?)*

*The United States position was characterized, with much mockery, as
"capitalism is the best contraceptive." Maybe it is not the best. But fast
economic growth does correlate with market economics and reduced fertility.
As Casey Stengel said, "You could look it up." The proper designation for
the case we put forth in Mexico City, as expressed here, is "supply-side
demographics."*

Indicators: *Demographics*

A. Fertility rates have fallen almost everywhere.

1. Total Fertility Rates and U.N. Projections

Area	Children per Woman			
	1965–70	*1985–90*	*2005–10*	*2020–25*
Less Developed Countries	6.0	3.9	2.9	2.3
More Developed Countries	2.4	1.9	1.9	1.9
Sub-Saharan Africa	6.7	6.5	5.2	3.2
Northern Africa	6.9	5.3	3.2	2.3
Mexico	6.7	3.6	2.5	2.3
Kenya	8.1	6.7	5.3	3.0

2. Total Fertility Rates (TFR) Since 1950 (Children per Woman)

Country	*50–55*	*55–60*	*60–65*	*65–70*	*70–75*	*75–80*	*80–85*	*1990*
U.S.	3.45	3.71	3.31	2.55	1.97	1.93	1.82	2.0
Canada	3.70	3.90	3.61	2.51	1.97	1.77	1.66	1.7
Japan	2.75	2.08	2.01	2.00	2.07	1.81	1.76	1.6
USSR	2.82	2.81	2.54	2.42	2.44	2.34	2.35	2.5
Poland	3.62	3.29	2.65	2.27	2.25	2.26	2.33	2.1
France	2.73	2.71	2.85	2.61	1.31	1.86	1.87	1.8
Italy	2.32	2.35	2.55	2.49	2.27	1.92	1.55	1.3
Sweden	2.21	2.23	2.33	2.12	1.89	1.65	1.66	2.0
U.K.	2.18	2.50	2.82	2.52	2.04	1.72	1.80	1.8
W. Ger.	2.08	2.32	2.48	2.33	1.62	1.44	1.36	1.4
E. Eur.	3.08	2.72	2.45	2.42	2.29	2.27	2.15	2.08
W. Eur.	2.40	2.54	2.72	2.51	1.99	1.85	1.67	1.58

B. Islam will encompass a growing proportion of the world's population.

Projections of Islamic World Population, 1988–2050

Year	Population *(in Thousands)*	Percentage of World Pop.
1988	983,977	19%
2000	1,319,745	21%
2015	1,761, 504	23%
2025	2,050,817	24%
2050	2,663,575	27%

Source notes are on page 396.

C. The U.S. will grow substantially. Its competitors will not.

Population Projections (in Millions of People)

Nation/Region	1990	2000	2025
United States*	251	276	336
Canada	27	29	32
USCanada*	278	305	368
Mexico	89	107	150
Japan	124	129	128
West Europe	361	360	350
East Europe	140	148	160
Unified Europe	501	509	510
World	5,321	6,259	8,491

* Current estimated "most likely" projections

Population Polemics in Mexico City

I have just returned from a week's service in Mexico City as a member of the U.S. delegation to the U.N. International Conference on Population.

The major themes of the conference—as trumpeted by the press—were well established by the time the delegates took their seats for the inaugural ceremony.

First, Mexico City was described as a place drenched in pollution, poverty and, especially, inundated by too much population. "Under the human volcano" was the way the *New York Times* described it. *Time* magazine saw the city suffering from "the population curse."

Robert McNamara went high profile to remind the almost 5 billion earthlings that we all face potential catastrophe as population climbs higher in the decades to come, and nations "explode, literally and figuratively."

The U.S. policy position was assailed and ridiculed. It was said to stress the idea that economic growth tended to reduce the birthrate. That was called "voodoo demography." It was said that rigid, politically motivated positions on abortion policy would upset the apple cart of the global effort to reduce population growth rates.

And so, the issues were presented as an "either-or" situation. Either you're for economic growth or for family planning. Either you're for noting progress or noting problems. In the most tortured issue—either you're against funding organizations that promote abortion, or in favor of population programs. And either Mexico City, bursting at the seams, is a symbol of a dark and crowded future, or the viewer has not eyes with which to see.

In contrast, the official U.S. position paper was that the issues were not essentially "either-or." The U.S. view was "both." A bizarre thought: In the old phrase, we think we can walk and chew gum at the very same time.

Thus, it is generally recognized that economic growth is not only good in its own right, but usually associated with a drop in birthrates. It is also generally understood that freer economies tend to grow somewhat faster than less-free economies. Indeed, that is why in the industrial world, in China, in Hungary, even in the Soviet Union, as well as throughout the developing world, people are trying to figure out ways to encourage markets, decentralization, and incentives.

One can hold that view while *also* believing that family planning is very important. That, in fact, is the U.S. position. It is stated in our policy paper. It is backed up by the steady rise in funding for U.S. population aid programs—an increase that has been going on over recent decades under Democratic and Republican administrations, liberal, moderate and conservative in ideology. And it is backed up by a budget request for next year that still further increases family planning aid. (See data on fertility rates, page 159.)

Thus, one can claim that there has been enormous demographic and socioeconomic progress in the developing world, and *also* note that major problems remain. The critical "Total Fertility Rate" has gone way down—further than the gloomy publicity would have us believe. There have also been very positive trends in life expectancy, literacy, health care and per-capita income—all achieved while population was allegedly exploding malignantly. At the same time, it is *also* true that huge numbers of people remain trapped in human misery. Progress—and problems. "Both," not "either-or."

Thus, the fact that the United States proposes not to give monies to organizations that "promote" abortion does not mean that we will not *also* invest heavily in other population programs. In fact, if monies should actually end up being cut from an organization involved in abortion, such funds will be redirected to other family-planning agencies.

The U.S. delegation spanned a broad spectrum of views on a number of issues, particularly abortion. Former Sen. James Buckley and Jacqueline Schaefer, for two, are "pro-life." William Draper, chairman of the Export-Import Bank, and your author are "pro-choice." But the delegation was united about defending the official policy paper that called for U.S. family planning assistance at higher levels.

And, finally, poor Mexico City. There are plenty of people and plenty of poverty and pollution—although, as it happened, our week there was often sunny and crystal-clear.

But let me tell you something else that is *also* true about Mexico City. All those cursed people under the volcano have built themselves a beautiful and fascinating place. I want to go back soon—as a tourist.

August 14, 1984

Supply-side Demographics

Shortly after I returned from the United Nations Population Conference in Mexico City last summer I received a call from an editor of a leading magazine.

"Something's going on," he said. "Until recently all I ever heard about was 'the population bomb' and 'the population crisis' and 'the population explosion.' But now I hear some experts saying there's no bomb, no explosion, no crisis. What's happening?"

Something important is indeed happening regarding thinking about population. Even those who still believe in bomb-crisis-explosion sense the ground shifting beneath their feet.

In an important article in Foreign Affairs earlier this year, Robert McNamara—a super-explosionist—wrote this: "Many . . . believe that the world in general, and most countries in particular, no longer face serious population problems. . . ." He goes on later: "Editorial writers and commentators in the mass media have been quick . . . to take up this theme, announcing the end of the population explosion, or declaring rapid population growth to be 'another non-crisis.' " Of course, McNamara also stresses: "Such a view is totally in error."

What is going on is a rare occasion where reality and theory swing into confluence, yielding to a new argument.

Thus, birthrates have been coming down around the world. In the industrial world they are actually "below replacement," that is, less than the 2.1 children per woman necessary to keep a population stable over time. Of course, fertility is still quite high in the less developed world, but it too has come way down: from six children per woman a few decades ago to four children per woman today—and still falling.

This calming development has allowed people to concentrate on an earlier question: Does rapid population growth hurt economic growth?

The classic modern response has been a resounding "Yes." More people, it is maintained, mean more mouths to feed, and more resources consumed. More people, in short, mean more trouble.

But there is another view about people: They not only consume, they also produce—food, resources, whatever. Hence a sort of "supply-side demography" has grown up. Population growth need not be bad; it may even be good in some cases, say the supply-siders. They note that every baby comes equipped with two hands as well as a mouth.

As it happens, I had the opportunity last week to chair a seminar entitled "Are World Population Trends a Problem?" The seminar was part of Public Policy Week at the American Enterprise Institute, where I am a fellow. The demand-siders were there from the United Nations and from leading population organizations. Leading and influential supply-siders were there: Lord Peter Bauer, emeritus from the London School of Economics, author Julian Simon (*The Ultimate Resource*) from the University of Maryland.

Perhaps the most interesting responses, however, came from the non-committed academic world. Samuel Preston is the president of the Population Association of America, and director of the Population Studies Center of the University of Pennsylvania. He referred to the tentative conclusions of a report he is now preparing for the National Academy of Sciences: ". . . rapid population growth in most times and places is a relatively minor factor in reducing per-capita income and other indicators of welfare."

Dr. Allen Kelley of Duke University, whose academic field is precisely the relationship of population and economics, applauded the revisionist thinking. He said it "places population in its proper perspective. Population is neither a villain nor a hero in the economic development story. It's instead an important actor in a complex plot."

Interesting, and heartening, is that the two sides don't disagree on goals. Both want to expand the availability of voluntary family planning around the world. Both want to spur economic growth in the less developed world.

But ideas have consequences. If we get away from the idea that population growth is simply a geometric, catastrophic, economic horror, we can look at real problems and begin to focus on real solutions.

December 11, 1984

The National Academy of Sciences report issued in 1986 is, by my lights, one of the most important pieces of research published in recent years. Because it goes against the grain, it has been largely ignored. It generally confirms the central thesis of supply-side demographics, that culture is what counts. Please note particularly the statements about the relationship of population growth to environment. It is at the heart of the great environment–population debate.

In brief: there is little relationship. Bad policy causes pollution— as we have seen in Eastern Europe. Better policy, as we have seen in Western Europe, which is a more densely populated place, keeps the environment healthier.

Population Bomb De-fused

How does the world work?

Little noticed, the National Academy of Sciences has just issued a report that should change the way most people think it does. In brief, it changes the answer to this key question of our time: Does rapid population growth harm Third World nations? The old answer was "Yes, it's a disaster." The new answer is, "Uh. Well, maybe a little bit."

The document is entitled "Population Growth and Economic Development: Policy Questions." It is the fruit of two years of work by a specially appointed panel of 15 eminent scholars. It includes 17 research papers which review the current state of knowledge and, in some cases, break fresh ground.

Oddly, this revolutionary and revisionist study makes its case by using the most timid sorts of language. Thus, some evidence "is extremely varied," some statistical correlations "provide little insight," some points are "debatable." In short, this is real science in an uncertain field. It stands in refreshing contrast to the apocalyptic scare-mongering certitude offered by (for one example) Jimmy Carter's "Global 2000 Report."

Consider some of the ways the study challenges the conventional wisdom:

It's been said that we're running out of non-renewable resources and this will hurt us. No way, says the NAS: "The impact of rapid population growth on resource exhaustion has often been exaggerated. . . . (It) is at most a minor constraint on economic growth." Why? Because as a resource gets scarce, the free market responds first by higher prices and then by conservation, better technology and cheaper substitutes. Indeed, this NAS report stresses the role of free markets on almost every page.

The issue of renewable resources—particularly food—is more complex. The study acknowledges that rapid population growth can strain Third World agriculture. It also notes that with the exception of Africa, "per capita agricultural output has risen in most developing regions during the recent period of rapid population growth." In Africa, the study says that the best food policy is not slower population growth (although that would help) but the reform of "long-standing political inadequacies" that have penalized farmers. The need for political change is another key theme of the study.

On pollution, a similar view: Slower population growth "might allow somewhat more time" to deal with it. But the real solution is "socially negotiated access rules," which is a fancy phrase for political action of the sort taken in the richer countries, where pollution rates have come down in recent years.

On urbanization, the study attacks the argument that ever-bigger cities have been a tragedy for the Third World. Just the opposite: "Urbanization . . . plays an important beneficial role in the development process, providing . . . relatively high-wage employment, education, health care," etc.

On the broad questions of how population growth affects economic growth, the study offers a mixed bag. Rapid population growth does not impede improvements in health, but slower growth may help somewhat in education. Slower population growth, encouraged by family planning programs, can increase per capita income, though this effect is "relatively modest . . . (and) by no means appears to be a decisive influence." (After all, people produce as well as consume.)

In sum: Slower population growth in itself is of only limited benefit.

This clear thinking should yield better policy. The fact that family planning aid is of limited benefit for economic growth is an argument for it, not against it. Limited benefit is still a benefit (and, in any event, family-planning aid is justifiable on personal if not economic grounds). But it is only one of many tools. Most of the other tools, however, don't concern the numbers of people but how people act. When by political action, people make their economy more free—they prosper. When they don't—they don't.

March 13, 1986

Birth Control Chinese Style

We saw the unmasked face of totalitarianism last week on American television—and heard some foot-shuffling apologies about it.

At issue is a fascinating film entitled "China's Only Child" that appeared on PBS's "Nova" and was condensed on CBS's "60 Minutes." The documentary concerns China's official population policy which, since 1980, has sought to prevent Chinese couples from having more than one baby.

Now, there is nothing new about a nation trying to persuade its citizens to lower its birth rate—or raise it, for that matter. But the Chinese program is taking place in a country that is totalitarian—as in "total."

When the state controls your job, your house, your neighborhood and the education of your child—it might be said that the state has some pretty good tools of persuasion at hand.

In China they use the tools.

The film, originally produced by England's BBC, shows us how it works in Changzhou, a city of a half million. Changzhou is regarded as a showcase for family planning, Chinese style.

Factory workers must receive permission from the factory to get married and to get pregnant. In a typical factory there is an informer for each 16 women. Here is what one informer says: "We watch for women who start to eat less or who get morning sickness. If a woman isn't as active as she usually is—that's a sign of pregnancy. It's very difficult to escape . . . the attention of us family planning workers. No one has ever become pregnant without one of us finding out."

There is a back-up spy network as well. Back home, there is the "Granny Police." Neighborhoods are divided into units of 16 families, each under the eagle-eyed scrutiny of an official snoop on a regular pregnancy patrol.

What is the penalty if a woman seeks a second child? It can be a little thing—like a fine that could amount to a full year's wages.

But in Changzhou things don't get to that stage. Madame Chen is the population policy officer and she tells us of a case of a woman seven months pregnant: "There was a pregnant woman in Wazan factory. We

persuaded her to have an abortion. We took her to the hospital. That
night she changed her mind and escaped. She ran off to Shanghai. The
Shanghai people helped us find her . . . and we brought her back . . .
to the hospital for abortion."

Another case history, this one shown on camera, involves Junghu and
Manxue, a couple on a commune who want a second child. When Manxue
is six months pregnant, their plan is discovered. Manxue is "persuaded"
by nightly visits from top-ranking officials. We then see the abortion taking
place on our television screens.

Why all the concern? The Chinese believe they have a population problem. Indeed, China is already the most populous country in the world—
about a billion people. If they don't push population rates down, they
say, they'll grow at a faster rate than they want, and have difficulty feeding
their population.

There are several things very wrong with all this.

There is a major argument about the nature of population growth in
the less-developed world. It is high, but it has been declining sustantially
in most countries in recent years—without draconian policies. There is
also an argument about whether population growth harms economic growth.
In just two centuries, America grew from 4 million people to 250 million,
and we managed to improve our standard of living.

Beyond that is a human rights issue. The right to reproduce is an elemental
human right. It is not unreasonable for two parents to want two children
to replace themselves with. People who favor legal abortion (the right to
control your own body) must surely oppose Chinese-style coerced abortion
(which denies that right).

Yet, both the PBS and CBS programs are strangely silent about all this.

On CBS, Morley Safer concludes the program by saying China's methods
may not be civilized, "but there may be no other choice."

And on "Nova," the narrator tells us this: "If we were faced with this
future, how would we try to deal with it? First, we would educate and
convince everyone there is a problem. Then limit births. And, finally,
insure the rules are applied equally to all. That's what the Chinese are
doing. It is harsh. But is there an alternative?"

And so, a new message from civil libertarians: the end justifies the
means.

February 21, 1984

*As recently as the end of 1989, Dr. Paul Ehrlich and Lester Brown,
the head of World Watch, were publicly writing that the Chinese
population policy was peachy.*

Islamic Explosion

The "Islam bomb" is thought to be nuclear. More likely, it is demographic.

Islam is on the front page again, flexing muscles the rest of the world didn't even know existed. Ayatollah Khomeini has decreed extra-territorial capital punishment for Salman Rushdie, an allegedly blasphemous author. Booksellers in America received death threats and quivered.

About the same time, in what is now called the Islamic Republic of Afghanistan, heroic mujahedeen whipped a Soviet army previously regarded as invincible. If you can trash the United States and bash the Soviets, you're in the big leagues.

There are almost a billion reasons to suggest that Moslem influence will grow. A report by the Population Reference Bureau sets out the global playing field ("The Demography of Islamic Nations" by John Weeks and Saad Gadalla).

In 1950, there were 375 million Moslems in the world. There are 983 million Moslems today. By the year 2020, PRB projections show almost 2 billion. In 1950 only 15 percent of the global population was Moslem; today it is 19 percent; in 2030 it will be 25 percent.

By far, the Islamic nations are the world's fastest growing. The number of children born per woman is 1.7 in modern developed nations, 2.1 in Soviet bloc countries, and 4.5 in non-Islamic less-developed countries. In the Islamic nations the rate is 6.0!

It is a mistake to generalize about the Moslem world. The American mind often tends to equate "Moslem" with "Arab," yet the largest Moslem nations (Indonesia, Pakistan, Bangladesh, Turkey, Iran) are not Arab. Some Moslem nations are pro-American; others are pro-Soviet. Fundamentalist Moslems are often powerfully opposed to modern Western values; many other Moslems seek Western-style progress. Some few Moslem nations support terror; most don't.

The key question: Is there something about the growth of Islam that is seen as a potential threat to other nations and cultures?

There are about 50 million Moslems in the U.S.S.R., already making up 17 percent of the total population and growing about four times more rapidly than the Russian population. The Russians, always fearful, are haunted by a new political environment exemplified by Moslems thrashing Russians in Afghanistan.

As Moslem immigration in Western Europe has increased, anti-Moslem sentiment has grown. Some European nations are not only trying to keep Moslems out, but are trying to oust those who are already there.

Indeed, most of the Moslem world itself is fearful of the power of those fundamentalist Shiite Moslems who have endorsed terror. Those Shiites are a small minority, but they have blocked modernization in many parts of the Moslem world and were responsible for the assassination of Egypt's Anwar Sadat.

The estimated number of Moslems in United States range from under 2 million to more than 5 million, with the higher numbers most likely correct. What is uncontested is that the Moslem population—through immigration, high fertility and conversion—is growing much more rapidly than the American population as a whole. Most Moslems have moved quickly into the American middle class.

Unlike Europe, the United States has not experienced a sustained anti-Moslem backlash, even after the Ayatollah took American hostages. But potential storm clouds are visible. *U.S. News & World Report* maintains that networks of Iranian terrorists are in America and speculates that, "Some ordinary Moslems here, aroused over the perceived insult to Islam in the Rushdie book," might heed "Khomeini's call to arms." That could blow the cork.

None of this was predictable 20 years ago. It is hard to know what the next 20 years will bring. But as Islam grows rapidly around the world, we may find out whether the Islam bomb comes equipped with a sizzling fuse.

March 2, 1989

Tomorrow: The Population Explosion Is Ending

The population explosion is ending in all the areas of the Third World, and the potential impact of the lower fertility rates, especially in economic and environmental terms, is enormous, positive—and subject to debate.

From 1960–65 to 1985–90, according to the United Nations, the fertility decline has been sharpest in Asia. For example, India's rate went from 5.8 children per woman to 4.3, South Korea's from 5.4 to 2.0, Indonesia's from 5.4 to 3.3 and China's, partly due to coercive government policies on childbearing, declined from 5.9 to 2.4. In Latin America, Brazil's fertility rate fell from 6.1 to 3.5, while Mexico's dropped from 6.8 to 3.6. Mexico's lower rate is of particular importance to the U.S. because slower population growth can eventually mean less immigration pressure. Also, because lower fertility usually correlates with economic progress, it may be an indicator that Mexico will become more prosperous and thus a potentially better trading partner.

Now, fresh data from Africa has completed the demographic puzzle. While Egypt's rate dropped from 7.1 to 4.8, sub-Saharan Africa was thought to still have unyielding high rates. But a new survey generated by the Institute for Resource Development shows Kenya's rate of 8.1, formerly the world's highest, declined to 6.7. Rates also fell in Zimbabwe and Botswana.

For environmentalists who believe that population growth causes pollution and drains resources, the new numbers should be good news, even if the full effect is distant. Those economists who believe rapid population growth dilutes economic growth will also welcome the news. Others, however, argue that poverty in Less Developed Countries (LDCs) has not been caused principally by the population explosion but by the lack of free and productive economic systems. Prosperity, the argument goes, depends on how well people produce, not on the number of people or how fast they multiply. But even by those standards, falling fertility may be seen as an indicator of economic progress attributable to other factors such as market-oriented policies. Either way, falling fertility means more people will be of working age with fewer resources needed for children and more available for investment.

Although fertility rates will surely fall much further, the population of LDCs will keep growing. Because there are so many potential mothers in LDCs today, even with fewer children born per woman, the population will likely double by about 2050 before leveling off. In fact, the LDCs' fertility is not yet close to the "replacement level" of 2.1 children.

The fertility decline is due partly to more family planning, lower infant mortality, better education for women, and advancing economies. But lower rates also reflect a broader idea: modernism itself. The dramatic political changes occurring in Eastern Europe attest to the power of modern communications in affecting individual aspirations. People see how the modern world works, and many want to buy in. The same emulative revolution, with different aspects, such as smaller families, is also going on in less developed countries.

December 18, 1989

"Before leveling off": even I say it and write it. Yes, world population will almost surely "level off" in the century to come. But that will likely only be a way station toward population decline. In a modernizing world of the future, most of the nations will likely have what the more developed countries now have: below replacement fertility. As that plays itself out over many decades, far in the future, total world population will probably decline.

Environmentalists would maintain that will be good for us. Financial analysts, looking at sales and profit curves of existing businesses, would say, "Sell."

The hardest point to get across in the population argument is that two entirely different situations can exist at the same time in different places on the same planet. The situations, being different, can yield different terrain in different places.

As has been noted here, in the less developed countries (LDCs), there has been a population explosion, which continues, but is now in a long process of ending.

We turn now to the more developed part of the world, where there has not been a population explosion, but a Birth Dearth. This is the first time in human history that a large group of nations, over an extended period of time, has had fertility rates well below what is required merely to keep a population stable. The key question now is this: is that Birth Dearth still continuing?

The latest communiques from the demographic front indicate this: the United States, as described in the piece immediately following, may be coming out of the Birth Dearth. (There were over four million births in 1989, for the first time since 1964.) Japanese fertility is falling, almost dramatically, from low to very low levels. European fertility is mixed; on balance, the situation is roughly stable at quite a low level of fertility.

The recent developments in the United States are startling. If they are confirmed, and they continue, the new trends will probably yield substantially positive results. The changes in fertility, when coupled with the likely changes in immigration, mean an extra 45 million Americans in the next four decades, and the difference between an America that is receding demographically and an America that is growing.

From the point of view of existing businesses, that is the difference between organic and fairly easy growth, or the zero-sum murderous competition that is involved in fighting for a larger share of a non-growing market. Financial advice: buy stocks, buy with vigor when it becomes apparent that an immigration bill, at higher levels of legal immigration, will really pass. Nothing, long term, is more bullish.

Take some time and play with the chart on the bottom of page 74. It is as important as any in this book, particularly for people in business.

New customers are being created wholesale. Barely noticed developments in fertility trends and immigration law will likely yield an additional 8 million people in the 1990s. Housing industry, take note: they will all have to live somewhere. Clothing industry: they will all wear clothes. And so on.

By the year 2010, not so far away, the "unexpected" additional people will amount to about 17 million.

Now, projections aren't predictions. Things can change, and probably will, up or down. But projections are a whole lot better *than guessing. They tell you what will happen if things continue to go on as they are going on now. That is not a bad base to start from, subject to the test of reasonableness. The assumptions here are reasonable.*

But it's not just businesses and markets. That may be the least of it. Let us posit that there is indeed a contest for "Number One" in the world—politically, commercially, technologically, and culturally. Let us further assume, as is generally assumed, that the contest is between the United States, Europe, and Japan. If Europe and Japan are either losing population or simply remaining at no-growth levels, and the United States is still growing vigorously (and Canada is growing too)—what does that mean?

It means, in combination with other factors discussed in this volume, that the United States has a strong chance to remain Number One, in my judgment likely to be more influential than ever, indeed, as mentioned earlier, to become the most influential nation in history. Take that.

If this sounds like a refutation, by me, of that seminal book The Birth Dearth, *by me,—it is not.*

The Birth Dearth speculated (that is the word used in the first and last paragraph of the book) about what would happen if, in the industrialized nations, low fertility and then-current immigration patterns remained roughly constant. Under such a scenario, I suggested, there would likely be some harmful economic, geopolitical, and personal consequences. The consequences, I said, would likely be more severe in Japan and Western Europe, because fertility was lower there than in the United States and opportunities for increased immigration were less likely.

Since then fertility has gone up in the United States, and immigration increases seem much more likely. Fertility has not gone up in Europe or Japan; immigration increases are resisted vigorously.

Why has the United States done so well? The answer is obvious: because people in the United States took the time to read, and heed, The Birth Dearth. *The solution for Europe and Japan is elementary: read and heed it too.*

Is the Birth Dearth Over?

Although no formal announcement has yet been made, newly available government data reveals that fertility rates in the United States are up, and for the first time in nearly a generation American women are bearing an average of more than two children. The new trend will likely have profound and positive effects.

The turnaround is probably not happening in Europe, and certainly not in Japan.

In early May, the National Center for Health Statistics computed the estimated annual U.S. Total Fertility Rate (TFR). Simply put, the TFR is the number of children, on average, that a woman bears in a lifetime. It is both a bedrock demographic statistic, perhaps the most important one, and a primal cultural indicator.

The new TFR is remarkable. Consider the recent sequence:

U.S. TOTAL FERTILITY RATE

1976–86: 1.74–1.84 children per woman

1987:   1.87   children per woman

1988:   1.93   children per woman (estimate)

1989:   2.00   children per woman (estimate)

The precise new number is 2.0009. In short, the Birth Dearth in America still exists, but may be ending.

What's going on? There are solid clues. What does it mean? Good things for us, problems for our competitors.

The biggest reason for the change is that thirty-somethings are having more kiddy-somethings. The sound we hear is the snooze alarm on the biological clock, a final-chance collective understanding of a demographic axiom: "fertility delayed is fertility denied."

From 1977–87 the general fertility rates of women aged 30–39 rose from 40 to 50 births per thousand women. The new data indicates that this increase among older women apparently continued through 1989, more than overcoming a slight ongoing decrease in the fertility rate among teen-agers and twenty-somethings.

The rise puts the United States within range of returning to the TFR "replacement level" of 2.11. That is the rate required to keep a population just stable over time, not counting immigration. But because America accepts a solid number of immigrants, we may already be at, or slightly above, the replacement equivalent.

Accordingly, when the Census Bureau does its next projections, the "most likely" calculation will probably no longer show America losing population in the next century. The difference between the 1.8 TFR used in the recent projections and the current 2.0 rate generates more than 50 million additional people by 2050. Instead of a declining population of 300 million at that time, there would be a growing one of 350 million. (Again, see the table on page 74.)

The potential economic effects are great (particularly if augmented by moderate immigration increases now being considered.) For example, the

Social Security shortfall would be cut (because of more contributors), and growing American markets would likely boost existing businesses.

America's competitors are in no such happy mode. The Japanese TFR is falling, now down to 1.57, an all-time low. The recent growth of feminism in Japan will likely lower the rate further.

European rates are more complex. Three of the four big nations have, for the moment, stabilized at low or extremely low levels. England and France remain at 1.8 while Italy is holding at 1.3. The West German TFR is a very low 1.42, but it is up somewhat. At the least, the demographic freefall in Europe seems to have ended.

The biggest European demographic news comes from Sweden, where the TFR went up from 1.65 to 2.02 in four years. That follows newly instituted pro-natal policies, including better paid leave for women.

While the Swedish increase might be a precursor of things to come, birth rates are simultaneously dropping in Poland, Yugoslavia, and Romania. Long term, it seems as if Europe and Japan, both with low fertility and resistance to immigration, will end up with non-growing or somewhat shrinking populations in the next decades. By contrast, America will be growing demographically—and in economic and geopolitical influence.

There are caveats. Fertility may be up in the U.S. only because the economy has been healthy. The newest numbers are only provisional estimates, which can be revised. The trend is of short duration. America is still below the 2.11 replacement rate.

But there is intuitive sense to what is happening. Many young adults are sensing that a life without progeny can be unfulfilling. Moreover, perhaps related, perhaps not, the society, partly through changing day care and taxation policies, is beginning to respond.

An era may be ending.

May 9, 1990

The two following pieces, about "Nogrowthia" and the Rural Renaissance, were written prior to the projections based on new fertility-immigration assumptions, discussed earlier in this chapter. If the new projections hold up, the numbers used in the two columns would have to be amended upward somewhat. Still, they show an important directional (if not absolute) situation. Particularly if you live and work in a rural area, or the Midwest, or the Northeast, or sell goods or services in those areas, or are interested in the future of America.

"Nogrowthia" vs. "Popgainia"

In the 1990s, for the first time in American history, an entire region of the country will lose population! That stunning fact is perhaps best understood by viewing America as a tale of two countries. These countries can be named "Nogrowthia" and "Popgainia."

The data for such an interpretation comes from new Census Bureau projections. The diminishing region in question is the Midwest. From 1990 to 2000 that region is projected to lose 181,000 souls (even after receiving immigrants). That is a trivial amount. But like the famous talking dog, the remarkable thing is that it talks at all, not that it misquoted Shakespeare. It's the first such loss ever, and it provides a tip-off about what will happen not only in Nogrowthia, but in the rest of America and the Western world.

Nogrowthia is a large country. It is made up of the American Midwest and the American Northeast. In 1990 Nogrowthia will have 110 million people, roughly the combined population of England and France. In 2000, and in 2010, its population will be 111 million. No growth in Nogrowthia.

Why? Part of the reason, often mentioned, is migration—people from the Frost Belt are moving to the Sun Belt. But there is another critical factor: birth rates. It's low in Nogrowthia. Massachusetts has a Total Fertility Rate (TFR) of 1.45 children per woman per lifetime. That's almost one-third below the 2.1 rate required to merely keep a population stable over time. The TFR in New York state is not much higher: 1.63. Ohio is at 1.8.

What about that other country, Popgainia? That nation is created by combining the Southern and Western region of America. In 2000, the two most populous states will be California and Texas, both Popgainian. The TFR in California is 1.90 children per woman; in Texas it's 2.11. (Texas is 46 percent higher than Massachusetts! Part, but not all, of that differential is due to large Hispanic populations with higher fertility rates.)

From 1990 to 2000, recall, the total population in all of Nogrowthia will rise by just one measly million. (Slight gain in Northeast, slight loss in Midwest.) At the same time the number of people in Popgainia will go up by about 17 million!

Two countries. One is warm, somethat fecund, and growing. The other is cold, not even close to reproducing itself, and not growing.

It is a fascinating demographic laboratory. The trends may touch us all in ways we don't usually think about. Is business better in a place where there is growth, or stability, or decline? (New Jersey will grow; Ohio will shrink.) If you already own a house, will resale value be better in a place with few potential buyers, or many? Where will people be happier—in a place with few grandchildren, or many?

The demographic conditions in the two-country America reflect in slow motion what has happened, and will happen, in the Western world. In the '90s Western Europe, now near population stability, will begin losing population. In America, Nogrowthia will go from population stability to shrinkage by about 2010 (Poplossia?), while growth in Popgainia will slow down.

Other new Census projections, to be issued shortly, show America as a whole losing population by about 2030. (If you're under age 40, you may well be alive then.) At the same time the developing world will still be growing rapidly.

Is all this sure to happen? No. Demographers carefully distinguish between projections and forecasts. Projections only show what happens if the future arrives in a manner consistent with the patterns of the past.

If Americans don't like the future that is projected, they can act to change it. How? By making it economically easier for young people who want to have babies to have babies. By allowing more legal immigrants into America. We ought to do both.

November 24, 1988

Revisiting "The Rural Renaissance"

Wouldn't you like to live where you'd like to live? Many urban Americans don't. How would you like to be pushed to live where you don't want to live? That happens to many rural Americans. It's a problem, and the seeds of a solution are on the farm.

Polls show that about half of all Americans (not me) would like to live on "farms" in "small towns" or "rural areas." But only about a quarter actually do. There are about 60 million unrequited ruralians.

Further, more than half the rural counties are losing population. The folks who leave are not usually leaving because they want to.

The cultural indicators are also pro-rural: country music, jeans, tiny tractors in the back yard, cowboy movies, coin-operated bucking horses at the shopping mall. There are lots of people who would like to be away from urban crime, drugs, racial tensions, crowding, traffic jams. Some people (even me) think trees are prettier than cement.

So why don't the urbanites move? And why do the ruralians keep on moving? There are no jobs in rural areas.

There is a germ of a national policy in this situation. If urbanites feel crowded, and ruralites complain that they need people, , , ,

There was a time, during the '70s, when it was happening. It was called "The Rural Renaissance." There were new rural recreation and retirement communities, a booming market for farm exports, factories moving to the countryside, new oil discoveries and high demand for minerals. For the first time, rural areas grew faster than the urban ones.

The big recession in the early '80s wiped it out: oil, mineral and food prices plunged. Manufacturing went overseas. Since 1980, urban areas have grown much faster than rural areas.

The Rural Renaissance dream makes sense. In a high-tech world, urban advantages can be enjoyed in the country: The fax is a messenger service, VCRs and cable television provide entertainment, computers do everything else, including medical diagnostics.

Can it happen? Or will we become irrevocably more urban, more of us living near the oceans and fewer of us in the interior heartland?

Demographer Calvin Beale, of the U.S. Department of Agriculture, is mildly optimistic. Farm income is up. The decline in mining and manufacturing jobs has plateaued. Growth in rural retirement and recreation communities never stopped. The rural unemployment rate is coming down.

Should we try to encourage, via legislation, a reignition of the rural renaissance? Sen. Max Baucus, D-Mont., thinks we should. "We've always had an affirmative rural policy in America: railroad building, land grant colleges, rural electrification, interstate highways." Telecommunications, he says, "are the interstate highways of the future."

The Senate and a House subcommittee have now passed rural development bills. Each act tries to make it easier for rural businesses to get credit, and each encourages better infrastructure such as sewers, water supply, airports and computer-compatible phone company switchboards. But the monies are trivial. The Senate version adds $300 million to the $6 billion that USDA spends on rural development. The House bill spends less.

The efforts are sound, but of marginal use. Alas, the legislators say, there is no money in the budget for big expenditures.

There is. Subsidies to farmers—primarily for wheat and corn—still run about $10 billion per year. For the 98 percent of Americans who are not farmers, those subsidies, and others in the food realm, yield two swell general results: higher taxes and higher food prices.

The answer is obvious. Break the stranglehold of the agricultural lobbyists. Phase out the money from farm subsidies and put it into water supply, roads, sewers, airports, fiber-optic switchboards.

That could create jobs, letting some country boys in the cities get back to the country. It could make it easier for some country boys to stay in the country. And, in another farm crisis, it could help farmers stick it out.
December 13, 1989

There is a great deal of optimistic talk about enormous economic growth in Western Europe coinciding with economic integration scheduled for 1992. It is probably correct. There will probably be another bump as the nations of Eastern Europe move toward market-based economies. But the demographic projections for Europe—West or East, or both—are flat, stale, sterile, and ultimately diminishing. It's bad; almost as bad as the picture for the Japanese.

Is Europe Vanishing?

When I was growing up there was always much good-natured humor about the large size of Italian families. Bambini, bambini, everywhere bambini!

Question: What country today has the lowest fertility rate? Answer: Italy!

That answer is by courtesy of demographer Carl Haub of the Population Reference Bureau in Washington, D.C., which recently issued its annual, and always fascinating, "World Population Data Sheet." Using updated statistics, Haub has calculated some Total Fertility Rates (TFR) to two decimal places. (The TFR expresses the average number of children that women will bear.)

Haub estimates that West Germany, the former holder of the least-children record, has increased its TFR by from 1.28 children per woman to 1.36 children. At the same time Italy has dropped from 1.42 children to 1.35.

Now, statistically speaking, there is no real difference between 1.36 and 1.35, and the slight swings may be temporary. There is also no statistically significant difference between Haub's estimate of the TFR for all the free nations of Western Europe for 1985—1.62 children per woman—as opposed to a minuscule drop to 1.61 children for 1986.

What is significant, however, is the lack of major change. No news can be big news, and this probably indicates the changing nature of the European economy and European geopolitics in the 1990s.

The nations of Western Europe have the lowest fertility rates of any region in the world. They have had the world's lowest rates for about 15 years. Those rates are well below the rate required to merely reproduce a society over time. (It takes a TFR of 2.1 to keep a society stable over time. Western Europe's rate of 1.6 is almost 25 percent below that.)

The rates are the lowest in all recorded history! Moreover, the recent politics in Europe show clearly that immigration will not be an easy remedy. The surprise vote-getter in the first round of the French elections was Jean-Marie Le Pen, who not only wants to stop most immigration into France, but deport some immigrants. To one degree or another, that kind of anti-immigration attitude is pervasive in Europe.

So what? A few years ago French Prime Minister Jacques Chirac said, "Europe is vanishing." That is a bit overstated, but the thought is on target. There were about 330 million people in Western Europe in 1985. By the middle of the next century, unless rates change solidly in an upward direction, the population will be about 290 million. By the end of the next century, it will be down to about 200 million and still sinking. C'est la vie.

Meanwhile, most of the rest of the world will be growing. In 1988 there were 231 million people in the European "big four": West Germany, Italy, the United Kingdom and France. These nations today are the 14th, 15th, 16th and 17th largest countries in the world (according to PRB.) By 2020 those four nations will have about 210 million to 215 million people, and they will rank 24th, 25th, 28th and 29th. The total population of the big four at that time will be just about that of one Asian nation— Bangladesh!

So what? European markets will be less important relative to the rest of the world. The geopolitical power and potency for European countries and for European culture will be diminished.

June 16, 1988

What is the opposite of "lebensraum"—"shrinkensraum?"

There has been discussion about a unified Germany becoming another superpower, and perhaps a nasty one.

Not to worry. The Total Fertility Rate (TFR) in West Germany is 1.4 children per woman, tied for lowest in Western Europe. The East German rate is 1.7, the lowest in Eastern Europe. The TFR for a unified Germany would be about 1.5.

As Germany reunifies it will indeed be the biggest country in Europe—and losing population the most rapidly. By 2035, the population of France will be as large as that of a unified Germany. Of course, the French (like much of the rest of Europe) have recently made immigration much more difficult. Like the rest of Europe they are petrified of "Africanization" and "Islamization."

The demographic picture, in broad strokes, looks like this: Japan will lose *population. Europe, either Western or all Europe, will* either lose *population* or stay stable at a no-growth level. *The United States or the United States-plus-Canada* will grow *with some vigor.*

My guess about European demographics is that the Europeans will end up for a while with the worst of two worlds: population stagnation and bitter fights about immigration. Later, rather than sooner, they will realize that pluralism is the only answer to what ails them.

The Japanese situation is more serious, for the Japanese. Pluralism does not seem to be a serious cultural option over there.

The facts of the matter are fairly simple: a modern country with fertility well below replacement levels either takes in immigrants or raises its fertility rate—or slowly goes out of business.

Nations

8

America in the World

*W*e *are becoming a universal nation at home; we come from everywhere.*
We are a "wondrous race," although, Lord knows, it's not always easy,
and we self-inflict more than a few wounds. Still, as demonstrated, it's
worked, and it's working.

But that is only part of the equation necessary to become the omni-
power, the mega-, maxi-, uni-, ultra-, hyper-, multi-, magna-, supra-power.
It is the thesis here that America is not only becoming a successful universal
nation at home, but abroad as well. The overseas influence of American
popular culture, ideas, foreign policy, science, language, business, politics,
military force and universities are of tidal wave proportions, more so than
ever before.

Jean-Jacques Servan-Schreiber had it right: Europe faces "an American
challenge." Richard Barnet had it right when he described the "global reach"
of American commerce.

We now examine America's global impact.

To understand the terrain of "American foreign policy" in the nineties,
it is wise to start by looking at the "American" part first. The essence of
our global role is a reflection of American public opinion.

Part of that public opinion concerns what we do not believe. For example,
we do not believe that Vietnam was an immoral war. We do not believe,
nor have we ever believed, that our military fellows are the bad fellows.

We do believe that we are the good guys of history and that we still have a mighty role to play in shaping a world that is changing quite remarkably.

What should we do?

The global situation is conducive to it, and domestic public opinion is prepared to support a simple U.S. global strategy in the coming contest for the culture: neo-manifest destinarianism.

The Myths of Vietnam

The 10th anniversary of the fall of South Vietnam has led to a bull market in the cottage industry called "The Lessons of Vietnam." Fair enough. It was a tragic and complex war; we should try to learn from history. What's happening, however, is that many of the lessons are springing from myths— most set in motion from the left of the political spectrum, but some from the right—designed to prove only what the myth-marketers want to prove.

Thus, it's said Americans didn't support our soldiers during the Vietnam War. That's wrong, with a mountain of public opinion data to prove it's wrong. The vast majority of Americans honored our soldiers—during and after the war—and scorned the anti-war demonstrators.

It's said that the public came to reject the policies of the various presidents who were in command. That's wrong, too. Of course, strategy evolved during the war. But the polls show that most of the public generally supported the policy at any given moment. There were good tests of this. George McGovern lost the election in a landslide.

It's said that Vietnam proved that the so-called domino theory didn't work. Wrong. It proved the opposite. As soon as South Vietnam fell to the communists, down came the dominoes in Laos and Cambodia.

It's said by some that the "blood bath" never came to pass. It's true there was no genocide by the communists of the sort that Stalin or Mao unleashed. But 10 years after the war the communists still have people in "re-education camps," where horrid conditions kill people just as surely as a firing squad.

Other common statements are much more complicated. It's said that Vietnam was the only war America ever lost. Not quite right. We began in Vietnam by supporting a nation threatened by subversion and invasion. When we left, the internal Vietcong threat had been crushed and the external North Vietnamese threat was stalemated. We then tried to turn the war over to the South Vietnamese—something we should have done earlier. They fought for two more years without us—and then were conquered. We tried to help. We failed. But our allies lost a war—not us.

Finally, it's said—mostly by those on the right—that the Congress pushed our South Vietnamese allies over the cliff. Congress did pass laws that irresponsibly limited the U.S. military role and undercut our allies. But even at the time of the collapse in 1975, the United States was sending hundreds of millions of dollars in military aid to a large and well-equipped South Vietnamese army that had fought well on many occasions. There was reason to think they could fight well enough to hold the line. They didn't.

There is a tortuous paradox regarding our role in Vietnam. The case can be made that we pulled the plug; it can also be made that for seven long years we spent more in life and treasure than any nation has ever given to another when the strategic stakes were so distant and so far out in the geopolitical future.

The war was a great tragedy. The Vietnam Memorial, with more than 50,000 names carved in stone, shows the full scope of the disaster.

Why then pick over the falsehoods and the facts? Because we do not honor our lost young men by building a new foreign policy on myths—that the American people don't support their soldiers, that they reject any policy that may involve the use of force, that communists are not expansionist, that communists are no longer barbarous. Nor ought we believe that we were defeated in combat by a Third World country, or that we should be ashamed because we bugged out. That's not the way it was.

Because that's not the way it was, we can remain a powerful, credible and moral factor on the world scene—an idea that makes the left nervous. Because that's not the way it was, we need not engage in macho muscularity—a course that some on the right sometimes yearn for. Steady as she goes.

April 11, 1985

What Jane Fonda Didn't Say

That was an interesting half of an interview Barbara Walters had with Jane Fonda on ABC's "20/20." It was good to hear Fonda apologize to American Vietnam veterans for some of her actions during the Vietnam War.

As "20/20" documented, in Hanoi in 1972, Fonda made a propaganda broadcast calling American officers "war criminals." She also was photographed, grinning, in the gunner's seat of a North Vietnamese anti-aircraft gun—the kind that shot down American pilots. Later, when returning POWs said that they had been tortured, she said "I think they're lying."

Talking about these incidents on the program, Fonda addressed Vietnam veterans, explaining: "I was trying to help end the killing, end the war, but there were times when I was thoughtless and careless about it and I'm very sorry that I hurt them. And I want to apologize to them and to their families."

That's a personal apology. Fine. We believe in redemption. Fonda is a gifted actress, entrepreneur, and political activist. In a time of healing, it would be churlish to remain distressed about a woman of such talent, once she has apologized for grievous past errors.

But the Walters interview doesn't do that. Jane Fonda was more than "thoughtless" and "careless," and she wanted more than "to end the war." Walters naively asked Fonda, "when so many people protested the war . . . why are your actions today still being criticized? Why is it still so painful?"

There is reason for the pain. Tens of millions of Americans were against the war, just as there were tens of millions (including this writer) who supported it. But most Americans who opposed the war were just that— opposed to American involvement in the war. When they demonstrated, their placards read "Negotiate now" or "America out of Vietnam." But Fonda, and some other radicals, had a different idea. Their followers carried flags of the National Liberation Front and chanted "Ho, Ho, Ho Chi Minh: the NLF is gonna win."

Remember, our adversary was the North Vietnamese totalitarian Communist government, supported by arms from the Soviet Union, and they were actively trying to kill American boys.

What did Fonda think about all that? The "20/20" program barely touches it. Walters cites a Fonda quote: "As a revolutionary woman I am ready to support all struggles that are radical." Walters then accepts without further comment Fonda's response: "It was preposterous that I described myself then as a revolutionary woman. I didn't even know what that meant."

Didn't know what that meant? A look at the record will show that upon arriving in Hanoi she said, "I come as a comrade." Back in America she said the Vietcong was the "conscience of the world," and that they were "driven by the same spirit that drove Washington and Jefferson." To a student audience she said, "I would think, if you understood what communism was, you would hope, you would pray on your knees, that we would someday become communist."

It is hard to avoid a simple thought: Fonda favored the victory of the other side. Fonda owes more than a personal apology. She owes a political apology for supporting the enemy; she owes a national apology to the South Vietnamese. Remember, that when the comrades invaded, South Vietnam was turned into a totalitarian slum, and fleeing "boat people" were drowned at sea.

Remember, too, that when these horrific events were publicized, many prominent anti-war activists (like Joan Baez) publicly denounced the actions of the communists. Fonda had a different response. She said that the charges "weren't fully substantiated."

During the show, Fonda says, "I am proud of most of what I did and very sorry for some of what I did."

Fonda gave half an apology. Accept it halfheartedly.

June 23, 1988

The Rise and Fall of Paul Kennedy

A wonderful debate is suffusing the intellectual community and has spilled over into our national politics at just the right time. The issue concerns the Decline of America.

The trigger of the argument has been the publication of a long, academic book entitled, *The Rise and Fall of the Great Powers: Economic Change and Military Conflict from 1500 to 2000*, by Professor Paul Kennedy of Yale.

Kennedy's theory: Great powers come into being because they have the most prosperous economy. Using this economic might, they build a powerful military force to take advantage of other nations. But—here's the rub— the costs of major military and geopolitical power are enormous, and the great power gets drained economically, victim of what Kennedy calls "imperial overstretch." Thus weakened relative to other nations, the great power succumbs, usually militarily, to another power, an economically rising one, because that power hasn't been burdened by costs of empire. Kennedy cites examples of stretch-marked empires: Spain, England, France, Holland.

What makes Kennedy's thesis provocative is that he thinks it's happening to the United States—now. Our adversaries in this contest, he says, are not the Russians, who are also in economic trouble, but other industrialized nations, particularly the Japanese, who are beating us economically. The task of our leaders, says Kennedy, is to manage our decline gracefully. He says we ought to cut defense spending and reduce our global commitments.

It's a useful argument—even though it's wrong, wrong, wrong.

Wrong because America is spending proportionally much less on defense now than earlier: about 6 percent of the gross national product vs. about 10 percent in earlier postwar years.

Wrong because our standard of living is still way higher than the Japanese. Japan is a nation hampered by archaic retail and farm policies. It is the world's most rapidly aging society and will soon pay the piper when pension and health costs soar.

Wrong because America, remember, defends Japan—a country located in a dangerous neighborhood.

But wrong even more because Kennedy doesn't really understand America. He's an Englishman. He emigrated here as a young adult. My sense is that he hasn't got the whole message yet.

The American empire is not like earlier European imperialisms. We have sought neither wealth nor territory. Ours is an imperium of values. We have sought to boost a community of ideas—political democracy, free market economics, and science and technology. These days those values are advancing, not eroding.

Seen in that light, America is not in decline. No way. Our foreign policy has been designed precisely to help other democratic nations become more prosperous. That Japan and the countries of Western Europe have become competitors is the good news, not the bad news. Would we really be better off if those nations were still poor? Surely not; they are our allies.

So why is Kennedy's book useful? Because it has made American politicians think afresh about America's role in the world. American politicians aren't allowed to talk about gracefully managing America's decline. Voters won't stand for it. So politicians are forced to figure out ways not to let it happen. Thus, Democrats chant their mantra: "We'll make America number one economically again." And Republicans chant: "We'll make sure America stays number one as the geopolitical leader of the free world."

Number one economically. Number one geopolitically. Soon our politicians, stimulated by the Kennedy thesis, are going to notice the commonality of these themes and say, "Eureka, let's be both." That idea will form a consensus and capture the votes of all the Americans who want to be number one. Which is most of us.

May 19, 1988

On Churchill and Summitry

Since Oct. 12, I have been musing about how the past impacts on the present, and how the present often can send us some dim glimpse of the future.

Oct. 12 was the night that President Reagan and his negotiating team returned from the Iceland summit.

It was also the night of the final episode of the eight-part series "Churchill: The Wilderness Years," aired by the Public Broadcasting Service.

Having now read more than enough about the Reykjavik summit, I am convinced that the Churchill programs explained more about what's happening to us than all the Iceland commentaries rolled into one.

The PBS programs brilliantly dramatize Churchill's lonely uphill fight during the 1930s to alert England to the threat posed by Hitler's military buildup. We see Churchill plead for more English arms and for a stern Western diplomatic response to the growing Nazi war machine.

The British military intelligence community sends Churchill a stream of secret documents detailing the German menace. Churchill makes eloquent speeches. But his alarmist and hawkish views are rejected by the English people and derided within his own Conservative party. He is frozen out of the Conservative Cabinet.

Limp-wristed Conservatives tell Churchill that the country won't stand for cutting the social welfare budget to increase the military. They say

Churchill is exaggerating the Nazi threat, that he sees Nazis under every bed. (Sound familiar?)

In 1938, Prime Minister Chamberlain goes to a summit meeting with Hitler in Munich and comes back assuring us there will be "peace in our time." He says that what is needed is more arms control, not more arms, and that he will deal with Herr Hitler. Later, Chamberlain says, "Our policy of appeasement is beginning to work." And the British public applauds the appeaser. Within months, Hitler is on the march. Sixty million people will die before the war is over.

Cut to Iceland. Another summit, almost half a century later. It's more than a little confusing about who did what to whom in Iceland, but several things come into focus. Reagan went to Iceland having already presided over a large American military buildup following a decade of Soviet adventurism. And he surely was not pushing Star Wars—whatever its merits—to appease the Soviet Union.

As soon as the Iceland summit ended, many liberal pundits criticized Reagan for not making the arms control deal of the century. Why, we could save a trillion dollars if we dumped Star Wars! And we have a deficit and poor people to think of.

Reagan, the Churchillian hawk, returns to America. But this is not the 1930s: Reagan's popularity jumps. Public support for Star Wars goes up. In some Senate races it is used as a symbol of whether the candidates are for a strong America. Suddenly, everybody in politics seems to be stressing support for some version of Star Wars and for a strong America.

Now, PBS is sometimes criticized for having a left-wing, dovish tilt. Yet, let it be noted that the Churchill story is still the most intelligent and potent case to be made for the hard-liner view that peace comes from strength.

The obverse view yields the lesson of the '30s: that weakness yields chaos for the democracies. Remember, the '30s was the decade when Ronald Reagan came of age. And after all the talk of a "successor generation," it is the tragic events of the '30s that still frame the view of the world as seen through the eyes of policy makers in Europe and America.

Reykjavik and Munich. Both on our television on Oct. 12. History does not always repeat itself.

November 6, 1986

George Bush was a young teenager interested in public affairs at the time of Munich; a few years later he was a Navy pilot. Bush says, "Read my lips." Better: read his mind. He, too, was shaped by the sad history of Western flaccidity. He keeps using the word "prudent." My sense is that he means "tough."

Reagan's Doctrine

Ronald Reagan has finally claimed full paternity of a matured version of "The Reagan Doctrine."

Interestingly enough, the first use of the phrase came from a columnist, the incisive Charles Krauthammer. Secretary George Shultz, who can be pretty incisive himself, has given speeches about it.

Reagan, of course, by both rhetoric and deed, had helped the birth process along. His 1982 speech in England endorsing a National Endowment for Democracy was noteworthy.

And surely, the flow of events in recent years has played a large role in the doctrinal evolution. Rather suddenly there were insurgents fighting communists: mujahedeen bucking the odds in Afghanistan, Jonas Savimbi beating Marxists in Angola, and, of course, *contras* in Nicaragua fighting the Sandinista betrayal of democracy.

At the same time, democracy was on a roll in authoritarian countries of the right: in Brazil, Argentina and Central America. Recent events in the Philippines and Haiti underlined the point.

But Ronald Reagan wove the strands together last week: words and music—polemics, policy and politics.

Reagan's written message to the Congress was formally entitled "Freedom, Regional Security and Global Peace." But its real message was summed up in a phrase well into the interior of the document: "The Democratic Revolution." In brief, the Reagan Doctrine says that the forces of freedom—moral and material—must now go on the offensive.

Ever since the debacle in Vietnam, the idea that we need a new idea in foreign policy has been growing in the American body politic. There was a beginning of it in the early '70s when Sen. Henry Jackson introduced "The Jackson Amendment," directed against the totalitarian left. It said, in effect, that human rights counted for something real in American diplomacy.

I recall, in 1976, at the meeting of the Democratic Party platform-drafting subcommittee, the Jackson forces were represented by (now Sen.) Daniel P. Moynihan and me. As described in Josh Muravchik's new book *The Uncertain Crusade*, we Jacksonites argued that the Democrats ought to condemn human rights abuses in repressive communist nations. Jessica Tuchman and Sam Brown (both later served in the Carter administration) argued that a human rights policy was fine but ought to be focused on repressive nations of the right such as South Korea and Brazil. The solution in the platform: make human rights an across-the-board issue covering repression from both left and right. The chairman of the sub-committee was the new young governor of Massachusetts, Michael Dukakis.

Of course, it was Jimmy Carter who promoted the human rights policy in a way that only a president can. Many of us thought his execution of the policy was peculiar, but, to his credit, he moved the policy from backroom meetings to the front page.

Reagan has now extended the policy by linking human rights to the political form that promotes human rights: democracy. Reagan is saying let's go for it. He says he's done his part with rightists in the Philippines. His speech to the nation challenged the Democrats to join him against leftists in Nicaragua.

The "rebuttal" speech by Sen. James Sasser, D-Tenn., only confirmed Reagan's thesis. After hithering and thithering, Sasser said let's just test those bad Sandinista folks one last time; if they won't be reasonable, it may well be necessary to fund military action. It is fairly clear that even if Reagan "loses" a first vote in Congress, the Democratic "compromise" now forming will give him what he wants: military pressure on Nicaragua.

If the Democrats are smart, they should go along with the Reagan Doctrine. After all, they helped form it over the years. But for political reasons, they should soon rename it. They could call it something strange, like "bipartisan American foreign policy"—"Bipfip" for short. And they could note that it was just such a bipartisan policy that made America the most potent superpower the world has ever seen.

March 20, 1986

Sentencing Reagan to History

What about George Washington? He was the father of our country.

How about Abraham Lincoln? He freed the slaves.

Franklin Roosevelt? He gets two sentences. Fought the Depression. Won the war.

Lyndon Johnson? A struggle, still, between two sentences. He got us into Vietnam. He helped the poor and blacks.

Millard Fillmore? James Buchanan? Grover Cleveland? Nothing, nothing, nothing.

It was a theory of the late Clare Booth Luce that important presidents were remembered by only a single sentence, occasionally by two. The sentences are terse, sometimes unfair or simplistic, but that's all that one gets from history. Sorry about that. Lesser presidents don't even get that much.

What, then, about Ronald Reagan? In the past few weeks there has been much written about his accomplishments and failings. He made us feel better about ourselves. He rebuilt the military. He cut taxes, inflation and regulation. He oppressed the poor. He showed that capitalism worked. He ran up a gonzo deficit. He was lazy, inattentive and presided over a rogue White House. He paid ransom to the dreaded ayatollah. He made peace with the Russians. He cut back nuclear weapons. He started Star Wars.

Sorry, too much. Under Luce's rule that just won't do. One sentence, maybe two. You say that's not realistic? Too bad. That's the rule.

What does Reagan get?

Feel better about ourselves? Dubious. Too fuzzy. "We" never felt so bad; anyway, we may start feeling that way again.

Taxes, inflation and regulation? They are important, but they may go back up. Not necessarily a lasting change.

Bashed the poor? The poverty rate is lower.

Lazy and inattentive? Me too. Not the stuff of history. Ransomed hostages, Iran-contra? Poof! Another blip.

There are only two serious candidates for lasting single-sentence Reaganesque historical simplicity. Both are hostages to history.

One is the deficit. It is big. One can have fun by imagining what Ronald Reagan would say about it if it had been run up by Jimmy Carter.

There are some people, even economists, who believe that we are in for a major crash, crunch, bash or bump. If it happens, it will surely be ascribed to Reagan's promiscuous budget debt. No matter that the relationship between economic apocalypse and national deficit is, at best, unclear. In popular history it will be Reagan's fault. His sentence will then be: "He started the Crash."

I don't happen to think the economic apocalypse is now. I think it is the apocalypse-mongers who are headed for a crash, crunch, bash or bump. Accordingly, I doubt that Reagan will get a bad sentence.

His sentence, and it is a good one, will more likely be in the realm of international affairs. The ones generally offered are too neutral, tactical or factual. No pizazz. Started Star Wars. Cut back on nukes. Rebuilt the military. Made peace with Russians. Too limited.

But something big did happen on Reagan's watch that is fraught with substance. For almost 50 years we have been grappling with the Soviets about the nature of the world. That struggle is called the Cold War. That Reagan was able to participate in it is a debt he owes to two generations of Western statesmen, politicians and taxpayers who hung tough against the Soviets. They kept us in the game.

But it happened to come together on his watch. He helped make it happen. He reacted in the right way. If Reagan is lucky, if the great struggle indeed winds down soon, there will only be one proper sentence for the

Gipper, perhaps simplistic, perhaps unfair, but there it is, in big neon letters: "He won the Cold War."

If George Bush is lucky, and tough, he'll be included: "*They* won the Cold War."

January 12, 1989

Testing Bush's Vision

Early this year George Bush appeared to stumble over the most important requirement for an American president: vision, or as it was put, "The V-Thing." By summer Bush not only had a vision and spoke out about it, but it was the right one: "Freedom works."

Now, as Bush assembles a foreign policy and defense team, he and his minions should once again Think Big. Thusly: Is there a relationship of the Big V to the likely, and peculiar, nature of the 1990s? Yes. And it is more important than Star Wars, START talks, or trade balances.

To think this through, the Bushniks should trot out some old military criteria: What is the terrain? What are the conditions? What is the goal? How do you get there?

The global terrain of the '90s can be summed up in a word: "different." To begin a long list: an economically united Western Europe, a turbulent Eastern Europe, a roiling, more open Soviet Union, a booming Asia, China in a U-turn.

The global conditions, from an American point of view, are stunning. Despite talk about the economy-in-disarray and America-in-decline, there is this fact: Never has the culture of one nation been so far-flung and potent.

Consider: last year alone, 40 million VCRs were sold; the cassettes that go in them show mostly American movies and music. Important newsstands around the world now sell three American daily papers: the *International Herald-Tribune*, the *Wall Street Journal*, and *USA Today*. There is now a near-global television news station: Cable News Network.

There is, at last, a global language: American. It is the language of "Dallas" and silly sit-coms that are due for explosive growth in viewership as much foreign television is privatized and expanded.

Foreign students flock to American universities. Immigrants come to America; we take more legal immigrants than all other nations put together!

Democracy is becoming the system of choice. American political consultants peddle their wares and their wisdom in the strangest places these days. Free-market economics are touted everywhere.

Does this help us? You bet it does. Our goal in the global game is not to conquer the world, only to influence it so that is is hospitable to our values. These values should not be slavish American imitations, only rooted in ideals we have pushed forward in the global arena: political, economic, intellectual, and scientific freedom. As Bush says: "Freedom works."

Vision is the primary commodity in geopolitics today. Before his death, Germany's Franz Josef Strauss asked this: How can you change the world? He answered: Military force is now unthinkable, revolutions are usually crushed, but the contest of ideas is more potent than ever.

The pieces of the global jigsaw puzzle will be scrambled in the turmoil of the '90s. But what will the world be like when the pieces come together? If those American values are safeguarded and extended, then Bush can count himself a success.

How do you do it? You figure out what you're trying to do and build on what you've got. America has a mighty private communications business. Several government agencies do important work. Is there a need, or a way, to stimulate or encourage either public or private sectors? Is there a better way for Bush himself to make the values case in a prominent way? Are there better ways to talk publicly to the people of communist nations?

The Cold War may end in the '90s. If and when it does, the cultural equation that is then in place will determine who won it.

Culture counts. That's why freedom works. Decades ago Henry Luce wrote that the 20th century ought to be the American Century. It is George Bush's job to lead us to another century, different to be sure, but still American-inspired.

December 1, 1988

Waging Democracy

Long before there was a Soviet Union, there was a U.S. foreign policy.

That is important to remember after almost a half-century when one stark word defined our foreign policy: "anti-communist." Because that one-word foreign policy is getting harder to maintain, we should look back to our roots and get on with our job.

There is nothing wrong with a bumper sticker foreign policy, when the bumper sticker is accurate. "Anti-communist" was the right strategy when the Soviet Union was on the march and the intellectual banner of communism was flying high.

Now the Soviets are at least temporarily on the defensive. Its army was humiliated in Afghanistan. Their economy is failing. The idea of communism, Soviet-style, has become laughable.

This makes it hard to build a foreign policy based on anti-communism.

The Russians aren't coming, at least not now. That makes it difficult to keep our defense establishment well fed—even though defense is the insur ance policy needed to prevent Soviet imperial recidivism. No readily apparent threat equals no easily appropriated money.

Beyond that, America has serious interests that cannot be expressed as "anti" anything. It is time for a new bumper sticker. An American foreign policy, to be successful, must quicken the public pulse. Americans have a missionary streak, and democracy is our mission. The new sticker should read "pro-democracy." That's what it was before Lenin.

Woodrow Wilson pledged to "make the world safe for democracy." Theodore Roosevelt sought to export democracy. It wasn't perfect policy, but American values were spread.

What would make up a pro-democracy foreign policy? First, let's help some government agencies that are already in the business. The National Endowment for Democracy gives grants to private organizations in nations seeking greater freedom. NED gets about $16 million per year. Raise it to $50 million per year now and then to $250 million over time.

Radio Liberty and Radio Free Europe broadcast to the Soviet Union and the East European satellite nations. Thanks to glasnost, jamming has stopped. The stations are widely listened to, pushing communist governments to open up even further. Raise the RFE/RL budget from $200 million per year to $250 million. Wage democracy first class.

The United States Information Agency, which includes the Voice of America, runs on a budget of almost $1 billion per year. Raise it: build new VOA transmitters, reopen budget-savaged cultural centers. Budget cuts have slashed State Department spending, closing American consulates. Ridiculous! Give State more money. It's almost as if we've been running a muzzle-America foreign policy.

The foreign aid budget has been cut. It ought to be increased and sharpened—and offered only to nations defending democratic values or moving toward them.

Where is the money going to come from? When you switch from "anticommunism" to "pro-democracy," you can take some money from the defense budget. Democracy-peddling is defense spending. The best defense is an offense. Democracy is our lance.

Foreign and economic policy has a big role to play. Support pro-Western Savimbi in Angola. Keep the heat on Ortega in Nicaragua. Support El Salvador. In Latin America we should offer debt relief to democratic governments that are moving toward market-oriented economic reforms. (Typically, that debt was run up, and squandered, by earlier dictatorial regimes.)

Eastern Europe, the ancestral home of tens of millions of Americans, is where the rubber meets the road. That's where anti-communism and pro-democracy become the same policy. We ought to offer serious help as, and only as, those nations try to move toward freedom.

It's a beginning. It's the least we can do. Democracy is our destiny.
March 9, 1989

> *I'd like to publicly thank Pat Buchanan and Jesse Jackson. Whenever I have doubts, these two are always around to make it easier for me to focus my mind. They may both run for president in 1992. Buchanan is a better writer.*
>
> *Buchanan's article bashing democracy (reproduced below), which bashes my article supporting democracy, may sound bizarre, but it is a position with a lot of isolationist American history behind it.*
>
> *Too bad for Buchananite anti-democratists. Their view has been overtaken by events. There were indeed instances in the past when it could be said, with some merit, that America sometimes had to work constructively with non-democrats. After all, they were anti-communist and anti-Soviet, the Soviets had all those missiles pointed at Chevy Chase Circle, and our proper primary objective was American security. The collapse of the Soviet Union makes it easier for us to support democracies everywhere, which, in any event, are blossoming everywhere. Does Buchanan really think that's bad?*
>
> *There is another Buchanan rebuttal on page 264 and several Jackson critiques in Chapter 13. Golly, it's good to be a centrist.*

Rebuttal—by Patrick Buchanan

With Moscow's empire in crisis, anti-communism no longer seems cause enough to justify an internationalist foreign policy; hence, left and right are casting about for a new rationale.

"It is time for a new bumper sticker," Ben Wattenberg writes. "An American foreign policy, to be successful, must quicken the public pulse. Americans have a missionary streak, and democracy is our mission. The new sticker should read, 'pro-democracy.'"

A Humphrey Democrat, Wattenberg wants the GOP to "wage democracy first class" by pumping the budget for the National Endowment for Democracy 18-fold, spending more at the U.S. Information Agency and Voice of America, and beefing up the Department of State. "Budget cuts have slashed . . . spending, closing American consulates. Ridiculous! Give state more money. . . . The foreign aid budget has been cut. It ought to be increased and sharpened." In Wattenberg's vision, you and I would start paying off the huge foreign debts of Latin nations that move toward market reform. "Democracy is our destiny."

"Messianic globaloney," Dean Acheson's phrase, needs dusting off; and Wattenberg needs to take a long, cold shower.

We are not the world's policeman, nor its political tutor.

Whence comes this arrogant claim to determine how other nations should govern themselves, or face subversion by NED, the Comintern of the neocons?

What have the "democracies" done for America lately?

When we were fighting in Vietnam, Gen. Park Chung Hee of South Korea and Philippine President Ferdinand Marcos sent troops; the democracies traded with the enemy.

When Richard M. Nixon rescued Israel in the '73 war, authoritarian Portugal permitted the use of its Azores base, while other NATO allies said no.

Democratic India sided with Moscow in Afghanistan, while Gen. Mohammad Zia ul-Haq, at the cost of his life, gave us one of the triumphs of the Cold War. Who was America's friend, the democrat or the autocrat?

Of late, NED has been funding the opposition in Chile and South Africa. Why? A soldier-patriot like Spain's Francisco Franco, Gen. Augusto Pinochet saved his country from an elected Marxist who was steering Chile into Castroism. Why was he an enemy to be subverted?

The Boer Republic is the only viable economy in Africa. Why are Americans collaborating in a U.N. conspiracy to ruin her with sanctions? Anyone think the ascension to power of the African National Congress will be better for them—or for us? What the devil are we doing down there?

Years ago, when we learned that Pretoria might secretly buy *The Washington Star*, we were full of high dudgeon about this co-opting of the free press. What, then, entitles us to subsidize newspapers undermining regimes that have done no injury to the United States?

Conservatives exploded when Earl Warren gutted federalism to impose his one-man, one-vote dictum on every state, county, city and school board in America. How, then, demand that other peoples be governed by this democratist ideology?

Conservative principles do not sanction democracy worship; it is liberal idolatry masquerading as conservative orthodoxy.

There are 150-plus nations in the United Nations. Wattenberg's Mission Democracy is a prescription for endless and seditious meddling in the affairs of nations whose institutions are shaped by their own history, culture, traditions and values, not ours. Democracy *über alles* is a formula for permanent conflict and national bankruptcy.

In the Moslem world, there are few democracies; yet, when President Ronald Reagan needed aid for the abandoned Contras, the sultan of Brunei and the king of Saudi Arabia answered the call, while Europe sent money to the Sandinistas. Who proved to be America's friend?

In South America, democrat is synonymous with deadbeat; in Africa, with dead. ("Your black African does not like dissent," the foreign minister of South Africa lectured me years ago, "and he does not long tolerate dissent." Was Botha wrong?)

Will Namibia be better off if the majority Ovambo tribe votes into power, democratically, of course, Marxist guerrilla Sam Nujoma?

Whether the man who rules in Bujumbura or Buenos Aires wears a business suit or a military blouse is not our concern, so long as he does not make of his nation an enemy of the United States.

Have we forgotten our history? In our war for independence, we were allied to the King of France, Louis XVI, against the Mother of Parliaments; in the War of 1812, our enemy was the Duke of Wellington; our de facto ally was the dictator Napoleon.

"We should go back to our roots," Wattenberg avers. Yes, indeed; but those roots go back before the bankrupt internationalism of Woodrow Wilson. A century before Wilson retired, a broken man, John Quincy Adams said:

"America does not go abroad in search of monsters to destroy. She is the well-wisher to the freedom and independence of all. She is champion and vindicator only of her own. . . . She well knows that by once enlisting under other banners than her own, were they even the banners of foreign independence, she would involve herself beyond the power of extrication in all the wars of interest and intrigue, of individual avarice, envy and ambition which assume the colors and usurp the standards of freedom."

Wilson forgot this wise counsel; and, when this Cold War is over, America should come home.

September 18, 1989

Pat Buchanan, Come Home

Did some liberal at the Harvard Lampoon steal conservative columnist Patrick Buchanan's computer slug and file a spoof that then appeared in newspapers under Buchanan's byline?

Judge for yourself. In a recent column Buchanan deals with whether America should vigorously encourage the growth of democracy around the world. Buchanan says no.

Buchanan says that real conservatives can't sanction "democracy worship," and that from its outset America has been on the team of dictators and monarchs. Buchanan speaks admiringly of Pinochet, South Africa and Marcos. Buchanan says let's cheer for the non-democratic Moslem nations.

Buchanan—yes Buchanan, not Jane Fonda—says America ought to "come home" because we're "not the world's policeman nor its political tutor." He asks, "What have the 'democracies' done for us lately?"

It does sound like a put-on. After all, it's what liberals have said Buchanan-ism is about—ham-handed, neanderthal conservatism—and liberals are wrong about those things. In real life Buchanan is a very smart fellow: premier conservative controversialist, author of a splendid autobiography (*Right from the Beginning*), counselor to presidents.

But, alas, Buchanan's creed against exporting democracy is no parody. Columnist Charles Krauthammer, a wise man, says it figures: paleo-conservatives like Buchanan will head back to isolationism as the Soviets fade away.

Perhaps. I hope not. Buchanan's primal scream may be Buchanan-specific, and possibly transitory. Most conservatives, even the old-fashioned kind, have gotten smart.

Buchanan was rebutting a column of mine in which I said that as the Cold War ends our foreign policy ought to change from "anti-communist" to "pro-democracy." Why? Because it's in our national interest, and it's moral. Most conservatives, even the old-fashioned kind, know that.

Buchanan says democracies haven't helped us recently. But West Europeans drafted their youth, and spent trillions, to join us in holding the line against Soviet expansionism in Europe.

More important than what democracies do is what they don't do, like start wars against other democracies. More democracy means we spend less on defense. But dictatorships, right and left, often do nasty things to democracies. We've seen it too often during this bloody century, and most conservatives, even old-fashioned ones, know that.

Democratic governments don't blow up our airliners; the Libyans, Iranians and Syrians who do are run by dictators. Most conservatives, even the old-fashioned kind, know that.

We should also peddle democracy to those who want it because freedom is moral, and its economic handmaiden—the free market—yields prosperity. Conservatives, especially the old-fashioned kind, know that.

In the 1930s, American conservatives were mesmerized by the slogan "America First," which left us naked to our enemies. But recently, fortunately, conservatives have been among the best champions of democratic internationalism (along with sensible liberals). Not accidentally, American values flourished everywhere. Most conservatives, of all stripes, know that.

Ironically, even some isolationist hyper-liberals now know it. Disgusted with China, buoyed by reform in Eastern Europe, reading election returns, there are exotic liberals who are becoming commie-bashers and democracy worshippers. They waffled on the Vietcong and Sandinistas, but now want to drive a stake through communism's heart in Poland. Just when we get some left-right togetherness, Buchanan jumps ship!

The goal of recent American foreign policy has been to create a user-friendly world for our values. We still need all the help we can get. Philosopher Leszek Kolakowski notes there are other goblins out there besides communists. (Anarchy and fanaticism are two.) Without many democratic allies, our values may not end up regnant. An America First policy can yield a world where America isn't first.

The Cold War is probably ending. Let's not only end it, but win it. Play offense, America. Extend democracy.

Pat Buchanan: Your troops won't follow you on this one. Conservatives have wised up. Come home, Buchanan.

September 27, 1989

Another Peace Dividend

Let us say a word about the folks who brought us the spectacular summit in Malta, and the end of the Cold War. They shaped the modern world. They may keep on doing it.

Who did it? Americans, that's who. For almost half a century they ponied up both the bucks and the votes to lead an alliance to success in the effort to keep the Soviets in their pen until they finally came to their senses.

What do those successful Americans think about things now? Americans are bored. And cautious, hopeful, ready to help, and ready to do business. They are also damn proud. Americans don't know it yet, but they are going to get an unexpected bonus from all of this.

Bored? Of course. When things are going well people in democracies are bored by public affairs, perhaps properly so. Accordingly, the television programming about the incredible political events in Eastern Europe have not drawn big ratings. Poland. Then Hungary, East Germany, and Czechoslovakia. Enough already. Message received. Americans are saying, and it's great. Now, let's see some pictures about a kid trapped in a well, an earthquake, trapped whales, or those crooked politicians.

And cautious. You bet. Americans are smarter than experts. That's clearly revealed in the "public opinion report" section of the forthcoming wonderful brand new magazine called *The American Enterprise,* published by the American Enterprise Institute. (I work at the American Enterprise Institute. The preceding will be nominated for a Guiness-level mentioning spasm.)

The collected recent public opinion surveys (from Gallup, Roper, NBC, etc.) show that most Americans believe that Gorbachev is different from previous Soviet leaders, that he can be trusted more, that he is more peacefully inclined, and that he is sincerely trying to open the Soviet economic and political systems.

But most Americans also believe that communism is the worst form of government. They believe that the Soviet Union is still a major global actor, potentially aggressive, and that it might revert to evil ways. (Gorbachev's Maltese stonewalling on Central America offers a hint.) Most Americans believe that the United States should go very slowly before drawing down its defense budget. They do not believe that George Bush has been too slow in responding to Gorby's dramatic moves.

Americans like Gorbachev a lot. Gorby has learned Reagan's secret: If you denounce Soviet life and Soviet policy, people think you're wonderful.

Americans, despite their cautious skepticism, are ready to play in the new world. Foreign aid is almost invariably regarded as a bummer by Americans. Yet, today, Americans favor economic aid to Poland, Hungary and East Germany.

Alas, pollsters don't always ask all the right questions. The unasked question in the survey is the most important one. This: Are you proud of what the United States has done?

But you know the answer. It is *Yes*. That affirmation will provide the political force to let America keep on shaping history. Americans like what they did, and they're going to keep doing it.

In years to come, Americans will get a dividend from what they have accomplished. Human beings seek a transcendent role in life; they want to do something larger and greater than themselves.

Shakespeare said it in *Henry V*. The king addresses his troops prior to the battle of Agincourt. "He which hath no stomach to this fight, let him depart . . . But we in it shall be remembered; we few, we happy few, we band of brothers; for he today that shed his blood with me shall be my brother. . . . Gentlemen in England now a-bed shall think themselves accursed they were not here, and hold their manhoods cheap whiles any speaks that fought with us upon St. Crispin's day."

Americans were there on St. Crispin's Day. They held the line. They won probably the most important, and certainly the most costly, ideological conflict in history. They shaped the world. They should tell their grandchildren war stories about it, or rather, Cold War stories. They're entitled.

December 6, 1989

Peddling Neo-manifest Destinarianism

The argument now concerns The American Purpose. If it can be defined, perhaps we can do something about it.

It can. We can. What? Consider neo-manifest destinarianism.

Until recently, our national purpose was imposed: Keep the free world free. As communism collapsed, options expanded. Theories bloom.

The Declinists said America would no longer be "Number One" because we were "over-stretched" militarily. Their remedy: Cut the defense budget, manage our decline gracefully. We will cut defense. The Declinists still want us to decline ourselves. They don't like being Number One.

Pat Buchanan bangs the lead tambourine for The Isolationists, a conservative rap group. His recent contribution, in *The National Interest* magazine, is "America First—and Second, and Third." Buchanan says our foreign policy should only be in our national interest. How original. To Buchanan that means we should "come home" and stop peddling that silly democracy stuff. But doesn't the spread of democracy enhance our national interest? His title is two-thirds accurate. The Buchanistas would make it more likely that America would be second or third.

Charles Krauthammer and Joseph Nye, coming from different directions, make more sense. Both know that America will remain Number One. Both believe ideology will play a lesser role. Both know that we must remain a big time global actor. But toward what end?

Krauthammer sees a "unipolar" world. America would coalesce with its democratic industrial allies, establishing stability and "binding political connections." He says this means "the conscious depreciation not only of American sovereignty, but of the notion of sovereignty generally." Gulp.

Nye's book, *Bound to Lead*, solidly rebuts the Declinists. America should aim at "managing transnational interdependence" to form a free, peaceful, prosperous, free-trading global community. You get to MTI through the global organizational alphabet soup: GATT, IMF, NPT, IEA, IAEA.

All right. But no one is going for the gold. And so we come to neo-manifest destinarianism.

We ought to wage democracy—remembering that the mansion of democracy has many rooms. Democracy American-style, a way of life as well as a political system, is not the same as, say, the pinched stultification of Swedish-style democracy. And in Eastern Europe today, it's said by some that the newly free countries should go Swedish.

American taxpayers didn't spend trillions to create more Swedens. Not long ago we were troubled by the Swedish—read European—model. It was seen as stagnant, decadent and even "creeping socialism." Fortunately, since then, they and we have gotten better.

If the world evolves toward European-style social democracy, or some democratic hybrid, or some unipolar transnationalism, so be it. We and our allies will have won a free world. But that result is only acceptable. As the last superpower, we ought to try to shape evolution.

Americans have always felt they had something special to offer. This sense of mission was once called Manifest Destiny. At times it went overboard, into distant geographic expansion and wild-eyed cultural imperialism. We know now we can't clone the world American-style.

But American democracy has distinctive features. Most Americans believe most of them are beneficial. Individualism, pluralism, opportunity, dynamism, and the absence of a rigid class structure come to mind.

As democracy surges, different features of many free systems will be pushed toward synthesis. There will be a contest for the culture.

We ought not be passive players. We have the most, and best arrows in our quiver. These include our global entertainment monopoly, immigration, the spreading English language, the prime tourist destination, the best universities, the most powerful and far-flung military, an opportunity society and a worldwide information operation.

Without going sky-high on foreign aid, or neglecting the home front, or leaning too much on government, or becoming messianic—how can we, in our self-interest, go about boosting the writ of the American vision? That will be the topic of a later piece.

In the meantime, remember this about American Purpose: A unipolar world is fine, if America is the uni.

March 21, 1990

The Contest for the Culture

The elusive search for a new emphasis for American post-Cold War foreign policy need not be so elusive. It is as close as a dollar bill.

To review the bidding, as described in this space earlier:

- In large part due to modern communications, democracy is winning the world series. The global contest will not concern whether, but what kind of, democratic values will be influential.
- Today, America is No. 1, more powerful than ever, the omni-power. In the future, the No. 1 country will be the one that is most successful in shaping the global democratic culture.
- Only the American democratic culture has legs. Only Americans have the sense of mission—and gall—to engage in benign, but energetic, global cultural advocacy. Hence, the doctrine of "neo-manifest destinarianism," to help form a world that is user-friendly to American values.

If communications of values is the key, how do we get fully engaged? How to assure that American concepts of (for example) pluralism, capitalism, upward mobility, individualism, and opportunity become better understood?

There are things that government can do. There are conditions that government can only encourage. (There are plenty of things the government ought to stay out of.) Here are a few examples, big and small:

Our government communication policy is penny-wise-penny-foolish. Because of budget strictures, the Voice of America (VOA) recently had to consider cutting language services. Ridiculous.

Some budget-cutters say we should cancel a new American short-wave transmitter, now under construction in Israel, designed to carry VOA and

Radio Liberty into the Moslem areas of the USSR. It's said the Soviets are no longer our adversaries. Maybe. But won't the omni-power (us) still have something to say to the Moslems of Central Asia, when Moslems are the fastest growing and most volatile segment of the global population?

Most Americana, luckily, is spread by non-governmental means. But shouldn't the government, if possible, encourage such enterprises?

All commerce is not equal. The export of widgets is important. But more important is that American television programs and movies have fair access in other countries, that the English language spreads, that it is easier for tourists, teachers, and students to come to America.

The global entertainment business is largely American. Yet, television programs and movies are not included in the General Agreement on Trade and Tariffs (GATT). That makes it difficult for us to keep foreign markets open and fair. But one reason entertainment is GATT-less is that Congress is under domestic pressure to keep the American maritime industry un-GATTed. That gives foreigners a case to keep entertainment out of the GATT negotiations. GATT it? In the American interest, box office beats boats.

America is the No. 1 tourist draw. People aren't coming here just to see the Grand Canyon. Tourists absorb a sense of the American experience and take it home. Yet, of the free countries, we have the most stringent visa requirements. Other nations subsidize hostels so that young foreigners can visit. We don't.

There are 50,000 Russian language teachers in Eastern Europe. These are skilled instructors—but now without students. They want to learn English, and teach it. Let them study in our universities. In return, they could teach American students about the nature of evil empires. More important, they could teach it to our faculty members.

We ought to help more foreign students study here. About 2 million per year want to, but only about 350,000 can afford it. We also ought to help American universities set up branches overseas.

We ought to take in more immigrants; they are the greatest global gossipers.

Emphasizing the contest for the culture wouldn't diminish other forms of foreign policy. Promoting American-style democracy doesn't contradict promoting just-plain-democracy. It should not diminish traditional diplomacy, or necessary military muscle, or geopolitical gamesmanship. The policy is enhancement, not replacement.

Why? On the dollar bill, you will find the Great Seal of the United States with the Latin words "Novus ordo seclorum"—"a new order for the ages," words as old as America and as fresh as tomorrow. It's what we do for a living.

May 2, 1990

*The Bush administration has not done a very good job on this. A
vigorous expansion of America's effort in public diplomacy has the
following advantages: it is inexpensive, it would have enthusiastic
bi-partisan political support, it would be very popular with the
American people, it would demonstrate that there is vision in
high places. It has an added advantage: it's the right thing to do.*

It is hard to believe the transformation of the role of the media
during the 1980s in the great game of geopolitics. Early in the decade,
on a certain level, in certain ways, in the ongoing attempt to wage
the struggle for hearts and minds, journalists could often be a first-
class pain. No more; now they're the good guys.

What geopolitical lessons were in the air in the early 1980s? Those
that came from the advent of important new communications tools
such as lightweight television cameras and television satellites. Alas,
in the beginning, in a powerful manner, the communications
lessons made it more difficult for free nations to operate in the real
world.

Remember the wars: Afghanistan, Iran-Iraq, El Salvador, the
Falklands, and Lebanon. And consider, from yesterday's vantage point,
the rules of the road.

Communist countries could wage brutal wars and pay little for it.
The nightly news almost ignored Afghanistan because the television
cameras couldn't get in to witness the poison gas and the maimed
children. No access, no horror. So too for non-free, non-communist
countries. The Iran-Iraq war was a slaughter, but no television cameras
were allowed to record the young Iranian boys blown to smithereens
as they served as human mine detectors. No cameras, no news. No
news, no outrage. No outrage, no penalty.

But the new rules for democracies were quite different. They could
wage tiny wars on tiny islands, like Grenada and the Falklands, where
they could control the press for a few moments.

But if the battlefield was in an open country, it was very tough
sledding. America provided military aid and 50 advisers in the civil
war in El Salvador. The advisers were outnumbered by journalists.
The coverage made the Americans appear at times like conspiratorial,
lying butchers. They weren't.

And in a real land war involving a democracy, beware of the wrath
of the world. Israel and Lebanon hosted plenty of television crews.
Because censorship in open countries is porous, the horror, chaos,
and deceit that any war produces were almost immediately in the

Indicators: *Communications*

A. Video cassette recorders (VCRs) took off first in Western Europe but are now more prevalent in the U.S.

1. VCRs in Use as a Percentage of Western European and American Households

Year	W. European	American
1982	13%	3%
1983	17%	6%
1984	21%	11%
1985	26%	21%
1986	30%	36%
1987	35%	49%
1988	41%	58%
1989	46%	65%
1990	52% (est.)	68%

B. English, which barely existed one thousand years ago, has become the global language. Although about the same number of people speak Chinese, English is much more widespread.

English Speakers in the World (in Millions)

Year	Total English Speakers	Secondary English Speakers*
900	0	0
1600	6	0
1960	583	300
1986	700	375
1990	1,000	610

* See note.

Source notes are on page 397.

C. Countries receiving Super Bowl telecasts

Year	Countries
1967	2
1978	6
1990	60

D. Cable TV is attracting viewers the world over.

Countries Receiving CNN Signals

Year	Countries
1982	2
1983	6
1984	12
1985	20
1986	44
1987	55
1988	73
1990	90

E. American film companies' sales in foreign markets are climbing rapidly.

Major Studio Revenues Coming from Exports (in Millions)

Year	Exports	Total Revenues	Percent
1984	$ 654	$1,967	33%
1985	$ 620	$1,729	36%
1986	$ 798	$1,963	41%
1987	$ 935	$2,180	43%
1988	$1,020	$2,434	42%
1989	$1,347	$3,127	43%

global living room with a new intensity and thoroughness, thanks to
the new technology. In war, access will equal horror.

The Israelis complained that they were unfairly held up to a double
standard. It was more serious than that. The new rules of media
warfare established a double standard for all open societies.

That was important. The use of force and, more crucially, the
threat of the use of force or the possibility of the use of force, is
always a part of the global geopolitical equation. The nature of
television demands that it show whatever horror is available. Our
adversaries' horror was not available. (Not then.) Ours was. That
imbalance unwittingly presented our adversaries with a great gift.
Relatively untouchable by public opinion, at home or abroad, due
to censorship or lack of access, they could use the threat of force in
a harsh world. It was much more difficult for us. Although there
are some airhead correspondents, this situation was not, at root, the
fault of television; it was the burden of the glory of a free press.

Remarkably, by the end of the eighties, much of that equation
had been neutralized. The lightweight cameras, satellites, radio beams,
fax machines, VCRs penetrated further than imagined: in the
Philippines, in Chile, and in the communist lands. American networks
covered rebellion in China, ethnic unrest in the Soviet republics,
stark demand for democratic change in Poland, Hungary, East
Germany, Romania, and Czechoslovakia. They did a mediocre but
useful job of setting the stage for free elections in Nicaragua.

There was, finally, a somewhat reachable public opinion in unfree and totalitarian lands.

Moreover, because of economic failure, the totalitarians needed
public support from the free nations. They wouldn't get it if they
were seen to be murderers, appearing on television sets all over the
world.

The playing field of public affairs media became more level, and
on a level playing field, the good guys win.

The writ of modern communications extends far beyond public
affairs. As never before, movies, television, radio, music, magazines,
and books show an alternative life-style to the world's billions. Because
the United States—for poetic, mystical, and quite rational reasons—
runs a near-monopoly on international entertainment, we have a
long leg up in the contest for the culture.

VCRs Change the World

It was reported last week that in the month of October more than 1 million video-cassette recorders were sold in the United States!

In a season of summitry, we might consider how popular technology—like VCRs—can change global politics more than even Reagan and Gorbachev.

Some numbers: There are now VCRs in about 30 percent of American households. There are about 100 million sets in the world. (See page 207.) Costs have come way down. You can get a basic model now for $190.

Who gains from this technological explosion? The Japanese build the sets. But Americans make most of the movies. They have the hardware. We have the software.

You can make money on both, but the software has a political payoff as well. The advent of the VCR vastly multiplies the numbers of people who will see the movie version of America.

It's happening everywhere. In Western Europe our movies are more accessible than ever before: A rental fee is cheaper than two theater tickets and a baby sitter. In poor countries, people watch "E.T." in remote villages that do not even get a television signal. There are no movie theaters in Saudi Arabia: the sheiks stay home and watch "Beverly Hills Cop."

The tantalizing question concerns to what extent the VCR will penetrate the Iron Curtain. It is already common in some of the satellites of Eastern Europe.

The Soviet Union is a tougher nut to crack. Yet, it is happening. The Soviets tried to produce VCRs, but, alas, the sets turned out so badly the government can't even unload them on yokels in the provinces. However, it is legal for Soviet citizens to buy foreign VCRs in Eastern Europe. Soviet visitors returning from the United States stock up on VCRs before going home.

Pre-recorded tapes are another matter. They are deemed subversive. They cannot be legally brought in to the Soviet Union but they have arrived. It is already enough of a problem that an entire group was arrested for watching a Western movie.

The VCR is a danger to a totalitarian state. Unlike a foreign radio signal, it can't be jammed. Unlike a book, a tape can be easily reproduced. And what the tapes show is devastating; they are popular, musical, thrilling, violent, vibrant, visual, seamy and sexy—just what people like to watch.

Many of us in America complain that American movies and television only show the bad side of things. But that is a relative view. If "Miami

Vice" is shown in Moscow, what the viewers will notice is that even American slum-dwellers own cars.

The Soviets always try to stop the penetration of technology that disseminates free ideas. And they are always only partially successful. Despite jamming, Western radio signals get in. Audio cassettes ("Magnitizdat") are used to record protest songs.

It won't be many years until taped American movies and television may be a somewhat familiar, if illegal, sight in the U.S.S.R. Just imagine: "Rambo" in Russia! "Kramer vs. Kramer" in Kharkov! "Nine to Five" in Novosibirsk! "Ghostbusters" in Gorki!

Does all this help America? You bet. After all the summit talk of missiles, let's remember that the ultimate contest between East and West will probably be settled in the minds of men.

Gorbachev came to the summit spouting off that America is the land of monopoly repression, a land that is anti-Semitic and anti-black, full of hungry, homeless and unemployed people.

Our movies, now proliferating everywhere, show a different view to the foreign eye: materialism beyond belief, excitement, technical virtuosity and the freedom to be critical—very critical. Which is a pretty good menu of what the rest of the world wants.

November 21, 1985

America's Global Culture

The most recent figures showed the U.S. trade deficit growing deeper again. The usual suspects have tsk-tsked that America is a debtor nation, that everyone everywhere is out-competing us, that we're not innovative enough or productive enough, that Japan is a rising sun, that America is a setting sun.

But for another view of how the world spins, consider some other trade facts and figures:

In France the movie theaters basically show French movies and American movies.

In Japan the movie theaters basically show Japanese movies and American movies.

In Japan they show almost no French movies. In France they show almost no Japanese movies.

In America the movie theaters basically show American movies.

What's going on? American movies—from "Rambo" to "Rain Man"—are very popular around the world. In 1988, foreigners paid $1.1 billion dollars for the rights to show American movies. That's up 41 percent just since 1985.

If you think movies are off the charts, consider television. "Dallas" and "Hill Street" are on the air everywhere. This time series, compiled by the Security Pacific Merchant Bank, shows the sales of American programming to foreign broadcasters:

> 1987—$1.0 billion
> 1988—$1.3 billion (estimated)
> 1989—$1.7 billion (projected)
> 1990—$2.3 billion (projected)

By comparison, in 1988 America paid about $100 million for the rights to foreign movies and television programming combined. (The ratio is about 25 to 1.)

There are similar reports from the music, book and VCR businesses. Foreigners listen to our music, read our books, watch our tapes. We don't much read, watch, or listen to their stuff.

Is it that Americans are provincial, insular, parochial boors? More likely is that we have a taste for just what the rest of the world now enjoys: American popular culture. American mass culture—for all its ills and all its glory—has become the only broad-based global culture there is.

That fact has some ramifications.

First· Perhaps we ought to stop complaining about "foreigners buying up America." Are you concerned that the office building in which you work is owned by a Japanese bank? Don't be. The building is going to stay right where it is: you'll never know the difference. But how would you like it if you turned on your television and saw Japanese sitcoms? Or went to the movies and saw Japanese feature films? That's real invasion, and more important than who made the widgets in your car. Other nations fear American cultural penetration. Sometimes they try to repel it via "cultural protectionism." Some Europeans are trying that now. But, sooner or later, it becomes pervasive.

Second: This trend is likely to grow. Cable and satellite television are expanding as Europe moves toward economic integration in 1992. More people everywhere are moving into middle-class brackets that allow some time and money to enjoy entertainment.

Third: Foreigners are trying to buy some of our popular entertainment companies. Germans own Doubleday; Sony now owns CBS Records. Japanese interests are looking at Hollywood studios. But the sale of an American entertainment company is different from other takeovers. Foreign companies don't seek to replace American popular culture with their own. They are buying in order to make money by selling more American culture to more places. As Jack Valenti of the Motion Picture Association of America says,

"Entertainment isn't fungible. You can't clone an American movie. It must be infused with American talent, or it won't feel American."

And finally this: We are the most culturally potent nation the world has ever seen, and becoming even more so. Is it possible that such a nation, or a culture, is in decline?

April 27, 1989

Well, it is said, sure, American popular culture is washing across the global flood plain, but who sez that's good? American popular culture is glitz and sex and violence and vapidity and materialism and raucous music.

That is true, but incomplete. American popular culture is also musical comedy, NBA, basketball, jeans, Katherine Hepburn, Bill Cosby, Dixieland, progressive jazz, CNN, James Michener, Paul Newman, Archie Bunker, Beverly Sills, the International Herald Tribune, *Steven Spielberg, Michael Jordan, Kermit the Frog, John Updike, Simon and Garfunkel, Jack Nicholson, Berlitz schools, and Berlin songs.*

American popular culture, we are told, is also anti-establishment and left-wing, and, alternatively, a hidden tool of capitalist interests. (I lean toward the former view.)

That's not the point. The point is that it is market-tested. The Hollywood people, the news people, the cable people, the cassette people are trying to sell something in a highly competitive arena. They are very good salespersons. Why, just in April of 1990 the California glitz-merchants held a trade exhibit called the Academy Awards. It was watched on television, in 94 countries, by about a billion people. They watched because, typically, they are at least mildly addicted to American programming, the only universal currency in the entertainment business.

Some global buyers like glitz and glamor. Some like Sills and Spielberg. Some like basketball and Bunker.

Our media merchants sell them what they want, including mud wrestling.

As technology and media deregulation flower almost everywhere we can make this statement: for the first time in history most people in the world will be able to watch, read, and listen to what they want. What they want, for the moment at least, is American. That is to our advantage, and probably theirs.

The only alternative is elemental: someone, somewhere, will tell the global audience what they should like and try to control the choices. And if it's not me doing it, I'm against it.

Which leaves the question of "Why?" Why is American popular culture so potent so far from home?

It is not because Americans happen to be the best moviemakers and television show makers, although they are.

It's not because American journalists, authors, musicians, and essayists are better than non-Americans; they are not.

It is not because all those American lefties in entertainment-land have such a beautiful and coherent vision of how the world ought to work; they don't.

There is an invisible hand at work, and American cultural potency is important because that hand is working. Our movies, television, music, books, and journalism reflect American values, the American way of life if you will.

It is that content, whether reflected favorably or unfavorably, that brings people to the box office. That content is more powerful than politics or economics. It drives politics and economics.

Alright, but what is it? Here are some words, make your own sentence: open, mobile, individualistic, anti-establishment, pluralistic, voluntaristic, populist, dynamic, and free. My favorite is the last one. It's the word that is changing the world in every way you can think of.

Still the Heavyweight Champ

Big trouble in Washington. It was nut-shelled recently on ABC's "Nightline." Here are excerpts:

> TED KOPPEL: As foreign news continues to dominate the headlines and the airwaves, the question is becoming more persistent: is Washington becoming less important?
>
> DAVID BRODER (*Washington Post*): This is a city which has accustomed itself to thinking of itself as the center of the political universe. . . . It's a bit of a shock to recognize that we're no longer there.
>
> JEFF GREENFIELD (ABC): That sense was crystallized by David Broder, perhaps the single most influential journalist in Washington, in a recent column that became, literally, the talk of the town.
>
> DAVID BRODER: It was as if somebody had said, "Oh, the emperor really does have no clothes." Sometimes you get the biggest reaction by stating the obvious.

Among the notables endorsing the Washington-in-Retreat theme are David Brinkley, elder statesman Clark Clifford, liberal historian Arthur Schlesinger, Jr., and editors of *The New Republic* magazine.

They discovered that this year's Washington news is just like last year's

(Brinkley), that the age of superpowers is over and the government doesn't spend enough (Schlesinger), that the thrills are gone (Morton Kondracke, *The New Republic*), that Washington is in decline because America is the biggest debtor nation, that Congress doesn't play enough of a role (!), and there are too many murders (Clifford).

The television cameras, notes Broder, have gone overseas. That is one indicator that Washington's claim to being the "most important city in the world" may now be "as dented as Mike Tyson's heavyweight crown."

Wrong. Washington did not lose the heavyweight championship of the world. It won it.

There is some topsy-turvy logic to the shrinking-Washington thesis. Can Washington be less important, Tyson-wise, because communism collapsed, or was whipped, or both? Did Joe Montana become less important when the 49ers won the Super Bowl? Did Dwight Eisenhower, or America, become irrelevant when World War II was won?

There is journalistic myopia in it. The coverage of Lithuania is in significant measure an American and Washington story because it is about the collapse of the Soviet empire, a process that can lead to a second American Century. Hiroshima and Vietnam were American stories, even though the cameras were far away.

There is governmental myopia about it. Broder quotes politicians saying that Washington is politically gridlocked. With the tax-and-budget Snore Summit in motion for the 173rd time, that is hard to rebut, except frontally.

Washington is indeed not as much about government and programs as it was. But is that bad? Americans (and people everywhere) have been voting for the idea that there are more important things than government programs.

There is a yearning for the bad old days:

> HENDRIK HERTZBERG (*The New Republic*): People are talking about how it doesn't matter anymore, looking back with great nostalgia at things like Watergate. Remember Watergate?

Yup. Watergate was Washington as the politics and morality capital of America. Journalists and liberals loved it. We haven't been close to such a rich scandal since Iran-contra pooped out.

Now, Hertzberg makes sense about the personal reaction to communism's demise: ". . . that kind of struggle . . . infuses your whole life and gives it meaning. When it's over, there's a terrible letdown." True. And for those in Washington who have been energized by programs, politics and scandal, the letdown is worse.

But Washington is moving beyond programs, politics and scandal. It is the capital of the whole United States, reflecting America's flaws and America's flowering.

It is no accident that Washington is growing rapidly, a burgeoning center of international trade, with high-tech wonder suburbs, home to most of America's business and trade associations, still the news capital of the world, shaping telecommunications at the Federal Communications Commission and the future size and composition of America via a new immigration law.

All that and more flows in large part from the fact that Washington is the capital of the nation that won the heavyweight title and remains the most important place in the world.

May 16, 1990

9

The Soviet Union

In the course of writing and putting together this book, I have learned a firsthand, if once-removed, lesson about the sweeping effects of the changes in the Soviet Union.

Reading through my columns of the past few years, I attempted to sort out those that retained relevance from those that didn't. I found out several interesting things. The Soviet erosion touched almost everything, rendering some columns overtaken by events but also making some prescient columns irrelevant because they have subsequently come true. (Both categories have been mostly eliminated. Would you really like to know that I wrote early, very early, about how the Soviet public was turning against the war in Afghanistan? Pin a rose on me.)

What changed? East–West relations, obviously. Central America, yes. Our defense budget, of course. What we can spend money on because we think we won't have to spend it on defense, you bet. (Children's allowance, anyone?) Japan's attitude: They can be much more cocky if they don't need us to keep the Soviets at bay. Israel's situation: the Arabs don't have a superpower patron any more, but that also means that the United States has more options to squeeze Israel, because Israel cannot as powerfully or credibly plead potential apocalypse. Iraq: lacking Soviet support, in a crunch, they were weakened immeasurably.

What about the Democratic Party? As shall be noted subsequently, a case is made by some that the Soviet erosion can help the Democrats.

It's easier to ask what hasn't been affected.

The Soviet collapse not only causes change, it was caused by change. The market economies boomed while the communist economies failed. The West went on an ideological offensive and was persuasive. Modern communications were able to penetrate the Iron Curtain. Global hatred, literally hatred, for the Soviet system grew.

The entries that follow deal with cause and effect, effect and cause. When all the geopolitics and georhetoric is stripped away, it becomes apparent that the most destabilizing factor in the recent modern world has been that one of the superpowers has not had democratic governance. Democracies are not aggressors. As, and if, the Soviet Union continues to move further down the path of democracy, the world will become more peaceful and productive in the nineties. And, of course, the United States will be the only superpower left, an omni-power.

Reader: a confession. Until the very final page proofs of this book were edited, in August of 1990, there were contingency plans to drop some new material into pre-existing slots within this chapter on the Soviet Union. The new stuff would deal with the breakup, collapse, fragmentation, civil war, anarchy, or total chaos in the Soviet Union. However, by August 1990, none of that had quite happened. That doesn't mean at least some of that won't happen. There are plenty of signs.

There are some other things I don't know about the Soviet Union. There is that nice story about who's in control of the nukes. Don't worry, some say, they're all in the hands of highly disciplined Russian KGB folks. Worry plenty, others say, ethnic groups in the various Soviet republics could grab some of those weapons. If it will let you sleep any better, you might consider this: if some of the ethnic groups do get control of a couple of weapons, they'd be much more likely to point them at Moscow than at the United States. Sleep tight.

Regarding the Soviet economic future: Somebody has got to tell those people that a market economy is what you get when you do nothing. It kind of grows. Then you regulate it. You don't get it by regulating, re-regulating, and figuring out new governmental planning schemes. In mid-1990 I was at a conference where a grand Soviet economic thinker told the group that the Soviets were so far behind in economic thinking, they would have to spend a generation educating an economic elite so they could get to a market economy.

Help! Dropping an economic elite upon a nation is what you do to an enemy. If you think you must teach sex to teenagers in order to get sex, then it is logical to believe that you must teach market economics to new elites in order to get market economics. Markets are doin' what comes nachurly. The growing Soviet black market is the best thing they have going for them. They ought to encourage it, then regulate it.

Indicators: USSR

A. There has been a marked shift in attitudes towards the Soviet Union.

Q. Is the Soviet Union more a force for peace in the world or is the Soviet Union more a threat to peace in the world?

Year	Force for Peace	Threat to Peace
1983	6%	90%
1989	46%	38%

Source notes are on page 397.

B. Americans disapprove of Communism.

Q. Thinking about different forms of governments in the world today, which of these statements comes closest to how you feel about Communism?

Year	The Worst Kind	Bad, But No Worse Than Some	All Right for Some	A Good Form
1973–4	47%	27%	22%	3%
1980 & 82	60%	26%	13%	1%
1988–9	49%	34%	16%	2%

C. Americans no longer find the Soviet Union objectionable.

Q. Are your opinions of the Soviet Union generally favorable, generally unfavorable, or neutral?

Year	Favorable	Neutral	Unfavorable
1979	15%	38%	41%
1987	15%	40%	41%
1989 (May)	30%	43%	24%
1989 (November)	30%	54%	13%

D. Americans have come to see the USSR as more of a rival than an enemy.

Q. In your opinion, which of the following best describes Russia's primary objective in world affairs?

Year	Only to Protect Itself	To Compete with the U.S. for Influence	Global Domination Without Risking a Major War	Even Risking a Major War
1978	7%	25%	34%	23%
1980 (Feb.)	5%	18%	34%	39%
1980 (Nov.)	5%	21%	38%	28%
1983	9%	23%	34%	29%
1985	8%	29%	35%	20%
1988 (Jan.)	12%	34%	33%	11%
1988 (July)	10%	40%	29%	9%
1989 (Aug.)	12%	41%	26%	11%
1990	16%	44%	18%	7%

218

Soviets Decimated and Diminished!

As we approach the dawn of a new decade it is asked: What kind of shape is the world in?

We argue about that shape in political and economic terms. But you would think that we could agree about it geographically. We don't, although the National Geographic Society has just made a notable contribution that may move the argument part of the way toward consensus and, moreover, tells us something about the world of the future.

Maps tend to reflect not just land masses, but politics, culture and power. The earliest serious maps are of the Mediterranean: that's where the cartographers and navigators were. Early European maps don't show North America: it hadn't been "discovered," although folks lived here.

More recent maps have, but there is another problem. It is impossible to do an accurate flat rendition (a map) of a round object (the earth). The cartographer's "projection" must distort either shape or area. When that is done, someone complains.

Flemish geographer Gerardus Mercator's projection (1569) yielded what is still the most recognized world map. Africa and South America look like cute bunches of grapes, hanging from the main stem of life, which is the Eurasian land mass and North America. German historian Arno Peters said that's not fair: Mercator shows the world as imperialists would see it. The Peters map (1973) shows Africa and South America as huge bunches of bananas, dwarfing their northern hemisphere stalks. (Peters is regarded by many cartographers as an ideological, pro-Third World promoter.)

Until now, National Geographic used a map of the earth based on a 1904 projection by Alphons van der Grinten. Like Mercator's projection, this one exaggerates northern latitudes. The Soviet Union appears 223 percent larger than life. It looks like a great thick dagger pointed at the United States.

Comes now the Geographic's centennial and a new world map, based on a 1963 projection by Professor Arthur Robinson. It's been used before, but now 10.5 million copies will be going out in the December edition of the magazine. John Garver, the Geographic's chief cartographer, believes it will become the standard general reference map of the world because the compromises it makes between shape and area cannot be much improved.

Surprise! It too reflects culture, politics and power. Robinson, 73, is a kind and crusty gentleman. His global projection has some comforting features to it. He says its northern "central meridian" (the one with no distortion at all) roughly tracks "the old U.S. 40," which traverses Columbus,

CURRENT PROJECTION

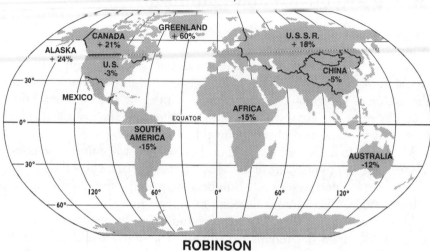

ROBINSON

PREVIOUS PROJECTION

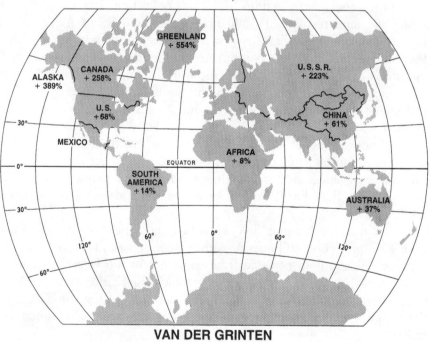

VAN DER GRINTEN

Percentage figures represent
area distortion on each map.

The Soviet Union Reduced to Size. Reproduced with permission of *National Geographic*.

Ohio. The Soviet Union is the nation changed the most by Robinson's middle-latitude view. Robinson out-perestroikas perestroika. His restructuring takes the Soviet Union's 223 percent distortion and reduces it to a mere 18 percent. Viewed another way: Mercator had the Soviet Union 332 percent bigger than the United States, Van der Grinten had it 250 percent bigger, and Robinson has it at 174 percent. The real difference is (only) 136 percent.

No longer will generations of American schoolchildren see the Soviet Union as a thick dagger pointed right at us. Neither will the secretary of state, the secretary of defense, nor the network anchors—all Mercator-users. (Headline: "SecDef Distorts Red Threat!") Robinson's projection squishes the northern distortion: the Soviet Union is now nothing but a rolling-pin pointed at Labrador. As Robinson notes, "It's less ominous."

Well, the Soviets are indeed not as ominous as they used to be. Neither will the future of the world be decided by Africa or South America, as Peters suggests. Robinson's U.S. 40 is not a bad guess for the future locus of global power. When extended, it not only runs near Columbus, but near Beijing and Tokyo.

November 17, 1988

Time Out for Gorby

In the approach to the Summit Conference there is a big propaganda battle going on between Ronald Reagan and the Soviet Union's General Secretary Mikhail Gorbachev. It's an interesting competition.

Suppose I told you that the No. 1 news magazine in America—*Time*—had just run an exclusive interview with Reagan. *Time* precedes the interview with a portrait of Reagan. He has—we are told—"naturally controlled energy." Reagan, *Time* tells us, "dominates a meeting with three extraordinary tools." What are Reagan's remarkable tools? Why, his eyes, his hands and his voice.

His eyes—oh, his eyes. They will "lock into a listener and not let go until the listener gives some sign of acknowledgment, agreement—or flinches." What else about those eyes? They "are neither harsh nor kind. They are big and strong, and sometimes quick, too."

How about Reagan's hands? They "have a variety of specific functions." (Stop the presses!) The right one holds his glasses. But "the left hand talks." It can "lecture" or "declaim" or "thump . . . karate style"—but "always quite gently." (A gentle karate chop?)

And his voice? It is "deep, but also quite soft . . . melodious." But sometimes, "without warning, his voice can cut across the room . . . not angry or bullying, just stronger than any other sound in the room."

Reagan! What a man! Put it all together: "Occasionally the eyes, the hands, and the voice reach peak power at the same time, and then it is clear why this man is president."

Oops, sorry. "General secretary"—not "president." The howler above is from *Time*'s cover story on Gorbachev, not Reagan. *Time* submitted six puff questions in writing in advance to Gorby—a practice rarely offered to American politicians. Then five top *Time* journalists spent two hours talking to this remarkable leader who actually has eyes, hands and voice. Their questions make a slow-pitch softball pitcher look like Dwight Gooden.

Here are some of them: What are your impressions of President Reagan? Do U.S. anti-satellite testing and spy-dust charges damage the summit? Do you enjoy mingling with workers? Are people afraid of you? Only one question—about why the Soviet Union is taking an all-or-nothing position on space weapons—even half-challenges Gorbachev.

Time did not ask a question about Afghanistan, and why the Soviets are committing genocide there—a million people have already been killed. They did not ask about human rights in the Soviet Union, did not ask about the health of Andrei Sakharov or Anatoly Scharansky. *Time* did not ask why the Soviets feel it is all right for them to have space weapons, but not us. *Time* did not ask about the Soviet repression of Poland. They did not ask why communism has lost its appeal around the world.

Time's editors did not even have the sense of decency to laugh out loud when Gorbachev—who came to power as the protege of former KGB chief Andropov—said that his policies "have led to a . . . flowering of our democracy." They did not laugh when Gorbachev sorrowfully noted a global condition where "hundreds of millions of people go hungry"—including those in Afghanistan whose food supply is being scorched by the Soviet military.

Would *Time* interview Reagan without challenging him about his problems—South Africa, deficits, civil rights?

It has been noted that there is an unfair aspect to the propaganda battle between us and the Soviets. We have a free and critical press: they have a controlled applause factory. That lets them try to play our media like a violin without fear of being undercut at home. We can live with that imbalance, and even prosper. But it is not asking too much of our press to—at least—be as critical of our adversaries, as they are of us.

There is much talk in Washington these days about how the Soviets are winning the Summit propaganda battle. But sometimes it's no battle. *Time* has shown it can be a pushover.

September 12, 1985

Campaigning, Soviet-style

After a bruising election campaign someone always trots out that tired Churchill chestnut: "Democracy is the worst form of government, except for all the others."

That's wrong. Even with negative campaigning, sleazy commercials and shameless candidates—democracy yields absolutely, unequivocally, the very best government.

For proof, I offer fantasy.

Suppose, after Brezhnev's death, there had been a free, American-style election in the Soviet Union. What would have happened?

Picture if you will: Yuri Andropov arrives in Kharkov to press the flesh. His advance man says the best place to find groups of voters is on the lines outside of the food stores. Off they go. The candidate, hand outstretched, approaches the line of people, shivering in the cold. "Andropov," a man yells angrily at him, "if you want my vote, end the food lines!" The crowd roars: "Right-onsky!"

Politicians in a democracy learn quickly. At the next corner, Andropov approaches a food line and announces, "If elected, I will end the food lines in Kharkov." An old lady runs up to him and kisses him. A man offers him a slug of vodka.

Comrade T. Whitesky, working on a new book to be called *The Making of the General Secretary, 1982*, scribbles in his notebook. "In Kharkov, as the sun set behind misty clouds, Yuri Andropov had found his theme."

In Moscow that night Andropov's media adviser—Garthovitch—is at work preparing a dazzling television commercial on the theme "No More Food Lines." The biggest time buy in Soviet history is arranged: 11 time zones, 42 languages, a million rating points. For one last check, Andropov calls Pyotor Hartsky, famous pollster. "Da," says Hartsky, "food lines good issue. Good for men. Good for women. No Gender Gapsky."

Hooray, say voters in 42 languages, no more food lines!

Plot thickens. Enter Andropov's opponent, the wily Konstantin Chernenko. Meets with own media advisers. New 11-time-zone commercial next night. Theme: "Andropov Is a Demagogue—Has No Plan to End the Food Lines." Press picks it up: In Pravda, dean of columnists Giorgy Willovich quotes Cicero on demagogues, makes analogy.

In Kazakstan, at a speech to Future Farmers of the Soviet Union, Andropov says he does too have a plan. Way to end food lines is to end food shortage, he says. Only way to end food shortage is to get rid of collective farms. Need family farms. "Have name for plan," says Andropov, "is called 'deregulation.'"

TV reporters query opponent Chernenko as he boards campaign plane. "Ha!" he says, "it can't be done. Would require tractors for 25 million private farmers. No money in treasury. No more taxes. Andropov still demagogue!"

In Pinsk, Andropov fights back, issues position paper. Title: "Re-Ordering Priorities." Theme: Cut U.S.S.R. defense spending by 3 percent; use money for tractors.

Chernenko says in television interview: "Cut in defense spending means opening window of vulnerability with America." Off on the side, Chernenko's media adviser Ivan Deardourfsky murmurs: "Window of vulnerability," he says. "Good phrase; wish I'd thought of it."

Day of big television debate. Andropov back on the attack. Points finger at Chernenko. "Is safe. Is safe. Defense cut is safe because of history, Chernenko." Wiggles finger at him again. "History lesson: democracies never go to war with each other. Voters don't like it. America is democracy. Russia is democracy. Nothing to fear but fear itself, Chernenko."

Chernenko flustered; can not think of democracies that have gone to war with each other, because there are none.

Is big landslide for Andropov. Russia cuts military budget. America cuts military budget. Taxes are cut. Peace dividend declared. Moral of story: liberty yields peace, and peace yields prosperity, in exactly that sequence. Elections come first.

Everyone lives happily ever after. As it happens, most of peace dividend goes for political commercials. Democracy strikes again. Is best form of government.

November 23, 1982

Scharansky: Humor and Heroism

Scharansky. The name had taken on mythic qualities during his nine years of incarceration in the Soviet Gulag. Now he is free, and the man is as good as—even better than—the myth.

He was jailed by the Soviets in 1979 on charges of being a CIA agent. The claims were patently trumped-up. The real reason for his incarceration was obvious to all: The Soviets were trying to break the Jewish dissident movement, and Scharansky had become its most visible spokesman.

They never broke his spirit. On the day of his release, his KGB guards tried to take away the Jewish book of psalms that had been sent to him by his incredibly devoted wife, Avital. He lay down in the snow and wouldn't move until the book was returned. When the moment for his release came, he was told to walk in a straight line across the bridge to the American ambassador's waiting car. Instead, he walked a zigzag course.

When he got to Israel he talked to the world. Two of the themes he stressed have particularly impressed me—one personal, one political.

On the personal level he talked about, of all things, humor. "I think the sense of humor is one of the most important weapons by which you defend yourself. I think the moment I would have lost it, the moment when I would be unable to look at what's happening a little bit from the side, I would have failed. . . . (I tried) to look at everything that happens like theater."

That is profound advice not only for courageous prisoners being starved by KGB brutes. It has relevance to the rest of us mere mortals in everyday circumstances. It happens to be the essential theme of Woody Allen's remarkable tragi-comic new movie "Hannah and Her Sisters," which is a work of great artistry. Allen plays a raving hypochondriac, who comes to the conclusion that human existence is futile and goes into deep personal depression. He finds salvation by watching a wacky old Groucho Marx movie! For as he watches it, Allen understands the absurdity, the humor and the theater of a cruel world, and resolves to re-enter it constructively.

Now politically, Scharansky is stressing the need for "real detente." The release of one symbolic Jewish dissident is not enough, he says. Hundreds of thousands of others are waiting: Jews, Pentacostalists, Crimean Tatars, Baptists, and others.

So, Scharansky is saying keep the heat on, test the Soviets to move from symbolism to reality.

My sense of the Soviet situation is this: The leadership can be viewed as the political equivalent of powerful thugs wearing bloody T-shirts. They desperately want to be invited into the dining room of the best gentlemen's club in town. But they won't take off the T-shirts or put on a coat and tie.

Real detente—as opposed to the one-way giveaway of the 1970s—means trying to get the Soviets to put on a coat and tie. What would be the signs? Freer emigration. Relaxation of repression in Eastern Europe. Taking their butchers out of Afghanistan.

When that happens—as that happens—if that happens—the free world would begin to sense a real transformation of Soviet attitudes. The Soviets would gain credibility and standing on all the other issues of the day, including arms control. Those issues could be negotiated on their merits. The Soviets would gain entry into the club of powerful moral nations.

Will they do it? I don't know. I'm skeptical. But we ought to make sure that the choice is always available to them and always made public. With spokesmen like Anatoly Scharansky playing a super-star role in a great political and human drama, we know that the choice offered the

Soviets will be very public indeed. And it will be offered by a man of great sensitivity who can even see absurdity in the stark political tragedy of the Gulag.

February 20, 1986

Moscow's Fabulous Fabulist

Most of you, alas, may have only seen or heard America's new media star Vladimir Posner: He's been on with Phil Donahue. He's a near-regular on Ted Koppel's "Nightline," he's been on CNN's "Crossfire" in the early evening and on late at night with Larry King.

I am more fortunate, I guess: We had Posner in person at a question-and-answer session at the American Enterprise Institute (my home base).

It seems there is a big argument about Posner in American media circles. He's often billed as a Soviet "journalist" or a Soviet "commentator." (He works for the government-run State Committee for Television and Radio.) Some American journalists, who believe (properly) that a real journalist has to have the right to criticize his or her government, believe that Posner is not a journalist at all. They claim he is a "propagandist"; in fact, Koppel described him that way on the air recently. More neutrally, Posner could be called a Soviet "spokesman." Some conservatives have said, take him off the air.

What the argument on terminology is about is whether Posner speaks for himself or for his government. Observing him firsthand, I can now offer my own description of Posner. He is surely no journalist or commentator in the Western sense. You could call him a propagandist or a spokesman. He'll speak for his government, or about his government, he'll even say he's speaking for himself (of which, more later), but whatever, he is a slick piece of work, very good at his job. And his primary job is that of a "fabulist."

Now, a fabulist is one who tells fables, and some of Posner's fables are beauts. Consider: He was asked, was it not a tragic mistake for the Soviets to invade Afghanistan? Here are excerpts of his answer: "I think that there exists a vested interest to keep the Soviet Union in Afghanistan, especially in the West. Because it's a beautiful way of . . . exploiting the anti-Soviet sentiment. It makes people very angry and very upset . . . The majority of (Russian) people support (the war). . . . I think it has to do with the Soviet heritage . . . to fight a revolution. . . . There are some people who remember that. It's almost like if there were Americans around who remembered George Washington."

Fable connoisseurs, attention! It's all our fault that Soviet soldiers have killed a million men, women and children in Afghanistan. And George Washington would be on the side of the killers!

Consider: Posner was asked why he refuses to appear on television with Russian emigres, like the heroic dissident Vladimir Bukovsky. Posner said: "I have always felt that anyone who betrays his country by going over to the other side is a traitor. . . . I have nothing to do with those people, and I will not discuss—not only on television, I wouldn't share the same bathroom with them."

Interesting fable: Bukovsky did not "go over to the other side." He was deported in handcuffs! (Posner's taste in bathrooms is his own business.)

But in all fairness, in Russian propaganda terms, Posner is a fabulist with a difference. In order to gain credibility with Americans, he has apparently been given the franchise to express "a personal point of view." And so he says his personal view is that anyone who wants to leave the Soviet Union ought to be able to leave. He says his personal view is that the Soviet jamming of all Western radio programs is "counterproductive." Yet, when asked if, as a Soviet journalist, he will write publicly of these personal views in the Soviet Union, the answer is "nyet."

So Posner wants it—and gets it—both ways, or three ways: He appears on U.S. television, he says, because as a journalist he reports the Soviet government view. At the same time, tugging his forelock, he will tell just you his personal views, very personally, on American network television. But they are a secret; he won't tell them to the Russian people.

I say keep him on our air. He is a fabulous fabulist!

June 12, 1986

The Worst Is Yet to Come

It is being said that the Soviet defeat in Afghanistan can be equated with the American loss in Vietnam: two superpowers that went too far, stayed too long and were driven out with their tails between their legs. There is some truth to that—and some critical differences.

Recall some facts: Vietnam fell more than two years after American troops left. While American troops were actually there, South Vietnam was a fairly stable place.

Not Afghanistan. The Soviet troops are there right now, under attack. Unlike Vietnam, it is superpower troops that are fleeing. The Soviet army lost, not their surrogates. It is the first Soviet defeat since World War II.

There is also a logistical difference. Americans were fighting 12,000 miles from home. The Soviets were fighting next door—as if the United States were fighting the Canadian province of Manitoba. The Soviets had an easier military task. Their defeat is therefore that much more telling.

The biggest differences concern geopolitics, the domestic situation, and timing.

America didn't have a ring of conquered nations nearby, nor scores of nationalities within her borders, all yearning to be free. That's what the Soviets have in Eastern Europe and inside the Soviet Union. What message does Afghanistan send to those restive peoples? Might they be looking at Moscow and saying, "That dog won't hunt?" Perhaps. Remember: Even with a sure-fire Soviet military threat, there have been uprisings in Eastern Europe—in Hungary, Poland, and Czechoslovakia. Within the Soviet Union we have seen nationalist sentiments expressed recently in Armenia and Kazakhstan. The Ukraine smolders. So do the Baltic states.

Domestically, America was in the midst of an economic boom during the Vietnam War. But the Soviet economy is a shambles: that's why Gorbachev is trying perestroika (restructuring) and glasnost (openness).

And there is timing. We already know what happened in the 15 years since Vietnam. We cut defense spending, but then raised it. We backed off in some Third World spots as Soviet influence expanded but now we are pushing back. We heard isolationist rhetoric, but our grand alliance is still intact. Our European allies went for missile deployment, forcing the Soviets into a treaty. American ships now patrol the Persian Gulf. We are the brokers in the Middle East. China looks toward America, not Russia. And all over the world the American cultural imperium is stronger than ever. American movies, television, and music are everywhere. The 150 million VCRs in use today, including those in Iron Curtain countries, are pumped full of American tapes. Nations experiment with democracy and free markets. But in intellectual centers all over the world, the idea of communism has lost its luster.

Of course, it's not all been peaches. The ongoing intramural war in Congress about Nicaragua shows that the "No More Vietnams" syndrome in America remains potent.

But the 15 years following the traumatic Soviet defeat in Afghanistan haven't happened yet. Will there be an uprising, or major turbulence, in Eastern Europe? If there is, will the post-Afghanistan Soviets march in— just while Gorby is trying to show how peaceful he is?

Will the nationalities in the Soviet Union grow even more unruly? If glasnost is taken away, will they grow still more restive? Will perestroika-capitalism succeed—an economic theory as much like capitalism as root beer is like real beer? If it does work, will that yield some greater political democracy, and if it does, will that shake the Soviet foundation? And if perestroika doesn't work, doesn't that also shake the Soviets?

In America we know what trouble Vietnam hath wrought. The Soviet experience was worse, and they will only learn how much worse as the years roll on and the 1980s become the 1990s.

April 28, 1988

Now that's a pretty prescient column. That dog didn't hunt.

Labor's War on Communism

If it really is the end of an era, if the Cold War really is over, we ought to ask: Why?

Part of the answer is "Irving Brown," whose memorial service was held, appropriately, on May 1—May Day—in the marble and mosaic grand lobby of the AFL-CIO headquarters building in Washington.

Brown died in February of this year in Paris. He was 77. For four decades he represented the American trade union movement in Europe.

Many Americans do not know that American labor has a foreign policy and has been a potent player in American statecraft. Over the years that policy has generally been consistent and describable in straightforward phrases: "anti-fascist," "anti-communist," "anti-totalitarian," "pro-democracy."

There are many reasons, from patriotic to parochial, that labor is so concerned with foreign policy and so passionately pro-democracy. One reason, as AFL-CIO President Lane Kirkland likes to say, is that, "We don't want to negotiate with an employer who also owns the police, the army, the courts and the atom bomb."

Irving Brown arrived in Europe as World War II was ending. The continent was destitute. Politically, only the communists were well organized. The Soviet Union had taken over the eastern half of Europe, and they were trying to gain influence in the western half. Their chosen instrument, their greatest potential prize, was the trade union movement. The communists knew that whoever spoke for the unions could credibly claim to speak for the workers. They knew that if they could capture control of unions, they could roil the waters of the West, for example, by subverting the Marshall Plan.

Backed with the authority and resources of American unions, Brown helped European unions fight communist doctrine and control. It was not an easy task. The European union movement came out of a leftist tradition of bitter class struggle and class consciousness alien to the American experience. Brown and his American colleagues stressed that the biggest issues at stake went beyond left vs. right and on to the contest between free vs. non-free. In most European countries, through the toughest times of the Cold War, the communists were denied the domination of the unions they sought.

Later, Brown was influential in the creation of the International Confederation of Free Trade Unions, which has worked globally to keep unions free and out of communist hands.

And so, in the course of time, the force of totalitarianism was stymied. Not, of course, by the trade union movement alone. There was allied military strength, a trillion dollars worth and more. There were courageous

politicians of many democratic ideologies. There was the example of the
fruits of a vigorous and often creative private business sector. But the unions
were a prime target, and thanks in some large measure to American trade
unionists like Irving Brown, the prize was denied to the oppressors.

Now, the tide of totalitarianism seems spent. They say it's the end of
an era. But if so, why? It is a long tale, with many tale-spinners, but let
us remember that, in the first instance, totalitarianism foundered because
it was prevented from succeeding.

At the memorial service, Kirkland spoke of the role of trade unionism
in the new era: "For years a silent army has been assembling on the path
(Brown) trod, but they are silent no more. . . . they have raised the banner
of free trade unionism in Poland, and they are changing the course of
history. In China they have taken to the streets . . . demanding democracy.
In Hungary they are forming independent trade union organizations. They
have marched in the streets of South Korea and Chile. In South Africa
they are tolling the death knell of apartheid. Wherever working people
are rising from their knees and walking erect, they are choosing the path
of Irving Brown."

May 4, 1989

*Brown died early in 1989, before the astonishing flowering of freedom
at the end of that year. He would have been delighted, of course,
and justifiably busting his buttons about labor's role.*

*Labor unions are not the most popular of institutions in the United
States. As George Meany used to say, "When a plumber charges
you $18 an hour, he's not going to be popular." In recent years it
has also been said that unions are losing all their battles.*

*I surely do not agree with all, perhaps nowadays with most, of
the policy positions of the AFL-CIO or their constituent unions.
But then again, I am not a plumber, or a garment worker, or a
mailman.*

*Labor unions in America usually do a pretty good job for their
members; they are powerful and necessary part of the fabric of an
adversarial democratic society. The American labor movement is far
more responsible (and in terms of wages, more successful) than its
counterparts elsewhere in the world. I don't believe the labor movement
is even close to an unrecoverable tailspin in America.*

*In any event, the American labor movement deserves eternal thanks
for their key role in bringing freedom to Eastern Europe in the 1980s.
The trigger of the upheaval was the activity of Solidarity, the Polish
labor union, which received lifeline support from its fraternal comrades
in the AFL-CIO.*

In 1981, I was in Gdansk doing a television documentary about Solidarity. I desperately needed a wrap-up interview with Lech Walesa, who can be a pretty cantankerous fellow. Word was sent in to him that I was a longtime friend of Lane Kirkland, president of the AFL-CIO. Word came back: "No. Every American journalist who wants an interview with me says he's an old friend of Lane Kirkland's."

Later, I got the interview. I think he reconsidered and decided to play it safe.

I'm told that the Chautauqua conference in Riga in 1986 was a sort of turning point. The glasnost was only about half-full then.

The attitudinal conditions described in the speech that follows were not unknown to the Soviets. I believe that condition—global hatred for the Soviet Union—played a bigger role in the Soviet turnaround than is commonly understood.

Over the years, the Soviets came to understand that, until and unless they changed, they would be hated and feared. As long as they were hated and feared, they would suffer economic consequences.

Two notes from Riga.

I was wearing a lapel-button Latvian flag when I came into the hotel lobby and said hello to a cluster of Soviet diplomats. One of them saw the flag and asked his colleague a question in Russian. An answer was offered, and general laughter erupted. I asked for a translation. Diplomat number one had asked what the flag was. Diplomat number two said it was the flag of Latvian fascists and that no one in Latvia today would even recognize it. It's the flag we now see waved on television.

When asked about political conditions in Lithuania, an American diplomat said the idea of democratic ferment there was most unlikely, the place had no spunk, it was dormant, finished forever. One actual phrase he used to describe the Lithuanians was "brain-dead." Who was brain-dead?

Latvian Landscape

RIGA, LATVIA. Some reflections on six days here, where I served as a member of a delegation engaged in a dialogue between Russians and Americans. The conference was sponsored on our side by the Chautauqua Society and the Eisenhower Institute.

We left America when Nick Daniloff had been released from jail, but only to the custody of the U.S. ambassador. Some American delegates, most notably Jeanne Kirkpatrick and Richard Perle, felt the best way to show outrage over Daniloff was to boycott the conference. I and some others thought it better to show outrage by coming here to express it. I think both positions are responsible.

I can offer only a blur of thoughts. The two delegations were housed together in the best hotel in Riga. We ate all our meals together. The old pros of the diplomatic corps often swapped rumors about who was up and who was down in their departments. The professional friendship people talked about conference logistics. The rest of us made small talk. Evenings a fine troupe of American musicians gave concerts, joining Latvian performers.

During the day, the delegates waged verbal combat. My sense is that the Americans were on the offensive. Every American speaker hit on the Daniloff affair. American speakers made the point that the United States does not recognize that Latvia is even a part of the Soviet Union. (It was invaded by the Soviets in 1940 under the terms of the Nazi-Soviet pact.) Our speakers made sharp references to the lack of human rights in Russia.

During the public question periods, a number of Chautauquans made critical references to issues in America—the use of drugs, for example. But no member of the Soviet "public" voiced criticism of anything in Russia. In fact, some of their "typical" Latvians were experts brought in from Moscow. The rest were basically handpicked organization types from Latvia.

After a while the American delegates began teasing the Soviet audience asking them to say just one little old thing wrong with Russia.

Our side was better prepared. Our statements were usually written out and thought out. Most of the Russian speeches were off-the-cuff and boiler-plate rhetoric.

They wanted to talk about arms control (very technical), the need to avoid war (agreed), and the need for the peoples on both sides to be friends, good close friends, just like at this friendly conference.

My opinion of the shrewdness of our adversaries has gone down. In many cases they sound like plain fools. Their top delegate carefully explained that the Berlin Wall was really built to keep West Germany from invading East Germany! His proof that Latvia was part of the Soviet Union was that the delegates flew there in a Soviet plane with Soviet visas.

Their scheduling of the conference in Latvia was a blunder. It gave more attention to the restive Baltic republics than those little states have had in decades. Young Latvian-Americans (traveling with the Chautauquans); passed out pins with the old Latvian flag on them. The local Latvians were euphoric that someone cared enough to come.

Does it all matter? What happened in the hall itself is irrelevant. After all, even 2,000 people are only a handful. But some of our tough speeches were printed entirely in the Latvian press without comment. Some of our harsh remarks appeared uncut on Latvian television. Others were blanked out. Similarly, some of our remarks were broadcast, in context, on national television. Other statements were purposefully distorted. Some of mine were.

Vladimir Posner, of *Nightline* fame, moderated the Soviet side of the program and was the only Russian official to publicly criticize something about Russia. He said that more Americans should appear on Soviet television. To dramatize his point he said let's even put Wattenberg on.

Something strange is going on in the Soviet Union. Their foreign policy hasn't changed since Gorbachev took over. They still murder Afghan children. They are still repressive internally. But some new cracks may be appearing in the information curtain.

I was asked by Gov. Charles Robb (one of our speakers) to accompany him and his wife to the apartment of some Jewish refuseniks in Moscow, Mr. and Mrs. Alexander Joffe and Mr. and Mrs. Igor Uzpenski. The refuseniks said they felt the information window widening somewhat.

Is the window opening up a little bit in Russia? Perhaps. I don't know. I do know that in an age of TV, VCRs, audio cassettes and international radio, it's getting harder for the Russians to keep the lid clamped down. It may mean something, perhaps a great deal, one of these days.

September 25, 1986

Why Everyone Hates the Soviets

(*Address to the Chautauqua Conference on U.S./Soviet Relations, Riga, Sept. 1986*)

Let me begin by saying how appreciative our delegation is of the personal warmth, graciousness, and hospitality shown us by our official hosts here in Latvia and by the people of Latvia whom we have met.

I say this for several reasons: speakers generally say that sort of thing. In this case, it is entirely true. And it should set to rest the notion that the troubles in our world are because people are the big problem. People are not the problem. Governments are the problem.

Let me give you an example. Here from a recent public opinion survey, from a major country, are the responses to a simple question:

Question: "What does it mean to be living well?"

The top five responses were these:

"Having financial security."
"Having a good family, children."

"Having an interesting job."
"Living in peace and social justice."
"Being healthy."

Security. Family. Work. Peace. Health. I would submit that these values, with only minor variations, could have been elicited in any nation in the world, certainly in the United States. (Indeed, most of the themes listed formed the basis for President Reagan's election campaign in 1980; and free elections, as we shall see, are also a powerful indicator of public opinion.)

As it happens, this particular public opinion poll was taken in the USSR and was reported in *Agitator*, a Communist Party Central Committee Journal. The data come from the Institute of Sociological Research of the Academy of Science in Moscow.

So the problem is not the nice people we analysts meet anonymously on the print-outs of the public opinion polls in either the Soviet Union or the United States. People everywhere want family, work, peace, health, and economic security.

So, people being similar at root, I propose this morning to speak about *governments* and people's *attitudes* toward governments. I want to talk—very candidly—about the facts about opinions.

I believe a conference like this one in Jurmala can be a useful one, but only if both sides tell it with, as we say, "the bark off." I intend to do that.

My counterpart on this panel (ambassador Vladimir Lomeyko) has talked about the United States. I propose to talk mostly about the Soviet Union. I propose to tell you what people think about the Soviet Union. I confine myself to the views held by the peoples of those major modern nations where we have some regular ability to test public opinion.

At our nice hotel where the Soviet and U.S. delegations are staying (and enjoying each other's company) I have heard one word many times from our Soviet colleagues. It is "misperception." "The Soviet Union is misperceived," they tell us. Indeed, it is a crucial question of our time.

I have spent some time recently examining the survey research results to see just what these perceptions are. Let me share them briefly with you.

Consider first the major nations of Western Europe. Here is a collection of poll results taken only last year in Great Britain, France, West Germany, and Italy. Those four nations comprise well over 200 million people.

Here is one question asked of respondents: "Which nation (in the world) would be most likely to use military force to attain its goal?" Of the people responding in Britain, 81 percent said, "The Soviet Union." In France, in response to the same question, 77 percent of the people replied, "The Soviet

Union." In Italy, the figure was 75 percent. In West Germany, 77 percent.

These responses, obviously, are very high. Among the peoples of Western Europe, almost 8 in 10 think the Soviet Union would be likely to use military force to attain its goals.

There are other similar sorts of polling results. Again from the four major countries, when the question was asked, "What country seeks domination over other countries?" ("seeks domination" rather than "uses force"), 70 percent of the people answered, "The Soviet Union."

When the question is asked, "(Which) nation spreads lies in other countries to attain its goals?"—78 percent of those with an opinion said, "The Soviet Union."

Let me just briefly mention a few country-by-country specifics. The French organization *Institute Français de Demoscopie* reported last year that the Soviet Union was characterized by the French public (in addition to those attributes already mentioned) this way: "cannot be trusted to keep its commitments," "supports subversive groups in other countries," "does not seek peaceful resolution of international conflicts."

Or consider a poll taken last year by the Italian public opinion organization DOXA. Rather than repeat the earlier list, I add the results of only one additional question, and I quote from the conclusion: "Among the major countries of the world, the Soviet Union is the most imperialistic. . . ."

The views in Japan are roughly the same as in Europe: The Soviet Union spreads lies, supports subversion, uses military force, wants nuclear superiority, cannot be trusted, does not seek peaceful resolution of conflicts.

Well, you may say, what do you expect? These are American allies.

Let us look at Eastern Europe, an area which is, shall we say, under heavy Soviet political influence, not to mention the tanks and troops that are either permanently stationed there or on call if necessary.

I mentioned earlier that free elections can be excellent barometers of how people feel about an entire variety of issues.

Well, as you may know, more than 2 million travelers and vacationers from Eastern Europe visit Western Europe every year. (Most of them, alas, are usually not permitted to travel with their entire families for reasons of state security. That is, the states involved fear defections.)

Over the years, nine independent opinion research institutes in different Western European nations have interviewed these Eastern European tourists. The results of these polls are tabulated and compiled by Radio Free Europe (and I should mention here that I am the vice chairman of the Board of Radio Free Europe and Radio Liberty, and very proud of it.)

I want to mention one particular survey. The nations polled were Hungary, Poland, and Czechoslovakia. The tabulations used were 3-year rolling averages, to minimize fluctuations.

In essence, a model of a free election was conducted in those countries, offering the respondents choices of political parties, as they are typically arrayed in a Western European election. Here are the results:

Parties	Czechoslovakia	Hungary	Poland
Conservative	8%	9%	7%
Peasant	3	11	15
Christian Democrat	29	26	34
Democrat Socialist	43	42	35
Communist	3	7	4

Of course, all of these nations are ruled by Communist governments, yet only about 5 percent of the people would *vote* Communist in a free election.

Moreover, another question asked of Czechs, Hungarians, and Poles was this very general one: "Are you favorable to, or would you side with, the United States or the Soviet Union?" The aggregated responses:

Side with: United States, 61 percent; Soviet Union, 10 percent

Now consider the United States. In many ways, we hold similar views to what we've already heard about in other countries.

The magazine I co-edit, *Public Opinion*, has recently pulled together the most recent data. I think from the point of view of the policy-makers here, one key fact should be remembered. It is this: the latest polls I have seen show a great majority of the American people saying they "trust Reagan to make the right decisions when it comes to what the U.S. should do in world affairs." Over 70 percent of the public felt that way, and they also felt that way when queried specifically regarding whether they trusted Reagan in his dealings with the USSR. Interestingly, trust in Reagan has been growing steadily in the last two years, just when Reagan was supposed to be a "lame duck."

Other American views may be of interest as well. Americans believe that the Russian people are much more friendly than is the Russian government. Another item: the American public wants another summit, in fact, wants one every year (which was Walter Mondale's campaign position, but not Reagan's).

We have talked about Western Europe, Japan, Eastern Europe, and America.

What about the Soviet Union? I will spare you the arrogance of telling you about your own country, with only two exceptions:

(1) Our polls, gathered in roughly similar ways to the Eastern European methodology mentioned earlier, show that about half of the Soviet peoples are against the war in Afghanistan.

(2) Our polls show massive numbers of people listening to foreign radio: Voice of America, BBC, Deutsche Welle, Radio Liberty, and Kol Israel.

When asked why, the respondents say they listen because they don't believe what the government of the USSR is saying on Radio Moscow.

I have one conclusion, and some comments. The conclusion is this: The peoples of the modern world, insofar as it can be measured by survey research, believe that the government of the Soviet Union is the most hostile, aggressive, and subversive nation in the world.

And there is more. What I have mentioned so far doesn't include attitudes on human rights in the USSR: the lack of a free press, the inability of workers to organize, or the lack of freedom of religion, all of which only add to the view that the Soviet Union is a power that is unfriendly, even malign.

What can be done about all this? As I said earlier, I know that our Soviet hosts say this portrait of the Soviet government is based on "misperceptions of the Soviet system."

There are two ways for a nation to clear up a misperception.

The first is this: Think about opening up the country. Show us we're wrong. Let us talk to Sakharov in Gorki or, better yet, let Sakharov out of Gorki. Think not only about letting out the Jewish prisoners of conscience—like Abramov, Begin, Berenstein, Brodsky, Cherniak, Eldentstein, Koifman, Levin, Lifshitz, Magarik, Murzhenko, Nudel, Nepowiniaschy, Shaloshvili, Shefer, Vishubsky, Zelichenok, and Zunshain—but also about letting out any Soviet citizen to travel or emigrate if he or she wants to. Let them come and tell us what it's really like in the U.S.S.R. Let foreign tourists to Russia go anywhere they choose (except military installations); let them talk freely to anyone they wish, with no reprisals threatened.

The second strategy is to consider, and reconsider, whether a misperception really is a misperception. If it is not, think about changing it. You will be surprised how quickly the peoples of the world will change their mind about the USSR from negative to positive.

An example: reconsider the presence of the Soviet Army in Afghanistan. Is the Soviet Union really merely aiding "a fraternal ally"? Are the estimated one million Afghans killed there really "fraternal allies"? Are the five million who have fled Afghanistan "fraternal allies"? Remember, there is only one foreign army in Afghanistan, and it is the Soviet Army.

Another example: stop sending arms to Nicaragua in an attempt to set up one more Soviet surrogate state, this one in North America.

And a final example: Think about some form of legitimate elections in Eastern Europe—in Czechoslovakia, Hungary, Romania, Bulgaria, and Poland and in Estonia, Lithuania, and Latvia. Show us who the people want as their government. Make us eat our own misperceptions.

You will not then have to worry about perceptions of using military force or of dominating the world. Instead, Russia will be perceived, quite properly, as one of the great nations of the world, with a deep culture, a profound literature, and a nation that could become the natural partner of the United States in defusing tensions around the globe. That would lead to a world where people, all the peoples of the world, will no longer be concerned with war, violence, and nuclear catastrophe, but about economic security, family, work, and health.

Afterword, July 1990: The Soviets are out of Afghanistan, the Eastern European satellites are free from Soviet control, Soviet emigration is at all-time highs, although still not available to all who might seek it. The Baltics seek freedom and seem to be half-way there. The Soviets still support Cuba.

After-afterword, August 1990: Oops! The Soviets are pulling the plug on Cuba.

Glasnost Insurance

The questions were triggered by Mikhail Gorbachev's announcement at the United Nations that the Soviet Union would reduce its troop strength by 10 percent. Will that do it? Will that end the 40-year struggle?

Don't hold your breath: great powers don't often give up great armies. And the Soviets have made troop cuts before.

But something else happened at about the same time that will have a greater chance of calling the whole thing off. With no fanfare the Soviets ended the jamming of the U.S.-backed Radio Liberty. After 35 consecutive years, the harsh, crackling static beamed out by more than 2,000 jamming devices was gone.

The Soviets don't like Radio Liberty. Most international radio stations broadcast news of the world and news of their country of origin. (Thus: Much of the programming of the Voice of America is about the United States.)

But Radio Liberty broadcasts about life in the Soviet Union, and it does so in 15 of the major languages spoken in the U.S.S.R. It's not programming in the American style. Here we have a plethora of stations. With a push of a button we can hear rock 'n' roll, all-news or classical.

But in a closed society such as the Soviet Union's, a different menu has been necessary. For decades Radio Liberty served as news broadcast, editorial page, literary review, town meeting, church, history classroom and language teacher—across a country covering 11 time zones and composed of over 100 nationalities.

For decades the Soviets attacked Radio Liberty. They said it was a bellicose, confrontational, argumentative tool of the imperialist Cold War.

But what the Soviets were hearing was the unfamiliar sound of freedom. Free speech and unfettered thinking are not always pleasant, to either the receiver or the sender. I have served on the Board of Directors of Radio Liberty for almost seven years. I have witnessed some monumental arguments among RL broadcasters with different points of view and different backgrounds: nationalist and democrat, gentile and Jew, Russian and non-Russian, hawk and dove.

Sometimes it was as raucous, or even worse, than the tension one can observe on a major American newspaper or television network. Such is the sound and fury of free speech.

Even with the jamming, an estimated 20 million people per week in the Soviet Union tuned to RL to hear what was going on in their own country. At times they listened even when doing so might mean going to jail.

And the Soviet leaders complained. Regularly and bitterly. Stop it, the Soviets said. To our credit, we didn't. Instead, the Soviets stopped the jamming.

They did it, I think, for several reasons. They are authentically pursuing glasnost. And the vast web of modern communications (including the advent of the VCR) has made it very difficult to keep the news of the world bottled up. News is now everywhere.

Well, with glasnost, is there still a need for Radio Liberty? Now more than ever. Glasnost has only begun; the Soviet Union is a long way from an open society. (They have just announced that they will still not allow publication of the works of Aleksandr Solzhenitsyn.)

Will glasnost proceed? The unjammed existence of Radio Liberty makes it much more likely. Now that RL can be heard clearly, the Soviets will be forced to answer—by publicly addressing the internal issues that are standard fare on Radio Liberty: economy, ethnic identity, bloated military budgets, religious life, immigration, the Soviets role in the world.

If, over the years to come, the Soviets do a real good job at countering Radio Liberty, they will become a free country. When they become a free country, the Cold War will end.

December 15, 1988

As this is written in mid-1990, I am vice chairman of the Board of International Broadcasting and, in a linked arrangement, of Radio Free Europe/Radio Liberty as well. To say the least, my service on those boards since 1981 has been extremely fulfilling.

Cognoscenti of the Washington scene know the Radio/BIB board is the best one there is. Frank Shakespeare (former director of the

United States Information Agency and former president of RKO
General) was the chairman from 1981 to 1985, and the driving force
in setting it up in its present form.

It is a citizen board; not even the chairman works full-time at it.
Malcolm Forbes, Jr., succeeded Shakespeare in 1985 (at age 37)
and has done a magnificent job. Among the others: Lane Kirkland,
President of the AFL-CIO, works hard at it; James Michener served
actively for many years, as did Ed Ney, formerly chairman of Young
& Rubicam and now ambassador to Canada; my AEI colleague, author
Michael Novak, is a valued board member, as are Ken Tomlinson,
former director of the Voice of America and now managing editor
of the Readers Digest, Arch Madsen, former president of Bonneville
Broadcasting, and former 5-term Congressman Clair Burgener.

In the early 1980s, the Radios took a lot of heat. They were, we
were told, "a relic of the Cold War." They were said to broadcast
material that was anti-Semitic, anti-Catholic, anti-religious, pro-
religious, anti-democratic, too democratic, nationalist, anti-
nationalist, pro-fascist, and pro-communist.

There were, indeed, lots of problems in broadcasting in 21 languages,
in some of them 24 hours a day, often through intense jamming.
That is doubled when the broadcasters are primarily émigrés, many
of whom don't have a Western journalistic background, many of
whom carry some of the competitive poisons of Eastern Europe and
the Soviet Union with them to the RFE/RL studios in Munich. All
that they had in common was a passionate repugnance for Communist
tyranny.

The hardest thing to deal with was that the contradictory charges
were often originated by the people who worked at the Radios.
Sometimes the charges were made publicly, more typically they were
leaked to the press or the Congress in order to strike a factional blow.
Watching the émigré fratricide, I was often reminded of the quote,
"I've just travelled around the world, and you know what? They hate
each other!"

It is the job of the Board to oversee the Radios, and to make their
case. Accordingly, in such a climate, we were periodically roughed
up. It is not a whole lot of fun defending an institution charged,
inaccurately, with being anti-Semitic, or fascist. But after some ritual
banging-upon, we always got good support from the Congress.

When the Cold War ended, it became apparent that all those
exaggerations we had put forth were understatements. Lech Walesa
explained that Solidarity couldn't have made it without the Radios.
Vaclev Havel was a particularly strong supporter; one of the charges

that put him in prison was that he collaborated with Radio Free Europe. The Minister of Communications of Poland in 1990 had been an RFE stringer in 1989.

With all their flaws, the Radios worked. They played an important role in the freeing of Eastern Europe and the liberalization of the Soviet Union. One Romanian diplomat said the Radios were more important than NATO. America has supported these stations for four decades. The roster of honor is long. It was, and is, a great enterprise, one that should be an on-going source of American pride.

In early 1990 I visited the Radio bureaus in Poland and Hungary. Incredible. Radio Free Europe offices in places where only a few years earlier we were reviled as provocative imperialist swine!

It is said by some that the Radios should be cut back now that the Cold War is over. No; not now. I came away from that visit with the view that we ought to be spending more, not less. It will be a few years until we see what Eastern Europe looks like. At least until then, while these nations are making decisions, we ought to be broadcasting less hard news, (which is covered now by free journalists) and more about how various democratic systems work, particularly the American one. There is still that intra-democratic contest for the culture going on.

Broadcasting into the Soviet Union now is as important as ever. In the 1990s the peoples of the USSR will be deciding what kind of place they want to have. That outcome will have a great deal to do with what the world looks like in the future. We ought to put our two cents in, pro-democracy, and pro-American-style democracy.

There has been some opposition to the building of a new VOA/ RFE/RL transmitter in Israel. The target area is the Moslem part of Soviet Asia. It would be crazy to renege on that project. Is it plausible to suggest that in the mid-1990s the United States will have nothing to say to 50 million Moslems in a situation that may well be near-anarchic?

Strictly from Hungary

BUDAPEST, HUNGARY—Who would have thought it? Publisher Rupert Murdoch just bought a 50 percent interest in a newspaper in a country with a nominal communist government. But it's all right. The government is leaving, and the Hungarian paper combines two aspects of modern free society: biting political commentary and undressed ladies.

And in Poland, another first: The TV guide for Warsaw cable has a naked woman on the cover.

So the West comes East. From news to nudes, freedom is arriving.
The American Generals—Electric and Motors—will do business here in
Hungary. Surprise! So will Suzuki.

But will Westernizing work? Can tired, poor, East European nations
revive? Logic answers: Why not? These are European countries, and free
European countries do well: West Germany, Italy, today even Spain and
Portugal. The Eastern Europeans, we believe, are only poor because they
haven't been free. Now the Soviet unperium shrinks and shakes. So shouldn't
the East Europeans make it, and quickly?

No communist nation has ever done it. It might have been nice to try
one laboratory experiment before mass production. That's not the way
the world works. Six East European nations are up for grabs, ten counting
Yugoslavia and the Baltics. Predictions by economists have not recently
been selling at a premium. So there are nervous experts here.

The stakes are large, representing a good piece of the nature of the
future. If these experiments work, they will be the showcases demonstrating
that freedom works.

These are backward countries. In the drab slum that is Warsaw the
phone system is sub-Third World. Hungary is the most advanced of the
lot, and they still don't know about credit cards, stock markets, insurance
and checking accounts. The phones are on hold here, too, and housing
is usually grim and scarce.

Technology is the least of it. Serious people here wonder whether the
sweet communist governments not only killed and jailed people, but also
fried the brains of the proletariat. Did motivation survive? Why work if
there is no incentive? Why work if everything is taken care of—poorly—
even if you don't work? Why let anyone else work hard if he shows you
up?

To unlock their minds, the East Europeans are going the free market
way. In Hungary, subsidies have been cut. Privatization is beginning. But
when subsidies go down, prices go up while wages don't, and folks are
strapped and fearful. As unsubsidized, inefficient firms go bankrupt, unemployment rises scarily during the transition.

The devil may be in the details, which may be decided in the Hungarian
election two months from now, the first wholly free one in Eastern Europe
in 40 years.

Forty-two (!) political parties have formed. The key contest is expected
to be between the Hungarian Democratic Forum (HDF) and the Alliance
for Free Democrats (AFD).

The argument confuses an American. In the United States, the hyper-
free-enterprise party has also captured the traditional values and populist

issues. But here the HDF trad-val-pops mostly lean to a Swedish-style social democratic economy, with a dash of Hungarian nationalism.

The Free Democrats started as dissidents (mostly Jews from Budapest). Now they seem to be gathering national support as they bang the media drum. But, hold on, these urban intellectuals are described by their opponents as right-wing capitalist free market extremists!

The terrain is not only confusing but dangerous. Can the psychological stagnation of communism be repealed simply by elections, free expression and foreign investment? If democracy doesn't respond quickly, will autocracy, or anarchy, or restyled communism take over? What kind of democracy? America's Cold War goal was to establish democracy—but is Swedish-style really the best around?

And if democracy works in Hungary, how much does it matter? It could be a model. But brooding Poland remains, three times as big as Hungary and much poorer. Poland is where the revolution began. It is a kingpin in the future of freedom, and the topic of a subsequent column.

January 24, 1990

Reach Out and Touch Poland

WARSAW, POLAND—Even a few hours in the brand-new Marriott hotel here tells you something about Poland today.

The hotel gleams and shines, towering above the other tall building in town: the grotesque, Stalinesque, Soviet-designed Palace of Culture (from which, it is said, one gets the best view of Warsaw—because you don't see the Palace of Culture). The Marriott staff, specifically not selected from the ranks of people who learned hotel-keeping communist-style, are mostly young, bright, bright-eyed and friendly Poles. It's a novelty to hear a chambermaid speaking English, anywhere.

The carpets are new, the paint and the flowers are fresh. The phones in the rooms are new also. But, alas, the pretty new phones are not hooked up to a new phone system.

The Marriott, like some other places in Warsaw, is not wholly plugged in to the main telephone network. And so, sometimes, after failing to reach a number, a guest will call the hotel operator for help. The operator will call a friend in another part of town. The friend calls the party the guest wanted to reach—and asks that party to call the hotel guest. That call—don't ask me why—can get through. Reach out and throttle someone.

So the Poles are trying. Lord, they are trying. But it's uphill all the way. Could Poland end up as the little engine that didn't?

Sen. Andrzej Celinski worries. "If only we could skip 1990," he dreams aloud. This is the year that the Poles go cold turkey. No halfway measures to free enterprise here, they say. Things are too bad for gradualism. So price controls have been canceled; the cost of bread is soaring; hard-pressed young people are helping out the scared old pensioners; the Poles are praying that the magic of the market grabs hold soon.

Except for the crescendo of freedom at its end, the '80s were not a good decade for the Poles. Poverty and repression drove an estimated 1 million Poles to emigrate, most of them young. A woman in her early 30s reports that 80 percent of her classmates at an elite Polish high school are now residing out of Poland, many in America.

The crowds still form by the U.S. Embassy, trying to get tourist visas. Of those who come to "visit" America, about half return to Poland.

Poland is by far the most populous country in Eastern Europe (38 million). It was the daring political exploits of Poland's Solidarity activists that started the democratic domino effect. Still, Poles worry they may get lost in the shuffle. West Germany will nurse East Germany. Hungary and Czechoslovakia are more advanced industrial nations, natural targets for foreign investment. Where does that leave Poland? Down with Romania and Bulgaria, the backward basket cases of Eastern Europe. A leading Polish journalist talks about "the civilization gap" between Poland and the industrialized countries.

Celinski heads the Solidarity caucus in the newly elected Polish Senate. Like Lech Walesa, he looks to America for guidance and help. "The West European foreign policy is craftsmanlike," he says. "Only America has a foreign policy based on values. Americans have the pioneering spirit that can invest in a place like Poland where both the risks and the rewards are higher." He hopes particularly that American businessmen of Polish descent will take a shot in the land of their ancestors.

Poland will likely rise or fall depending on whether foreign investors, probably Americans, will put a chip on what may be the world's barometer nation. If Poland makes it, East Europe makes it; if East Europe makes it, we've won.

Will it happen? Will the investors come? The good news is that some young middle-level managers at the Marriott are leaving their jobs. Newly arrived foreign investors are paying better salaries. The bad news is that, for a while at least, they will still have to use the same phone system.

January 31, 1990

10

Defense: We're Number One

*P*ower, *including military power, perhaps especially military power, especially in America, comes from the barrels of guns labelled "culture" and "politics." The nature of our culture and politics will define our military role and capability in the 1990s.*

The pieces here suggest the terrain. Our culture is technologically potent, attitudinally vibrant among the broad public, and proud of the major triumph gained in the eighties. One of the people who helped create the triumph was Caspar Weinberger, Secretary of Defense from 1981 to 1987.

Ironically, it was also Weinberger who most publicly exposed a softness in the culture. That squishiness is not in the mass public, but it is in the military elites, who apparently think that squishy liberal elites control the broad public. Generals, admirals, Cap Weinberger: read the election returns, read the public opinion polls.

Indicators: *Defense*

A. Defense spending is declining as a percentage of GNP.

National Defense Outlays as a Percentage of GNP and in Billions of Constant 1989 Dollars

Year	Percent of GNP	Total
1940	1.7%	$ 14.7
1945	39.1%	$571.5
1950	5.1%	$ 70.6
1955	11.0%	$197.7
1960	9.5%	$201.6
1965	7.5%	$199.3
1970	8.3%	$261.1
1975	5.7%	$199.4
1980	5.0%	$201.6
1985	6.4%	$291.3
1989	5.9%	$303.6
1990 (est.)	5.4%	$296.3
1991: OMB Estimate	5.1%	$303.3
1991: Norman Ornstein Estimate	4.8%	$287

B. The American people have adopted a wait-and-see attitude regarding defense cut-backs. (Jan. 1990)

Q. How do you think U.S. defense spending should be affected by the changes taking place in Eastern Europe?

Make cuts right away	7%
Wait and make cuts after things develop	78%
No cuts in the foreseeable future	13%

C. After defense increases and the diminishment of the Soviet threat, American attitudes toward defense spending have reversed.

Q. Do you think we are spending too little, about the right amount, or too much [on national defense]?

Year	Too Little	Right Amount	Too Much
1969	8%	31%	52%
1976	22%	32%	36%
1981	51%	22%	15%
1982	16%	31%	41%
1986	13%	36%	47%
1990	10%	35%	50%

D. American foreign aid has declined from its apex in the mid-eighties.

Foreign Aid (in Billions of 1989 Dollars)

Period	Total	Economic	Military
1970	$19.9	$11.1	$8.8
1975	$14.8	$10.5	$4.3
1980	$14.4	$11.2	$3.1
1985	$20.8	$14.1	$6.7
1986	$18.6	$12.0	$6.5
1987	$15.9	$10.2	$5.8
1988	$14.9	$ 9.3	$5.6
1989	$13.4	$ 8.1	$5.2
1990	$14.3	$ 8.9	$5.4

Source notes are on page 397.

Generals Top Clergymen

Generally speaking, in what American institution do you have the most confidence?

Until 1986, if you were a typical American asked that question by Gallup pollsters, you would have responded "church or organized religion." Moreover, the clergy had been in that first place spot for many years.

No more. The 1986 Gallup data shows a major drop in confidence in the church, from 66 percent in 1985 down to 57 percent in 1986.

And who would you think is in first place now? The Supreme Court? Congress? Newspapers? Television? Banks?

None of the above. According to Gallup, the most popular institution in America is—get this—the military! The Harris Poll and the Gallup Poll don't always agree, but on this one the 1986 year-end Harris data concurs: Americans, says Harris, have the most confidence in "the leaders of the military"—more than leaders in medicine, universities, the Supreme Court and organized religion.

One has to be careful in handling poll data, but these two sets are pretty good; Gallup and Harris have asked the identically phrased questions over many years. When polls are solidly based, they can send important messages. There are at least two such messages in these data.

Why have the clergy fallen?

The president of the Gallup organization, Andrew Kohut, has an answer, ". . . religious figures and institutions have become controversial and more political." Indeed they have.

The Presbyterian Foundation and the (Presbyterian) Board of Pensions recently voted to carry divestment beyond South Africa. They're going after other bad guys, too: Now they will purge their $2.4 billion portfolio of any investments in America's major corporations that deal in national defense. James Woolsey, former undersecretary of the Navy in the Carter administration, and a leader of a common sense organization called "Presbyterians for Democracy and Religious Freedom" has described his church's actions in just one word: "flaky."

The Methodist bishops recently adopted a position that was not only anti-military spending and anti-Star Wars—but anti-nuclear deterrence as well. They will apparently defend America with hymnals. (But one official Methodist committee tried to delete "Onward Christian Soldiers" and "Battle Hymn of the Republic" from the hymnal. Luckily for us, public outrage forced them to recant.)

The Catholic bishops' recent pastoral letter on poverty has been described as a negative, sometimes hostile view of American society. An earlier letter came close to telling Catholics it was immoral to work in the production

247

of nuclear weapons. What do Catholics think of their church's activity in politics? Gallup asked that question in 1986. The answer: 27 percent positive, 63 percent negative—by far the most negative answer in a series of questions about recent Catholic Church activity.

So, the message for churches: People want religion not politics coming from the pulpit—sacraments not Sandinistas, worship not weapons, divinity not divestiture.

There is a message here, too, for the military. It is well understood in Washington that the most dovish and nervous branch of our foreign policy establishment is the Department of Defense. Why? Still living in a time warp of the Vietnam era, they have spooked themselves into believing that the public won't support the military. Should any military activity prove to be necessary, our brass believe that the press and television will be out to mug the military. Accordingly, they usually say, let's not get involved.

Generals and admirals, attention! The American people think you and your services are doing fine. You're No. 1, says Gallup. Not only that, but the same poll puts television dead last.

Forward march!

January 8, 1987

Hidden Player at the Table

When nations lock horns about dividing up power—which is what will be happening at the Geneva summit—it is a process that deals with more than mere military force and hardware. Competing cultures are on the table. Accordingly, there may be hidden players to watch for.

Thus: At the center of the Geneva negotiations will be the Strategic Defense Initiative, alias SDI, "Star Wars"—the projected super-high-tech missile-defense system. In Washington, needless to say, Star Wars is seen as a grand governmental, military and political thrust: It's Ronald Reagan's proposal, it's being run out of the Department of Defense, it's funded by Congress. There is some validity to this, of course. But one of the key reasons SDI has become so important—and why the mere idea of it has driven the Soviets batty—is that so much of it came not from our government, but from our culture.

Here is the history: In the later 1960s and early 1970s, particularly after the Anti-Ballistic-Missile Treaty was signed, the government took only a low-key interest in defensive technology. There was the Ballistic Defense Command at Huntsville, Ala. There was some exploration of high-energy lasers and charged-particle beams. Military research into micro-electronics continued. But it was all mostly on the back burner. And for good reason:

The technology for a comprehensive defensive system simply wasn't available.

At about that time, however, the private sector was going ape in high tech—in places like Silicon Valley in California, on Route 128 near Boston, but soon in other communities as well.

Americans, with dollar signs in their eyes, were working on some trivial aspects of computerization. Young entrepreneurs, anxious to make a killing, were inventing video games. (One of the early ones was called Missile Command.) Using new basic theory of surface physics, a new infra-red sensor technology was developed. One commercial use: activating the automatic doors in hotels.

At the same time, the aircraft and automobile industries needed new materials that were strong and light—to provide transport that was fuel-efficient. (Thanks, OPEC.) The space program—governmental, but not military—needed the same sort of stuff. Another new technology came on line: carbon-carbon composites.

Products came to market. Ideas were exchanged. Young high-tech hot-shots jumped from job to job; many of them started new firms. Their former bosses got angry, but their jumping around cross-pollinated the new technologies.

So, for a decade, American entrepreneurs and scientists fiddled around with the products, processes and ideas that were to become the building blocks of Star Wars: miniaturization, speed, sensors, space travel, light-weight materials, mass production. By 1981, former Secretary of the Air Force (and now chancellor of the University of Texas) Hans Mark was able to note in a speech that there had been a "Private Technological Revolution." Dr. Mark, a physicist, does not use the word "revolution" lightly.

Is it any wonder the Soviets are so afraid of Star Wars? They know we have the whip hand. They can't match it. When they try, they have to do it all via a ponderous communist government in a tight-lipped society that doesn't think much about video games, automatic hotel doors or light-weight car bumpers. It's not a culture where engineers jump from job to job or start their own business. (It is not a good idea to get your boss angry in the Soviet Union.)

So when you hear all the talk about high-profile politicians engaged in Star Wars negotiations these next few weeks, remember that there's also another presence at the meetings. On a crass level, you may view it as the spirit of a lot of Americans doing what Americans do so well—trying to make a buck. On a more elevated level, and a more accurate one, you may consider it as a blessing that the culture of freedom bestows upon its practitioners.

November 7, 1985

Stockmania

The gist of David Stockman's new book is in the title: *The Triumph of Politics: Why the Reagan Revolution Failed.*

How failed? Stockman says it failed because our icky politics did not allow big tax cuts to be matched by big spending cuts. And so, we ended up with a big deficit, which, he says, will likely prove to be a disaster. (Hard to notice on Wall Street these days.)

The necessary reason for all the tax and spending cuts (says Stockman) was to smash the state—the welfare state. Those monies diverted from little programs like Social Security were to finance Stockman's supply-side state, chock-full of economic growth and entrepreneurism. This would free people from the heavy hand of government.

Reagan's problem, says Stockman, was this: "Despite his right-wing image, his ideology and philosophy always take a back seat when he learns that some individual may be hurt." Eek!

The villain in Stockman's book, however, is not Reagan: It is Caspar Weinberger. If Weinberger writes a memoir it will be called "How the Reagan Revolution Succeeded."

There were always two Reagan Revolutions at work. Stockman's was domestic. Weinberger's was international. Stockman got a piece of his: He didn't roll back big government, but he slowed its growth. So we will continue to live in a capitalist country with a medium-level safety net (which is fine with me).

Weinberger—the villain who wouldn't let money be taken from his defense budget—saw a different problem in the world. It wasn't the welfare state. It was the totalitarian state.

The conservative view of the globe when Reagan took office was this: The Soviets had gone through the biggest peacetime military buildup in history. They had built a "blue-water navy," with which to "project power." And, they said, the Soviets were indeed projecting power—on the horn of Africa, in Mozambique and particularly viciously in Afghanistan—and probing in Central America.

And America? In the conservative view, we were sucking our thumb. While the Soviets were building and pushing, we kept a flat military budget, idealistically worrying about the relationships of rich countries to poor ones (remember Andrew Young?) rather than the relationships between us and our superpower adversaries. Worst of all, they felt, we had a wimpy president who said we must rid ourselves of an "inordinate fear of communism." Hawks said Carter's foreign policy was not only weak, but incoherent.

So, backed by Reagan, Weinberger got big increases in defense and gave Stockman a case of deficititis.

Now there are very smart analysts who say the Reaganauts didn't spend the new military money as wisely as they might have. They have also said—often correctly—that Reagan's foreign policy leaves something to be desired and (like Carter's) is incoherent.

But, when all is said and done, there is this: When Reagan had a choice between an important revolution (halting totalitarians) and a chimerical one doomed to failure except at the edges (rolling back Social Security, health care, education, etc.)—he made the right choice. That's so even if he foolishly ran up big deficits.

So the real Reagan Revolution succeeded. It may be cause-and-effect, it may be happenstance, but the Soviets are now more cautious in the power-projection game, they are negotiating, and suddenly it is said that democracy is on a roll, not totalitarianism.

Of course, we still have an incoherent foreign policy, but at least it is incoherent from a safer base.

May 1, 1986

Is Weinberger a Wimp?

Secretary of Defense Caspar Weinberger has surfaced and sanitized a naive, dovish and dangerous idea that has been simmering in the Pentagon. It bubbles up every time there is any talk that the United States might use force anywhere in the world—Central America, Lebanon—anywhere.

Speaking before the National Press Club last week, Weinberger said, "before the U.S. commits combat forces abroad, there must be some reasonable assurance we will have the support of the American people and their elected representatives in Congress."

What does "reasonable assurance" mean? During the Vietnam War it was the peace activists who said, "Hell no, we won't go." The current demand for reasonable assurance is the military version of no-go.

Mind you, the Pentagon view that Weinberger megaphones is taken with the best intentions. The military wants public and political support. They deserve it. They are solid professionals who still put their lives on the line when called. But even the best intentions do not excuse naive thinking. Nor do best intentions mitigate the consequences of such thinking.

Much of Weinberger's speech is reasonable, full of caveats and recognizes subtleties. Indeed, one of his major points notes that the real challenges to peace and democracy in the years to come will not be as a result of frontal geographic attack. More likely, he says, are "gray area conflicts" like proxy wars, guerrilla action and terrorism.

Such subtlety, however, does not reveal itself in Pentagon thinking about either politics or public opinion. Our warriors believe that they were undercut in Vietnam by the politicians, the press and the public. There is some truth to this idea, but less than they suppose. To be sure, there was turbulence, but for seven long years—from 1965 to 1972—a solid majority of the public went along with the government's Vietnam policies. The voters elected a hawk (Richard Nixon) over more dovish candidates. The Congress appropriated the money for the war. And all the public opinion polls showed that the vast majority of Americans honored our troops.

To publicly demand "reasonable assurance" of public support for any use of force reveals ignorance of what happened in the past and lack of insight into what is likely to happen in the future. For "public support" or "political support" are not commodities that can be counted by Pentagon computers. Even allegedly learned political scientists throw up their hands at the ambiguities in the polls and in congressional votes.

Examples: Did the public support Grenada? Yes. Would they have supported it if it was a failure? No. Does the public or the Congress want to send troops to Central America? No. Do they want Central America to be taken over by governments that are pro-Soviet? No. But is the public or the Congress willing to send troops if the communists are taking over? Maybe.

The public might well support action if the president explains why we have to do it; if we do it quickly; if other nations support us; if we get lucky; if we win—or some combination thereof. But there is no way to know how any of this will play out in advance.

All we really know is that the public is pretty tough-minded. They supported hawkish Ronald Reagan. But it's not a 100 percent situation. The military must understand that they may have to get engaged in some tough ones, when there will be no political blank check available.

To publicly maintain that they shouldn't be asked to do that has consequences. It begs peaceniks in the United States to throw a public tantrum. After all, Weinberger has said if they can cause turmoil, he'll fold his hand.

And, despite its caveats, Weinberger's speech sends a message to our adversaries. Test us, it says. Just try us out and watch how difficult it will be for us to respond. You may even get away with it, Mr. Adversary.

President Reagan has had plenty of recent experience telling Americans that he was misquoted or taken out of context. Now he faces a tougher task: He's got to convince us that Weinberger didn't really mean what his speech said.

December 4, 1984

Making America Number One

Because Americans want America to be number one, we won't, and we shouldn't, make big quick cuts in the defense budget.

What do Americans do when their team wins a football game? They raise a forefinger and yell, "We're number one!"

Consider: From 1945 to the mid-'60s our leaders told us that we were the most powerful military force—number one, first in the world—and we loved to hear it. Then, Soviet military power grew and politicians began saying America was "second to none." By 1980 hard-liners were saying what we did not like to hear, that we were "second," or, in a variant, "unless we rebuilt militarily we would become second." Hmm. First. Second to none. Second.

In the 1980s America rebuilt—and as a partial result, some argue, the Soviets began self-destructing.

Now we must decide what to do about defense. The doves have an answer: (still in footballese) cut it back, cut it back, way back—and reap a big peace dividend. At last, the dove case makes some sense. It is, after all, rooted in the ancient hawk precept: "The American military budget is set in The Kremlin." With the Soviets weaker, say the doves (now), we can cut big and fast.

Why not? How could a hawk (like your author) oppose such logic? There are some rational reasons. And there is another reason, mystical, yet known to almost all.

Rational reasons: Big Soviet defense cuts haven't happened yet. Let's wait and see. It's hard to cut budgets quickly—contracts are committed. Research and development takes a long time and we don't know the future. We have other military responsibilities.

Then there is that other reason. If we play our cards right, we will be able to wave our forefinger and say we're number one militarily, and partly because of that, we'll probably be first in everything else too.

But is it good to be number one? It costs money, and it can periodically get you into trouble.

On balance it's fine. Throughout history, nations that had a chance at it, tried for it. When you're number one other folks don't usually mess with you in a serious way. They certainly take your phone calls.

Since colonial times Americans have wanted to be first. John Winthrop said America would be "a city upon a hill . . . the eyes of all people are upon us." Andrew Jackson announced that America is "a country manifestly called by the almighty to a destiny. . . ." It got a little out of hand; James Gordon Bennett wrote that "it is our manifest destiny to lead and rule all other nations." President McKinley used "manifest destiny" to justify annexing Hawaii. Reagan quoted Winthrop.

What do you do with it, if you're number one? Invade the world? Create a bunch of little Americas?

Of course not. If you have to ask the question, you don't understand it. But, if we're lucky, we'll find out what being number one is for. The Judeo-Christian God, remember, is a God who reveals himself as history unfolds. That's one reason the West has always been oriented to the future.

Ask a hundred Americans whether they want to be number one, and 90 will say yes. Why? Because we peddle the American idea. Americans today want to offer the world a kinder, gentler, optional, manifest destiny. When you're number one, people pay more attention.

We have an opportunity now to be first—and on the cheap. (Just when they were saying America was in decline!) The Soviet empire is unilaterally engaged in a going-out-of-business sale. So we can all agree to cut back our military. But by how much? How fast? We can do it in a spasm, increasing chances that there will be a world with no leader. Or, by cutting our military only slowly and cautiously, we can make it more likely that we will be what we want to be—number one.

February 7, 1990

11

Foreign Policies

*T*he ideas that are commonly held as the nineties begin are not the same *ones that were held when the eighties began. How come? There were new circumstances, surely. That is probably the biggest part of the matter. It can be said with merit that the statist dream ran out of gas in the eighties. It was probably going to happen sooner or later, and that's when it happened.*

But there were also people who helped make it happen, who made a difference by changing the way people thought. I believe the so-called neocon-servatives played an important role in that process. Jeane Kirkpatrick was perhaps the most visible of the neo-cons.

Late one morning, in early 1981, after she had been appointed Ambassador to the United Nations, Jeane came over to AEI (where, until recently, she had worked) to participate in a panel discussion. She had just been at a cabinet meeting and was bubbling with enthusiasm about the new president. "I love Ronald Reagan," she said. The cause of her joy was clear. Reagan believed in certain principles and was going to fight for them. They happened to be mostly the same principles she stood for.

In some ways Jeane understood Reagan's foreign policy better than Reagan did. He had a general sense, valid, I think, of how spun the world, of who the good guys were and who the bad guys were, and what we ought to do about it.

So did Jeane. But she had theorized about it, written about it, looked into the nooks and crannies of the arguments in an intellectual's way. Agree with it or disagree with it, she had a coherent world view.

She ended up in some monumental intramural fights within the Reagan administration. There were those in the State Department and the White House who said she was not a "team player." My sense of the matter is that she felt strongly that she was indeed a team player, that it was Reagan's team, and that, dammit, she knew what he really stood for.

Sometimes he backed her; sometimes he didn't for reasons of diplomacy, or politics, or disagreement, or perhaps changing conviction. But she was generally presenting him with "the Reagan option."

More important, perhaps, by using her podium, by appointing like-minded scholars, she helped present that view to a global audience, and in many places it resonated.

This process was replicated in many ways and in many places by many others in the neo-conservative movement, which itself runs across a fairly broad spectrum of views. Those ideas—fresh, bold, scholarly yet passionate— helped change the global terrain, the one upon which we now operate.

Ideas have consequences.

What Jeane Kirkpatrick Did

Jeane Kirkpatrick is leaving her post as U.S. ambassador to the United Nations. She has done a remarkable job there for two simple reasons: She understood what the job was about, and she figured out a way to deal with it.

The political part of the United Nations has little power because the major adversaries have the right of a veto. That hamstrings anyone from doing anything important. And so it is said that the United Nations has become a fudge factory, a smoke blower, a hot-air machine, a war of words.

Accordingly, most important nations regard the United Nations as irrelevant—and patronize those militant Third Worlders who try to use it as a serious bludgeon. It's all only rhetoric, the big powers seem to say; let's give the poor fellows a pat on the head.

Mrs. Kirkpatrick, however, is from the academic world. She is an intellectual. She takes words seriously. She believes, as do many intellectuals, that ideas have consequences. She believes further, that there is a war of ideas going on. That war is about whether the principle of human liberty is the essential one upon which to organize society. She knows that if we lose that war of ideas, the consequences will not be pleasant for us.

In the U.N. system—as in the world at large—if words and ideas are not challenged, they take root. Thus, what may seem like mindless socialist rhetoric about who owns the minerals in the sea-bed surfaces years later as an unworkable socialist heist designed to turn over billions of dollars to nondemocratic nations.

What seems like left-wing blather about rapacious multinational corporations soon reappears as an idea for friendly U.N. bureaucrats to regulate the global drug industry.

More verbal abuse of the free press soon turns out to be a code to license journalists so they can't say anything nasty about Third World thug dictators. Preaching anti-Semitic slogans like "Zionism is Racism" turns out to be a call to destroy Israel. Ideas have consequences.

Understanding the job in that way meant doing something that hadn't been done before: the mobilization of a corps of intellectual shock troops to do the actual combat.

In an earlier time, it was said that the U.S. government ought to keep intellectuals "on tap, not on top"—and certainly not in the trenches where hand-to-hand fighting went on. But Mrs. Kirkpatrick's U.N. staff was an all-star team of people from the world of ideas, most of them Ph.D.s, mostly from universities, think tanks, foundations, political-action organizations and little magazines with big ideas.

There were Alan Keyes from Harvard, Ken Adelman and Jose Sorzano from Georgetown University, Charles Lichenstein from Notre Dame, Marc Plattner from the *Public Interest* and the Twentieth Century Fund, Carl Gershman from Yale and the Social Democrats, Allan Gerson from Yale Law School, Joel Blocker from UNESCO and *Newsweek*, attorney and political activist Richard Schifter, to name only the top level.

When it came time to send delegates to international meetings—often the spots where the bayonet warfare of the U.N. battle takes place—Mrs. Kirkpatrick dispatched distinguished intellectuals like Michael Novak, Walter Berns and Peter Berger.

Did it work? The intellectuals performed with gusto and erudition. They fought for Western values in a world that was becoming cavalier about them. They won some fights: they lost some. But when it was over, they had changed the nature of the debate, perhaps forever.

These days, a U.N. debate on human rights includes references to Poland, Afghanistan and the Soviet Union, not just Chile and South Africa. These days, a U.N. debate about development notes without shame that free markets can boost an economy.

How important is all this? It's hard to measure. It's only one piece of a puzzle. Other things have been going on in the world. But five years ago it was being said that socialism and collectivism were the waves of the future. Nations were accommodating to that perceived tide.

Today, it is being said that democratic values and free-er enterprise are in the ascendancy—and nations are accommodating to those notions.

February 26, 1985

I grew up in a household that was vigorously pro-Zionist. My mother, Rachel Gutman Wattenberg, had emigrated from Odessa to Palestine as a little child in the early part of the century. Her family was one of the first to settle in a brand new suburb called Tel Aviv in the early 1900s. My father, Judah Wattenberg, came to Palestine from Vienna in 1919 as a "chalutz" (pioneer). They met in America when both were students at Columbia University and stayed here. Some years later my older sister and I were born.

Although as a boy my primary interests were basketball, stickball, and the Brooklyn Dodgers, the dinner table conversation at home frequently turned to Jewish and Zionist topics. It was a time of Jewish revival.

In those days the Palestinian liberation organization was the

Haganah, at least in our house. My father was then the first executive director of the American Technion Society. My older cousin David Guttman, now an eminent clinical psychologist, lived with us for many of those years. As a teenager, he had served in the U.S. Merchant Marine during the war. When the war ended, he sailed for both the Irgun and the Haganah, bringing in illegal Jewish refugees to that British colony called Palestine.

So those are some of the reasons I'm so interested in Israel. I have history, family, and emotion over there. When I emigrated to Washington in the 1960s, I came to know some people who were at least as pro-Israel as I was, but weren't Jewish. My coauthor Richard Scammon was one such. Political scientists Jeane Kirkpatrick, Austin Ranney, and Howard Penniman, who all later became colleagues of mine at the American Enterprise Institute, were others. Penn Kemble, of the Coalition for a Democratic Majority (now with Freedom House) and my political co-conspirator for many years, fell into that category. Why were they so pro-Israel?

They didn't have family or history there. They weren't in elective politics, looking for votes or contributions. Scammon explained it to me once. In some ways, he said, it was an acid test of American postwar foreign policy. If American policy wasn't about helping a threatened pro-American democracy, what was it about?

My current political beliefs were formed in the sixties, working on the LBJ White House staff at a time when we were trying to help South Vietnam, another threatened pro-American nation far away.

In any event, I'm a strong supporter of Israel. The Israelis have made some mistakes, but they are not alone on that score.

One huge mistake concerns the Israeli economy, which in recent years has only barely muddled through. This is a self-inflicted wound of major dimensions.

It's not just that the Israelis are poorer than they ought to be. But when their economy is sluggish, many Israelis leave. The clearest indicator of Israeli economic health is the number of Israeli cabdrivers on the streets of New York City and Los Angeles: the more cabdrivers, the worse the economy. Recently, Israel received a great gift: hundreds of thousands of Russian Jews. But these well-educated new arrivals may leave if the Israeli economy doesn't shape up.

Long-term, Israel's major problem is demographic. They need people to populate a land that is still sparsely populated, and I'm talking about inside the 1967 borders, particularly in the Galilee.

*I pretty well buy the conventional wisdom about why Israel's
economy isn't humming: too much socialism, too much bureaucracy,
too much government regulation. It sure isn't that they don't have a
head for business. If the Taiwanese and South Korean economies,
each with heavy military budgets, can take off and fly, so could Israel's.
The Israelis are moving in that direction, but it's slow going.*

*I part from pro-Israel orthodoxy about American economic aid.
We ought to give military aid. We've done that for the Europeans,
the Japanese, and the rest of the free world, in one way or the other,
for almost half a century. We've done it because it's in our best
interest. It's been in our best interest to help the good guys. It still
is.*

*But economic aid is another matter and ought to be looked at
afresh. Zionism wasn't about getting American money to make things
easier for Israeli consumers. An Israeli economy that was properly
harnessing the talents of the people there wouldn't need economic
help in the current magnitudes. And they would be more likely to
harness talents if they didn't have the crutch of American aid.
Sometimes taking away crutches pushes limping people to learn how
to walk sooner, and better. Americans don't like to give aid; Israelis
don't like to get it. Most of the non-military American aid comes
right back to the U.S. as interest payments for prior loans, which
were used to help the Israelis buy military equipment from the U.S.
in times of war. Those loans could now be forgiven, and any new
non-military aid stopped.*

*Israel has been banged around unfairly, I think. These columns
are mostly rebuttals.*

Israel and the Double Standard

The case is being made—mostly validly, I think—that Israel is being held
up to a "double standard" these days. Friends of Israel argue that a code
of one-way phony moralism is applied to Israel but not elsewhere. To
gain a flavor of this charge, it may be useful to put in one place a short
catalog of examples:

The point has been made that Israel gets aid and arms from the United
States and yet acts on its own, sometimes against the wishes of the United
States. This is supposed to be a novel and outrageous situation. We are
asked in mock horror: How dare an ally-client behave like that?

Well, if all our allies, clients and aid recipients listened to us and acted
the way we wanted them to, then the world would look like this: Japan
would quintuple its defense spending and let us sell beef in its markets,

West Germany would not be signing up for Soviet natural gas, France would not sell arms to Nicaragua, Saudi Arabia and Jordan would be part of the Camp David peace process, South Korea and Brazil would be more democratic, and most of the OPEC oil-producing nations would stop trying to screw us to the wall.

The only superpower that tries to get total obedience from its allies is the Soviet Union, and even it often fails. America heads a formal and informal alliance of free and independent nations—not a totalitarian lock-step empire.

Or take the argument that the Palestinians need a state of their own. After all, it is implied, every people must have a state. Well, some peoples have states: the French do, the Indonesians do, the Americans do, the Israelis do. But lots of people—maybe most of the peoples of the world— don't have their own state. Where are the states for the Kurds, Copts, Flemish, Basques, Scotch, Armenians, Azerbaijanis, Moluccans, American Indians, French-Canadians, Bretons, Estonians, and Tibetans—let alone the scores of African tribes, some of whom have more people than the Palestinians?

The hypocrisy is compounded when nations that do not offer their indigenous peoples either statehood or autonomy demand that Israel do just that. Is France for ever greater autonomy for the Bretons? Is Iraq or Iran for Kurdish statehood?

All of this is not to say that the Palestinians should not or will not get a state of their own. It may come to that, but history tells us that it is by no means a divine right that is automatically bestowed.

The double standard goes on and on: One hears Arabs complain bitterly that the Palestinians on the West Bank don't have free elections. That is truly unfortunate, but where in the entire Arab world is there a country with free elections? The last democratic Arab country was Lebanon—and that was rubbed out by the PLO and the Syrians.

One hears continuing reference to "wholesale killing" and "slaughter" in Lebanon by the Israelis. Yet, the original estimates of 10,000 to 15,000 dead civilians in Southern Lebanon were clearly exaggerated; many-on-the-spot observers say the number now looks more like 600. Yet there was very little public outrage when the PLO and the Syrians killed tens of thousands of Lebanese in the earlier part of the civil war there.

England's reconquest of a fly-speck 8,000 miles from home was found morally justifiable on the grounds of "national honor." But Israel's combat with two armies next door on the grounds of "self-defense" was often found immoral.

The English certainly did not tell the whole truth, nothing but the truth, about their military activities and goals in the Falklands while the war was going on. Nations at war rarely do. But when the Israelis either dissembled or changed their mind to take advantage of an opening target of opportunity—usually regarded as sound military policy—they were condemned.

Israel is denounced for not giving the Palestinians a West Bank state. But who denounced Jordan when it controlled the West Bank from 1948 to 1967 for not giving the Palestinians a state?

Now, when the Israel-is-a-bad-boy proponents are challenged on the grounds of the double standard, there is one all-purpose reply: "Israel should be held to a higher standard. It was set up as 'a light unto the nations'; it was to be an idealistic state that we all cherished."

Well, maybe. But that's not what Theodore Herzl, and many other founders of modern Zionism, had in mind. They thought the Jews could establish a real state again only when, for good and for ill, they behaved like everyone else in the world. They speculated about the idea of a Jewish state that would have not only intellectuals, mechanics and farmers, but prostitutes and criminals just like every other nation. They might just as well have added "nationalistic, security-obsessed prime ministers and generals" to that list. Just like other nations.

All this is not to say that everything that Israel has done recently is right. I, for one, don't believe that. Nor are Begin and Sharon exactly my idea of charm school graduates.

There is, indeed, a whole other catalog of authentic geopolitical arguments—pro and con—regarding the Israeli action. These arguments stem from a single-standard view of the world as it is. They are arguments that are surely worth a thorough venting. But spare the sermon.

July 27, 1982

Will Arab Weakness Yield Peace?

TEL AVIV, ISRAEL—We have heard a great deal about stark political change wrought in the Middle East by Yasir Arafat's alleged incantation of "the magic words" concerning Israel's existence. But one question has been generally absent from the discourse: Why now?

Why, after so many years of resistance, did Arafat and many Arab states make the big rhetorical push just now? In the answer to this question may possibly lie the essence of the Middle East's future.

Certain pieces of an answer, offered in a somewhat different context, surfaced here recently at a conference at Tel Aviv University on "Prospects for Arab-Israeli Cooperation 1988–2000."

One panelist, Prof. Eliyahu Kanovsky of Bar Ilan University, sketched out what the plunge in the price of oil has meant to the Arab nations. Back in 1981, oil revenues for Saudi Arabia were $112 billion, and we were being told that the world would be owned by the petro-princes. But by 1987, Saudi oil revenues were down to $20 billion.

Today, pity, the Saudi petro-plutocrats are running deficits, drawing down their petro-hoard and borrowing money. The oil-price drop inflicted even greater damage on the economies of the Arab countries that are not large oil producers. During most of the fat years, Egypt, Syria and Jordan got major financial aid from the big oil producers. Their citizens went to work at good pay in the oil-rich states. No more; the oil crunch is on.

That's the past and the present. U.S. Energy Secretary John Herrington then looked to the future for the conferees.

These days, there are oil analysts who say oil prices will be going up soon. Don't believe it, says Herrington. When OPEC ran the price of oil up from $2 to $35 a barrel, a mighty force was unleashed: self-preservation via the free market. Many non-OPEC nations went out and discovered oil. Cars were designed to burn less gasoline. Natural gas, coal and nuclear energy became competitive fuels in many nations.

Super-efficient ceramic automobile engines are around the corner. So are photovoltaic energy sources. America uses the same amount of energy today as it did in 1973, although our economy is one-third larger! In short, says Herrington, there will be plenty of energy supply to meet demand, and oil prices aren't going to go up in the 1990s.

Now, suppose one puts the Kanovsky and Herrington messages together. A political truth emerges that offers help in answering that crucial question: Why now?

Consider the Arab situation. They have squandered their windfall. They have imported 42 percent of the world's arms in recent years! Corruption is hyper-endemic. The public has been bought off with socialist goodies, but those bills can't be met now. A serious modern market economy has not emerged.

When the petro-dollar was king, the Arabs believed that time was on their side. They would get richer and stronger as the years went on. Sooner or later, they could overwhelm tiny Israel. That was good reason not to negotiate seriously.

But Kanovsky says they are getting poorer and weaker. Herrington says things are not going to get better in the future. Isn't this one reason for Arafat and his patrons to look for a deal now?

For the Israelis, all this poses a problem. They don't know whether Arafat said what he meant or meant what he said. They don't know if Arafat is a terrorist or only an ex-terrorist.

In the past, suicidal Arab politics let the Israelis sit still and validly say there's no one serious to negotiate with. Now there may be a partner aborning. It is a foe that is weaker than before. It may be a good time for the Israelis to see if the Arabs, finally, are serious.

December 22, 1988

> *Even beyond low oil prices, the Arab hand is weaker than it has been in a long time. The apocalyptic threat to Israel has not been just "Arabs who want to throw them into the sea," but Arabs who want to do that and were backed by an aggressive super-power, i.e. the Soviet Union.*
>
> *The Soviets now seem to be out of that business. Their former Eastern European satellites, who typically helped the Arab states in many ways, are certainly out of it.*
>
> *And, of course, hundreds of thousands of Jews from the Soviet Union are expected to emigrate to Israel.*
>
> *It's a pretty good picture. You would never know it from reading the news about Israel, or for that matter, talking to most Israelis. The media ink flows to the turbulence on the West Bank, and the bizarre Israeli political system that seems to guarantee political deadlock.*
>
> *Those are serious situations. But if, a few years ago, anyone looking at Israel's future who said that oil prices would be way down, that the Soviets and East Europeans would be de-fanged, and that hundreds of thousands of educated Jews would be pouring into to Israel—would have been regarded as a nut.*
>
> *Arab weakness and Israeli strength make it a good time for the Israelis to try to make a deal, if there is one around.*

Is Buchanan Mushy on Middle East?

Who would be the last public man in America to be described as a) wishy-washy, b) media-manipulated, c) defeatist? Answer: Pat Buchanan.

Over the years, as both a private commentator and a public figure. Buchanan has been the crystalline, hard-line conservative. Agree with him or not, he has been consistent, coherent and clear-headed. Above all, he takes a position. Hamlet he ain't.

But consider Buchanan's views now on Israel. Over the years his position has been staunchly "pro-Israel." He has generally maintained that Israel is pro-Western, pro-American, and that the Arab radical states, and the PLO, have been pro-Soviet and pro-terrorist.

In the broad sense, Buchanan is still "pro-Israel." For example, he favors continued American military aid to Israel. But his views have been evolving in an uncharacteristic way. On this issue he now sees a vast terrain colored in shades of gray.

Consider a recent column of Buchanan's. He asks, early on, "Can a Jewish state survive in the Middle East?" He offers a string of melancholy responses. One is that America "is not the imperial power it was in 1958." The old Buchanan would have said: Let's make America assertive again. The new Buchanan simply sighs.

The new Buchanan says that Israel is paying a price for her fight against the rebellion by Palestinian Arabs on the West Bank. That price, he says plaintively, is measured by "the coarsening of her army, in relations with America, in her own self-esteem." The old Buchanan would have remembered that the "coarsening" and "self-esteem" arguments are ones that the New Left used against the Vietnam War. The old Buchanan knew war is hell, that warfare depicted on television is doubly hellish, and that coarsening and diminishing self-esteem can be acceptable prices when the alternative is destruction. The old Buchanan would not just note that American public opinion is changing. He would talk about how bang-bang television coverage of rock-throwing kids challenging an army can erode even the most solid of cases.

The new Buchanan stresses the enhanced power of Syria and Iraq. The old Buchanan would say that is all the more reason to help Israel remain strong.

The old Buchanan would have seen Israel as an anti-Soviet bastion in an area where the Soviets are still powerful and mischievous: the Soviets recently sent bombers capable of reaching Israel to kinder, gentler Libya.

The new Buchanan asks, "What difference does it make to us who governs Hebron or East Jerusalem?" The old Buchanan would be explaining why the web of American superpower activity is necessarily of global character, extending from Europe, to Japan, Australia, Vietnam, Nicaragua, Cuba and to Israel and the Arab nations.

After much agonizing, Buchanan writes that the Israel-Palestinian situation "is a historic tragedy yet to unfold: a case not of right against wrong, but of right against right." Yet Buchanan also notes that Palestinian demands could lead to an attempted dismantlement of Israel itself.

In one big sense, surely, Buchanan is correct: there are, indeed, two rights in question, and Israelis have made some mistakes recently. But it is not so hard to list the grievances of a situation pro and con. Such examination is a precondition to a harder task: forming a solid opinion. In recent years, conservatives have needled liberals for seeing too many sides of too many issues, and coming up with mush. The old Buchanan assayed the Israeli and Palestinian cases, found one stronger, and went for it. My sense is that, on balance, he still sees greater merit in the Israeli case. Unfortunately, he's writing about it now like a liberal.

April 20, 1989

Dual Loyalty

A couple of months ago, the far-left novelist Gore Vidal wrote a vicious and, I believe, anti-Semitic article in the left-wing magazine *The Nation*. Among other things, Vidal accused neoconservative writers Norman Podhoretz and his wife, Midge Decter, of being stooges of Israel, more interested in Israel's well-being than America's. It was worse than the old anti-Semitic charge of "dual loyalty."

Podhoretz recently wrote a column quite properly denouncing Vidal and denouncing *The Nation* for running such vile material.

For the record, in my judgment, the charges are outrageous: Podhoretz is a deeply committed American patriot.

The question of "dual loyalty," however, is a particularly interesting one in American society, and not only in the Jewish context. America, after all, is the model pluralist nation in the world. Unlike the people in most other nations, Americans come from everywhere.

And so, many Americans feel an affection for other nations. And they act upon these feelings. Greek-Americans lobby with vigor against America sending arms to Greece's archenemy Turkey. They often wield great clout, even though the State Department says that it is in America's interest to arm the Turks.

Another example concerns the "Captive Nations" constituency: Americans whose ethnic heritage stems from the Eastern European countries subjugated by Russia. Now, the United States has plenty of other good reasons to oppose the Soviets, but it has been claimed that we are too tough because ethnic Americans play tough politics here.

Recently, some American blacks have taken a passionate interest in U.S. policy in Africa. The anti-apartheid movement has moved American foreign policy. Again, there are some who say that the demands of American blacks go too far and do not serve broader American interests.

And, of course, there are the Jews in America, most of whom vigorously support the existence of the state of Israel. Many Jewish organizations have put pressure on politicians. Jews in America have always been active in campaign funding; now there are scores of political action committees interested in the Israel issue. And, of course, the charge is made that America is too pro-Israel because of Jewish pressure. (Gore Vidal says we ought to give no help to Israel.)

How to resolve this? American pluralism needs two components. First, surely, is a foreign policy that is in the American interest. Second is a foreign policy that is in the interest of Americans, including Greeks, Jews, blacks and ethnic Europeans. After all, they vote; they pay taxes.

Those interests—"American" and "of Americans"—are usually compatible. Most Americans, of whatever heritage, are pro-freedom-around-the-world. Sometimes, however, there is some distance between the two interests. Then the executive and congressional branches battle one another. A healthy compromise is the usual result.

All this is not new. America's most famous diplomatic "special relationship" has been with Great Britain. Why? Because so many Americans came from England. That "special relationship" was one good reason we gave military aid to England to fight our hemispheric neighbor Argentina during the Falklands war.

And special interest foreign policy isn't going to stop. It's just starting. The latest waves of immigrants to America have come from Latin America and Asia. Cuban-Americans have become a serious political force. Down the road, there will be more political influence by Americans of Korean, Taiwanese, Filipino, Central American, South American and Arab heritage.

And the problem—and the glory—of our global role will remain what it is today: trying to create a foreign policy that is both in the American interest and in the interest of Americans.

May 29, 1986

A powerful nation that is universalizing will end up with a universal foreign policy, which makes it more powerful.

The longer I watch the scene, the more impressed I am with the old saying that "God helps drunks and the United States of America."

We came perilously close to screwing it up in Central America in the 1980s. There is a lot of retrospective blame for that, and I would lay most of it on the liberal Democrats who were still skulking in the shadows of Vietnam.

We did prevail, in a contest that really put the last spike in communism.

There were several key factors. We held the line in a bumpy and chaotic sort of way. It was very important that we do so. Nicaragua became a symbol of whether the United States could prevail when it correctly felt threatened and in circumstances when it could easily prevail, if it marshaled the will to do so. Superpowers that don't do that, or are not perceived to be able to do that, can have difficulty remaining superpowers.

The Nicaraguan people showed they were like people everywhere, and given an opportunity to vote to choose democracy, of course they did. (I'm very proud of my column predicting Mrs. Chamorro's victory. It appeared 11 days before the election. I believe I was the first of the very few columnists who called it the way it turned out).

And, for all the talk about, my, wasn't it terrible, we're putting Central America in a big-power cold war context—it clearly was in that situation, like it or not.

From 1986 to 1988, my son Daniel was special assistant to Eliot Abrams (assistant secretary of state for Latin American Affairs). He passed along a story to me about the first negotiating meeting between the Sandinistas and the Contras in 1988. Before the meeting began, the Sandinista officials taunted their Contra adversaries. "The Yankees will sell you out," they said. "They sold out their allies in Vietnam, and they'll do it to you too."

But the taunting went the other way as the Soviets collapsed. That was one big factor that forced Daniel Ortega to hold a mildly free and fair election in 1990, which he lost and which changed—forever, I would guess—so much of the romantic malarkey we have heard about communism as the wave of the future in the developing countries.

Third Worlders now understand that if they want the interlinked blessings of democracy and markets, they have to go to democracy and markets.

Keeping Our Neighborhood Safe

The contra vote has been delayed again, this time by cutesy congressional manipulation. Sooner or later, we will make up our mind. When we get around to it, I hope the central issue has been framed properly. Here is how I see it:

Periodically, American generals and admirals are brought before the Congress and asked this question: "Sir, would you rather be in the military position of the United States or the Soviet Union?"

Our highest ranking officers invariably answer, "We'd rather be in the military position of the United States." They say this despite the fact that the Soviets have more troops, more tanks, more guns, more planes and a nuclear arsenal that is at least equal to, and in some ways more potent than ours.

Why? Mostly because the Russians are surrounded by peoples who hate them—a potentially high crime area, if you will. On the other hand, we live in the geopolitical equivalent of a nice, safe, suburban neighborhood.

Consider: Within the Soviet Union itself are restive peoples, from the Balts in the north to the Muslims in the south, many of whom feel as if they have been swallowed up by the great communist bear. Then there are the peoples of the Soviet "satellites"—who know that they are "captive nations." Periodically, eruptions boil over: Hungary in 1956. Czechoslovakia in 1968, Poland of Solidarity days. Add a billion Chinese who are feared by the Russians, as well as the people in the socialist fraternal state of Afghanistan who are being killed by and are killing Russians every day. The Soviets have reason to be worried about their neighborhood.

And America? We have oceans on our east and west borders. Peaceful Canada is on our north. To the south is Latin America. At least until recently, the Latins have not caused us much serious trouble. Cuba has been a thorn, but after a failed attempt to foment revolution in our hemisphere, they've been sending most of their young mercenaries to kill and advise how to kill Africans in Africa.

The root of the present contra problem—from the U.S. point of view— is that the current situation might change. Behind all of the (important) talk about who's a Somocista, a democrat, a freedom fighter or a Marxist-Leninist, is this issue: Will the United States continue to live in a safe neighborhood?

The current Nicaraguan Sandinista government is supported by the Soviets and the Cubans. If the Sandinistas survive and flourish in Central America, there will logically be a linkage of their activities and those of the Soviets. The Soviets will want to try to get the pot boiling under the United States. The Sandinistas, as the one lonely Soviet surrogate on the North American mainland, will be seeking compatible neighbors to ensure their survival. To do that, they will almost surely try to subvert their neighbors: The Sandinistas even have a phrase for it, "a revolution without borders." Together, these pot-boiling activities may well serve to make our safe neighborhood unsafe.

As has been pointed out, the contras are not the perfect force to stymie the Sandinistas, and the $100-million package may not do the trick. The contras lack training. In the past, some of them have been involved in human rights violations. Some of their leadership—but not most—are old Somocistas. Perhaps there may be a better military plan to put the squeeze on the Sandinistas.

But at the end of the argument there is this: It is extremely important to us. We should try something, particularly if young Nicaraguans are willing to do the hard part. If it doesn't work, we may have to try something else later.

If we don't, at some future congressional hearing, a general may well be asked who's in better shape militarily, the United States or the Soviet Union. And he will throw up his hands and say, "I don't know."

April 24, 1986

Tip's Contra Passion

In the first game of the World Serious, the Tippers beat the Gippers. Speaker Thomas P. "Tip" O'Neill is as passionately against aid to the Nicaraguan contras as President Reagan is for it.

O'Neill is a tough foe: he is a man of honor, deeply patriotic, serving his last term, with a record more right than wrong over the years, properly lauded as a great American at testimonial dinners by Reagan and Bob Hope. O'Neill used wit and muscle to rally just enough Democrats to beat Reagan's contra plan.

It is a battle of giants over the nature and future of American foreign policy. Both men are emotional about it. Reagan thinks Central America is the place to start rolling back the red tide. But what are the roots of O'Neill's emotional commitment? They are both ordinary and extraordinary.

On the ABC news the other night, Tip gave clues. The ABC sketch by Peter Jennings showed that O'Neill opposes contra aid for some obvious reasons: he particularly fears a Vietnam-style escalation. But the piece also stressed that O'Neill's passion has another powerful dimension. He is a devout Catholic, within a deeply divided Catholic community. O'Neill listens to those who oppose U.S. policy; O'Neill's much-beloved aunt was a sister of the Maryknoll Order; O'Neill particularly heeds the Maryknolls' counsel. "When they come in to see me," O'Neill told ABC, "they are women of the cloth, people of God. . . . They are not going to mislead me.

If Tip's emotions on the issue are tipping the balance, if the Maryknolls are a key influence on Tip, then the Maryknolls are very important. Who are they?

They are a small Catholic order. Many of their members devote themselves to serving the poor.

But the Maryknolls also practice political action. Their publications have praised the foreign policy of Castro's Cuba. Maryknolls have supported the communist guerrillas in El Salvador and in the Philippines. They have supported the current Sandinista government in Nicaragua. Ironically, that is the same government that most of Tip's Democratic colleagues characterize as "Marxist-Leninist." It is the same government that the primate of Nicaragua, Cardinal Obando y Bravo, has denounced as "totalitarian." The Sandinista foreign minister Miguel d'Escoto is a Maryknoll priest. He has said, "Marxism is one of the greatest blessings on the church."

Yet Tip O'Neill—who is as far from Marxism as you can get—has never gotten the word. Last year he said: "We've followed the (Maryknoll) order all our life. . . . When they come and talk to me, I have complete trust."

It goes beyond Maryknolls. O'Neill has said one reason for his opposition to the contras goes back to an incident when a friend of his, a 17-year old Marine, was stabbed in Nicaragua—more than 50 years ago. The Marine, says Tip, told him the reason he was in Nicaragua was "to take care of the property and the rights of the United Fruit Co. I got stabbed for United Fruit."

Oh my. Since the Marines left Nicaragua in 1933, the Soviets have become imperialists who penetrate the Third World, Cuba has become a Soviet stooge, Cuba and the Soviets are pumping Nicaragua full of arms, Latin America has had a revolution in favor of democracy, and Latin countries are begging American companies to come in and provide jobs. Yet, O'Neill harks back to the old world of United Fruit.

Using masterful political strategy, O'Neill beat Reagan in round one, even though a majority of the House believes that military pressure must be part of the package to push the Sandinistas to free elections.

It is a torturous issue for many legislators on both sides. O'Neill—still trusting Maryknolls and still remembering horror stories half a century old, tying all that together with more ordinary concerns—will continue to try to defeat, delay and dilute contra aid. He still may succeed.

He's a great American all right, and making a great mistake, leading his Democrats in the wrong direction, based on bad memories and bad advice.

March 27, 1986

"20/20"-gate

ABC News has discovered why the Iran-contra scandal happened. You may not choose to believe it—I don't—but they do.

"A clear picture has emerged," Barbara Walters told us at the top of a special edition of "20/20" on Thursday, Dec. 18. "President Reagan is the reason it happened." says Walters.

Consider ABC's view of the contra story. Walters says it begins with "Ronald Reagan's battle with communism"—we are shown a clip of the president saying, "They are the focus of evil in the modern world."

Soon Sam Donaldson explains, "If Lt. Col. Oliver North is the evil genius of the present crisis, there stands behind him a framework of ideological zeal"—coming from Ronald Reagan, who is, says Sam, "driven by a fierce determination to combat communism, particularly in Nicaragua."

We see Reagan saying "To do nothing in Central America is to give up the first communist stronghold on the North American continent—a green light to spread its poison. . . ."

Ted Koppel provides the geo-political perspective: ". . . wherever this president can find men and women prepared to roll back the tide of Soviet communism, he will help. It is a policy that comes to be known as 'the Reagan Doctrine.'" We then see the gunfire of the doctrine at work: in Afghanistan, in Cambodia, in Angola—and in Nicaragua.

John McWhethy informs us that there was a "mindset" and an "atmosphere" within the administration: they were "obsessed" with Nicaragua.

Walters returns to look at the big picture: "a Marine in the NSC who brought the 'Rambo' spirit to life, a management style in the White House that let things get out of control."

Koppel sums it up: "if the question is whether President Reagan created the political and operational climate that made the deal possible, if not inevitable, the answer is yes."

Mindset. Climate. Atmosphere. Inevitable. Powerful words of psychological predestination. It just had to happen. That's ABC's theme. The political and operational aspects are linked. There was an "obsessed" administration, infused with "ideological zeal," led by President Rambo—is it any wonder that policy became scandal?

Well, yes. Did Reagan make it happen? I think Daniel Ortega is the more likely culprit. His Sandanistas subverted a democratic revolution and turned Nicaraguas into a Soviet-Cuban outpost.

It is not obsessive to understand that a Soviet proxy state in Central America can indeed "spread its poison." It is not zealotry to support the Reagan Doctrine. Usually, Congress approves. No one complains about helping the Afghans. A liberal congressman (Stephen Solarz, D-N.Y.) led the fight to give aid to Cambodian rebels. And if Nicaraguan policy is zealotry, why did Congress vote to send $100 million to the contras?

Is it zealotry for a president to fiercely oppose communism? If so, why has every American president since World War II shown such ferocity?

Now: Is it a scandal if free-lancing White House staffers broke the law to fund the contras? Yes. If it happened, find the malefactors—whoever they are.

But consider: Is there a journalistic scandal in painting a psycho-hypo mumbo-jumbo picture that says that a "mindset" of anti-communism "inevitably" leads to a policy that leads to a sordid scandal? Yes.

After all, if that formula is valid, shouldn't this be asked: has our (obsessive) policy of support for NATO, for Israel, for Japan—indeed 40 years of ideological zeal to help protect free nations from the Soviets—also been inevitably linked by climate and mindset to scandal? If not, why not?

There is policy. There is scandal. We will all be better served if we talk about whether serious policy is sound policy—and then look at scandal to find out if the butler really did it.

December 25, 1986

North at the Pearly Gates

It is the distant future. Trumpets blare at the gates:

"Oliver North, this is a preliminary hearing, prior to meeting your maker. Are you ready?"

"Yes, sir."

"You lied to Congress. Not just to congressmen, whom you may scorn, but to the U.S. Congress and its majesty."

"Yes, sir."

"You destroyed evidence. That was wrong and illegal."

"Yes, sir."

"You did stupid things. Not the fence to protect your family from terrorists. That wasn't stupid. But you violated the first commandment of covert work: separation. You let Iran be linked to contra. When Iran was uncovered, so was the diversionary funding to the contras. Cluck! You were in over your head."

"No excuse, sir."

"And you violated the laws of the land regarding helping the contras."

"Well, no, sir. Perhaps. I don't really know."

"You don't know?"

"There were so many different amendments, so many Boland amendments and others, too. They were worded ambiguously on purpose, as a political compromise within the Congress. There were zealots in the Congress, too."

"Suppose it was never done. All of it—the dumb money diversion, and the other things, too, the third-country help, the quids and the quos— all of it, never done. What would have happened?"

"What do you mean?"

"I mean, suppose the whole executive branch had decided to follow the letter and spirit of all the laws—as the liberals interpret that letter and spirit."

"But I don't agree with their interpretation. Lots of people don't. Certainly not on third country and quids and quos."

"Don't trifle with me, Colonel North. I said suppose the liberal interpretation had been followed, what would have happened?"

"The contras would have been in terrible trouble."

"Would they have collapsed? Disappeared?"

"With no money, no American political muscle to back them up, no third-country help, yes sir, they might well have collapsed and disappeared."

"But, later on, in 1986, when the U.S. Congress did vote money to the contras, wouldn't they then have been all right?"

"With respect, sir, no. That's not the way a military force runs. It takes years to put together. If it's disbanded, it's chaos. It could take years to resuscitate. It might not have worked at all. Probably not."

"So the contras might have gone out of business. They might never have been around in 1986 and 1987 to put military pressure on the communist government in Nicaragua?"

"Correct."

"So what?"

"Without military pressure by the contras, the communists probably wouldn't have started negotiating in 1987."

"Is it also true that eventually real elections were held in Nicaragua?"

"That is correct."

"And democrary did finally come to Nicaragua—and all of Central America?"

"Yes, sir."

"And you think the Reagan administration had something to do with bringing democracy to Central America?"

"I do, sir. We made some errors, but we helped."

"You include yourself in that effort?"

"Yes, sir, but because I and others did wrong and stupid things, there was a scandal, and that hurt the cause."

"But you're saying there might not have been a cause left . . . ?"

"Yes, sir."

"Very interesting. Stop smiling, Colonel. A very interesting case. Did stupid and illegal things. Lied. Probably helped freedom flourish. Very interesting. You can go to the main hearing now, Colonel North. I said stop smiling."

May 11, 1989

Media Piranhas, Where Are You?

If the election is even moderately fair, and it may turn out to be barely so, it is not a bad bet that on Feb. 25 Violeta Chamorro will be elected president of Nicaragua. If it happens, yet one more communist dictator, the Sandinista's Daniel Ortega, will fall.

That, of course, is not the story we've generally been hearing. Most of the journalists reporting about Nicaragua are perhaps too sophisticated.

You see, Chamorro's party, the National Opposition Union (UNO) doesn't have much money for electioneering. UNO is a 14-party wall-to-wall left-right coalition—and they bicker in public. They haven't been successful at organizing voters. They don't have cars, phones and Xeroxes.

The Sandinistas, on the other hand, are giving out cigarette lighters, tee-shirts, belt buckles, beach balls and briefcases, all with the Sandinista logo. They have organized. Their posters are everywhere.

You know what that means. Money, organization and inside baseball are what drive elections, right? And not only that. Chamorro broke her knee on Jan. 2, and *The Washington Post* says, "Many analysts wrote UNO off as a lost cause."

Polls, too. Bizarrely, the *Post* reports that "almost all polls show Ortega in front." A *Los Angeles Times* editorial says "only two public opinion polls among many" taken in Nicaragua show Chamorro "even close" to beating Ortega, and urges the United States to get ready to support a freely elected communist (Oxymoron.)

They just don't get it. You'd think that they might after Eastern Europe. These are not elections. They are referenda. The referendum question is "Do you want to be ruled by totalitarians?" People everywhere, given half a chance, vote no. When they're scared, as many Nicaraguans are, they tell pollsters "no opinion," "undecided" or even lie. With all that, Chamorro has been ahead in many of the better polls.

The communists turned Nicaragua into a repressive slum. The living standard has fallen by 90 percent. About 20 percent of the population has fled. Inflation is too high to measure.

Given such circumstances, says Costa Rican President Oscar Arias, "It is inconceivable that the Sandinistas could win a fair election." Arias says Costa Ricans wouldn't tolerate the election abuse going on in Nicaragua.

UNO gets 30 minutes a week on television. The Sandinistas keep the rest and use putative news programs to market their wares. They use government resources to finance their campaign. They have threatened, harassed, jailed, beaten up and even killed UNO supporters. They have claimed that Chamorro supported Somoza's National Guard: it was her martyred husband that led the anti-Somoza opposition.

The press, which in the United States goes ballistic if a candidate boosted an expense account, which faints at Willie Horton commercials, has quietly bought in to the subversive idea that what ought to be judged in Nicaragua is whether it will be an "acceptable" election. Hey, press, do your job. Hey, piranha fish, where are you when we need piranha fish?

My guess from far away is that the Sandinistas are probably going to lose. They became drunk with power. Ferdinand Marcos thought the opposition could never unite on a single candidate. Hello, President Aquino. The Sandinistas made the same mistake.

They'll probably lose because even with Sandinista skullduggery, there are a thousand international observers in place, many of them straight shooters. There are hundreds of international press, and, sooner or later (it will be later), the press will do their thing about dictators and corruption and saintly ladies drawing big and passionate crowds who want freedom now. Headline: Vi's Got Big Mo. Hey, press: the whole world is watching.

The Sandinistas cut a deal to get their Central American neighbors to dump the contras in return for free elections. It's hard these days to shut down an election while the spotlight is on. If Chamorro wins, the Sandinistas may even have to let her govern. The process is forcing the Sandinistas, in a grudging and ugly way, to compete. It's becoming Poland, not Cuba.

February 14, 1990

Mrs. Chamorro received 55 percent of the votes; Daniel Ortega, 41 percent. The American press, for the most part, never did get the hang of it; the Sandinistas are a Marxist-Leninist party and people don't vote for that kind of party.

Fidel, Here's the News

Finally, Radio Marti is on the air, broadcasting into Fidel Castro's Cuba. Marti has been criticized, not just by Castro, but by Americans. The complaints fall into two categories—geopolitics and programming.

The geopolitical gripe is based on the idea that Marti will harm relations between Cuba and America and that it might lead Castro to jam American radio stations. This view deserves only a short amount of shrift. We shouldn't worry about harming relations with Cuba. It is Castro who needs good relations with us. It would help him in many ways: trade, tourism, technology, legitimacy.

What we want from Castro is a change of behavior. We don't want Soviet troops next door, or Cubans trying to export communism to Central America, or Cuban soldiers serving as Soviet mercenaries in Africa. If Castro changes his behavior, he'll get good relations with us. If not, it won't hurt us. We can live without Cuban cigars.

Will Castro jam U.S. stations? Is a mouse likely to challenge a lion? Jamming is misunderstood. When a nation jams its own airwaves, it's unfortunate and ugly, but probably legal. Thus, Russia can, and does, broadcast static in Russia in order to try to prevent Russians from hearing the news from abroad. It is a partially successful technique.

Castro is also afraid to let his own people hear the news. So, he can try to jam Radio Marti—in Cuba, using "ground wave" jamming that stays in Cuba. But he is not entitled to do it through "sky wave" jamming that could obstruct an American station in Rochester, N.Y. That would be akin to an act of commercial warfare not unlike having Cubans tell us what supermarkets we may shop in.

Castro would be foolish to try it. It might give Ronald Reagan, conqueror of Grenada, the sort of ideas that Castro should not want Reagan to consider.

What about programming? It is said that Marti will be a propaganda station. Or, it is said, it will replicate the Voice of America. This is silliness. There is a third option—a "surrogate home service."

The distinctions are important. A propaganda station—say, Radio Moscow—is an organ of government peddling a party line. The VOA is different: it's a non-propagandistic national radio service for an international audience. The programming deals mostly with American and global news. It is broadcast by professional journalists in English and other languages.

What is a "surrogate home service?" As it happens, I am a member of the board of directors of Radio Free Europe and Radio Liberty. These radios broadcast in 21 languages to the Soviet Union and Eastern Europe. We are, we believe, professional and non-propagandistic.

But, unlike VOA, the Radio Free Europe/Radio Liberty stations do not deal primarily with America. Our charge from the Congress (to use one example) is to try to put on the air the kind of journalism Poles might have if Poland were a free country. So we hire the best Polish emigré journalists and let them broadcast about Polish news, culture, economics and politics. (And Poles in Poland listen. It has been said that the Solidarity union could not have happened were it not for R.F.E.)

That's the sort of mandate Radio Marti has: to broadcast Cuban news, Cuban culture, Cuban politics, Cuban economics, to Cubans in Cuba. That sort of news can't be gathered and broadcast by either VOA or private Spanish stations in Miami. After all, shouldn't Cubans know how many Cuban boys have been killed in Angola?

I wish the Marti team well: Adelante! Theirs is a tough job. With lash marks from Radio Liberty political wars on my back to prove it, I guarantee that the Martinis will be harshly criticized, mostly unfairly. But there is a bonus. Theirs is a noble task: to shine a fair light in a dark place.

Broadcasting the truth often causes problems for governments, even in free countries. In those sick parts of the world where tyrants try to strangle the flow of information, the truth can be particularly scary. It makes dictators very nervous. That's why Castro is trying to keep Marti out of Cuba. That's why we're putting it in.

May 30, 1985

Indicators: *Freedom*

A. 1990 is the first year in which there are more free countries than not-free countries.

Number of Free, Partly Free, and Not-Free Countries

Year	Free Countries	Partly Free	Not Free
1973	44	38	69
1975	41	47	64
1980	51	55	55
1985	53	59	55
1989	60	39	68
1990	61	47	59

B. The percentage of free people has surpassed the percentage of not-free people in the world. (If China were suddenly to become free, the percentage of not-free people would be cut in half).

Percent of the World Living in Freedom

Year	Free Countries	Partly Free	Not Free
1973	32%	21%	47%
1975	35%	23%	42%
1980	37%	21%	42%
1985	35%	23%	42%
1989	39%	20%	41%
1990	38.8%	22.5%	38.6%

C. America's perceived allies: China down, USSR up.

Q. For each country [listed below], tell me if you believe that country has acted as a close ally of the U.S., has acted as a friend but not a close ally, has been more or less neutral toward the U.S., has been mainly unfriendly toward the U.S. but not an enemy, or has acted as an enemy of the U.S.?

Country	"Close Ally"/ "Friend" Combined	
	1985	1989
Great Britain	83%	84%
Japan	68%	62%
West Germany	60%	48%
Israel	50%	47%
South Korea	41%	42%
Egypt	33%	32%
India	30%	26%
Mainland China	31%	16%
Soviet Union	3%	16%
Pakistan	10%	13%
El Salvador	15%	11%
Nicaragua	6%	5%

Source notes are on page 397.

In early 1986 I was asked by the White House to be a member of the official U.S. team to observe the Philippine elections. It was where the People Power wave began. It was an exciting and glorious moment. There are some aspects of the situation that should be better understood.

A few thoughts:

It was a fiction that the United States played a neutral's role in the process that led to the unseating of President Marcos. We intervened. The American embassy was a player, early and often, despite somewhat disingenuous protestations to the contrary. When the crunch came the American government did its best to help Mrs. Aquino gain power. (We even refueled military helicopters.)

Question: if we can properly help democrats dump a friendly right wing authoritarian regime in the Philippines, why did we have such an argument about helping democrats dump an unfriendly communist regime in Nicaragua?

The power of an international press pack is awesome. Our delegation had split into eight small teams, each headed by a member of Congress, and we helicoptered all across the archipelago to do our observing. We saw a very public, relatively peaceful election. When we returned to Manila, many delegation members spoke with their families back in the United States, and we began to understand how the election had been covered. Our relatives were petrified: Did the goons get you? Did you see gunfire? It's so terrible that those thugs stole the election!

The actual election was quite good. If all the ballots had ever been counted (they weren't), if the election campaign were wholly fair, my guess is that Cory Aquino would have won a narrow victory.

It is said disparagingly of some public figures that they cannot walk and chew gum at the same time. The same must be said of a hungry press pack, particularly those from television: They cannot cover two stories at once. There was only one story in the air in Manila, preprogrammed from the moment the good lady challenged the bad dictator: fraud, corruption, and violence. The reporting was surely not a lie; it was only unrepresentative of the total reality on the ground.

Should we be concerned? After all the good lady was indeed a good lady. She won, and the bad dictator lost. But we ought to understand what happened. The media wave drove U.S. public opinion, which drove the Congress to a feeding frenzy regarding who could be more democratic-than-thou. Ultimately, Reagan's executive branch went along as well. To some extent, it was politics-by-media.

As noted earlier, the politics of the media wave is working mostly in our favor now. That was certainly apparent in the coverage of the glorious then ghastly events in Tiananmen Square. That one made everyone an anti-communist.

But, I confess, I am still leery about media-wave politics. That's my trauma from Vietnam. The unelected media should not be mindlessly and reflexively running the railroad.

The Fourth Wave of Freedom

MANILA, PHILIPPINES—Beneath the apparent electoral chaos, corruption and confusion that is playing itself out in the Philippines, something is going on that is of enormous global significance. It is more important than whether Ferdinand Marcos or Corazon Aquino "wins" this close and controversial election.

For despite all the charges of fraud, thuggery, theft, violence, harassment and goonery—strange as it may seem—democracy has won a mighty battle.

For wittingly or unwittingly—probably unwittingly—Ferdinand Marcos let all the genies of freedom out of the bottles of liberty.

The first game, of course, was the election itself. The Philippines have a genuine democratic tradition. As Americans, we should be proud that it stems from a time of American colonial rule. That tradition was so sturdy that it did not vanish during the years of the Marcos-imposed martial law. In such an open culture, an election can have the power of a tidal wave; it is, in fact, an uncontrollable force.

The second genie Marcos let loose was the National Citizens Movement for Free Elections (NAMFRL). Now, there is simply nothing like this organization anywhere else in the democratic world. It is as if a conservative U.S. president, facing re-election, signed an executive order deputizing Common Cause and the National Council of Churches to become a fourth branch of government during the election period, and that new fourth branch—while authentically stressing and policing the precepts of good government—worked against the hated president with a passion. In the Philippines, there were half a million(!) NAMFRL volunteers watching the process—very, very closely.

This good-government genie interacted famously with a third genie that Marcos underestimated: a ravenous international press corps. The basic, all-purpose story—it may be true, it may be false—was graven in stone the day the election was called: Marcos will try to steal it. All that was needed were the details, and a few good video bites.

The fourth genie was collective: the U.S. embassy, and the free-floating international electoral observer corps. I was privileged to be a member of the team sent out by President Reagan and headed by Senator Richard Lugar. We received a non-stop tattoo of allegations of fraud, corruption and harassment. Some of the charges were even confirmable.

In short, all the pent-up forces of democracy were let loose upon poor Ferdinand Marcos.

There was a final factor: Marcos and his thugs may indeed be corrupt—but they are surely inept. Watching them operate, one wants to present marksmanship medals to The Gang That Couldn't Shoot Straight. Surreptitious is not a word in their vocabulary. These palookas couldn't get away with the smooth theft of an election in the dark of night, let alone with all the genies jumping up and down in broad daylight.

As this is written, no one really knows whether Marcos or Aquino got more votes. (My guess is Aquino.) No one knows (yet) what machinations the players will use to make their will felt. Marcos still has plenty of power left, which he may still try to use illegitimately.

But the Philippines will never be the same. All the president's horses and all the president's men will not be able to put the toothpaste back in the tube. There will be an opposition party—either Marco's or Aquino's—that will have probably received 48 or 49 percent of the vote. They will organize, complain, bang the drum—in short, do all the things that happen in a contentious and fractious democracy. The sanctimonious faction will be sanctimonious. The bully boys will be bully boys. The press will keep the kettle boiling.

But at the end of the day, I hope in 1986, but maybe a little later, the Philippine Islands—55 million people in a developing country—decent people, friendly to America—will be a nation squarely in the column called "free."

That is no small matter. Popular democracy is on a hot streak. It blossomed in the modern world in America 200 years ago. In a tortuous way, Europe followed. After World War II, there was another surge.

And now we are witnessing the fourth wave. Latin America is going democratic in a quite remarkable way. Even perhaps Haiti. Parts of Asia have already made it, other parts, like the Philippines, are closing in on it.

If it indeed happens here, it must be understood that it is more important to us than our military bases, or the control of the sea lanes, or whether the communist guerrilla army is a little stronger or a little weaker. For our national interest is to see to it that the fourth wave of the democratic process surges. When it does, we ride it on a superpower surfboard that can't be stopped.

February 13, 1986

"The Whole World Is Watching"

Our three-man observation team is on the road early in a U.S. Embassy van to catch the opening of the polls at 7 A.M. When we arrive at our first school, San Pascual Central, long lines already snake around the courtyard: The mood is calm and festive. These people know more about election fraud and political corruption than any U.S. anchorman. But a country can be both corrupt and free; so the voters are up early this morning to exercise their franchise.

There are two schoolteachers at each voting table. And two party reps—one from Marcos's New Society Movement (KBL), one from Aquino's UNIDO. And a volunteer poll watcher from the National Citizens Movement for Free Elections (Namfrel). In order to cast a ballot, a voter's thumb must become a printing press, affixing a thumb print in five places. The voter must sign his name in four places. When the ballot is cast, the voter's right index finger is marked with indelible ink, to prevent multiple votes. The ink is trademarked "Comelec," the acronym for the Commission on Elections. The ballot boxes are locked with three separate Comelec locks. The polls are closed at 3 P.M., so that ballot boxes can't be switched in the dark.

In Manila and in the provincial capital of Batangas, the rumors are as thick as the sugar cane in the fields. The indelible ink, it is said, won't last 24 hours. The military will take over the country if Aquino wins. The warlords of the north won't let Namfrel observers in. The Muslims of the south won't let Namfrel in. Marcos is spending billions to buy the election. The Army will cause trouble. The troops won't be confined to their barracks, they will intimidate the voters. Yes, they will be confined to their barracks, they won't keep law and order.

Are the rumors true? Even paranoids have real enemies. There is a historical record to go by, and it is not nice. Many observers believe that Ferdinand Marcos, once a hero, has raped the democratic process in the Philippines.

American political consultants are selling and spreading election techniques around the world: TV spots, press conferences, audio bites, media spin. But Namfrel could give the consultants a few lessons. The day before the election, our full delegation is briefed in Manila by the head of Namfrel, Jose Concepcion. Comelec can't be trusted, he says. Only 85 percent of the precincts will be covered by Namfrel. I have here a phone message from our observer in the north—a death threat—they need a media team right away. I have a message here from the south—there are reports of teams of "flying voters," ready to vote early, often and everywhere. I have here a phone message that pro-Marcos goons will cause commotion and switch ballot boxes. A wag in our delegation says it sounds like pledge night on a Jerry Lewis telethon.

Concepcion has worked his hustle well. His unstated message: if Cory Aquino doesn't win, it's a rigged election.

If he needs it, Marcos will try to do whatever he can get away with. But how much could he get away with? The ultimate answer to that question is being played out back at the San Pascual Central School. It is already 2:30 P.M. The voting lines have dwindled. More than 80 percent of the registered voters have cast their ballots.

The election, at this moment, in this one remote corner of the archipelago, is no longer in the hands of the low-ballers, the thugs, the priests, the Army, the warlords, or any of the other stock characters from central casting of modern democracy. There is a new player in the game, Felicisima P. Reyes. She is a no-nonsense schoolteacher and she is preparing to supervise the counting of the ballets of Precinct 48 in San Pascual near Batangas. She arranges the desks so that seven officials will watch and record the count. Loudly she reads out the first ballot: "Marcos."

Again: "Marcos." And again. In the back of the classroom, the people of the precinct have crowded in. I count 40, jamming the room. I look at the slatted windows: nothing but wide-open brown eyes, trained on Felicisima Reyes. Another 30 people. The silence is total.

"Marcos," she says. And then, "Aquino." And "Aquino," again and again. The eyes in the room and in the windows relax. It is Aquino country, one of the least corrupt areas in the Philippines. The final vote is Aquino 164, Marcos 110.

Most important, everyone knows the tally. When the retail vote is public, it's hard to cook the books wholesale. Almost one-third of all the voters have stayed to hear the count. They care. Don't let anyone ever tell you that only industrialized countries can exercise democracy. Right now, what has happened in Felicisima Reyes's schoolroom is the center of the geopolitical action in the world. Is democracy on a roll? It is in many places. If it stays hot: America wins.

There is a poster in the classroom, titled "Rules for Reading Aloud." Stand straight. Read with expression. Stop at periods, pause at commas. Group the words correctly. Pronounce the words clearly.

That's where we are 36 hours after the vote. The Filipinos have stood up straight to try to regain their democratic birthright. There will now be a pause. The powers that be will try to figure out whether they can pull some tricks that all those eyes in all those slatted windows won't see. It won't be easy. It's too public. My guess is that the government will ultimately have to respond to the people one way or another, for the Filipinos are grouping their words correctly, and pronouncing them clearly. And the whole world is watching.

February 17, 1986

Don't Let China Get Away with Murder

If the Chinese thugs are allowed to get away with murder, we will pay for it in the decade to come.

The ultimate tool in the enforcement of totalitarianism has been the credible threat to ruthlessly murder any opposition. The great wave of democracy rising now in the world is due in some large measure to the fact that in recent years murder has become unfashionable and unrewarding among many totalitarian butchers. It has not happened because they are kinder and gentler but often because television cameras are gaining more access, even in unfree lands. The cameras tend to show the murderers at work, just as they have in China, even after the government tried to pull the media plug.

When people in free countries see murder, they do not like what they see. They often tell their governments to punish the capos. A denial of trade, technology, and investment are usually the chosen instruments. The people's revolution is fueled not only by brave dissenters but by the free people who can see the dissenters and help them. The Chinese man who stood in front of the tanks may have won the war.

The butchers have murdered people in China. The blood flowed in Tiananmen Square. But at issue is more than the lives of brave students, more even than the future of freedom in China. The fate of the global democratic surge may well be at stake.

If the Chinese Communists can prevail because they slaughtered their adversaries, they will have reinstated murder as a form of politics. And the word will go forth: Murder works: it is an acceptable policy tool to scare off the opposition.

Insofar as such a precept regains ground in the international community, it diminishes the chances for the freedom wave to swell. It is a message that will reverberate in all those lands where freedom may be just beginning to bloom—in Poland, Hungary, the Baltic states and in the Soviet Union itself. We should not forget that the governments in those places are still the people with the machine guns.

But suppose the community of nations gets tough with the Chinese gunners. Suppose the community decides that China can no longer hide under a human-rights double standard. China has entered the modern world. The government has pledged itself to economic progress. China has recently become a part of the global commercial grid. Running such an economy without foreign markets, foreign technology or foreign investment would be more than a little difficult.

Such sanctions can be useful in proportion to the degree that the great commercial nations can credibly threaten to act in concert. Free-market philosophy can sometimes be best served by selectively denying it.

Because China is by far the world's largest nation, because we are at the edge of a new political era, because the media have penetrated where they have not been before, the potency of the signal that eventually comes from China will be enormous. Indeed, it may be the hallmark of the oncoming decade. It can determine whether Americans will live in a world that is user-friendly for democrats.

If China is turned around and is forced to forswear violence, we can enter an era where the pre-eminent human command can also apply to governments: Thou shalt not kill. When thou can't kill, it's a lot harder for thou to oppress.

June 8, 1989

The Bush administration has generally done pretty well in foreign policy. I give them a B+. When your adversary is destroying itself it's usually not a bad policy to sit back and applaud. If the train is leaving the station, and it's headed in the right direction, that's fine.

But America is not just a super-power, or an omni-power. We are those because we have established ourselves as a moral force for free values. Now, there are some sound geo-political reasons for the United States to continue dealing with mainland China, just as there is a sound reason to give the Soviets some running room on the Baltics.

But those positions can only be wisely maintained if the President is successful in making the public, and passionate, case that he is spokesman for liberty in the world. The two tracks are not neccessarily mutually exclusive. Reagan had other flaws, but in this regard he was first rate. Bush has not yet pulled off the rhetorical flourish to go with the common sense prudence. He may still do it.

I have a dream. Deep into the next century, when population growth around the world pretty well ceases, the cards will be cut and we may well see who the power players are for the next millennium or so.

As that reckoning approaches, the United States and the values we represent will be well served if the U.S.–Canadian bond is tight

*and strong. The Free Trade agreement was a powerful step in that
direction, particularly so because it came at a time when Canadian
views of the United States are at less than an all-time high.*

*In early 1990, as the Quebec issue heated up again, there was
talk about several of the Canadian provinces joining the United States.
I went up there to get a sense of how the land lays. Of course, as a
neo-manifest destinarian, I liked the idea.*

*There is also talk about statehood for Puerto Rico. I have mixed
emotions—concerning language. Intuitively, I'm for it. Maybe some
day, some way, Mexico would like to hook up. But I have reservations.
Look at Quebec; maybe language differences are too great to overcome.
Rest assured: I will take a position. Columnists do that.*

North American Anti-Americanism

Somebody up there doesn't like us: Canadians.

In a recent poll, a sample of 1,000 Canadians were asked to describe
Americans in just one word. Brace yourself: Eight of the top 10 responses
were "snobs," "pig-headed," "aggressive," "powerful," "obnoxious," "indif-
ferent," "stupid" and "rich." (The other two answers were—whew!—"good"
and "friendly.")

It's pretty clear that it's not just our acid rain policy that's been bothering
them.

The poll was taken by Decima Research in Toronto and appeared in a
July issue of *Maclean's*, Canada's largest circulation magazine. Devilishly,
Maclean's/Decima simultaneously also polled an American sample.

Would you like to know what single words Americans used most frequently
to describe Canadians? "Friendly," "nice," "neighbors," "wonderful," "satisfied," "normal" and—ugh!—"delightful."

It's an odd couple: the fat klutz waltzing with the demure damsel.

Curiously, American cosmic geopoliticians are concerned about anti-
Americanism everywhere else in the world. If poll results like those above
came in from Bangladesh or Burundi, there would be a task force at work.
Results like that from Japan tend to shake the international economic
system. In Europe, when Americans are described as obnoxious pig-headed
snobs, we shudder about the future of NATO. Everyone is concerned
about what Mexico thinks of us; you know, it's our back door, and there
are Communist guerrillas in Central America.

The standard solution for anti-Americanism is well-known: teach 'em
about America, let 'em see our movies and television shows, let 'em read
our books and hear our music, let 'em come visit. There is a small problem
with that remedy for the Canadian situation: They do know us. They're
the largest tourist group we have. And Canada is drenched with U.S.

popular culture: An overwhelming proportion of Canadians live within range of a U.S. television station.

What's bugging them up there? *Maclean's* cited some verbatim responses of what Canadians least liked about Americans: "they are self-centered," "they don't try to understand what is going on beyond their borders."

Truth be told, the poll reveals clearly that we are indeed ignorant about our friendly, satisfied neighbors. Only 12 percent of Americans knew that Canada was our largest trading partner. (Erroneously, 69 percent thought the answer was Japan). Only 11 percent of Americans knew that Brian Mulroney was the prime minister of Canada. (By contrast, 35 percent of Canadians knew that Dan Quayle was the American vice president.) Only 57 percent of Americans knew that the United States and Canada had recently signed a Free Trade Agreement—but 97 percent of Canadians knew it.

Maybe we ought to take a short course about our wonderful northern neighbors. We could begin by noting that not long ago (1964) a substantial percentage of Canadians (29 percent) thought it would be nice if Canada became part of the United States. Ho, ho! Today the rate is down to 14 percent. By contrast, 66 percent of Americans think it's a peachy idea.

Is all this a problem? It is a symptom of the problem that one even asks the question. If the nice Canadians were not such compatible neighbors, they'd surely be a big problem. We share 5,527 miles of common border.

What should be done? Maybe we should start a reciprocal dislike campaign. We could call them obnoxious snobs. There are those who say the United States needs a large northern enemy. With the Soviets collapsing, we could get angry at the Canadians. But, alas, the Canadians are not obnoxious snobs. They're wonderful; the poll says so.

Anyway, with the new Free Trade Agreement, the United States and Canada are now embarked on a monumental economic enterprise that will compete directly with the European common market juggernaut, which comes into being in 1992. We'd better be pals.

There are times in the course of human events when the best thing to do is not much. Maybe we just ought to leave bad enough alone.

August 9, 1989

How About a New Country—Right Here?

QUEBEC CITY—If what almost just happened in Canada—national suicide—had gone on in Moldavia, or Israel, or South Africa—it would have been at the top of the news.

But because Canada is, well, Canada—nice, near, neighborly and non-violent—Americans ignore it. We shouldn't. Recent events in Canada can shape not only Canada's destiny, but America's. Ours for the better, and perhaps theirs too

After wrangling, the premiers of Canadian provinces compromised about the "Meech Lake Accord," amendments designed to get Quebec to ratify the Canadian constitution. The process had a price: bitterness, and a stipulation that French-speaking Quebec is a "distinct society."

The agreement, assuming it is finally consummated, does not change the reality behind the tempest: French-speaking Quebeckers are indeed a distinct society. Francophonia is often their defining, and passionate, dimension. A majority seem to care more about the cultural and linguistic survival of Quebec than about the political and geographical survival of Canada.

Demographic imperatives suggest that the feeling will grow. Quebec has lower fertility than the rest of Canada. It draws proportionately fewer immigrants. It has difficulty keeping, and Frenchifying, the immigrants it gets.

Thus, Quebeckers are becoming a diminishing fraction of Canada, a small French island in a large North American ocean of English. Accordingly, the formula for retaining Francophone culture is elemental: Use it or lose it.

Using it—establishing language rules, forbidding outdoor signs in English—angers other Canadians. A town in English Canada declared itself a French-free zone, held a meeting and laid down a doormat with the Quebec fleur de lis on it. Television showed English shoes trampling the French flag. The clip enraged Quebeckers, bringing joy to those promoting separation.

Separation could shatter Canada. Quebec has almost a quarter of the population. If it leaves, the country splits. It would be as if a tier of Midwestern U.S. states seceded, leaving America in two unconnected parts.

In Canada, one unconnected part would be the four Eastern maritime provinces. If Quebec goes, it's said that the maritimes will apply for U.S. statehood. If that happens, the people in British Columbia, Canada's Pacific province, will also likely look for a new arrangement.

Some observers say the maritimes are so poor that America won't want them. Silly. God isn't making any more real estate. Texas was poor only yesterday. And British Columbia? It's not poor, and it would connect Alaska with the Lower 48 states. The rest of Canada, landlocked, might see that the original Canada was finished. Of course, English Canada doesn't like such thinking. They don't want to be "taken over." What's in it for them?

There are three non-Spanish cultures in North America: English, French-Canadian and American. Two of them seem happy about who they are. The English Canadians are less so. They often define themselves as "not American." (Call a national psychiatrist. These folks need a big couch.)

But all three peoples also have an identity as North Americans. It's a remarkable place. When the New World opened up in 1492, mankind started over again, and did a good job here, in a different way.

A new consolidated nation would be the most powerful, influential country in history, rich in land, resources, people, wealth and culture. Talk about identity.

North America is changing. New immigration, much of it Asian, is creating a pluralist nation in Canada, not unlike the United States. The U.S.-Canada Free Trade Act has created a common market. America will soon have a European-style financial allowance for children, something long available in Canada. We can learn from each other.

Will English Canadians go along? Not now. Pride is at stake. What could we do? Eureka! Let them take us over. Change the U.S. Constitution and call the new place "Canada." Details to come.

If, in time, the language gap proves surmountable, Mexico might join; we could then call the whole shebang "Mexico." After that comes Puerto Rico and then Quebec. And one day, far in the future, we can gather together under our real name, "North America."

June 13, 1990

The Meech Lake accords were not passed. There is talk now of the western Canadian states joining with American northwestern states in a special trade zone. Neo-manifest destinarians, stay tuned.

Playing with Blocs

The geo-political jigsaw puzzle is being scrambled. It's a great moment. The focus is on Europe. The bloc-builders are at work. Will a newly free Eastern Europe and an already-free Western Europe unite commercially? Politically? Culturally? Will Europeans inherit the earth? But wait a minute. Wasn't America supposed to inherit the earth?

The 1992 European Community will be made up of 12 West European nations with 320 million people, all pledged to free trade and unhampered migration. The six once-captured nations of Eastern Europe comprise 115 million people. Add Yugoslavia and non-EC nations of Western Europe (like Sweden), and the grand total is—half a billion people!

That's twice the number of people in the United States. Most of the Europeans are already wealthy and modernized. The rest can get there quickly. It will be a monumental trading bloc. Should we worry?

If we're going to play blocs, let's start by counting right. Add 30 million Canadians to our side; we have a free trade agreement with the Canadians. That gives us North Americans about 280 million, not much less than the existing EC '92 bloc. Moreover, we take in immigrants and are growing. The ECs have mostly plateaued

So call it a match between North America north of the Rio Grande (mostly English-speaking) and the current EC '92. The Europeans go ahead only if Eastern Europe hooks on.

If they get East Europe, what about Mexico? There are about 90 million Mexicans, and growing. The GNP per capita in Mexico is $1,830—not much different from Poland ($1,930) or Hungary ($2,240). Demographically, that puts a North American bloc up around 370 million, short of the all-Europe total, but not by much, with our gang growing.

A magic word almost slipped by: English. Might not the English-speaking nations of the Pacific—Australia and New Zealand—be figured on our side in the bloc-meistering game? Add 20 million.

And is it still in America's interest to push England into the EC? Do Scotchmen really have more in common with Greeks than with Americans? (Given the large Greek population in the United States, don't Greeks have more in common with America than with Scotland?) With England on our team we'd be more populous than the EC right now. (Who lost England?)

(Is Poland commercially and culturally closer to Italy or America? Why did Lech Walesa say "Poland can be the America of Europe?")

Another magic word: Pacific. Are those Pacific nations going to be a separate bloc led by Japan? There are more Koreans in America than in Japan. And more Taiwanese, Chinese, Filipino and Vietnamese. Maybe it will work out that the United States will be the common denominator of the Pacific.

There is a purpose to this exercise. Let us remember, as the pieces of the puzzle get reconfigured, that America is unique. We are a large, prosperous, influential nation, made up of people from everywhere. We are the only universal nation. If there are rules of blocs that matter to other nations, they may not matter to us.

Do trading blocs matter at all? They are convenient ways to lower trade barriers. Fine. But if West Europe can bloc with East Europe, and the United States can bloc with Canada, won't the blocs keep on blocing? Ever-bigger blocs lead toward global free trade, which is good for all, not zero-sum.

The most meaningful competition among the modern nations in the years to come will not be commercial. We're all going to be richer.

The competition will concern the nature of the global culture, and in that game the numbers can be counted in many different ways. The central question will be: What ideas and values will hold sway in the global community? Will they be oriented toward America, or Europe, or Japan, or toward some non-democratic systems?

That's a far better roster of potential outcomes than the one that used to include the Soviet Union. But it's still a competition. Our children and grandchildren will live with the results.

In that contest, in a universalizing world, the nation that is universal—that's us—has a head start.

November 22, 1989

American Politics

12

The Political Terrain

Our political system works fairly well, despite its abuses. Beware of experts and elitists; all hail the voters. Because the system works pretty well, don't count on major changes in the structure. What you see is what you'll get.

I exempt the savings and loan crisis from this mildly sanguine view. That is an incredible and repugnant story. It was predictable in one sense; if you have a system that guarantees deposits to 100 percent, there is no market test of a bank. Accordingly, the crooks can go a long way before the political system (as opposed to the market system) halts them. Lots of people ought to go to jail for that one.

Even there, I must remind non-Panglossian readers that the magnitude of the situation, said to be "half a trillion dollars," is nowhere near that. If someone said what is the value of your house? You could say what you paid for it, say, $300,000. You could say $400,000, the current market value. Or you could say $700,000 which is the total amount you pay for the house, counting interest on the mortgage for a full thirty years. All three statements have some meaning. But the one that really tells you what your house is worth is the current market value. The current market value of the debt accrued in the S&L situation is in the realm of $90–120 billion, according to an estimate by Alan Greenspan, chairman of the Federal Reserve Bank. The "half trillion" is the equivalent of paying a thirty year mortgage on the debt. If Uncle Sam wrote out a check, today, to pay off *the whole indebtedness in one shot, it would be in that $100 billion range, about 2 percent of one year's GNP.*

Terrain watchers: this is a bonus time for those looking for road maps of the future.

The politics of the 1990s will be shaped by the 1990 census. Some decennial censuses only apportion for two presidential years, the "4" year and the "8" year. But the 1990 census apportions for three presidential elections, the "2" year, the "6" year and the next "0" year. In the present case that's 1992, 1996 and 2000. In politics, that's as far as the eye can see and a little farther. The states showing the big electoral gain are Southern and Western, the ones that have been trending Republican in recent years.

Indicators: *American Politics*

A. Americans are eclectic—and anti-communist.

Terms with Which Americans Strongly Identify (1987)

Term	Percentage
A supporter of the gay rights movement	9%
A liberal	19%
A Republican	20%
Pro-Israel	25%
A union supporter	27%
A supporter of the NRA	27%
A conservative	27%
A supporter of business interests	28%
A supporter of the women's movement	29%
A Democrat	31%
An anti-abortion movement supporter	32%
An environmentalist	39%
A supporter of the peace movement	46%
A supporter of the civil rights movement	47%
A religious person	49%
Anti-communist	70%

B. The cost of a Congressional seat has levelled off after a steady climb.

Mean House and Senate Campaign Expenditures (Constant 1989 Dollars)

Year	House Seat	Senate Seat
1974	$119,916	$ 982,714
1976	$140,939	$1,144,659
1978	$183,865	$1,598,413
1980	$216,869	$1,566,737
1982	$276,637	$2,161,342
1984	$271,785	$2,621,127
1986	$276,406	$2,970,583
1988	$273,811	$2,802,118

Source notes are on page 398.

C. House members who run for reelection almost always win . . .

1. Incumbent's House Reelection Percentage

Year	Reelected, as a Percentage of those Seeking Reelection
1964	87%
1970	95%
1976	96%
1980	91%
1982	90%
1984	95%
1986	98%
1988	99%

2. (cont.) . . . but there is more turnover than is apparent.

Percentage of New Members (Elected Within the Previous 3 Terms of Each Year Given) in the House of Representatives

Session	Percentage of New Representatives
83rd (1953)	44%
86th (1959)	38%
89th (1965)	44%
92nd (1971)	34%
95th (1977)	48%
98th (1983)	41%
101st (1989)	28%

D. Although the number of political action committees has septupled in the last 15 years, the growth seems to have come to a halt.

Number of Registered Political Action Committees, 1974–1989

Year	Total
1974	608
1976	1,146
1978	1,653
1980	2,551
1982	3,371
1984	4,009
1986	4,157
1988	4,268
1989	4,178

Courting the Neo-moderate Liberals

The recent Supreme Court decisions, typically denounced or saluted as "conservative," have shown again that in America today most conservatism can be described more accurately as Neo-Moderate Liberalism.

Here is how to test the NML idea:

Consider the four big recent court decisions. Consider how the other linked parts of our political system will probably react. Consider what liberals wanted in, say, 1960—before liberals started going off the deep end. Consider where we are today and where we're likely headed given the temper of the public. And then ask: Is this conservative?

The big four court decisions are flag burning, affirmative action, the death penalty and abortion.

Flag-burning is the easiest. No one favors burning the flag, but the decision is hailed by liberals as a near-ultimate expression of free speech. Of course, the public thinks it's a bummer. Accordingly, the decision may be overturned by a constitutional amendment. But it will be tightly drawn, dealing with one particular act. The decision's potent impact will remain. Free speech, including symbolic speech, is a very broad concept—the traditional liberal position.

The affirmative action decision is said to be conservative because the court has returned to a "colorblind" society. No. Colorblind was the marching anthem of liberals during the great civil rights debates. What the court has modified are the concepts of "reverse discrimination" and quotas, which were, in truth, antithetical to real liberalism.

What about the death penalty? The liberal view was either to prohibit the death penalty or curtail it. The recent court decisions mildly expand the reach of the death penalty, but due to earlier decisions, and coupled with how the lower courts now actually practice, we remain with a curtailed death penalty.

Abortion: In the early '60s it was illegal. Liberals said it should be legal. The new court decision says that for now abortion will remain legal nationally, according to Roe v. Wade, but that the states can impose some restrictions.

But almost whatever the court does next, one can expect that a very great majority of women will be able to get legal abortions in the very great majority of cases. If Roe v. Wade remains in force, abortion is a constitutional right. If it does not, many states will make it legal.

Seventeen states had at least somewhat legal abortion prior to Roe v. Wade. Assume, for model-making purposes, that only those states would again have legal abortion. Today, those states have a population of about 100 million people. But there are almost another 90 million people living in states that adjoin those states. Typically, although not always, a cheap bus ride could then get even a poor woman from an illegal state to a legal state where abortion would be safe, relatively inexpensive and perhaps even free.

In total, that's almost 80 percent of all Americans. The rest might have to travel further—not likely to be a big problem for the non-poor. Private philanthropy would then have an important logistical and educational role to play to see to it that poor women are not denied an option available to the middle class.

That's where we are now: Conservatives accepting and ratifying some earlier common-sense liberal beliefs. But will Neo-Moderate Liberalism continue? Or might this court now start to roll back authentic aspects of liberal thought?

Dubious. The system, and that includes the Supreme Court, is reflecting the broad sweep of sensible public opinion, which is measurable in polls. Americans want a colorblind society, not a racist society or a quota society, they want a legalized death penalty, not a blood bath: they don't want the flag burned, but they want plenty of free speech: they want abortion to be neither criminal nor capricious.

The public, moderately liberal on these social issues, is getting what it wants.

July 12, 1989

College for Presidents

It has been noted that there is something gamy and demeaning about the presidential election. The candidates and the networks team up to give us 10-second televised sound bites. Balloons soar: candidates are seen in front of monster-size American flags. Demagoguery is not forbidden.

Learned scholars complain that the real issues are never discussed in any depth, even, or especially, during debates. We hear silly arguments about the Pledge of Allegiance. We see conflict; anti-abortion demonstrators breaking up a candidate's rally. A candidate rides around in a tank to prove that he will defend the republic. Serious economic policy issues are dealt with thusly: "Read my lips—no new taxes."

Well, yes. But there is another side to the story, and it should not go unnoticed. Ours is a most-peculiar election system, but it does have at least one enormous redeeming feature. It is a powerful learning experience for those who would be our leaders.

Whether or not the Pledge of Allegiance is a valid issue, it is important that Michael Dukakis—if he becomes President Dukakis—know just how intensely Americans feel about it, right to the marrow of their bones.

Dukakis—if he becomes President Dukakis—should know just how intensely some people feel that abortion is a terrible thing. And Vice President Bush—if he becomes President Bush—should know just how intensely some people feel that outlawing abortion is a terrible thing.

A President Dukakis should understand, in the marrow of his bones, that people really don't want to pay more taxes, and this feeling is intensified if it is felt that government programs aren't helping much. A President Bush should understand that a hard-working young couple who feel they can't afford a house, also may feel that they have been cheated by the system, no matter how wonderful some national economic statistics may look.

Democracy is not a perfect political system (Flash!).

But linking up with our election procedures, it offers some monumental benefits. It allows people to let off steam. When people are angry, about pro-life or pro-choice, about too much government or too little government, they can let their anger be known in a very public way, particularly so at election time. That public display of discontent, when offered official succor, even in the form of demagogic sound bites, lessens the anger quotient. It also reminds politicians that the poeple who elect them, the people who make them powerful and famous, can also make them unpowerful and less famous. That makes candidates listen. Intently.

That double dynamic—anger and dealing with anger—helps bolster democracy's strongest suit: responsiveness. When citizens feel that they have some control over their destiny, some control over their government, when they get response and succor, they cool off. They are then much less likely to, say, try to overthrow the government, an act which is not usually good for governments or nations. Thus calmed, people are more likely to get some work done during the day and have a beer at night. Responsiveness yields a stable society, which is better than an unstable one.

So—if you're feeling that the presidential campaign is simplistic or silly— you too can calm down. Remember it is serving a mystical democratic purpose: it's making the nation healthier and sending your next president to school.

September 29, 1988

How to Become President

Keep your eyes on the power brokers and the delegates, it's said. They'll pick the next president—right? Wrong. The voters will pick the next president. Let's keep our eyes on voters.

If we look at the most recent polls, we'll know what the voters think—

right? Wrong. The public opinion polls, as ever, are complex and contradictory. Still, they're the best game in town.

From the pages of *Public Opinion* magazine, we find this:

In 1981, 70 percent of Americans volunteered that inflation was the nation's most important problem. Today, only 2 percent say so. Interestingly, no single problem is cited by more than 13 percent of the population. No big problem—right? Wrong.

If instead of asking for volunteered responses, the pollsters offer a card listing "personal concerns," the top three choices draw big votes—"drug abuse" (43 percent), "crime and lawlessness" (36 percent), and "relations with foreign countries" (27 percent).

How about politics? With Reagan in office and Republicans elected to the White House in four out of five presidential elections, this must be a mostly Republican country—right? Wrong. By about 4-to-3, voters identify themselves as Democrats over Republican. By the same margin the voters also think that the Democrats are the party best able to handle the major problem. Sounds clear enough—pro-Democratic, right? Wrong.

By 2-to-1, voters regard themselves as conservatives, not liberals. They also believe—by 5-to-3—that "the federal government creates more problems that it solves." That was Ronald Reagan's message.

Is that clear? It shouldn't be. Solid majorities still favor more government spending on education, health, crime and drugs. Got it? Spend more, right? Wrong. By better than 4-to-1, Americans say they don't want a tax increase. Want more, don't want to pay for it—smart people.

How about defense? A big majority in 1980 (60 percent) said spend more on defense. Today, only 18 percent say spend more. We're not for a strong defense anymore—right? Wrong. More than half of us (53 percent) say to keep defense spending where it is, which is about $300 billion roughly 50 percent higher than in 1980.

Nicaragua? The contras? By about 2-to-1, Americans are against aid to the contras. That's the popular position, right? Wrong. When given this statement: "The U.S. should aid the rebels in Nicaragua to prevent communist influence from spreading to other countries in Central America"—Americans agree by 2-to-1! (Funny what the addition of that word "communist" will do.)

Look now at some social issues. By 2-to-1, Americans say it should be harder to get a divorce. 90 percent say extramarital sex is wrong, 81 percent say homosexual relations are wrong. Solidly conservative on social issues, right? Wrong.

The issue of legal abortion is about a 50–50 split. Only 25 percent believe that "women should take care of homes and leave running the country to men." More than 90 percent are pro-school integration. It didn't use to be that way.

Complicated? Indeed. Voters are complicated people. for example, by 5-to-4, Americans say that "after eight years of Ronald Reagan we need a president who can set the nation in a new direction."

OK. But what direction? That's for candidates to figure out. A fellow could do worse than come on as a conservative Democrat, concerned with drugs and lawlessness, against big government and tax increases, but for an involved government, pro-military strength but against defense increases, aware of the Nicaraguan threat, socially conservative in a liberal society. Right? Right.

March 10, 1988

I have a theory. Washington pundits and pundettes tend to reflect, forever, the basic perspective of their first Washington job. Compare a reporter who becomes a columnist with a congressional aide who becomes a columnist. They see the political world quite differently.

My first job in Washington was at the White House. I still tend to support presidents. I didn't even do much Carter-bashing.

Arrogance or Power?

And so we hear once again the old chant about the "arrogance of power" in the White House.

The phrase gained currency during the Vietnam War when critics claimed that President Johnson was waging war over the heads of Congress. How dare he? said the critics—conveniently forgetting that the Congress was voting funds to continue the war.

Now we are told about "arrogance of power" in the Reagan White House. Just imagine, there was this reckless lieutenant colonel (Oliver North) running the foreign policy of the United States—and from the White House basement! What arrogance!

About a hundred years ago I worked on the White House staff of President Johnson. With that credential, allow me to offer a generic perspective on what I sense a large part of this arrogance-power battle is all about.

What it's not about is an allegedly reckless light colonel in a "basement." You should have such a basement. It's at street level, one flight of stairs away from the president's office. It's where top National Security Council staffers are housed.

What it's also not about is whether a 43-year-old Marine was given too much authority. North was not working as a Marine. He had been detailed from the Marines and held a heavy title: director for political and military affairs of the NSC. As such, he was a member of the president's personal staff.

What the argument is about is that the "arrogance of power" is a phrase that concerns power more than arrogance.

Not only the president, but by presidentially delegated authority, the president's "personal staff" has great power. And White House staffers— smart ones and dumb ones alike—usually have one legitimate thought on their occasionally simple minds. This: The president, unlike any member of Congress, was elected by a majority of all the people.

Under the Constitution, and by law and precedent, the president has broad authority in foreign affairs, including the ability to go to war for 90 days.

For logistical purposes, the president delegates some of his powers. He can choose the secretary of state for one task. Or a member of the NSC. He can choose an experienced person for great responsibility or a young, less-experienced person like Ted Sorensen (age 33, on Kennedy's staff) or Bill Moyers (age 29, on Johnson's staff) or Hamilton Jordan (age 33, on Carter's staff).

The president will then be judged by the quality of his choices, and by whether or not he and they obey the law. If they don't, they are in trouble and deserve to be.

But many of our laws have ambiguities in them, put there by Congress to give the president some running room. (Even Congress knows that 535 politicians in Congress can't make foreign policy at once.) And so presidents end up pushing, testing, skirting and sometimes, so the court rules, breaking laws. That sounds terrible. But the White House often deals with brand-new laws whose limits have never been defined by courts.

The power struggle—from the generic White House view—does not involve a claim that Congress has little power. Congress has considerable clout, which properly checks the president. What often bothers presidents' men is the feeling that both Congress and the press use their power parochially, demagogically and sensationally.

What critics consider "arrogance" is often seen in a different light by the president and his staff. They feel that they—not the Congress—best reflect the nation's interest. That's not arrogance of power, they feel, its the responsibility of power.

It's a rich, interesting argument that has gone on for a long time and isn't going to stop now.

December 4, 1986

Junk-food Politics

The year is not half over. We have not even come to the slow-news months
of summer when the reportage of sleaze and scandal usually intensifies.
Yet we are already drenched in it. Tower. Wright. Coelho. And, it is
said, there is plenty more to come. More hearings, more trials, more
television stakeouts, more leaks and counter-leaks, more trivia, more serious
stuff, more partisanship, much more sanctimony.

Will it ever end? Should it end? Can it end?

It may not end for a long, long time. Remember, it's been 15 years—
since Watergate—that America has been on a rich diet of scandal.

It should end. At its core, scandal news is a junk-food diet for the
body politic. Like junk food, it is tasty and offers a quick fix. Like junk
food, if consumed in large portions over an extended period of time, it is
probably not healthy.

It is not healthy because, at root, it establishes a pernicious falsehood
that makes it more difficult to govern a vigorous democracy. Any individual
scandal story may be correct, they may almost all be correct, but the
totality of the impression yielded by the steady drumbeat of all the scandal
stories put together is not correct. Dear readers: This nation is not governed
by a collection of sleazebags, not in Congress and not in the executive
branch, not now and not earlier.

It is not healthy because, in the media age, firestorm television news
of sleaze devastates in almost equal measure the reputations of those guilty
of serious deeds, those guilty of trivia and those not guilty at all.

It is not healthy because the threat of a trial by television keeps good
people out of government service.

There are those who think it can end now that the lens is turned on
liberal Democrats, rather than conservative Republicans. After all, it is
said, most of the scandal targets have been Republicans, while most of
the sanctimonious scandal hunters have been Democrats. It is argued that
Democrats will now be getting their fair share of sleaze in the face. And
that, it is said, will stop it because everyone will sober up and see that
everyone is now destroying everyone. Don't count on it. Democrats have
taken scandal hits before. Remember Tom Eagleton, Billy Carter, Geraldine
Ferraro and Gary Hart? This won't lance the boil: we'll go right on boiling
Lance.

There are those who argue it will only end when, and if, journalists
turn the lens inward and scandalize each other, perhaps regarding speech
honoraria or prior political service. It's said that might make journalists
back off those appearance-of-impropriety stories. Wrong. Even if it happens,

even if big-foot journalists are cowed (a very doubtful proposition), there is an infinite supply of little-foot journalists who will man the howitzers.

Journalists say: Don't blame us for the scandal-mongering, we're only the messengers who bring the bad news. That is mostly bunk. How many messengers do you know who sort through a hundred potential messages and decide which three to deliver?

The journalists say that, even with the excesses, reporting on the sleaze and scandal cleanses the system. There is some truth to that: there is some real wrongdoing. But it is also true that, due to public disclosure regulations, there is probably less sleaze than ever before in our history— and yet the reporting of it is more prominent than ever. If the process is cleaner, shouldn't the headlines be fewer?

There is a glory to a free press and free politics—and also a burden. The glories far outweigh the burdens, which is why nothing can be done to muzzle anyone, in any way. The process may cleanse the system, but it also tarnishes it.

June 1, 1989

Putting Pressure on the Media

There was something heartening about the reaction to the conclusion of the Ariel Sharon vs. *Time* magazine case.

Consider: Normally—with but one exception—the view of the journalistic community is that the press does good work by putting the pressure on the major institutions in a democracy. Talk to your mainstream media man and you'll find out he believes that when the press puts the heat on government, then government cleans up its act. When the press puts the spotlight on business, Media Man says that will make business behave more responsibly.

There can be excesses in this view—I have, in fact, written about those excesses—but it is essentially true: Putting the spotlight on high beam tends to keep folks on the straight and narrow.

The one exception to this rule, to hear journalists tell it as they have heretofore told it, is the press itself. Pressure, we have been told, is not good for journalism. You see, it has a "chilling effect." If people criticize these tender flowers in medialand, we have been told, they will be afraid to stand up brave and strong and clean and true. (Just imagine a wilted Sam Donaldson.) If—heaven forfend—a politician criticizes the press, he is described as "Agnewesque," and the fear is that government will start pulling television licenses. If businessmen punch back, the fear is that they will hold back advertising.

But this time it was different. The press joined in the press-bashing. Almost every journalistic competitior called *Time* "arrogant." It's a pretty good word. *Time* was wrong: they seriously defamed a man: they have refused to acknowledge any real error.

The *Time* folks are all harrumphing about how they do not intend to change any of their practices. Don't believe that. The people at *Time* may be arrogant, but they are not stupid. They've spent millions of dollars on lawyers, been found guilty of two major charges by a serious jury, seen their reputation damaged, faced the scorn of their colleagues.

You'd better believe that they will review their procedures, and think twice before they again cavalierly imply that someone encouraged the slaying of women and children.

Pressure works. It works on government, just as the press says. It works on business, just as the press says. And it works on the press too, as the press has not liked to say. It makes them better.

Of course, the threat of a libel suit can cure only a very small part of what's wrong with the American press. Most items on television or in the newspaper do not touch on libel or defamation. Stories about politics, the economy, business and science may, on any given occasion, be wrong-headed, mis-emphasized, exaggerated, inaccurate and misleading—but they are not libelous.

But there are other forms of pressure that make journalists better, too. When conservatives began screaming that the media were too liberal, the reaction from the media moguls was about what *Time's* was to the Sharon verdict. Not us! How dare you! Chilling effect! But then they went back to their boardrooms and asked: Is there some truth to the charge?

There was. I sense the media are somewhat more balanced these days. Pressure works.

During the Lebanon war, the Jewish community in America jumped up and down about the perceived anti-Israel bias in the television coverage. The networks denied it, but took a second look. Coverage seems fairer now. Pressure works.

Public opinion polls have shown that many viewers are fed up with a steady drumbeat of sensationalized bad news. The networks have tried to respond.

The most constructive form of pressure on journalism—and the safest form—can and should come from other journalists. They can't be accused of chilling the press.

The press has become very wealthy and extremely influential in recent years. They must be treated as big boys and girls now, subject to the same intense scrutiny by the media that other big-time players get. The

CBS-Westmoreland trial verdict is coming up. If the networks handle the personalities involved in the same way that they handled, say, Hamilton Jordan, Bert Lance, Richard Allen or Ed Meese—you'll know that it's really happening.

(Author's note, 1990: Alas, they didn't.)

January 29, 1985

Reportorial Rules of the Road

Omigod! Holy Smoke! This is what I've been waiting for! I can't believe it: here is this guy offering me the briefing book for the Presidential Debate.

What am I staring at it for? Grab it. Read it. Write it for tomorrow's paper. Big scoop! Front page! Above the fold!

I get famous, my paper gets famous. The publisher will smile at the editor. The editor will smile at me. The *Columbia Journalism Review* will write all about it. The *Washington Journalism Review* will write all about it. I'll win a prize. I'll give lectures. That's good. Good? That's fantastic!

Grab it. Write it.

But wait a minute. Who is this guy? Who is giving me this leak? Why is he giving it to me?

Did he steal it? Is it stolen property? Is it stolen government property? Is it ethical for me to use this leak?

Ethical? Ethical—schmethical. My job is to get the news to the people. Grab it. See that it doesn't violate national security. Authenticate it. Write it. Print it.

But what if the guy did swipe it? What happens?

Scandal? Leak-o-gate? Scoop-o-gate? Journo-gate?

They wouldn't do that to a reporter! Would they? They wouldn't dare! Who's "they"; who's going to do it to me? Journalists don't expose other journalists.

Don't take it. It might be illegal. Look at what happened in Debategate.

Would the Justice Department do anything? Theft of government property? Receipt of stolen property with knowledge that it was stolen? Obstruction of justice by failing to report a theft?

They wouldn't dare. They'd end up in a blizzard of First Amendment charges. They'd end up looking like people who would pull out John Peter Zenger's toenails.

Debategate wasn't the press. That was a political campaign. Different. Very different.

Why? Our job is to tell people news—hindmost for devil. Their job is to—their job—is to what? Win the campaign for their candidate? Elucidate the issues?

That's their problem. We write about their problems. They don't write about our problems.

First Amendment. Maybe it's ethical for journalists to be unethical. It's unethical for others to be unethical. Is that hypocrisy? Hypocrisy is about other people.

Anyway, they'll laugh at me if I don't accept a leak. Snicker-gate. Maybe I should negotiate with the guy. Dicker-gate.

This is getting me upset. Irate-gate. My deadline is in half an hour. Late-gate. Take it easy, don't get excited. Sedate-gate. Everything's going to be fine. Elate-gate.

Anyway, if I don't use it, this guy will just take it down the street to the other paper. Some other reporter's editor will smile.

No way. It's my story. Let's have it, Mac.

July 5, 1983

13

Democrats

Once upon a time, I was a very partisan Democrat. I wrote anti-Republican speeches for President Johnson. In 1967, when some rough plans were being talked about in the White House regarding LBJ's 1968 re-election campaign, I was told I would likely be on the President's campaign plane writing Give 'em Hell speeches. That would happen, I was told, because the President knew that "I really hated Republicans."

Fast forward to the late 1980s. In Time magazine I am referred to as "the conservative's favorite liberal." What happened? By my lights, this: Democrats, many of them, changed. They moved to the left. That much is generally understood. But Republicans also moved to the left, toward the center, and that is usually not recognized. (Consider civil rights, social security, environmentalism, etc.) When the right-wing party becomes more centrist and attracts more votes than they used to, it's said that the country is moving to the right. That's not necessarily exactly what happened.

In any event, I think my basic political principles have remained essentially the same.

I believe the national Democrats have behaved foolishly in recent years, out of touch with the voters, out of touch with reality. Given such views, I'm often asked why I remain a Democrat. Several answers. First, the Republicans are a long way from peaches. Second, despite all the talk about the Democratic tropism toward suicide, in politics you can never tell what happens next. Suppose the Republicans nominate a turkey. Suppose there *is a terrible recession. Suppose there is a scandal. Suppose there is a bad war.*

Democrats could then win, and if such a Democratic administration came to be dominated by new-fashioned liberals, that could yield interesting but potentially addle-headed public policy. So it's useful for some of us paleoliberals to remain around to try to keep a moderate influence in what is still the plurality party in the nation that used to be called the leader of the free world. Now we are the leader of the whole world. Anyway, maybe a non-liberal Democrat can be nominated and elected. I'm not saying it will happen, only that anyone who says it won't happen doesn't understand the vicissitudes of political life.

The voters have behaved pretty wisely. Generally speaking, they'd rather vote for a Democrat than a Republican. But if the Democrats behave foolishly the voters won't go along.

There is a sad pattern to the pieces that follow. The first general grouping deals with the early stage of Democratic politics in the eighties. The second group deals with Reverend Jackson, and the Democratic pratfall in the mid-80s. The third part deals with the election of 1988, the events of 1989, and then Jackson and the party again in 1990. I apologize for being so consistent throughout and so Jackson-oriented, but, at least until very recently (perhaps) the Democrats have behaved consistently, and Jackson is the on-going symbol of the problem.

Is it possible that the Democrats will change? The two potential Presidential candidates that could best engender change are Senators Sam Nunn and Charles Robb, both exceptionally able and impressive men. (Unfortunately, in the run-up to the 1988 campaign Sam said Chuck should run. Chuck said Sam should run. Neither ran and the right wing of the left wing party had no standard-bearer.) Lloyd Bentsen is a solid possibility. (Perhaps Senator Bill Bradley could do it; I wait with open eyes and open ears.) My choice for Vice President is Senator Joseph Lieberman of Connecticut.

I think if Robb or Nunn had run in 1988, either one would have had an excellent chance of winning the nomination and the presidency. Either one would have a medium shot at winning in 1992.

Indicators: *Party Politics*

A. Democrats have been losing support . . .

1. Party Identification

Year	Democrat/ Leaning Democrat	Republican/ Leaning Republican
1980	53%	34%
1983	53%	35%
1986	47%	42%
1989	45%	44%

2. (cont.) . . . particularly among younger voters.

Party Identification Among 18–29-Year-Olds

Year	Democrat/ Leaning Democrat	Republican/ Leaning Republican
1980	54%	33%
1983	50%	37%
1986	41%	47%
1989	39%	50%

B. Despite losses in party identification, the Democrats have not been hurt in Congress.

1. Party Representation in the Senate

Congress	Democrat	Republican
96th (1979–81)	58	41
97th (1981–3)	46	53
98th (1983–5)	46	54
99th (1985–7)	47	53
100th (1987–9)	55	45
101st (1989–91)	55	45

2. Party Representation in the House of Representatives

Congress	Democrat	Republican	%
97th (1981–3)	243	192	56%
98th (1983–5)	268	167	62%
99th (1985–7)	253	182	58%
100th (1987–9)	258	177	59%
101st (1989–91)	260	175	60%

C. Democrats get a majority of congressional votes, and a somewhat disproportionately large number of seats.

Popular Vote and House Seats Won by Party

	Democrats		Republicans	
Year	Votes	Seats	Votes	Seats
1970	53%	58.6%	44.5%	41.5%
1972	51.7	55.8	46.4	44.2
1974	57.1	66.9	40.5	33.1
1976	56.2	67.1	42.1	32.9
1978	53.4	63.7	44.7	36.3
1980	50.4	55.9	48.0	44.1
1982	55.2	61.8	43.3	38.2
1984	52.1	58.2	47.0	41.8
1986	54.5	59.3	44.6	40.7
1988	53.3	59.8	45.5	40.2

D. Lyndon Johnson is the only Democratic presidential candidate to gain more than 50.1% of the popular vote since World War II.

Presidential Election Results

Year	President Elected	Popular Vote
1948	Truman (D)	49.6%
1952	Eisenhower (R)	55%
1956	Eisenhower (R)	57%
1960	Kennedy (D)	49.7%
1964	Johnson (D)	61%
1968	Nixon (R)	43.4%*
1972	Nixon (R)	61%
1976	Carter (D)	50.1%
1980	Reagan (R)	51%*
1984	Reagan (R)	59%
1988	Bush (R)	53%

* See note.

Source notes are on page 398.

Me Too

To understand what has happened, one must first understand that Ronald Reagan has pulled off the biggest political heist in American history. He swiped the whole party, the old Democratic one, leading to the "me too" dilemma.

Consider just a few aspects of that party. It was the old Democratic Party that first understood that totalitarianism (of right or left) was the menace of our time. It said that a strong, assertive America would have to play the role of world superpower. The Republicans at that time were isolationists, deeply concerned about the overextension of power.

The old Democratic Party was the party of "growth economics," of tax cuts, of what was then called "belching smokestacks." The pristine environmentalists of that earlier time were Republicans, usually called conservationists as well as conservatives.

The old Democratic Party was the party of "merit." The cards in the subway cars of the very Democratic city of New York showed a picture of white boys on a baseball field, with a black youngster on the sidelines. The leader of the white boys was waving the black youngster onto the field, remonstrating to his teammates: "What's his color got to do with it? He can pitch!"

The Republicans of that time were sitting on the boards of admissions of Ivy League universities, quitely enforcing quotas to keep Jews and blacks out of gentlemen's schools.

And now Ronald Reagan and his Republican cohorts have swiped most of the basic traditions of the whole damn party—or perhaps they only received them as a gift.

Reagan's the tough guy on the block (attacking Democrats for being isolationists). He's Mr. Growth Economics (attacking Democrats as environmental regulatory no-growthniks). He's for merit (attacking Democrats for being for quotas).

To add insult to theft, he's the fellow who says he'll protect "the safety net" (Social Security, Medicare, etc). that his party regularly opposed. To all that he has added some old Republican free-enterprise smaller-government ideas and—presto!—he calls it a "New Beginning." And the nation applauds.

How will the Democrats cope with this? There was no hint at the first post-Reagan-election gathering of the Democratic National Committee.

The Democrats are dedicated, as ever, to the theological fragmentation of their party. Their big issue was how to quota in women, blacks, Hispanics, Asians, etc. During the argument, someone must have risen to say: "Who cares if he can pitch? He's female!"

The dilemma may be exacerbated, but not resolved, by the DNC. The new chairman, Charles Manatt, has ritually vowed to favor "unity and cooperation." Other big-time Democrats said what the party needs is money and organization. They left unresolved only one simple question: Unity, cooperation, money and organization for what?

What does the Democratic Party stand for? One wing, unwilling to give away the game, says strength, growth and merit. Those ideas, they say, are our ideas: we can shape them better than the Republicans.

The other wing says, hey, those are Reagan's ideas. We can't be the "me too" party. Mind you, they are not exactly up-front for weakness, no-growth and quotas. They now say the Democrats need "new ideas." But they won't tell us yet what they are.

Democrats must face the music. They are not in trouble because they have no money, organization or unity. Exactly the opposite: They have no money, organization or unity because they are in trouble.

They are in trouble not because they stand for nothing but because they stand for two very different things. Some believe in the old Democratic beliefs (temporarily pilfered by Reagan). And some still believe in the new Democratic beliefs that got them into all the trouble they are in.

The Democrats' choice is unfortunately simple. They can go left, splitting up an ever-smaller liberal pie. Or they can go back to their roots, try to split off the Reagan voters who were stolen from them and do battle against the tough facts of ideology and geography.

Sooner or later in this game, ideas and philosophy are carried by Democratic candidates, not Democratic committees.

The potential nominees in 1984 will all be tempted to split the difference within the party. That is a tropism in American politics. They will be tempted to be for strength-but, growth-but and merit-but—just the policies that characterized the Carter administration.

If that happens, Democrats will have a party-but—a party, but without an idea, a posture, a direction or a stance, just those things a party needs to get elected.

Many Democrats now feel that if the party is to regain a fighting stance, there will first have to be a fight. Me too.

March 30, 1981

The Freeze, Frozen

It's a good exercise at election time to look at what did not happen as well as what did. It's an approach that Sherlock Holmes used profitably in "The Case of the Non-Barking Dog," (even though Holmes never ran for Congress.)

Earlier this year—about five big stories ago—long before double-digit unemployment, before Lebanon, before the Falklands—the big story was

the Nuclear Freeze. The gist of the story was this: A great grassroots movement was forming, it was the reincarnation of the anti-Vietnam-war movement except it had broad-based middle-class support, it would frame a
referendum on a great issue, it would be an enormous political force bowling
over all who stood in its way, it would raise money, recruit volunteers,
elect candidates, change the world.

Well, of course, what did not happen was just about all of the above.
The freeze is a cutting issue in only 1 to 2 percent of the congressional
races this fall. The Freezers have raised only comparative nickels for disburse-
ment to candidates. The issue is ranked so low in the latest Gallup Poll
index of "most important problems" that it is grouped with "all others"
below a 3 percent cut-off line. There will be referenda in nine states, but
predictably, their impact is much muted by the president's own freeze
plan.

What happens is now apparent: the press bought one more in a series
of by now ritualized post-Vietnam sucker stories. You may make your
own list, but I count at least five big ones that have used the formula,
"the (BLANK) movement is a mass-movement/reigniting the anti-war coali-
tion/enlisting middle-class support/changing our politics/bowling over all
in its way."

That is what was said of the anti-nuclear power movement at the time
of Three Mile Island. It was said about draft registration. It was said about
El Salvador. It was said about the ERA movement. (Remember NOW
activists vowing to start a new party to discipline defectors?) and it was
said about the freeze. And it did not happen.

(A similar phenomenon can also operate occasionally on the right side
of the spectrum. Remember all the stories about how the Moral Majority
and conservative political action committees were going to ride roughshod
over orthodox politics?)

Each issue engenders its own massive media wave with a temporarily
self-fulfilling cast to it. If television runs a special about a cause movement,
then the next demonstration will attract more rock bands and yet more
demonstrators, attracting still more television. Finally, however, the whole
proposition runs out of gas and collapses, the functional equivalent of a
journalistic Ponzi game.

There is a problem in all of this, most particularly when the stories
touch the foreign policy field. After all, what happens when it is accepted
by the media that a grassroots movement will change our politics forever?
What happens is that the media then has to report with a straight face
every jot and tittle of what the leaders of this-or-that very important mass
movement have to say.

Often, however, what the leaders of such movements have to say is silly, dangerous, or both. And so you hear physicians and actors on television telling you how to negotiate with the Soviets—which is equivalent to having Kissinger, Brzezinski and Schlesinger telling you how to treat gallbladder, or how to play a love scene. You hear that registration means a draft and a draft means war; that El Salvador is another Vietnam; that nuclear power plants are "death factories"; that civil defense yields a traffic jam but no civil defense; that Reagan doesn't want any arms control and toys with the idea of a limited or protracted nuclear war.

The nature of such conspiratorial stories points up what the post-Watergate press corps has not yet fully understood: if people say that the government lies, it doesn't mean that what those people say is the truth.

Now, of course, it's not that new movement-generated ideas don't deserve a hearing. Indeed, aspects of the women's movement, the environmental cause, even the freeze movement, have raised consciousness and quite properly moved into the mainstream. But by over-dramatizing and over-estimating the latest trendy cause, extra credibility is lent to some hardly credible notions that discomfit our friends, our adversaries, ourselves. That can force action on false premises, shape policy on flimsy predicates.

Do you think that journalists have now seen that the dog did not bark on this election day? Do you think that journalists will not get snookered in the future when the dog keeps right on not barking? If you believe that you will also accept the idea that Sherlock Holmes is leading a new mass movement that will reignite the anti-war coalition and change our politics forever.

October 26, 1982

This old column, with some amendments, will, I bet, be valid for the 1992 cycle of primaries. Democrats will get into a bidding contest regarding who can cut the most the quickest from the defense budget. This will allow the Republicans to be the responsible party of prudent, gradual defense cuts, as the evolving situation warrants. As the accompanying data indicate, voters are nervous about rapid defense cuts. Wisely.

Democratic DTs

The thirst for light bends plants inexorably toward the sun. There are also political tropisms. A notable one concerns Democrats running in presidential primaries, inexorably drawn into a bidding contest about defense, always bending toward an apparently sunny position that may be described as "Dovier Than Thou" (DTT).

There is some evidence that this process may be beginning. Just about all the putative Democratic presidential candidates pay ritual homage to a nuclear freeze. Just about all of them favor cutting Reagan's defense budget: some of them like to picture him as a fangs-bared nuke-rattler.

In all fairness, so far the DTT tropism is still in the responsible realm. The pro-freeze language voted on in the last Congress sprouted caveats not only big enough to base the MX in, but big enough to let moderates vote for it, grinning and bearing, fingers crossed, saying it's only optics, hoping it won't undercut America's negotiating position in bargaining talks with the Soviets. The Democrats are for cuts from Reagan's defense levels, but these are Washington-style cuts, a decrease in the rate of increase, yielding about a 5 percent per year addition to the defense budget, which is not bad as these things go.

Still, tropisms have a life of their own. The bend toward the sun is incremental and regular—bending, bending, always bending. On defense issues, Democrats tend to bend in primaries because they have been led to believe that the activist groups in the party are dovish, and that activist groups dominate the primaries. And so, the candidates bend and bid.

The classic horror story, of course, occurred in 1972. By the time the bidding ended, candidate George McGovern was on record for a 33 percent real defense cut. That's the equivalent of seven-no-trump, not a wise bid when Richard Nixon was sitting at the table with a fistful of aces.

We shall see whether it happens again this time around. But, now more than ever, Democrats will be wise to resist the siren songs of Dovier Than Thou. If it ever was valid doctrine, it is less so today. One reason concerns another inexorable tropism: the move to the sun-lands has led to bigger delegate catches in the more-hawkish Southern and Western states.

But even more important is the psephological calculus of the general presidential election, as opposed to primaries. Recall, the purpose of the running-for-president exercise is to become president, not to become candidate.

The record of presidential elections is instructive. The perceived and pronounced wisdom always seems to say, "Defense and foreign policy issues are not the big issues; Americans vote for president on domestic bread-and-butter concerns."

And yet, since 1940, with perhaps one exception, the foreign policy issues have been of enormous political consequences in the presidential elections. Just think of the issues: World War, Korean War, Middle East and Hungary, missile gap, Vietnam, Iran, and soft-on-defense.

And think of the winners: Roosevelt, Truman, Eisenhower, Kennedy, Johnson, Nixon—moderate hawks all. One can argue in several ways about

Jimmy Carter's policies as president, but remember that as a presidential candidate, he, too, ran as a Democratic version of a tough guy: a former career naval officer who clearly was not anti-defense.

Of Ronald Reagan we know: on his soft days he ran as a moderate hawk, on tough days he flashed his talons—and will again if he runs again. It helped him in 1980 and there is no reason to think it won't again, this time in moderated form: after all, it will have been four years with the button still unpushed, a term that by election time may even have yielded an arms reduction pact with the Soviets.

It is said that the 1976 election was not foreign policy and defense oriented. There was no Korea, Hungary, or Iran. That makes it all the more instructive. Republican pollster Robert Teeter reported in 1976 that while foreign policy was not the No. 1 issue, it was the key aspect that voters looked to in determining whether a candidate was in tune with "traditional American values." The voters, said Teeter, didn't choose a president on the criteria they used for other offices. They were looking for a stand-up guy who wouldn't be pushed around. They still are, he says.

If that image is violated by Democrats—then Democrats beware. The process that bends a plant to light is similar to the one that takes a moth into a flame.

March 1, 1983

Mondale's Moment

Memorandum to Median Voter:

Excuse this note, M. V. We haven't met personally, only statistically. I know you're a sensible person. According to data, you're very patriotic. You're for a strong national defense. You want to get government off your back, but at the same time you want plenty of services. You're for a clean environment, but not too much regulation. You're against busing and quotas, in favor of the death penalty, have mixed views on abortion.

Because you are the voter precisely at the 50th percentile, you are very important. Candidates who don't have your support are losers. And so, I thought I'd better get in touch with you now because all the real action next week will not be on the floor at the Democratic Convention in San Francisco—but in your living room!

For our political conventions have evolved into big shows with one basic purpose: to convince voters like yourself to vote for the nominee of a given party. And so, M. V., here are a few things to think about so you and I will be able to figure out what's really happened:

1) At the end of the week will you like Walter Mondale better than at the beginning of the week? If you don't—then Mondale is probably a solid loser in November. A nominee's poll rating should go up by about 10 percent during the course of a successful convention. Mondale is already 15 percent to 20 percent behind Reagan. He needs all the help he can get.

2) Were you turned on or off by the image of the Democratic Party you saw on your television set? The television folks will be devoting plenty of time to liberal activists: militant feminists demanding a woman vice president, gays demanding respect, freezeniks announcing that the world will blow up, Jesse Jackson supporters demanding drastic cuts in defense, and a ringing platform endorsement of racial entitlements.

It's not just the activists. The delegates themselves will be from the more liberal part of the more liberal party. Remember, M. V., all the right-of-center Democratic candidates—John Glenn, Ernest Hollings, Reuben Askew—didn't survive the first cut and consequently have no delegates on the floor.

The key question will be this: Was Mondale able to make it clear to you that he and the party he represents are more conservative than what you saw on your screen? He'd better: 74 percent of Americans regard themselves as either conservatives or moderates, including you, M. V.

3) What did you think of Mondale's choice for vice president? Did that choice make you think that Mondale shares many of your views and values? If the television anchormen don't say, "Well, Walter Mondale went to his right in choosing his running mate," he's hurt himself.

·4) At week's end, did you see much distance between Mondale and Jackson? Or is what's left in your mind's eye only a picture of Mondale and Jackson, on the podium, hands aloft and linked, all smiles, as the band plays "Happy Days Are Here Again"?

That won't help Mondale. Sometimes it's better to have combat than a love feast. Jackson has enthralled most black voters but inflamed many white voters. When Jackson was in Central America he applauded communist dictators and denounced the United States.

I know you didn't like that, M. V.

When Jackson came back to the United States, he and Mondale met, and Mondale said they are working together now. A Mondale aide in Minnesota was quoted this way: "There's a lot of truth in much of what Jesse has said in this campaign . . . He is one of us . . . He's a Democrat and true to Democratic ideals. He's never tried to mimic Reagan." Ouch.

Now Jackson is arrogantly threatening to tell black voters to stay at home in the fall if Mondale doesn't give in to Jackson's platform demands—as if Jackson controls them like an old-fashioned party boss.

What will you think about all that, M. V.? Was Mondale able to do something during convention week to show you that he vigorously disagrees with Jackson's positions? That Jackson doesn't represent the Democratic mainstream, or even the Democratic mini-stream? If he hasn't done that, M. V., you can bet we're going to have Reagan for another term.

I'll call you next week.

July 10, 1984

> *By picking Geraldine Ferraro, Mondale went to his left, not his right, for a vice presidential running mate. (My choice was Senator Daniel Inouye.) Mondale did not criticize Jackson's views in a serious public way. He did give an excellent, tough-minded acceptance speech, perhaps the best political speech of 1984. But it was too late, in what, in any event, was a tough race. I like Mondale; I think he's long since graduated from reflexive liberalism.*

Mugged

The Democratic presidential disaster brings to mind a harsh, apocryphal, but relevant story:

A liberal clergyman in a big city was mugged. He had always believed there were no bad boys, only bad societies. He sermonized against any hint of police brutality. He favored civilian police review boards. He said "law and order" were code words for racism.

As chance would have it, the clergyman was scheduled to speak to a group of elderly citizens a few days after he was mugged. He searched his soul to find meaning in his traumatic experience.

When he mounted the podium to address the elderly crowd, he said roughly this: "I have gone through a great personal trauma. I have thought again about my views on crime. And, despite the harsh and ugly act of violence unleashed upon me, I still believe in my liberal principles."

There was silence in the hall. Then an old lady in the rear cleared her throat and rumbled, "Mug him again."

The Democratic Party got mugged Tuesday night, losing the presidency by a historic electoral landslide—49 states. Like the mugged liberal clergyman, the Democrats are thinking things over.

Already we can hear the responses from some Democrats from the left side of the spectrum. It was, they say, a personal victory for Reagan—he's so amiable. Mondale wasn't a good candidate, they tell us. Young people are too selfish these days—that's what did it. It was Ms. Ferraro's finances that tripped us up. Reagan tricked us—he never came up with a plan. They outspent us—it was unfair.

Accidents, tricks, personal popularity. Everything but substance.

Strange—this is the message now brought to us by the folks on the far-out Left who earlier told us it was substance that was in the saddle.

They said that the nuclear freeze movement would freeze Reagan. They said the gender gap would sink the sexists. They said a tidal wave of black registration would establish the agenda of the Rainbow Coalition (and carry the South). They said Central America was another Vietnam, and Reagan would be quagmired.

These are the folks who believed the Civil Rights Commission must be the exclusive province of the quota-mongers. They said the baby-boom Yuppies could be enticed by social liberalism and neo-isolationism. They had no problems with establishing homosexual quotas in the Democratic National Committee—after all, they apparently believed, Democrats can always get the votes of people concerned with traditional values by waving plastic American flags at the national convention.

Now the Left tells us it was only because of an accident of personalism that they lost. They incant their new slogan, "The people really agreed with us on the issues."

There is just enough truth in that for it to be thoroughly deceptive. In national politics "issues" are subservient to "principles." And the voters supported Reagan's principles: strength, traditional values, merit, and initiative.

The activists of the Left were successful in only one aspect of their campaign. They managed to shape the public picture of the national Democratic Party in their own image. By doing that, they effectively destroyed any realistic possibility that any Democrat—even a decent and skillful one like Walter Mondale—could come close to winning the presidency.

Because they now maintain they only lost by accident, the Left liberals will insist that the Democrats do it once more their way, and with feeling.

They are very skillful and very active. Accordingly, it is plausible to suggest that the Left will prevail (once again) in party rule-making commissions. It is plausible that they will win in public relations combat. They may triumph in legislative battles.

But none of that will change the minds of the voters. What is implausible is to suggest that the Left will—ever—win a national election with their current viewpoint. That is too bad, for it robs the rest of the republic of the services of the national Democratic Party, which once was the political engine for sensible progress in America.

For if the activists of the Left succeed in shaping the image of the party again, the voters will merely shrug, and say, "Mug him again."

November 6, 1984

Sound Democracy by Sound Bite

Walter Mondale, Geraldine Ferraro, Tip O'Neill, Mondale's speech writer, and an irate letter writer to the *New York Times* all understand just what the problem is with the Democratic Party and with American politics. By George, it's television!

Here's an excerpt of what Mondale said in his morning-after press conference:

"Modern politics today requires a mastery of television. I've never really warmed up to television and, in fairness to television, it's never warmed up to me. . . . The thing that scares me about that [is that] American politics is losing its substance. It's losing the depth. . . . Tough problems require discussion. More and more it is these 20-second snippets. Those of us who want this office must be serious people of substance and depth and must be prepared not to handle the 10-second gimmick that deals with, say, war and peace."

Mrs. Ferraro also made a statement indicating that Mondale's problem was his televisability. O'Neil said, "Not even Paul Newman could have beaten Ronald Reagan this year." Martin Kaplan, Mondale's chief speech writer, was asked who could have beaten Reagan. His answer: "Robert Redford."

And one J. Gordon of Ithaca, N.Y., wrote to the *New York Times*, expressing extreme dismay because political advertising is "underrunning the structure of democracy." Gordon cites the Mondale "Missile" commercial and the Reagan "Russian Bear in the Forest" commercial.

He notes: "Advertisements using images of wide-eyed innocent children observing a nuclear holocaust (such as we have seen promoting Walter F. Mondale) or the foreboding shadow of a savage beast ready to pounce on one's family (part of the Reagan campaign) hardly direct themselves at the individual's ability to reflect, analyze, or draw a conclusion."

These stunning views are, in my judgement, dead wrong. More than that, they bespeak an attitude toward democratic governance that is in itself dangerous.

Start with the easiest aspects of the case. Recite the Ten Commandments at a moderate speed. How long did it take? Twenty seconds? Thirty seconds? That should demolish the idea that one can't say anything serious in a short time. You can say ten serious things in a short time.

Of course, it's difficult to say serious things briefly. There is an old axiom in the speech-writer trade that notes that it's harder to write something short than long. You have to know what you're talking about.

The fact is, the "Missile" and "Bear" commercials did present a pretty

321

good summation of what the two sides of the current geopolitical argument are all about. One side says stress peace: the damn missiles may go off. The other says stress liberty: the Russians are on the move.

And consider Redford and Newman. Breathes there a soul in this great land of ours who seriously believes that a liberal activist, no matter how pretty, would win a national election?

Voters—believe it or not—don't vote for pretty faces or people who "are good on television." It works exactly the other way: voters think that candidates with whom they agree are attractive and good on television.

Remember Jimmy Carter. In 1976, when Americans agreed with what he was saying, he was regarded as dynamite on television. His smile made all the covers of all the news magazines. But in 1980, when Americans did not agree with him, he was seen as a video version of a weak wimp.

Beyond the parochial argument about the role of television is something more serious. If voters are really swayable by a smile and a commercial, what are we saying about our democracy? That the voters are jerks.

I don't believe it. And I know that politicians who think their constituents are jerks aren't likely to get elected. I think deep down that Mondale, Mrs. Ferraro, and O'Neil know better. They know that voters vote substance. (Indeed that is the case they make about this year's congressional vote.)

They will serve their country and their party better if they acknowledge their real problem—which is the issues they have come to represent— than they will by trumpeting a phony one, that television did them in. A wrong diagnosis yields a wrong remedy.

November 13, 1984

Democrats and the Wizard

Democrats have been having meetings, trying to figure out how to save their party. My sense is that a bold and frontal strategy is needed, even if it breaks some old rules.

My logic flows, oddly enough, from the key scene in *The Wizard of Oz*, when Dorothy and her friends get a final audience with the Wiz. His voice is heard from behind a curtain. It is a booming voice, resonating across a great hall. Dorothy and her friends tremble before it. But not Dorothy's little dog, Toto. The dog grabs the curtain between his teeth, tugs on it—and down it comes! Revealed is not a potent Wizard, but a little old man, manipulating microphones to project a powerful image to a frightened public.

The story of the Wizard defines both the nature of, and the solution to, the Democratic dilemma.

First, note that our political system is one of party images more than direct party power. (Our parties don't pick the candidates, nor can they tell their members how to vote, as in European systems.)

Further, our system is candidate-oriented and particularly president-oriented. This is more true than ever because of heavy television exposure.

So, the image of the national Democratic Party is formed mostly in the context of the race for the presidential nomination. That Democratic image today is of a too-liberal party, beholden to the activist interest groups of feminists, gays, minorities, and peaceniks—among others. That's why Democrats lose national elections. That's why a mood of trickle-down panic is affecting most Democrats, who feel increasingly linked to that image.

This liberal image has affixed itself to Democrats because, in the presidential selecting process, there is a Wizard behind a curtain—the Wizard of the Left-Wing Veto. This Wizard thunders its message: "Agree with me, or our activists won't let you get nominated. We have a veto power in the selection process, because activists dominate the primary elections and the caucuses."

So Democrats running for president are forced to mouth liberal platitudes about every issue from gay rights to the nuclear freeze. A liberal image is formed at primary time, and it is very difficult to scrub off for a general election campaign.

But in reality, the Wizard of the Left-Wing Veto is not any more potent than the one from Oz. Contrary to common belief, the Democratic primary electorate is not a collection of left-wing activists. Almost 17 million people voted in the Democratic primaries in 1984. There aren't 17 million activists in America, or 7 million or even 700,000.

Working from exit-poll data, *The New York Times* has constructed a model of the 1984 Democratic primary electorate. Only 27 percent of the voters even called themselves "liberal"—not much more than the 21 percent who self-declared as "conservatives," and many fewer than the 47 percent who call themselves "moderates."

Only 18 percent of the primary electorate is black. That is less than the 26 percent who aren't even Democrats! (Some states allow independents and Republicans to vote in Democratic primaries.)

Other polling, among all Democrats, shows them in the mainstream: in favor of strong national defense, tough on crime, against high taxes, against high welfare—while favoring increased government help on health and education.

What to do in a situation of a too-liberal image and a moderate electorate? Fight. Tear down the curtain. Reveal the impotency of the Left-Wing Veto Wizard.

This means violating an axiom of party politics: Don't split the party.

But, under present conditions, such a strategy is not only plausible, but necessary. The image has already been cast—unfavorably. It must be recast—favorably. That is not easily done. Waving plastic American flags at the national convention in 1984 did not recapture the issue of "traditional values" for the Democrats.

Only a public fight for the soul of the party can recast the Democratic image, in a way that will be believed by the public.

That will require a candidate willing to engage in combat that will be party-shattering, but ultimately beneficial. That means finding a candidate who has the attribute that the Lion in Oz discovers in himself—courage. Let him or her now step forward.

March 28, 1985

Jesse Jackson is getting a bad rap. It's said "Jesse Jackson is what's wrong with the Democratic Party." Not true. What's wrong with the Democrats is the way the Democrats treat Reverend Jackson. No one is willing to say, upfront, that the emperor has few clothes.

I know about this strategy of silence firsthand, and I want to recommend an antidote.

In the spring of 1988 Reverend Jackson's campaign momentarily seemed to take off. (He won in Michigan with a smart campaign in a caucus state with a low turn-out and high black participation.)

When a candidate gets hot in the primaries, the media desperately need someone to play attack dog. There is usually no dearth of supply. There was this time. The Republicans and the conservative writers were not doing much Jackson bashing; it was too profitable to see the Democrats writhing in agony by their own hand. Nor, for the most part, were the mainline and liberal media attacking Jackson; they didn't take him very seriously, they didn't want to attack a black, and I think they didn't, and still don't, really understand the nature of his radical views and connections.

(The national director of Jackson's Rainbow Coalition is Jack O'Dell, a long-time and open pro-communist. The director of research for the 1988 Jackson campaign, Robert Borosage, was head of the Institute for Policy Studies, which describes itself as "radical." For amplification, I recommend a study by Penn Kemble entitled "The Rainbow Movement: Jesse Jackson and the Future of the Democratic Party," which is the best extended research of Jackson's ideological roots.)

Well, all right. Neither the Republicans nor the press were getting hurt by Jackson. But Democrats? Democrats were obviously getting clobbered by the linkage to Jackson. Still, no major public Democrats stood up and denounced the Jackson candidacy: They didn't want to

*seem anti-black, or they wanted Jesse's votes in the convention, or
they didn't want to lose black votes in November. They were fearful,
and for a reason that became apparent. When Mayor Ed Koch of
New York finally did make a moderate (yes, moderate) statement
regarding the reasons for his opposition to Jackson, he was scalded
by the press and calumnied as an incendiary near-racist.*

*So, with silence the order of the day, with Republicans, the media
and Democrats choosing not to speak up, who ended up on television
taking on Jackson?*

*Hah! Mostly me, or so it seemed. I had been writing about Jackson
and jousting with him since 1984. Suddenly, with no one else available,
there I was on the big television shows, on McNeill-Lehrer, Crossfire,
This Week with David Brinkley and many more, talking about Jackson.*

*I offer up this personal experience for one particular purpose: To
tell Democratic candidates how to run for President. I got an
astonishingly positive response from those appearances, and not just
from conservatives. Liberals went out of their way to tell me it was
grand that "someone stood up to Jackson"—privately, of course.*

*Jesse Jackson is smart to run for President. And the Democrats
are dumb for not challenging his views. He is a serious man, with
serious views. He has become the symbol and spokesman for the
American Left. He is an international superstar. Because his views
are so well known, he is a disaster when regarded as a symbol of the
Democratic Party, but for the same reason he is a potential gold-
mine if a Democratic candidate frontally challenges his views.*

*It is a crazy situation. Since early 1984—a lifetime in politics—
many Democratic professionals have privately described the
Democratic primaries as contests to see which candidate will be "the
last white guy standing." And then they wonder why they lose.*

If Jackson Were White

Some days ago, Reverend Jesse Jackson was asked where he would be in
the race for the presidency if he weren't black.

"Probably No. 1," he said.

Sorry, Reverend, you'd be last. Jackson's problem isn't that he's black,
but that he's Jackson, and that many of his positions are off the wall.

Just think about it for a moment. Picture in your mind the following
hypothetical white presidential candidate. He is 42 years old, a minister,
never served a day in public office. He frequently speaks in silly rhyme
("the text out of context is pretext"). He has been active in a federally
funded youth program that is under investigation for financial irregularities.

This hypothetical white candidate is running in the Democratic primaries—with many Jewish voters—and is regarded as pro-PLO, pro-Arab, pro-Syrian. He has used slurring stereotypes to describe Jews.

This hypothetical white candidate has a fanatical supporter—who travels with the candidate, warms up the audience for him, provides bodyguards, serves as his "surrogate"—and says that he's going to have a black reporter and his family killed and-or excommunicated because he wrote something unkind about this hypothetical white candidate.

What else? Well, this candidate is for a 25 percent defense cut—while 70 percent of the Democrats in America are for either keeping defense spending the same or raising it. The candidate is for a huge increase in domestic social spending, a distinctly minority view among Democrats.

To top it all off, this hypothetical white presidential candidate is for eliminating the runoff primary in the South, guaranteed to infuriate a majority of Southern Democrats.

Well, such a white candidate, no matter how fiery and charismatic, would not be running in first place in April of 1984. He would not even be running in last place. He would have been long out of the race—out long before Cranston, Hollings, and Askew.

The fact is Jackson is gaining, not losing, votes because of his race. He is getting so many black votes because he's black, not because of his sterling positions—blacks aren't in favor of an inexperienced, anti-defense, pro-Syrian candidate who surrounds himself with fanatics.

There is something both stirring and sad in this situation.

That a black has emerged as a major national political figure is good. That more blacks are coming to the polls is good. That blacks are voting for Jackson because he's black is no problem. Voting is often symbolic behavior. In 1960, millions of Catholics voted for John Kennedy because he was a Catholic.

What is sad is that the vehicle for this movement is Jackson. To see this, just think of another hypothetical candidate, this one black, who had Jackson's charisma, but also was in the ideological mainstream of American politics. Suppose, in short, such a candidate had Los Angeles Mayor Tom Bradley's views in Jackson's body.

Bradley won 49 percent of the vote in California last year—that's in a state that's only 8 percent black. That should have set to rest the idea that blacks can't get white votes in America.

They can. The right kind of black candidate—Bradley or Jackson—could have cleaned up this year in the Democratic primaries. In fact, such a candidate could have had a legitimate chance to be nominated.

The Jackson situation is compounded by irony. He became famous in the black community, and in America, not because of his Syrian connection or his anti-defense rhetoric. Recall that Jackson became famous as Mr. Discipline.

You are somebody, he preached, the doors are now open, he said, work hard, he said, stay in school, avoid trouble, and you'll go far. Those are themes that resonate among whites as well as blacks. In fact, those are themes that could attract a rainbow coalition.

Some presidential candidate who is black may figure that out one of these years and be in first place in April of an election year. It might even be Jackson.

April 17, 1984

Hands off Jesse

MANCHESTER, N.H.—Make no mistake about it. Rev. Jesse Jackson is one smart politician. I am not sure the same can be said for his competitors in the race for the Democratic nomination.

The debate among Democrats here on the Saturday before primary day was revealing. Six of the candidates looked like young boys engaged in a pillow fight: "Dick did a flip-flop," "Paul's going over the line." "Mike has no program." "Where were you during the long hot summer, Gary?"

The seventh candidate, Jackson, was above the juvenilia. No one attacked him. He attacked no one. He even tried to calm down the squabblers. His closing statement brilliantly took advantage of his situation: "You've heard some bickering and some pain on the stage today. Someone wants to be secretary of commerce (Richard Gephardt), someone wants to be IRS tax collector (Michael Dukakis), and someone wants to direct health and human services (Paul Simon). I want to be your president." Indeed, Jackson behaved most like a president.

After the debate, I asked several of the candidates why they laid off Jackson. The question was shrugged off; one of them told me we could talk about it privately sometime. Sen. Al Gore said he surely included Jackson when he critically said that none of the other candidates agreed with him that Reagan's toughness had been a factor in leading to the INF treaty. (Fair enough; but there was still no direct criticism of Jackson, by name, as there was of the other candidates.)

What's going on? Back in 1984 it was said that one reason Jackson wasn't confronted by the other candidates was that his poll ratings were so low he really wasn't even in contention. But this time he's been at or near the top of the poll ratings, and some pollsters say it's not just name recognition that's doing it. It's said he can't win. That's almost surely so, but it's also so that he will come to the convention with a huge bloc of delegates, perhaps 20 to 25 percent of the total. The candidates may want to soothe Jackson so that if there is a brokered convention they can get his delegates. And there is the issue of race. It's said that Jackson is unassailable because any attacker will be perceived as a racist. Of course, not disagreeing with Jackson just because he is black is the ultimate racism.

Despite some moderation of his views since 1984, Jackson is still a candidate whose opinions are at profound variance with those of mainstream Democrats. Listening to him, it is apparent that Jackson still blames America first in world affairs: he still thinks capitalism is a rip-off.

I asked Jackson why no one is going after him. His answer was truly shrewd. He said he was not being attacked because, after all, "the party is moving in my direction." He said he had been for military cuts first, now everyone is for them: he had attacked greedy multinational corporations first, now all Democrats do it.

Super Tuesday is just about upon us (March 8). As Jackson says in his very own way, "Super Tuesday is not superficial."

With the likelihood of three and perhaps four viable candidates (in addition to Jackson) still in the race, with many white voters likely to cross over to vote in the hot Republican primaries, Jackson's share of the Super Tuesday delegates will be large. He may possibly be the plurality leader in delegates.

Will the other Democrats keep giving him a free ride then? What will they say then, when he maintains that the whole party is moving his way? Will they agree and tell the whole country that the party is indeed in agreement, or in thrall, to far-out liberal thinking? Or will they finally get tough and challenge Jackson, a skillful and ever-more powerful force in American politics? And if they're going to have to do it after Super Tuesday—why don't they do it before?

February 18, 1988

Treat Jackson Equally

Do you remember in 1984 ever hearing anyone ask, "What does Gary want?" and "What will Gary get?" I don't. Yet Sen. Hart won 33 percent of the committed delegates to the Democratic convention. He got nothing.

Do you remember back in 1980 ever hearing, "What does Teddy want?" and "What will Teddy get?" I don't. Yet Sen. Kennedy won almost 38 percent of the delegates. He got nothing.

Strange. In 1988 it looks as though Jesse Jackson will get 20 to 25 percent of the delegates, and the questions on all lips are, "What does Jesse want?" "What will Jesse get?" and "Will Jesse be vice president?"

Has someone changed the rules? Did Walter Mondale put Hart on the ticket? Did Jimmy Carter make Scoop Jackson secretary of state or Jerry Brown secretary of planetary realism?

Now, Jesse Jackson is a genuine political genius and has run a brilliant campaign. But, is it possible that there is a double standard for Jackson?

Well, is there another Democrat whose record hasn't been assailed by competitors during the debating season? No. Nor is Jackson's likely to be. The Democrats in the contest feel that they may need Jackson delegates in Atlanta.

Will Republicans attack Jackson? You jest. They want the Democratic-Jackson bond to tighten, so Jackson's far-out policies can be draped around the Democratic nominee's neck.

Will the press go after Jackson? For the most part they haven't. Instead they echo his line—that if he's deprived of the presidency it's because he's black, that he's doing splendidly with the white vote.

Yet if held to the same standard as other candidates, Jesse has a lot to answer for. In 1984: He said in Cuba, "Viva Castro. Viva Che Guevara." In 1985: He threatened to bolt the Democrats and start a third party. He appeared with the Vietnamese ambassador at a celebration dedicated to "the heroic victory of the people of Vietnam." He said that American policy was to blame for Arab hijacking terror. In 1987: He marched with the Mobilization for Peace and Justice, a demonstration shunned by the AFL-CIO because of its "radical left wing" direction.

Does Jackson still hold these views and associations? He only says he's matured. Indeed, I think he has. That's fine. But does he recant? That's the question the press would ask any other candidate.

In the present campaign, Jackson has said that the defense budget could be slashed by "more than 10 percent" or, at least once, "by 25 percent." He opposes almost every weapons system that goes "bang." He's for "a code of conduct for American business, to ensure that its investment decisions are made in the best interests of the community." That sounds peachy, but also like shorthand for more government control. Is it? Will someone ask Jesse? Will someone ask him about his advisers from the Institute for Policy Studies, which describes itself very publicly as a center for "radical scholarship"?

Jackson has won less than 10 percent of the white primary vote (not caucuses or beauty contests; data complied prior to Jackson's home state Illinois primary). Will someone ask: Why is this regarded as remarkable when blacks like Lt. Gov. Douglas Wilder of Virginia and Mayor Tom Bradley of California won 46 percent and 44 percent of the white vote in statewide races?

Will the nature of Jesse's white vote ever become big news? Jon Margolis of the *Chicago Tribune* analyzed ABC's exit polls and noted that: Jackson's white voters appear to be "politically active homosexuals whose organizations have endorsed his candidacy, and the rest are the residue of the radical and counter-culture movements." (Jackson's savvy campaign manager Gerald Austin stresses Jackson's gay-lesbian support.)

Jesse Jackson may have a stunning future in American politics. But he won't have it, and won't deserve it, until he's treated equally.

March 17, 1988

Criticizing Jackson

I had the pleasure of appearing with Rev. Jesse Jackson on the PBS MacNeil-Lehrer News Hour recently. As always he is a man worth jousting with. The only part I didn't like was when Jackson said that I couldn't see the difference between him and Col. Moammar Gadhafi, apparently because some people think, in Jackson's not very felicitous words, that "all of us may look alike, but we are not alike."

I can indeed tell the difference between Jackson and Gadhafi. Jackson is the very smart American. Gadhafi runs the Libyan terrorist state that in the past gave money to Jackson's organization, People United to Save Humanity. When I mentioned that, Jackson artfully declaimed, dudgeon soaring, that "he had never met Mr. Gadhafi and never been to Libya," which I'm sure is true.

In any event, Jesse Jackson is top-drawer political goods. He's original and quick-witted. He's becoming at least slightly more moderate. He's a dynamic orator and a demonstrably fine candidate. Don't blame Jackson that he's put the Democratic Party in a position where one "party elder" (anonymous, of course) was quoted in the *New York Times* as saying that, if Jesse kept on his winning ways the party "would be in an impossible situation. We'd have the choice of turning our backs on Jesse and alienating the blacks, or nominating him and almost certainly losing in November."

That's not Jesse Jackson's fault. Blame anonymous elder Democrat and all the other Democrats this year who wouldn't say publicly that they disagree with Jackson's policies, not even some of them. What happens if they don't publicly disagree with him and he gets a plurality of delegates—which may happen? If an Anyone But Jackson strategy then emerges to deny him the nomination it will surely appear to be on the grounds of race, and that's a repugnant reason.

Gov. Michael Dukakis apparently doesn't understand what's going on, which may be why his "inevitable" candidacy lost to the heretofore "impossible" Jackson candidacy in Michigan by 2-to-1. After the massacre, the

New York Times reported Dukakis' views in the following fashion: "The governor said he saw no basic distinction between his message about the country's future and that offered by Mr. Jackson and the party's other candidates."

Dukakis may have missed his true calling. With zingers like that, guaranteed to gain votes for the Republicans, he could get a job writing press releases for the Republican National Committee.

In the nicest language possible let's put the situation this way: Jesse Jackson is very, very liberal. The Democratic Party has been losing national elections because it is regarded as becoming too liberal. Democrats like Dukakis are now quoted as saying they agree with Jackson's vision. Others merely say he is "the conscience of the party."

Do these people have beliefs? Are they really the same as Jackson's? Are these people professionals? Do they know how to add electoral votes? Are they looking for an electoral debacle of an order not seen before in this country—one that could pull down Democrats in the Congress, in the states and in the cities?

Will anyone speak up loudly and say, "I disagree"? Or will they be gulled by Jackson's plea that he can deliver the goods "if the party rallies behind me as I have rallied behind the party." Like many of Jackson's comments, there is some amount of truth there. It is also true that in 1985 Jesse Jackson was threatening publicly to bolt the Democrats and start a third party.

Jackson is no political saint. He is not the conscience of his party. He will be a better politician if he must deal with criticism of his views and his history. Just like everyone else.

March 31, 1988

"Love Feast" or "Blood Bath"?

Democrats seem to know only two ways to describe their quadrennial convention—either as a "love feast" or a "blood bath."

Democrats feel that history shows that the unity of a love feast sets up victory. Alternatively, they believe that the chaos and divisiveness of a blood bath yields defeat. There is a rationale. Much of the image of a party is formed during the heavily televised conventions. Americans show distrust of politicians who meet in order to beat upon one another with large wet fish. This month the Democrats will probably have a love feast in Atlanta. They are pleased. The mantra is recited endlessly: "We've never been more unified."

Still, the love feast may be oversold this time. There ought to be another phrase Democrats could wish for—more combative than a love feast and less messy than a blood bath. How about a "bold bicker" or a "rhetorical wrangle"?

The reason for such unorthodoxy is Jesse Jackson. So terrified are the Democrats of a chaotic convention, or of black voters not turning out to vote, that they are in danger of bending over backward to be super-nice to Jackson.

In general, it's fine to be super-nice. But Jackson comes with baggage. He has preached a message on the far left of the spectrum. He and his most vocal supporters say they have already made the party more "progressive" (i.e., liberal), and they have every intention of making it even more so.

That's not what voters want to hear. Quite the opposite: The perception of the Democrats being too liberal has been at the root of Democrats losing four of the last five presidential elections.

Jackson also exhibits certain party-crashing tendencies. In Boston, just before meeting the putative nominee, Jackson said, "In some sense, Mike Dukakis and I have the challenge of forming a new equation, a new coalition, to take our nation to another level of moral consideration."

Huh? Jackson lost in the primaries. What puts him in the new-equation-forming business? What happens if rank-and-file voters get the idea that a vote for Dukakis is a vote for Jackson's new equation?

It's tricky. The Jackson convention forces will likely bring up at least two major resolutions—cut defense, raise taxes—that the Dukakis majority will vote down. Yet, while these are important issues, the arguments already seem like a pre-programmed minuet, taking place in a certain context and atmosphere. The context is that there were about 40 Democratic debates, and Dukakis did not sharply disagree with Jackson. The atmosphere, I suspect, will be almost worshipful to Jackson. ("He's the conscience of the party, . . ." etc.)

So far, the Dukakis team has been wooing Jackson. One consultant, commenting on the campaign's maximum be-nice-to-Jackson effort and Dukakis' recent 10-point decline in the polls, said, "You could have a 20-point lead in the polls, and it would be worthless if you had a divisive convention." Wrong. Take the 20.

Dukakis finished first, largely because he was perceived not to have Jackson's view of the world. Dukakis should now make clear, publicly, that he has serious policy disagreements with Jackson. I believe that he does, and this is a time when honesty is the best politics. If Dukakis doesn't sharpen such distinctions, it will make more credible the attempt to paint Dukakis as the leader of a party that has gone beyond what was called McGovernization and on to Jacksonization. If that sticks, Dukakis will lose, despite an Atlanta love feast, or perhaps because of it.

July 7, 1988

Three Little Words

How strange. Not long ago every pundit on the block said this presidential election would be decided on "bread 'n' butter" issues. Yet now, George Bush is gaining by stressing social issues (pledge of allegiance, death penalty, prayer) as well as defense and foreign policy issues (Bush says Dukakis believes defense modernization went out with the discovery of the slingshot).

What accounts for the pundit pratfall? A confusion about problems vs. issues. Thus, the economy—bread 'n' butter—is surely a problem. There are deficits, fear of the future, jobs lost to foreign competitors. But there is not much difference of opinion about what to do about it: reduce the deficits, job retraining, bolster our competitive position, etc. Only Bush's plan to cut capital gains taxes (which helps rich people, says Dukakis), seems to fall into the Democratic ideal paradigm of "big-guy-vs-little-guy." There are economic problems, but because there is little disagreement about what to do, there is not much of a political issue.

Not so on social concerns, nor on defense and foreign policy.

There we find both problems and disagreements—made salient by two decades of Democratic party history. George Bush, nasty fellow, is trying to make Dukakis pay for that history; and Dukakis has not yet figured out how to deal with it.

Thus, consider the public perception of the national president-picking liberal wing of the Democratic Party. What have the voters heard over the years? The squeakiest part of the liberal wheel. Exaggerating for effect, it came out something like this: Law 'n' order is a code word for racism. America is a sick society, quotas and busing are necessary. Americans are racist, sexist, imperialist. Then the liberals cry foul when Bush tags Dukakis with prison furloughs, death penalty, the American Civil Liberties Union and the pledge.

So, too, on defense and foreign policy. The liberal Democrats condemned America's "criminal" and "illegal" conduct in Nicaragua, knelt at the altar of the nuclear freeze, opposed new defense systems, did not challenge Jesse Jackson's pro-socialist Third World tilt. But when Bush says slingshot, the lib-Dems say slingshot is cheap shot.

This banging-upon-the-Duke is paying off: Polls show Bush moving into what now looks like a small lead. What can Dukakis do about the central charge that he is a soft liberal?

Dukakis can say, right, we have been liberals, we still are, and proud of it. That's a loser.

He can dissemble. He can say he's not a liberal, that he's never been one, and neither has the Democratic Party been too liberal. I use the word "dissemble." The Republicans will say "lie." It will be found out. Another loser.

Dukakis can ignore it. He can say he stands for competence, not ideology. But Americans want a philosophy. Another loser.

The last choice is the hardest, but the most profitable. Three little words might save him: "We were wrong." Dukakis can say that Democrats have made mistakes and gone too far, that they understand their mistakes, and that they've changed. After all, DNC Chairman Paul Kirk, and others, have spent years of hard work changing things. Why? Because mistakes were indeed made.

Moreover, Dukakis has some credentials on the anti-soft side. He is a genuine governmental cheapskate, not a promiscuous program-proliferator. In the blazing decade of the '60s, when radical movements flourished—the Duke's big issue was no-fault insurance! Not only that, he knows the problem. That's why he uses the word "tough" so often; that's why he picked Lloyd Bentsen for vice president.

Do it, Duke. Say you and the Democrats have been wrong on some of these issues. Everyone knows it's true. American voters want to vote Democratic—if their fears are allayed.

September 8, 1988

Redefining Liberalism

The Democratic/Dukakis counterattack against the charge of "liberal" has gone from terrible to half-right—the easy half.

When Bush charged that Dukakis is a liberal, what did the Democrats do? They said Bush is running a negative campaign, without issues, with undertones of racism: that Bush lies; that the nasty polls are preordaining the results: and that the campaign sets a terrible model for future elections.

The charges are hypocritical, or silly, or exaggerated. These are the folks who mugged Robert Bork by peddling outrageous falsehoods. Meaningful campaigns are often negative—Roosevelt vs. Hoover, Johnson vs. Goldwater, Reagan vs. Carter. "Racism" has terrible connotations, but it has become a whip-word, so debased and promiscuously used that it typically yields only a backlash. Labeling opponents ideologically—like "liberal"—is not the mark of an issue-free campaign, but of an issue-oriented campaign. (In 1980 Democrats charged, "Ronald Reagan is too conservative.")

But what about the charge itself? What's the answer? For a long time—there was no answer. After all, the central deception in this campaign was set into motion at the Democratic convention when Dukakis said the race was not about ideology but about competence. Competence to move in what direction? Sorry, the Democrats said, we've got "unity," and by the way, we're ahead in the polls. What did they expect the Republicans to do, applaud?

Finally, behind by double digits, Dukakis responded.

He has defended, properly, the old liberalism of Presidents Roosevelt, Truman, Kennedy and Johnson. The liberal impulse yielded Social Security, Medicare, civil rights, collective bargaining, health research, environmental protection and much more.

But Dukakis must clarify. Has some recent liberalism gone too far? Yes. Principles of tough internationalism have often blurred into mushy isolationism. Merit has sometimes been transmuted into quotas. Traditional values have sometimes given way to permissiveness. Roosevelt-Truman-Kennedy-Johnson have been followed by George McGovern, Jimmy Carter, Ted Kennedy and Jesse Jackson—different kinds of liberals.

How should Dukakis amend it? By saying that some time on some issues some liberals have gone overboard and that Democrats have learned their lesson. That stated, attack Bush on the C-word! (Just as some liberals have gone over the edge, so have some conservatives.)

But Democrats and Dukakis (so far) will not admit that liberalism has gone too far. Their lack of recognition is stunning and repetitive. In 1968 when the phrase "Law and order" came into political vogue, many liberals said, "Law-and-order is a code word for racism"—and lost the election. Twenty years later—today—crime is properly raised again as an issue. Murder rates soar. And the knee-jerk, nouveau-liberal response appears again— "The prison furlough issue has racist overtones"—and they're losing again.

In the words of the '60s, "When will they ever learn?"

November 3, 1988

After November, 1988

To look to the future of the Democratic Party after yet one more presidential political trouncing, it is necessary to understand the nature of their current sad estate.

Consider this stunning, symbolic and real situation: Over the course of two election cycles—1984 and 1988—about 40 intra-party debates took place, all over the country. Fifteen major Democratic presidential primary candidates, from every region, were involved. And in those debates—no one disagreed directly and regularly with Jesse Jackson!

Incredible!

Here is a party vulnerable for 20 years for being "too liberal." And here is Jackson, a brilliant and electrifying candidate, preaching a set of views far to the left of liberal on foreign and domestic issues. And yet no candidate said, "Rev. Jackson, you have articulated some important issues with which I agree, but I have profound differences with many of your views and values."

Would it have made a difference? Suppose candidate Michael Dukakis had said it, regularly. When George Bush later attacked him for being—eek!—a liberal, Dukakis could have used the famous Latin defense: "Quis, Ego?" (Who, me?). As in: "Impossible. Why I'm the fellow who disagrees with Jesse Jackson."

Who didn't disagree with Jackson publicly? Liberals didn't: not Paul Simon, Alan Cranston, George McGovern or Michael Dukakis. Moderates didn't: not Walter Mondale, Gary Hart, Al Gore, Richard Gephardt or Bruce Babbitt. Conservatives didn't: not John Glenn, Ernest Hollings or Reuben Askew.

If we understand why Democrats have not disagreed with Jackson, we see what needs doing in the Democratic Party. It is partly because Jackson is black. That is the first hangup that has to go. It is not racism to criticize a black politician on substantive grounds. (In fact, it is racism to treat a black politician differently.)

But, Jackson aside, most Democrats believe that there is a "left-wing veto" in the presidential-selection process. That view is bolstered by the special treatment given to that superliberal, activist-dominated, "mug-a-moderate" parody of democracy (no secret ballot)—the infamous Iowa "caucuses." The Democrats have to take away Iowa's unfair status as the always-the-first-in-the-nation contest.

Then, potential candidates should scrub their brains of the notion of a left-wing veto. (Jimmy Carter won primaries and caucuses running as a Southern, anti-Washington moderate.)

Next, some of the Democrats who are of the right wing of the left-wing party (that's the American center) ought to get active, pronto. Sen. Sam Nunn and Sen.-elect Charles Robb are the two names that come most readily to mind. There could be others.

And then there must be a fight. Politicians in presidential primaries don't usually like to fight over substantive matters. In the back of their minds, bells go off: I want that fellow's delegates to come to me later; I want his supporters to vote for me later; a split party is a losing party, etc.

All normally somewhat valid concerns. But when a party loses five out of six elections, by mostly big margins, for roughly the same reason, and can't seem to stop nominating loss-prone, liberal politicians—the rules change.

The only thing that can make the Democratic Party competitive for the presidency is a head-on fight—hopefully decorous and reasonable—but a fight. The struggle for the soul of the party must be public—and start now.

The Democrats must finally decide one way or the other, whether they are a moderate progressive party, or a very liberal one. Doing it quietly, by compromise, won't help. The longer they dither, the quieter the argument, the more the image of "very-liberal" is cast in concrete. Splitting the differences can be considered later. For now, the marching banner must be, "No Compromises—Yet."

November 10, 1988

Ron Brown: Leader or Lemming?

Democrats have finally told us what the "L-word" stands for: lemming.

Professional politicians are usually the most accommodating of people. A little pressure often gets a lot of results. After the 1988 election, public pressure was on the Democratic party. It was said, by many Democrats and neutral observers, that the party was perceived as too liberal, that it was afraid to criticize Jesse Jackson, that it was in danger of being seen as the party of minorities. In normal times, in a healthy party, a response would be expected.

But when parties spin out of control, as in the case of the British Labor Party, some of their politicians go haywire. They don't accommodate; they don't respond to the public. Accordingly, they can end up losing even more votes. In short, they behave like lemmings, those near-mythical little animals that periodically march placidly into the sea, to their death.

Our questions of the day are these: Is the Democratic National Committee a collection of lemmings? Does it matter? If it matters, does it hurt Democrats? If it's harmful, is it redeemable?

Answers: If it quacks like a lemming, it's a lemming. It does matter. It is harmful. It may be redeemable.

Other candidates having withdrawn, the DNC is about to elect Ron Brown as its new chairman. Brown is an articulate, black super-lawyer. He formerly worked for very-liberal Sen. Ted Kennedy. In 1988 he managed hyper-liberal Jesse Jackson's convention campaign and forced pro-Jackson rules changes on the nervous and supine Dukakis convention.

From the outset Brown's campaign was about liberalism, Jacksonism and, unfortunately, race. Brown claims he's his own man and should not be regarded as Jackson's man, or a liberal, or a black. But it was Brown's liberal campaign that helped raise the race issue, making the hard-ball case that a vote against Brown would be seen as a vote against blacks in America.

The Brown campaign worked. Most party moderates took a dive. They had a strong candidate in former House Budget Chairman Jim Jones. But, as usual, moderate support was too little and too late. Who wants to fight about race with Jesse?

Many Americans are wondering whether Democrats have learned anything from the 1988 election. The message from the DNC is clear: Stop bothering us, we've got some serious wading to do and, yummy, the water is over our head.

Does it matter? The case has been made that the DNC is a collection of 400 politicians, many of them nonentities and nerds, barely elected in weird ways engendered by now-archaic McGovern reforms, representing no one, doing next to nothing, ignored by all. Partly true. But they are no longer ignored—at least their chairman isn't.

The media maw is bigger than ever. Television consumes political personalities with gusto. The party without a sitting president needs a spokesman. On many days to come, Democrat Ron Brown will be it.

Brown will be dueling with a Republican counterpart, Lee Atwater, who is a colorful, quotable, conservative white Southerner from the Reagan wing of the party. In the simplistic world of television, this is how the media match will begin: white Reagan conservative vs. black Jackson liberal. These images may not be wholly accurate, or fair, but it is the lay of the land. My own view is that a black politician can make it to any high office in America, but no politician can go high up the ladder identified as a Jackson-style liberal.

Is it redeemable? The Brown people say Chairman Brown will turn out to be like Nixon in China, like Reagan in Russia. As a black liberal, it is said, he can get tougher on Jesse than anyone else.

Chairman Brown, I am dubious. Prove me wrong. Make my day. Rescind the pro-Jackson rules changes. Give the marching Democratic lemmings the order: "About face."

February 2, 1989

In Unity There Is Weakness

PHILADELPHIA—Only one prepared paper was presented here at the recent annual meeting of the Democratic Leadership Council. Its final paragraph is a gutsy marching call that should be recited by serious Democrats concerned about the Jesse Jackson problem and looking to promote both partisan victory and the national interest.

The paper, "Rebuilding a Presidential Majority," was written by Dr. William Galston of the University of Maryland. Galston, a former issues director for Walter Mondale, lays out the current sad estate of the national Democratic Party.

The problems include geography and ideology. The reapportionment of electoral votes for 1992 will move more president-picking power to states that are already Republican (mostly Southern and Western). Voters see the Democrats as weak on defense. Voters feel that America has gone through "a severe breakdown in moral standards." And, says Galston, "for too many Americans . . . Democrats are part of the problem, not the solution. . . . We have become the party of individual rights but not individual responsibility; the party of self-expression but not self-discipline; the party of sociological explanation but not moral accountability."

Democrat-to-Democrat, in public, that is tough stuff. But Galston concludes on a yet-tougher note, a call to combat: "The changes we need cannot come from policy commissions or midterm conventions or party functionaries. They can only come from leaders—candidates for the presidential nomination—with the courage to challenge entrenched orthodoxies. . . . This will mean debate, controversy, even conflict. But it is far better than a barren and spurious unity. . . . We Democrats must at long last set aside the politics of evasion . . . it is the only way to rebuild a presidential majority for our party. . . ."

The DLC and Galston showed courage. Political organizations of elected officials don't often come out for conflict and against unity. That violates every partisan tradition. But, says the DLC, these are not traditional times. The Democrats specialize in losing the presidency. Only a victorious public fight for the soul of the party can turn the tide.

If it is hard for an organization to preach intramural combat, it is harder still for politicians. Most of those in attendance at Philadelphia did not. Indeed, many advocated old-fashioned, mindless unity. (One exception was Sen. Charles Robb, who engaged in a pointed exchange with Jackson.)

Will the politicians of the tough Democratic center have the brass to draw a line in the political sand? We shall see. "This was a good beginning, but only a beginning," says Alvin From, executive director of the DLC. "The debate should grow more specific and intense."

Indeed, the Democrats have a great opportunity to move this adversarial dialogue to centerstage. The opportunity has a name: Jesse Jackson. He has come to personify Democratic hyperliberalism. He will almost surely run for the presidency again. He has a coherent set of views. He has asked for, and earned, the right to a serious debate.

That's better than "unity." The much-touted unity at the 1988 Atlanta convention laid an egg. It only told voters that the party had no big problem with Jackson's views.

But most Americans do. A crackling debate, not the standard mush, can invigorate and redefine the Democratic party. A Democratic candidate who wins by opposing Jackson can redefine himself or herself right into the White House. That's the right time and place to consider what kind of unity is advisable.

March 16, 1989

Wilder Erases Race, Dinkins Doesn't

Two black men are running for high offices that have never been held by blacks. Both look like winners. One campaign is commonplace, but with an unfortunate twist. The other is new and can be a heartening turning point in black politics.

If black politics changes, so do Democratic politics and the future potency of some Democratic ideologies. If Democratic politics changes, so does American politics.

The two politicians are David Dinkins, running for mayor of New York City, and L. Douglas Wilder, running for governor of the Commonwealth of Virginia.

The Dinkins situation is familiar. There are many black big-city mayors. They have typically been first elected by capturing almost all of the large black vote, a large portion of a smaller Hispanic vote, and a small share of white votes. They have won in cities with huge Democratic majorities. The candidates have been quite liberal.

Dinkins qualifies, but with amendments. Blacks are a smaller share of the electorate in New York than in most big cities with black mayors, an estimated 23 percent. (Hispanics are estimated to make up somewhat less than 10 percent.)

And there is a disturbing subtext in the Dinkins campaign, sometimes stated, sometimes unstated. In the primary election (with Jesse Jackson working the streets) the Dinkins operation stressed that a vote for Mayor Ed Koch was a vote against "harmony" (i.e., racial harmony). In the current general election contest some Dinkins supporters (not Dinkins) say that voting for Republican Rudolph Giuliani is voting against "harmony."

Surprise: Only a vote for Dinkins will yield the treasured H-word. Although Dinkins might be a capable mayor, that theme is the politics of vote-for-me-or-else, the electoral equivalent of a potential temper tantrum. It is not politically healthy. Suppose next time Italians or Puerto Ricans or Jews—or whites—say there will be no harmony unless their candidate is elected.

By contrast, the Wilder campaign is fresh. There has never been an elected black governor in America, certainly not in a conservative Southern state only 17 percent black.

Wilder needs about 40 percent of the white vote to win. The polls say he can get it.

If he wins, black politics will be transformed. Blacks constitute 11 percent of the U.S. population but hold 0 percent of the highest elected offices. That circumstance has the appearance of de facto racism.

340

This sad situation has led to a circle of despair for many black politicians. Believing they could not gain higher office, they have typically accommodated the squeakiest very liberal wheels in the black community. So most black politicians are very liberal. To complete the circle, it is hard for any very liberal politician to win statewide.

A Wilder victory can change that. If a black politician wins on merit in Virginia, then a black politician could win on merit statewide anywhere.

The key to Wilder's good showing is that he runs not as a black politician, but as a Virginia politician. His campaign stresses that he is in the tradition of successful moderate Virginia Democrats, led by Sen. Charles Robb, who changed American politics by emphasizing that Democratic candidates need not be liberals, and if they're not, they can win, even in the South.

Wilder supports the death penalty and a tax cut. He did not bring Jesse Jackson in to campaign. He runs television ads featuring Robb's endorsement.

What happens if Wilder wins?

Many black representatives and mayors will aspire to higher office. That means moderate positions. Moderate black politics yields more moderate Democratic politics, which yields more moderate American politics. (Virginia moderates and conservatives get a national bonus by voting for Wilder.)

A Wilder victory may also have an impact on two main ideologies in the Democratic party debate—Jacksonism and Robbism. It makes Jacksonism less relevant. Jacksonism is the old-fashioned politics of resentment, rooted in the idea that blacks don't get a fair shake. The case for Robbism is more relevant. Robbism shows that Democrats, white or black, can win when they run right.

October 25, 1989

Jackson's Terse Verse Gets Worse

In the 1984 presidential campaign, the Rev. Jesse Jackson began his lifetime running-for-president career with terse verse. Remember, "From the guttermost to the uppermost," "From the outhouse to the White House."

Jackson's recent address to the Democratic Leadership Council in New Orleans shows signs of reversion, inversion, but not conversion. It was rhyme time again, right there up in the title of his speech: "Delighted to be United." Jackson missed one more rhyme, but it was inherent in his remarks: "re-ignited."

Jackson says that the Democratic moderates should be congratulated. Why? Because, he says, the moderates have finally understood that Jackson was right all along. Sweet. It is the political equivalent of amorous action from an anaconda, which hugs so hard it hurts. Left unchallenged, it is high caliber Republican ammunition.

In New Orleans, Jackson said that he was for big defense cuts all along, and now even moderates are for cuts. See?

No. There is a difference, and it's not only that today moderate Democrats are for moderate defense cuts, and Jackson is for huge ones.

For, unlike moderate Democrats, Jackson was for massive defense cuts when the Soviet military budget was climbing, when the Soviets were in Afghanistan, when the Soviets owned the turf and corroded the soul of Eastern Europe, when the Soviets were arming communists in Central America, when, unlike today, it was Reagan, not Gorbachev, who said the Soviet Union was an evil empire.

While Jackson was in Havana toasting communists, moderate Democrats were saying there was a real threat from the Soviet Union and we ought to stay militarily strong. Neither red nor dead, said rhyming moderates. But Jackson is no Castro convertible; he still publicly applauds his salute to Fidel in Havana.

Jesse is also messy with the facts about who is for what kind of affirmative action. He preaches the ruinous doctrine of racial "set-asides," which indeed belongs in quota marks. But the DLC's statement of principles issued in New Orleans goes precisely the other way: "We believe the promise of America is equal opportunity, not equal outcomes."

The DLC statement also says: "We believe the government should respect individual liberty and stay out of our private lives and personal decisions." Certainly—and unexceptional. But Jackson, surely looking ahead to the California primary, said he was very pleased because the context of the text revealed that the DLC, just like Jackson, was going out of its way to endorse gay rights. Or, as a Jackson-style rhyming headline might put it: "Dems say tres gay." But the new chairman of the DLC, Gov. Bill Clinton, said, "We never even discussed that."

Jesse Jackson has played a big role in transforming the image of liberalism into a far-out political movement, out of touch with the views and values of most Americans. That spreading perception about one part of the Democratic Party, has hurt the whole party. Now Jackson says that the whole party agrees with his views, and that he is now the new mainstream.

Most elected Democrats at the DLC meeting publicly laughed it off as preposterous. It's not. Jesse Jackson is not preposterous. He is now the principal voice of the American Left. He deserves to be taken seriously. That means choosing up sides, publicly and substantively, within the Democratic Party. Democrats can publicly endorse his views, which is what

Jackson says is now going on—and accept the political consequences one more time. Or Democrats, challenged now by Jackson's embrace, can publicly say they do not accept his views—and reap the benefits.

In rhyme: Agree and pay a fee, disagree and be set free.

March 28, 1990

As indicated, I didn't like the Dinkins campaign. He seems to be doing well enough as mayor. And Wilder is dynamite.

What a difference a percentage point makes in politics. Wilder won by a single point in 1989. Tom Bradley, the mayor of Los Angeles, who is black, lost for governor of California by less than a point in 1982. Had Bradley won, and been governor of the largest state, and one with a less than 10 percent black population, I think there is serious doubt that the Jesse Jackson phenomenon would have played itself out as remarkably as it has. The sense of black grievance would have been much diminished.

Chuck Robb is a gutsy fellow. When he went off to combat as a marine in Vietnam, his father-in-law was President Lyndon Johnson. Robb knew that if captured he could be used as a propaganda prize. He left a statement with Liz Carpenter (described in her book Ruffles and Flourishes) *to be used in the event of his imprisonment. He said in that statement that he thought he could withstand whatever pressure the enemy put him through, but if he couldn't, the statement should be used to publicly say that he supported American policy.*

The rap on Robb as a potential national candidate has been that he lacks platform charisma. That was not apparent at the Vietnam Memorial in Washington on Veterans Day in 1985 when he gave the keynote address. He followed both Leontyne Price, who sang "God Bless America" as if she were a bell in full peal, and her brother, Brigadier General George Price, who brought cheers from the vets when he said, "We never lost a damned battle in Vietnam, and we never will."

Robb, the ramrod straight ex-Marine, eyes moist, put away his prepared remarks. He moved the crowd with off-the-cuff Vietnam reminiscences and talked of healing and caring without bitterness or chest-thumping. He shrugged off the noisy overhead traffic from National Airport: "We don't mind it. Close air support pulled a lot of us out." Standing in front of the memorial with 55,000 names chiseled on it, Robb closed simply, speaking in a general and current sense: "There is a price for freedom."

Like another politician whose name begins with "R," Robb should not be underestimated. He has shown he knows at least two things: how to win elections and how to help other people, like Governor Douglas Wilder, win elections. Those aren't the only things you need to know to become president, but they are the first two.

Robb: Don't Knock Opportunity

Sen. Charles Robb of Virginia has offered a needed gift to his fellow Democrats: a philosophy to help them escape The Reagan Trap. Reagan said, several million times, that "government is not the solution—it's the problem."

Many Democrats took the bait. If Reagan said government was so very bad, and Reagan was such a silly fellow, then Democrats must therefore say government is so very good. Trap snaps! Republicans win the White House.

(Ah, Reagan. Read all about The Foolish One in a hundred books now out. The dunce actually said he would put The Evil Empire in the ash heap of history.)

As Robb explained it recently to the Democratic Leadership Council, too many Democrats believe their mission is to "affirm a positive role for government."

That pro-government mindset leads to trouble. It helps make Democrats patsies for every liberal special interest group looking for a federal feast or federal fix-up. That includes, but is not limited to, civil rights activists, feminists, poverty warriors, environmentalists and consumerists. (My list, not Robb's.)

Operating under such a rhetorical mindset, if a Democrat opposes what an interest group favors, the activists charge a moving violation of Democratic credo. Robb says the phrase "liberal fundamentalism" describes the phenomenon.

In politics, it is hard to oppose rhetoric enforced by fundamentalist ayatollahs who guard the scrolls. Rhetoric produces reality. So Robb thinks mainstream Democrats should change the rhetoric about affirm-the-positive-role-of-government.

He has good reasons: The idea is politically harmful, substantively unwise and historically inaccurate. Americans are not looking for ways to affirm big government. Ever-more, government is no cure-all for what ails us. And, says Robb, activist government has not even been a historically consistent central Democratic theme.

The real Democratic idea, he says, has been the expansion of opportunity for ordinary Americans. There have been times—mostly in the 19th century—when Democrats believed that activist government worked against individual opportunity.

Now Robb believes Democrats must again sort out the various roles of government. Which government actions help broad-based opportunity? Let's support those, even expand them. And which are aimed at more government for the sake of power or benefits to an interest group? Let's dump those.

Robb's formulation is useful. Formulations are useful. In politics, as in life, it's hard to move purposefully without a road map. Robb's road map can help Democrats think difficult but necessary thoughts.

Politicians often talk tough in generalities and then cave on specifics that challenge interest groups. Not Robb. He favors the authentic aspects of the good-guy issues—environmentalism, poverty, civil rights. But he takes his opportunity-not-special-interest theme to its logical and tough-minded end, to the sensitive realm of race-gender special preference, the clearest example of runaway governmentalism corroding opportunity.

He says ". . . we deplore the tendency to view all public questions through the prism of racial, gender, sexual and ethnic difference . . . It goes beyond a healthy pluralism to separatism; beyond the legitimate desire to dismantle barriers to equal opportunity, to demands that some groups receive special dispensation. It undermines the traditional American goal of assimilation and engenders resentment among those citizens who do not fit into any favored categories."

Pow!

Indeed, quotas and set-asides do offer government gifts to some special interests, but simultaneously deny opportunity to others. Because most professional race-gender activists are looking for just those "special dispensations" from government, Robb's point is hard for Democrats to be publicly specific about. It has only one advantage: Democratic voters, almost all of them, agree with Robb. They want opportunity, with or without more government.

Such is the nature of the Robb Counter to the Reagan Trap. Of course, the liberal ayatollahs say it means that Democrats will behave like Republicans. It doesn't. Opportunity transcends party lines. And for Democrats, opportunity knocks.

November 29, 1989

Sue the Democratic National Committee

With Bulgaria moving toward democracy—including such subversive devices as elections and secret ballots—perhaps the Democrats of Iowa, and the Democratic Party, should consider the same ideas in choosing a presidential nominee.

What exists now is a scam. The presidential nominating rules of the Democratic Party—whatever that may be—are made by a fascinating body called the Democratic National Committee. It's not democratic. It's barely a committee. If it's national, why does it always harm Democrats trying to win nationally?

There are 406 DNC members. There are quotas for blacks, Hispanics and women, but no one else. DNC members are typically self-perpetuating ciphers from state parties; sometimes they are appointed or muscled into their jobs; occasionally they are publicly elected, barely noticeable on the ballot. Thirteen members were handpicked by Jesse Jackson. No other current potential candidate picked any.

One DNC rule dictates that Iowa, and only Iowa, can have the first presidential selection event if it so chooses, and if it does, it must be done through caucuses. Under Iowa caucus rules it may take all evening to cast a vote—by non-secret ballot with the whole neighborhood and anchormen watching. Caucus turnout is small, thus providing a mugging field for liberal activists to extort far-out positions from the candidates.

Current DNC rules were established in 1988, in secret, at 4 A.M., by operatives of Jackson and Michael Dukakis, in a Dukakis sell-out designed to get Jackson to stop being a pest. Consider pest power: Only under such Jackson-demanded, European-style proportional representation rules can Jackson hope to get nominated.

Questions: 1) What would we say if Bulgaria did all that? 2) Because having exclusive right to "the first caucus" makes Iowans more politically powerful than thee and me—making us unequal—why don't we run a lawsuit against the DNC?

Comes now California. Jackson's choice for DNC chairman, Ron Brown, had pledged not to tinker with the rules. But on Feb. 14, the Brown-picked, and previously inconsequential, "Rules and Bylaws Committee," acting with no hearings or advance notice, moved up the starting date of the 1990 general primary season by one week. There was an understanding that California would take advantage of the ruling, changing state law to move its primary from last in the nominating process to what would become an exclusive "first big primary" slot.

Who gains? Theories abound. It's said California is great for deep-pocket candidates like Mario Cuomo, Bill Bradley and Lloyd Bentsen—folks who can raise money to buy expensive California television commercials. It could happen.

But one candidate doesn't need early big money. Jackson. He is already a super-duper-star and will get his media coverage for free.

The California-first rule also puts Jackson into the biggest state prior to the beginning of what is now called The Last White Guy Standing Syndrome. Jackson, it is believed, tends to lose to a white candidate when matched one-on-one after the winnowing of early primaries. The LWG wins. But in a split field, Jackson does well. California, if it goes first—before the winnowing—would guarantee a split field, probably a large one. It could catapult Jackson to a plurality victory.

Jacksonites like it. We know that because they haven't complained. When they don't like rules changes, they say it's racism.

This is no Jackson conspiracy. Californians didn't like being last in the process, reduced to apparent irrelevance by the LWGSS.

But non-conspiracies have been the root of much Democratic madness. Things happen randomly, and if they end up helping liberals, then liberal DNC members, who control the DNC, see to it that the item in question becomes untouchable. That happened with Iowa. It was once a gimmick caucus. But because it serves left-wing special interests, it now can't be budged from its superior status.

Unless there is a lawsuit. Which might properly be expanded to challenge the whole nature of the hardly national, non-democratic, quasi-committee.

February 28, 1990

Democrats Try Politicus Interruptus

Is Kevin Phillips a mole? Is Ron Brown serious? Are liberal Democrats—gasp!—going to do it all over again?

Political analyst Phillips (my colleague on CBS "Spectrum" broadcasts) has written an interesting and wrong-headed book, *The Politics of Rich and Poor* (Random House). He kindly informs Democrats how to win in the '90s. Interesting. Phillips is a Republican. His advice is suicidal for Democrats. Hmmm. . . .

Phillips says that in the '80s the greedy prospered and the needy suffered. The standard of living declined for the middle class. Phillips says it was the fault of sleazy, gluttonous, arriviste, rich Republicans who believed in terrible things like markets, capitalism, deregulation, lower taxes, less federal spending and free trade.

He says this can be seen in the political zodiac. See, there are these cycles. When Republicans take power they behave like plutocratic rats. They did it in the 1870s and the 1920s and were punished by a populist backlash. (Dubious.)

Phillips says Republicans were rats again in the 1980s. Ergo: punishment in the 1990s. Clockwork. Metronomical. All the Democrats have to do is become economic populists and run against Donald Trump.

The liberal Democrats, including Jesse Jackson (who Phillips thinks has the populism part right), said that all along. They like Phillips' philippics, and add their own stuff. Ron Brown, chairman of the Democratic National Committee, says it's a great time for Democrats.

Why? Well, the Cold War is over, and that's great, because Democrats were seen as weak on defense, and now there's nothing that needs defending. And great, because George Bush was caught fibbing, and endorsed the despicable idea of raising taxes, an idea abhorred by most Americans, an idea—oops!—promulgated by Democrats.

Other liberal Democrats say social issues have turned their way. Democrats are for abortion, and now it's clear that Americans are, too.

Message: The liberals were right all along. No apologies. No change. It's their turn. Hand it over. It was all an accident, don't you see? Americans really agree with liberals. It's just that Carter was a jerk. And Reagan was good on television. And Mondale was not good on television. And Dukakis was a puddinghead. And Bush tricks people.

Are mainstream Democrats in danger of being sucked in? Are they counting their winnings as calculated by a Republican cycle-meister? Mightn't it be wise to examine these issues?

Economics: Are the rich getting a larger share of income? Perhaps. The data is less clear than supposed. But the standard of living has been rising for the population as a whole. The poverty rate is down. Family, household and per capita income rates are up.

Will Americans vote by share, or by level? Is Trump on the ballot? Haven't Democrats lost when they use the politics of envy ? Have Democrats been shy about saying America's not fair? When does anti-wastrel-rich (OK) turn into pro-wastrel-poor (not OK)? Is sleaze a great issue? Did it work for Mondale and Dukakis?

Foreign policy: Is it a testimonial to say that on the central issue of our time—the defense of liberty—the liberal Democrats were weak but, ha ha, it doesn't matter anymore? Might voters ask which party will be smart about the next central issue that comes up?

Social issues: Might liberals overturn their deserved victory on abortion? Americans overwhelmingly favor parental consent for teen-age abortion, but pro-choice activists condemn it. Are liberals on the right side of the death penalty? On arts grants to perceived pornography?

Are Democrats right on affirmative action? They favor a bill that tricky

George Bush keeps calling "quotas." By pushing de facto quotas and set-asides, liberals established an issue that most Americans hate, and that ex-Klansman hate-monger David Duke exploits in Louisiana. (For a wise take on social issues, read Michael Barone's *Our Country*.)

Are there cycles? Could be. But there is the phenomenon of politicus interruptus. Cycles stall when the opposition doesn't learn its lesson. Phillips, and Brown, and the liberals are telling the Democrats not to bother. Which is sound Republican advice.

July 4, 1990

Maybe I'm just too crabby about the Democrats. Maybe they've turned the corner. Maybe they've finally learned.

Democratic Majority Leader Richard Gephart's attack on President Bush's foreign policy was from the tough side. Even if there was a cheap shot quality to some of it, it's a good sign. Speaker Tom Foley is attacked for being "too moderate." Isn't that terrible! Governor Douglas Wilder is making the case for moderation and social responsibility. I particularly liked the idea that Wilder went after Bush for being too easy with the Palestinian Liberation Organization. Forget the merits of the case for the moment; forget whether Bush is right or wrong; it's a sign that Wilder is ready to do battle with Jesse Jackson and the radical part of the black leadership.

Still, I'm nervous. There is still a reflexive quality to so much in the Democratic Party. Did the whole gang have to come out in favor of the soft-on-quotas 1990 Civil Rights Bill?

They go around saying there is a great political benefit to be gleaned from forcing the President to veto a civil rights bill. Sure there is. The Republicans will be saying Democrats are for quotas. The Democrats will be saying the Republicans aren't sufficiently pro-minority. I know who wins that one.

I have difficulty in figuring out why the Democrats do this. Were they mugged one more time by a special interest group, in this case civil rights organizations? Is it simply knee-jerk responsiveness? Or mindlessness? (The astute reader will have noticed long ago that I did not support the Democratic version of the bill.)

On other days, things look better. Maybe the end of the Cold War will help. On a weekend in August 1990, just after Saddam Hussein had marched into Kuwait, some conservative hard-liners (Pat Buchanan and James Schlesinger for two) were saying America couldn't respond, America shouldn't respond, America wouldn't respond. And Democrats, those weak-willed, limp-wristed Democrats were saying "go for it," which gave the President the running room to go for it. Even Jesse Jackson.

14

Republicans

T he Republicans get a much shorter political section than the Democrats. The Republicans have been in power, so what they do has been described and commented upon in sections about policy, not politics. That is a lesson that should be remembered by Democrats as they go down one blind byway after another. It may feel good, it may sound good, but you're not likely to govern.

I am still stunned by the amount of raw power a President has when he chooses to use it. The pop-talk is all about paralyzed government, about a weak presidency. And in late 1989, George Bush, suddenly, alone, acting in a complex situation with no clear mandate for a course of action, decided to invade the sovereign nation of Panama. The Congress said yes, boss, what a great idea.

Reagan, Mussolini, and the New Deal

His admirers and his adversaries don't agree on much, but they will get together on the idea that Ronald Reagan is a man of deep political conviction, our most ideological president in recent times.

Last week, in an exclusive half-hour interview to be aired soon on public television, I had the opportunity to explore some ideological byways with President Reagan, to talk about his view of recent history and his view of the world.

I found him an articulate and strong-minded man with certain views that some would see as unconventional—and others would see as revisionist or outrageous.

Consider the way he sees his own formative political years. We know Ronald Reagan thinks that federal government has gone too far, but, surprisingly, the scripture he cites is Franklin Roosevelt!

Reagan said: "I have known his (Roosevelt's) sons for years. I know their own conversations about what he believed. I think he always thought the things that were being done (during the Depression) were in the nature of medicine for a sick patient."

But, says Reagan, "my own analysis is that people attracted to government . . . in those years in many instances did not view the medicine as temporary."

Reagan chose to bring up his old grudge against those New Dealers in the 1930s who, he claims, saw some good in extreme versions of state planning: "Many of the New Dealers actually espoused what today has become an epithet, fascism, in that they spoke admiringly of how Mussolini had made the trains run on time. In other words, they saw what he was doing, a planned economy." Reagan also reminisces that New Dealer "Harold Ickes, in his book, said that we were striving for a modified form of communism."

Reagan's version of Roosevelt goes on: "I think that, had he lived and with the war over, we could have seen him using government the other way. Roosevelt at one time made a statement that the federal government had to get out of the business of—we didn't call it 'welfare' then, we called it 'relief.' And we didn't mean that you let people starve. But he (Roosevelt) explained that the federal government was not the proper agency for that and that the manner in which it was being done was demoralizing to the people that you were trying to help."

I asked the president if he wasn't carrying water on both shoulders, denouncing federal spending on the one hand and yet pointing with pride about retaining the "social safety net" of programs that he and his party had previously opposed. After all, even after all of his "cuts," the projections for the human services budget go up, not down; isn't he, then, really accepting much of the current form of a modified welfare state?

That is not the way he sees it. Those five-year budget projections, he says, are mandated by law. They are influenced by population growth, economic growth, inflation and so on. But that, he says, does not preclude continuing his plan to diminish the federal government's role. The private sector will pick up some of the functions, the states and localities will pick up other functions.

He sees this political time of ours as one that will not merely cap what we have but will be "a bridge" from one philosophy of government to another that he envisions. He will be happy to take us across that bridge.

Well, we shall see about that. I rather doubt it. When the fur and feathers settle, after years of political combat, I would guess (and hope) that the modified welfare state will have been capped but retained. But not because Ronald Reagan didn't try to turn it around. He is enjoying his job and relishes the idea of shrinking the federal role. After all, that's what he thinks Franklin Roosevelt would have done.

He believes that his views on the international circumstance also have an intellectual consistency. I asked him about the idea that has been raised in Washington that "Ronald Reagan has no foreign policy"; it is a view that maintains that there is no grand design and that what we have had is bluster without action.

Surprise! The president does not agree with that—although he did some heavy blustering. He said, for example, that the anti-American demonstrations in Europe "are all sponsored by a thing called the World Peace Council, which is bought and paid for by the Soviet Union."

He indicated wistfully that it might not have been a bad idea, years ago, "if the free world had been able to unite and quarantine the Soviet Union with regard to trade." But that didn't happen: now, alas, we sell the Soviets wheat, Reagan says, because if we didn't, they'd buy it elsewhere.

The president dismisses the idea that there is no grand design for U.S. foreign policy. Certainly, he says, there is one—only "I didn't announce it letter by letter and put it on the front page of the papers . . . I think that's kind of foolish to do, because much of a foreign policy must be concerned with rather delicate negotiations, quiet diplomacy, getting things done, not by challenging someone, putting his back up in the other country because politically he'll look like a weakling if he agrees with you."

To the question of whether we can, ought to, and are going to do something about Cuba, the president says "yes," indicates that he will not talk of specific options, and goes on to say that Cuba is "a puppet of the Soviet Union . . . with the Soviet Union using it as a forward base for the infiltration of subversion into the Americas."

The main story of the Reagan administration, it seems to me, is directional, not specific. Yet, most of the press coverage is focused at Reagan in the same way that it was focused at pragmatists like Carter and Ford: a budget cut here, a power clash there.

But one senses that there is a lot going on inside Ronald Reagan these days as he tries to square his philosophy and ideology with reality and events. It's not an easy chore for any man in public life, and particularly difficult for one who believes so vigorously and comes from a spot on the political spectrum that has been challenged for so long, for some very good reasons.

Some of his theology makes sense; some of it remains obscure, still outside the mainstream, in my view. But he seems to be a tough, smart fellow—and I would guess he will be challenging us for quite a while.

December 25, 1981

Savior of the Great Society: Reagan

Suppose it was a hundred years from now and you were an historian of American political economy, looking back at the flow of ideas and numbers over many decades.

What would our whole post-war era look like? And turning the focus tighter, scanning through three Reagan budgets, what would the Reagan years look like?

Try this double formulation:

By not opposing it, Dwight Eisenhower, in effect, ratified Franklin Roosevelt's New Deal. The big FDR programs were removed from political contention and became part of day-to-day American life. Only a Republican could have done that, and Eisenhower did it quietly and with grace.

Ronald Reagan, in effect, has ratified Lyndon Johnson's Great Society. Unlike Eisenhower, Reagan wiggled and squirmed, and fulminated. The press followed and spotlighted every curlicue of his anti-big government table-thumping. But three budgets into his administration, the numbers tell a clear story: the Great Society is still very much with us, perhaps in spite of Reagan, but in any event endorsed at least by indirection in the three consecutive budgets put forth by our most conservative president.

The evidence for this comes from both political rhetoric and budget numbers.

For all his kicking and screaming, Reagan from the first was pledged that he would "preserve the safety net." Strange language from a man who for two decades campaigned against instituting just such a level of social welfare expenditures, but then again, Ronald Reagan is not our first political schizophrenic.

The budget numbers provide verification for Great Society survival. Look at the "safety net" as a collection of all the federal programs dealing with welfare, food, housing, pension, medical care, veterans benefits, Social Security and unemployment. Then look at two time periods: from 1970 to 1981 (that is, from mid-Nixon, to Ford and on to the last totally-Carter budget) and then from 1981 to 1984 (to measure the impact of the Reagan years.)

In the first period, the amount spent on the Safety Net increased by 7.4 percent each year. In the second period it continued to grow, but by only 2.9 percent per year.

When viewed as a "share of Gross National Product," the Safety Net grew by 5.2 percent per year in the first period. In the second period, it continued to grow, but only by 1.2 percent per year.

The actual real-dollar increase in Safety Net spending went up by $16 billion per year in constant dollars during the first period, but by only $10 billion per year in the second period. That's less per year than earlier, but $29 billion after inflation (from 1981–84) is more than chicken feed.

Caveats: Some of the Safety Net spending goes to people who are not poor, but, then again, many of the people who are not poor, aren't poor because Safety Net programs like Social Security and medicare have helped move them well above the poverty line. Some programs for the disadvantaged have been cut, but then again, others have been raised. The current recession itself has automatically triggered some additional safety net spending, and that has nothing to do with Reagan's policies.

But with all the caveating, when viewed from our Olympian, hundred-years-from-now perch, one idea still comes through: after all the hoopla about cutting this and cutting that, the Safety Net is growing, albeit at a slower rate.

That should have been recognized much earlier. The press zeroed in on what Stockman-in-the-*Atlantic* had to say about trickle-down and Trojan Horses. But Stockman also talked about those massive "cuts" in social spending that had been so much in the news.

Stockman said: "There was less there than met the eye. . . . Let's say that you and I walked outside and I waved a wand and said, I've just lowered the temperature from 110 to 78. Would you believe me? What this was, was a cut from an artificial Congressional Budget Office base."

Or, as the *New York Times* so artfully put it the other day in a glossary of budget terms, "a cut is often just a smaller increase."

One acronym seems in so many ways to sum up the essence of our time. It is "DITROI"—"a Decrease in the Rate of Increase." But DITROI, remember, still means growth—lesser growth, but growth.

That is about what happened to our political, politicized economy in recent years. The moderate welfare state we have devised here survives—no question about it. (I've always wanted to give a prize for a politically acceptable synonym for "welfare state.")

That fact of survival can be handled different ways at different spots on the political spectrum. Liberals may bemoan the fact that we are no longer vigorously expanding our welfare state commitment. Conservatives may grind their teeth at not being able to roll back the welfare state. Moderate conservatives may applaud, by noting that the welfare state had to be capped at some point, and now isn't a bad point to start a plateau. Moderate liberals may scowl, saying it had to be capped alright, but the Reagan mix in the capping is wrong-headed.

Viewed historically, all that is politics, and blurred politics at that. The economics, however, are clear; the welfare state lives, its growth has slowed.
February 8, 1983

How Reagan Leads America

Ronald Reagan's brush with cancer reminds us that important political leaders—no matter how healthy—are always working toward creating their own glowing passages for history books that will be written long after they are gone. "What will be left behind?" and "What has been changed?" are the appropriate questions for both presidents and president-watchers to ponder. Such thoughts usually revive the old argument about whether "times make the man" or "men make the times."

I'm usually on the side of the times: technology, demography and geopolitics shape our world more than our leaders. Events, not people, are usually in the saddle. That's true with Reagan, but less so than is usual.

I've just returned from Europe. People there talk about "Reaganism" and "the Reagan philosophy." Like some Americans, some Europeans don't like Reagan, don't like his philosophy, don't even like dignifying a man they regard as a simpleton by awarding him a "philosophy" of his own.

But their terminology shows his impact. Reagan has influenced his time, and that is due to the fact that uniquely among recent American presidents he has a clear philosophy.

Could one have gone to Europe and heard about "Fordism"? Doubtful. How about "Carterism"? No. "Carterism," in fact, has become known as the philosophy of not having a philosophy. Nixon? He only had policies and doctrines. Kennedy and Eisenhower had bouyant personalities—important assets—but no consistent promulgated world view.

To get even a sense of a president with a philosophy, one goes back to Lyndon Johnson. But LBJ's public philosophy was reactive and legislative rather than ideological. There were problems regarding civil rights, poverty, the environment, and health care to be dealt with. Johnson acted boldly, and the hoped-for result of the problem-solving was called "The Great Society."

Reagan operates differently. Unlike LBJ, he operates from the general to the specific. Coming into office Reagan said big government was suffocating us, that traditional values were eroding, that America was being pushed around all over the world, that entrepreneurs were stifled. He dealt with themes more than with issues. The themes were the distilled essence of an ideology generated by his gut feelings and several decades of political testing out on the hustings.

Reagan has a legitimate case, although I think he exaggerates. In many ways, big government has been good for America. (Who wants to go back to a time when a third of elderly Americans were in poverty?) We were never as weak as the America-has-lost-its-nerve folks said. Our values remained strong; we have been the most religious of the modern nations. And our not-so stifled entrepreneurs managed to change the world with chips and biogenetics.

But that's not the point. What counts is that Reagan believes in Reaganism. He is trying to sell it. And history books will judge his presidency on how well he sells it.

As sidelights, such volumes could observe that he was not an intellectual president, that he was ill-informed on details, that he was a Great Communicator who gave some rambling, goof-a-minute press conferences, and his bark was worse than his bite—as in the hostage issue (at least so far).

But that would be peripheral. Reagan's real legacy should be obvious to historians: For all his flaws, he pushed America to think publicly about big things that were not on the anvil before he arrived. Were we too weak militarily? Was big government out of hand? Were we overtaxed? Were civil rights initiatives going awry? Was commercial innovation being smothered?

Now, asking questions doesn't answer them. But, in a democracy, you never get the answers you want if you can't surface your issues, in your way.

Reagan's achievement is that he has done that. He refocused the national dialogue. Agree with him or disagree, that is the hallmark of a man who has changed his times.

July 18, 1985

Trashing Bush-bashing

Early in 1980, as the presidential contests began to take shape, the people in the Carter-for-President campaign were hoping—really hoping—that their Republican opponent would be Ronald Reagan. After all, Reagan was known then as a right-winger and a bit of a far-out conservative kook. All Reagan could get in the general election, the Carter people reasoned, was Republican votes. What scared the Carterites was that a Republican moderate, not Reagan, might get the nomination. Such a candidate might get Republican votes and also plenty of independent votes—and even some Democratic ones. Someone, for example, like Howard Baker or Bob Dole.

Or George Bush.

Bush, in fact, made a pretty good run at it in 1980. He beat Reagan in the Iowa caucuses, and in primaries in Massachusetts, Connecticut, Pennsylvania, Washington, D.C., and Michigan. Finally, he was forced to drop out of the race, a victim of the Reagan juggernaut.

Comes now 1988. Bush will be the Republican nominee. Bush has done to Dole in 1988 what, in 1980, Reagan did to Bush: he wiped him out.

Of course, the sharks are circling. Bush, they say, is a preppy wimp. He is a boring speaker—Nembutal with a resume. He sold his manhood to Ronald Reagan in an eight-year spasm of vice-presidential sycophancy. He engenders no passion among his supporters. He has Iran-contra skeletons in his closet. When it was still a Bush-Dole race, one very well-known Democrat told me, "Dole beats any Democrat: any Democrat beats Bush."

We shall see. The rap on Bush is much overdone. Every vice president in recent times has become a caged political eunuch—but in those instances where he became president, he was able to act vigorously—consider Johnson, Nixon, Ford. We've also had plenty of presidents who were less than dazzling public speakers: Carter, Ford, Nixon and Johnson, to mention some recent examples. History shows that an Ivy League education or a wealthy upbringing has never before been a handicap for an aspiring president: consider Kennedy and Franklin Roosevelt. And Bush has been closely scrutinized for seven years while the serious scrutiny of any of his potential opponents is yet to come.

But there are some other things at work that the Bush-bashers ought to consider. It is indeed true that Bush does not seem to call forth passionate response. And intensity and passion among voters count for a great deal in a tight caucus or primary situation where voter turnout is a crucial determinant. But it counts for much less in a general presidential election where turnout is far higher and fairly consistent. Thus: if a voter had felt 99 percent passionate-positive about Ronald Reagan and now feels 51 percent passionate-positive about George Bush, he or she will still be likely to vote for Bush, and that vote will still count as just one vote. We count votes, not passion.

Moreover, the reasons the Carter people were fearful of a Baker-Dole-Bush sort of candidacy have not gone away. For good or for ill, George Bush is indeed intrinsically more moderate than Reagan. And even at the height of his popularity, Reagan scared away some voters who felt his conservatism was too rigid and doctrinaire. Structurally speaking, Bush can pick up some of these middle-of-the-road voters, even if they are not wildly impressed with his less-than-bulging kit of charisma. In short, Bush may be able to get conservative votes because of his Reagan connection, and independent and some Democratic votes because he's not Reagan.

Of course, an election is never the sound of one hand clapping. The voters will have a choice. If the Democrats nominate a candidate who will be able to appeal to the moderate center of the electorate, that candidate may well be competitive with Bush. But if Democrats should perhaps be dreaming that they've got a weak, wimpy, boring, elitist, guilty loser as an opponent—they're wrong.

April 21, 1988

Congress Is Gelous of Bush

A wonderful political indicator, at some variance with what we have been led to believe, appeared the other day in the *Washington Post*. A prominent headline announced, "BUSH, FOLLOWING HIS NOSE: THE PRESI-DENT-ELECT GOES SHOPPING FOR BATH GEL." Yup, big news: Bush himself actually entered a store in downtown Washington to buy some Christmas gifts.

You may ask: Why does this stunning event have massive political significance? I answer your question with more questions: Would there be a story, if newly elected Senate majority Leader George Mitchell, a Democrat, went shopping for bath gel? Would there be a story if House Speaker Jim Wright, a Democrat, went shopping for bath gel?

No. By the deeply ingrained standards of American journalism, bath gel is news only when associated with presidents.

The classic case in point was the great Ford English Muffin Caper. Have you ever toasted an English muffin? Was it big news? Answers: Probably yes, surely no. But when Gerald Ford assumed the presidency from Richard Nixon in 1974, it was learned (leaked?) that the new president tended to wake early and make his own English muffin in the White House toaster. Like, wow! A real man of the people; a clear signal of the death knell of the imperial presidency; how charming; how very American. Remake the front page!

This new-prez-worship is an important, sometimes temporary, often unconsidered part of the political power equation. More so than ever, media is power. Bush-o-mania is just beginning, and my guess is that the Squire of Kennebunkport is going to do pretty well with hyper-celebrity and the political power it yields.

The biggest laugh line of 1989 may be recalling the fact that in 1988 pundits actually said Bush had no charisma. Since the election I've seen Bush a few times at public occasions. He gives a fine impression: good looking, tall, trim, self-effacing, occasionally humorous. On television he appears decisive, crisp, knowledgeable—in short, presidential. Whatever happened to the foot-in-mouth wimp? What will we write about?

And all this before even becoming president. Just wait until the 53 grandchildren start visiting the White House! And add in Barbara Bush: she will be media dynamite.

Meanwhile, of course, the 535 members of the Congress will also be in the news. But their news will not be about bath gel and little children. No, indeed. It will be mostly about the world's most fascinating topic: the deficit. Sequestration. Targets. Shortfalls. Out-years. How very interesting. It is a topic that even the people who understand it, understand that they don't understand it.

This presidential media monopoly serves the president well, at least in the early years of a term when the publicity is almost invariably roseate. When the public is fascinated by English muffins, they are also inclined to listen, and often heed, what this wonderful president of ours has to say about taxes, defense, foreign policy. The Congress, ear to ground, senses this as it happens, but often not before. Hence, all the talk about how there "will be no honeymoon." There will be a honeymoon.

Only later, as and if policies and events don't work out well, the spotlight shows P-warts, and the media-public honeymoon ends. That's when you hear stories about Ford falling down and Jimmy Carter chasing killer rabbits.

On balance, though, our system is president-oriented. The president is commander-in-chief, negotiates with the Soviets, appoints and runs the executive branch, has the veto power and the media power. My colleague Richard Scammon has summed up the relationship between the Congress and the presidency rather well. "You can look all around Washington," he says, "and never find a statue to a Congress."

December 29, 1988

When the Anchors Are Away

Artful media manipulation for a worthy purpose, so slick that it is not slick at all, is the jackpot skill for a modern political leader. In Poland and Hungary, George Bush hit the jackpot.

There was probably more network television coverage of those countries in three days than there has been in the last three years. Nor was it mindless "photo opportunity" stuff. The network coverage had a theme.

The networks told us, with grace and virtuosity, the truth about communism today: that it has been a brutal failure, that democracy can be the wave of the future even in the Soviet rim-lands, that America will likely be the big player if democracy is to prevail as the Iron Curtain corrodes.

The good news is that the networks told the bad news. We saw the empty stores and long lines in Poland. We saw the Solidarity legislators tell us about their experiences in jail. We saw full stores in Hungary and heard about how hardly anyone had the money to buy anything. We heard Hungarian communist leaders announce that communism had failed. We heard a network anchor, NBC's Tom Brokaw, talk about "40 years of Communist oppression." In all, a vivid description of an empire that had been very evil indeed.

The quote of the week came from Lech Walesa, who said, "We have a chance to be the America of the East." Poles were sent to the slammer for less.

By the time the press corps got to Paris, CBS's Leslie Stahl was saying to Dan Rather that "President Bush comes here when the whole world is celebrating American values."

Why this outburst of televised geopolitical reality? First, what's happening in Poland and Hungary is remarkable. Second, President Bush decided to make the trip. Third, the new television technology gives the president more agenda-setting power than ever before.

Thus, all the major networks "traveled the anchor." Brokaw, Rather, Peter Jennings (ABC) and Bernard Shaw (CNN) not only went to Hungary and Poland, but took whole broadcast teams with them. Accordingly, the anchors typically introduced the stories on the death of Sir Laurence Olivier from Budapest.

Once the program comes from a faraway place, editorial logic dictates that there will be plenty of coverage beyond just what happened at the state dinner or what the communique said. We get the sort of full flavor that we saw from Eastern Europe.

Traveling the anchor is not a new television technique. It's been around since the days of gavel-to-gavel coverage of the national political conventions.

But it used to be enormously expensive and complex. Now, with satellite transmission, computers and lightweight cameras and editing equipment, it's easier and cheaper. And competition within the television industry makes it likely that if the story is good, and if one network travels the anchor, so will the others.

So when Bush said "I'm going," each network had little choice but to say, "Me too." And once the networks went, with their anchors, they served up broad coverage—sometimes five or six stories per night. Once they did that, they did it well. And once the networks did it well, the public paid more attention to Eastern Europe than they ever had before.

Cynics say that these sorts of geopolitical circuses are designed primarily to boost a president in the polls.

There's more to it. Bush has a difficult chore. As the Soviets appear to recede as a military threat, American foreign policy must be seen to have both a cause and a constituency. The cause is democracy. The constituency is the patriotic and proud American public. But the public reacts with political zest (and resources) only as it empathizes with the situation.

That empathy is bolstered in a media democracy when the big networks put on an intelligent circus. Bush took the circus horses to water. Anchors away!

July 19, 1989

Commerce and Business

15

Everything Is the Business
of America

This *whole volume, in some sense, is about the terrain that the business*
community will face in the nineties. That idea will be discussed at the
end of this chapter.

One brief vignette. In late 1989, Sony bought Columbia Pictures. Ameri-
cans were dismayed; "They're buying up America," it was said, and the
anchormen moaned that Japanese now owned that American patriotic classic
film, Mr. Smith Goes to Washington.

We should be clear what Sony did and why they did it. To sell their
remarkable hardware, they need software that interests audiences. So they
are buying up American software and the ability to produce American
software, which is the only kind that people around the world are prepared
to spill vast amounts of money upon. To close the circle: trillions of Japanese
yen are being invested to produce and distribute American popular culture
around the world.

Fortunately, in America, we don't nationalize businesses. But we have
quite a unique record of nationalizing businessmen. James Michener's book
Centennial *describes how the second sons of English lords and ladies were*
sent off to Colorado with a huge spread of Western land as a going-away
present. (No doubt, Americans said at the time, "They're buying up Ameri-
ca.") The young Englishmen married American girls. The progeny was Ameri-
can. When the English lord died some part of the inheritance came here.

All we got in the transaction was the investment, the talent, the progeny of talent, and a piece of the inheritance. Is that supposed to be the bad news?

Item: When Rupert Murdoch, an Australian, became a naturalized citizen, two billion dollars worth of wealth should have moved from "foreign ownership" to "American ownership." Does that show up in the balance of trade?

Item for the future: Let's count how many Japanese decide to relocate in the United States.

All well and good. Nice little anecdotes. Not enough to combat the notion that America is losing the business wars. But the statistics don't show that either. America's share of the world economy is about what it was prior to World War II. In the eighties, America's economic growth was more rapid than West Europe's. America's share of world manufacturing jobs has remained steady. American manufacturing exports are booming. American productivity in the eighties went up faster than in Europe. The cost of production today is lower in America than in either Europe or Japan. American per capita income remains the highest in the world.

Enough? Some other relevant data are scattered about the book; particularly note the material on page 368.

Tomorrow: American Exceptionalism

It was the Frenchman Alexis de Tocqueville who coined the phrase "American Exceptionalism" to express the idea that Americans were different. Recently, there has been a worldwide explosion of public-opinion polling, and the results suggest that, despite European unification and Japanese perestroika, the international terrain of the 1990s will be far from homogenous.

Many surveys in the industrialized nations during the 1980s show clearly that the distinctive and probably locked-in hallmarks of American character are independence and individuality. This shows up in polls about whether the primary goal of democracy is freedom or equality, a fair chance or a fair share. More than others, Americans opt for freedom. They are less likely to favor government redistributing income from rich to poor or providing jobs for all. America, says sociologist Tom Smith of the National Opinion Research Center, is "an opportunity society," not "a security society." Thus, Americans rank first in believing young people should have the chance to attend college. (See page 368.)

Americans' individualistic bent means they are less likely to vote on the basis of economic class—about half the British rate. They are far more likely to do volunteer work; they prefer to help the unfortunate independently. More than others, Americans value science: they believe individuals can shape destiny by manipulating nature. Some 58 percent believe science will help mankind. The all-Europe average is 35 percent. Americans are also more likely to view their jobs as their defining dimension, not just a meal ticket. Half say that a "feeling of accomplishment" is the most important aspect of their work compared with a 10-country average of about a quarter. Not everything fits the pattern. Americans are in the middle range regarding "life satisfaction"—lower than Canada, higher than Japan.

Among the major industrialized nations, America is the most religious. Sociologist Seymour Martin Lipset theorizes that one reason Americans feel that way is because religion has been wholly voluntary, separated from the state. Americans are more likely to believe that their church answers spiritual needs, more likely to believe in heaven, hell, the Devil and life after death. Some 65 percent of Americans believe there is a personal God, compared with 31 percent of Englishmen and 19 percent of Swedes.

Americans, pretty sure of themselves, have more confidence in their institutions. Polling regarding 10 institutions (including church, business, schools, military, labor unions, the judiciary and the media) shows Americans have an average 80 percent rate of confidence compared with 52 percent among major European nations.

Patriotism is vitally important to Americans. Fully 80 percent say they

367

Indicators: *American Exceptionalism*

A. Americans are different from other modern nations in a variety of ways.

1. Which Is More Important: Freedom or Equality?

Country	Percentage Choosing Equality	Percentage Choosing Freedom
U.S.	20%	72%
Britain	23%	69%
France	32%	54%
Ireland	38%	46%
Italy	45%	43%
W. Germany	39%	37%
Japan	32%	37%
Spain	39%	36%

2. Percentage of Those Who Agree That It Is the Government's Responsibility to Reduce the Income Differences Between People

Country	Percent
Italy	81%
Hungary	77%
Holland	64%
Britain	63%
W. Germany	56%
Australia	42%
U.S.	28%

3. Percentage Believing That Differences in Income Are Too Large

Country	Percent
U.S.	56%
Australia	58%
Holland	66%
W. Germany	72%
Hungary	74%
Britain	75%
Italy	86%

4. Percentage Believing That the Government Should Provide a Job for Everyone Who Wants One

Country	Percent
Hungary	92%
Italy	82%
Austria	80%
W. Germany	77%
Holland	75%
Britain	59%
Switzerland	50%
U.S.	45%
Australia	40%

5. Percentage Believing That Opportunities for Young People to Go to College Should Be Increased

Country	Percent
U.S.	69%
Britain	55%
Italy	39%
Germany	31%
Austria	19%

6. Percentage Believing They Have a Good Chance of Improving Their Standard of Living

Country	Percent
U.S.	71%
Australia	58%
Italy	43%
W. Germany	36%
Britain	36%
Hungary	33%
Holland	23%

Source notes are on page 398.

are very proud to be an American. The all-Europe average is 38 percent; the West Germans come in lowest at 21 percent. When asked if they would be willing to fight for their country, 71 percent of Americans say yes. The all-Europe average is 43 percent: the Japanese response is 22 percent.

Tocqueville had the right word for yesterday and tomorrow: "Exceptionalism."

August 7, 1989

The data about pride in work is incredible, but not non-credible. I believe the data is sound. Does that sound like a non-competitive nation?

View from the Corporate Suite

"Competitiveness" is one of the great issues of the 1988 presidential race. Every candidate is for it; we are told we've got to face up to the threat of foreign competition or the end may be in sight. It is relevant, then, to ask: "How are we doing?"

The old car commercials used to exclaim, "Ask the Man Who Owns One." In effect, that is what *Business Month* magazine (formerly *Dun's Review*) has done. They commissioned the polling firm of Yankelovich Clancy Shulman to conduct what is probably the most comprehensive survey ever conducted of American chief executive officers. A total of 609 CEOs were interviewed person-to-person for about an hour in their offices, about half before the Oct. 19 crash and half after.

I examined the poll, and, in fact, wrote an article for *Business Month* about it. It gives, I think, a fascinating glimpse of the top echelon of corporate America and provides some significant information. The poll shows deep inherent optimism about the future of our businesses, and the good news comes through as tempered and credible, rather than as mere boosterism.

The executives come back again and again to the "competitiveness" question. In a general open-ended question about potential threats to the American economy, the CEOs list "foreign competition" as public enemy No. 1.

If competitiveness is such a problem, why so? The CEOs—90 percent of them—say American business is too "short-term oriented." Said one CEO, "Everyone is working for the benefit of financial analysts—short term instead of looking ahead." And another: "The Japanese system is long term. They back their people 100 percent; we just pull the rug out when we see temporary losses." One specific remedy suggested by the

Indicators: *Competitiveness*

A. America is still #1 in many areas.

Industries in Which the U.S. Leads the World

Production

Coal
Hydroelectric and Nuclear Power
Primary Aluminum
Refined Copper
Plastic
Synthetic Fibers
Rubber Tires
Integrated Circuits
Computers
Telecommunications Equipment

Technology Exports

Aerospace, Airplanes
Scientific and Precision Equipment

Transport

Air Passengers/Air Freight
Motor Vehicle Freight

B. The U.S. economy shrunk, then rebounded as a share of the total OECD economy.

Year	U.S. Share (at Average Exchange Rates)
1950	59%
1960	54%
1970	48%
1980	35%
1985	46%
1988	45%

Source notes are on page 399.

C. The U.S. has been receiving a growing proportion of the Nobel Prizes in the sciences: The University of California-Berkeley alone has claimed more prizes than the Soviet Union.

Nobel Prize Laureates in Chemistry, Physics, and Physiology/Medicine

Year	Total	Americans	Percentage
1900–09	33	1	3%
1910–19	25	1	4%
1920–29	33	3	9%
1930–39	37	13	35%
1940–49	30	14	47%
1950–59	54	30	56%
1960–69	58	28	48%
1970–79	63	36	57%
1980–89	65	40	62%

D. After falling, exports are on the rise.

U.S. Exports' Share of Total OECD Trade

Year	Percentage
1959	22%
1969	16%
1974	17%
1979	18%
1985	14%
1987	16%
1988	18%

E. How much pride, if any, do you take in the work that you do?

	U.S.	Japan	Eur.
A great deal	84%	36%	37%
Some pride	14%	37%	44%

F. Japan has grown most rapidly among the Big 7 industrial nations.

Gross Domestic Product (GDP) of Selected Countries as a Percentage of U.S. GDP

Year	Canada	France	Italy	Japan	U.K.	W. Ger.
1970	8	23	16	33	22	30
1975	9	25	17	36	22	30
1980	10	25	17	39	20	30
1985	10	23	16	41	19	28
1987	10	23	16	42	19	27

CEOs is to change the Securities and Exchange Commission regulation that demands quarterly financial reports. Biannual or annual reporting, they say, would take off some of the short-term pressure.

Have the CEOs done anything about this problem? They maintain they have: 69 percent say they are spending more time on strategic long-term planning, 61 percent more on controlling costs, and 54 percent more time on marketing.

To a remarkable degree, they have also signed onto the "lean and mean" strategy. In the last two years alone, 39 percent of the CEOs say they have "down-sized" their companies. (Of the larger corporations in the sample, the figure was 48 percent!) The process is by no means over: Of those CEOs who have down-sized, 50 percent say they will do more of it in the next two years.

The CEOs, overwhelmingly Republican, nonetheless want government help to encourage competitiveness: 83 percent say the government isn't doing enough to stimulate research, 67 percent want tax incentives. (By contrast, only 16 percent say the government should spend more on social programs.)

Is the drive for American competitiveness working? Will it work? When asked a general question—"How would you describe your overall confidence in American business to meet the challenges it faces?"—only about half (51 percent) offered up a "most confident" rating ("5" or "6" on a 1 to 6 scale). But, far more relevantly, when asked the same question about their own company, 80 percent gave a "most confident" response.

The long-term response—for all business—is also positive. The question: "In the year 2000 will American business be stronger globally?" Answer: 53 percent of the CEOs said yes, 29 percent said no.

Reading the poll results, one gets this general impression: The CEOs think we're in trouble, they know what the trouble is, they're acting to remedy it, they will continue at it, and they believe they will prevail. In short: stress and success.

March 3, 1988

Why Foreigners Invest in America

What of our economic future—particularly in the 1990s? Will there be "a day of reckoning"? Will "the piper be paid"? Will there be a collapse, a relapse, a crash, a smash?

I am dubious. Frightened Wall Street Republicans have been making the case for disaster since the dawn of the deviously devastating double deficits—budget and trade. Now, under the flimsy flag of "economic nationalism," Democrats are joining in. It is said that foreigners are "buying up America on the cheap," that we have become "the world's largest debtor nation," and that all this can lead to chaos and catastrophe down the road.

We are told that one cause of the piper-paying will come about because foreigners are doing what economists call "financing our deficit." But in non-econ lingo, the same phenomenon can be described as something else: Foreigners are investing in America.

Thus: The money invested here is used to make up for our government's spending that exceeds our government's intake (i.e., it does finance our deficit). But that's only what it is used for; it is not necessarily why it is invested here. If we understand why, we may have a better sense of whether it is potentially dangerous.

Why? Because foreigners believe the United States is a very good place to put a lot of their money. Why? Well, indeed partly because of our deficits, which are a real problem. The budget deficit keeps American interest rates somewhat higher than elsewhere, the trade deficit (according to some experts) helped to push down the value of the dollar. Both conditions make investing here attractive.

But there is something deeper that pushes foreign investment over here. Consider: Suppose you were the manager of a Japanese or European pension plan. Two facts drive your actions. First, you have lots of money to invest. (These nations have been getting much richer. By golly, they're almost as rich as we are!) Second, you go to sleep each night remembering your primary responsibility: that workers who have invested in the plan are supposed to end up with a good pension for their old age decades from now.

Where do you invest all that money? Africa? Well, no. There is political turmoil; the traditions of investment capitalism are barely rooted there. Latin America? Better. But there is monumental debt; the democratic governments and capitalist systems are often new and nervous. Asia? Better. There is a good business climate in some places. But it's a dangerous neighborhood: China and Russia are still wild cards.

Why not invest all the money in West Europe and Japan—that is, at home? Well, much of it is invested there. But those countries are demographically dormant; some are already losing population, and that will hurt businesses. Where will the new customers come from? Will the Soviets remain docile in Europe?

What's left? Who's left? We are. A long and flourishing capitalist tradition. A large 50-state common market. A population market forecast that is troubling, but much better than in Europe and Japan. Geopolitical stability, with a kicker: As "leader of the free world," we not only protect ourselves but also our more exposed allies. If we should falter; they suffer first.

Adam Smith said that nations have "comparative advantages" in producing

products. True. They also have comparative advantages in attracting investment. We are the No. 1 investment-attractors in the world—by far. We
are a "debtor" nation because we are an investment-attractor nation.

There is no particular reason to suggest that this situation will change.
Foreign investment will probably continue; given the trends and conditions,
it may well grow. That is a sign of health, not sickness; of growth, not
collapse.

October 27, 1988

Yankee-trashing

Perhaps the Japanese are being picked on too much in the current dialogue
about trade. So-called "Japan-bashing" isn't fair. Most of the causes of
our trade deficit are our own fault. Most of the Japanese economic miracle
has been of their own making, through hard work and brilliant marketing.

But if Japan-bashing is wrong, if the Japanese get upset about it, they
would be wise to address their own deep-rooted xenophobia, a Japanese
distaste for anyone not Japanese. In particular, they'd better think twice
about "Yankee-trashing." To get a flavor of it, consider this stunning paragraph by James Fallows that has just appeared in *U.S. News & World
Report:*

> In Japan, (the AIDS epidemic) has led to discussion of their
> preoccupation—foreigners. "Japanese Only" signs, conveniently in
> English, have sprung up in the commercial-sex zones. One of the
> candidates (for) prime minister, the Liberal Democratic Party chairman,
> Noboru Takeshita, added a charming touch by linking America's
> economic decline to its new medical vulnerability. At a political rally
> . . . he joked that the ever-rising yen had made American sailors
> stationed in Japan too poor to afford Japanese bar girls. According to
> a newspaper account, which his spokesman did not deny, Takeshita
> said that the lonely sailors' only alternative was to stay on base and
> give each other AIDS.

Now, that is pretty rough stuff under any circumstance. It should be
understood that the Japanese government tries to stop such ugliness. Still,
the remark was made by the person who is the front-runner in the race
to become Japan's next leader. And, coming from a nation whose existence
is due to our sufferance, it can make a grown man damned mad.

Recall that the Japanese constitution, under whose democratic umbrella
their economic miracle has bloomed, was imposed upon them by the
United States after the American occupation in 1945.

Note that 60 percent of the oil used by Japan is shipped through the

Persian Gulf, while the figure for America is only 7 percent. Yet it is America that is talking about risking American lives and spending American treasure so that the gasoline tanks in those cars in Japan can stay nicely topped off. If the Japanese have offered applause, I don't recall hearing it.

And we should mention the central fact of Japanese existence: They are our wards. They live in a very dangerous neighborhood, close to some big bad countries who don't like the Japanese—Russia and China. The Japanese do little to protect themselves—spending just over 1 percent of their gross national product on defense, the lowest rate of any modern nation.

The big reason they spend so little on defense, they say, is because their voters are afraid of resurgent militarism. Japan, after all, almost destroyed all of Asia, including itself, when it ignited the Asian front of World War II. So now the Japanese are the ultimate double free riders: They spend stingily on defense and yet feel secure because the United States guarantees their security. The American guarantee is worth something because we spend 6 percent of our GNP for defense. And one reason Japanese goods have been so inexpensive is that their companies and workers pay so little in taxes for defense, thereby reducing costs of production relative to other nations' costs.

So, Mr. Takeshita ought not to make jokes about American sailors. If he does it again, perhaps we ought to tell him that we might bring the sailors home from Japan and from the Persian Gulf. That would leave Mr. Takeshita all alone to talk to his nice Chinese and Russian neighbors, while Japan's military power is near zero, and its gas tanks are in danger of registering "empty."

June 18, 1987

Helping Japan Beat the Blues

The results of the grandest public opinion project in the history of the planet have begun to come out. It is Gallup polling at its boldest and broadest, a survey research study taken simultaneously in America, in most of the European countries and in Japan. Soon to come: Australia, Hungary, Mexico, Russia and many more. Tomorrow, the world!

The first findings reveal some very sorry facts which have engendered a controversy in the social science community, and which I know will upset you. Brace yourself! The Japanese aren't happy. Not only that, they are not proud of their country. They do not take pride in their work. And— get this—the Japanese people do not have confidence in "major companies."

Such results run so much against the grain that some social scientists have caviled, questioning the accuracy of the Japanese part of the survey.

To make this cavil war more complex, there is a University of Indiana survey that backs up the Gallup Japanese results.

Just think of it! These are the same Japanese we have been seeing on television singing the Toyota corporate anthem as they do their morning exercises with a Toyota calisthenics instructor. These are the same Japanese, we have been told, who are so well-motivated in their work because major companies in Japan never lay anyone off and provide total security. These are the same Japanese who proudly produce radios, motorcycles, cars and cameras with such pride and skill that America has to lay off its workers. We have all seen them on our made-in-Japan television sets, happy in their work, puffed up about their nation's achievements.

Wrong, says the worldwide Gallup mega-poll. In America, 50 percent of the respondents have confidence in "major companies," in Japan, only 25 percent do—dead last among the nations polled. In America, 80 percent of us are proud to be Americans. In Japan, it's 30 percent, next to last in the rankings. In America, 84 percent of the respondents take "a great deal of pride" in their work—in Japan, only 37 percent do.

It gets worse. On a "satisfaction with life" scale, the Japanese are last again. Hispanics and blacks in America are twice as likely as your typical Japanese to be "very happy."

This is serious. Like so many Americans in recent years, I have been concerned about Japanese well-being. The fact that the Japanese are un-happy, un-proud and un-confident—makes me unhappy.

Can we help the Japanese?

Perhaps we can. I posit that the reason the Japanese are un-confident in their companies, un-proud of their work and un-happy generally—is because they are not proud of Japan. (A lot of positing goes on in the survey research community.)

Why aren't they proud? Japan, after all, is a beautiful, stable, democratic place with industrious, intelligent people.

I have figured it out: they are not proud because they depend upon America for two of the most important needs any nation has: defense and markets. How can a nation that will not defend itself be proud? How can a nation that depends so heavily on other people to buy its goods be proud?

I have a solution, and it is a solution that combines interesting aspects of the Reagan economic philosophy. I propose a "flat tax" and "user fees" to straighten out the Japanese malaise.

Thus: the Japanese spend 1 percent of their GNP for defense. We spend 6 percent. We protect them. Suppose they paid a flat user tax of $80 billion a year to make up the difference. That would make them feel proud. They would be paying their own defense.

They could also pay us a flat user fee for using our market. That would be estimated as the value of American goods that could be sold in Japan if they would only allow us to sell in Japan. Call it $70 billion. That would make the Japanese feel even prouder, playing fair and square with an ally.

There are no psychiatrists who treat entire countries. But if there were, $150 billion a year would be cheap therapy to guarantee national happiness. If they pay us a flat user tax, the Japanese won't have to visit the international shrink, and they won't feel bad. Because it will lower our deficit, neither will we.

March 29, 1983

Making Hurt English

Watch out for a new crisis: Import-English!

Talk about a trade war and protectionism. Everyone is, what with Japanese micro-chips and Reagan's tariffs. Will high tariffs save American jobs or raise American prices? Can trade retribution force fairer trading practices? Good questions, but they miss a key point: A secret trade war is being waged upon the English language. Fellow Americans, we need protection, if not protectionism!

I am staring incredulously at a toy that recently arrived in my home. My wife ordered it for our 3-year-old daughter from a mail order catalog. The catalog calls it "Magic Designer." I concede: It's a novel toy, allowing a child to draw with a magnetized stylus on a magnetized board and then erase the picture, with a quick whisk of a built-in lever.

Nothing in the game or in the instruction sheet tells where the game was manufactured. However, inductive reasoning has led me to the belief that it was not made in the U.S.A.

There is an instruction sheet that comes with the game. One instruction warns: "Don't make hurt by dropping heavy things."

Another instruction notes, "On screen, some bubbles can be occurred, but you have no difficult on operation."

A third reads exactly this way, line for line:

> Let's draw each
> two lines with b-
> readth and len-
> gth, can enjoy l-
> ike Chess gam-
> es.

You get the idea. There ought to be a law. We screen imports for insects. We worry about whether they are being dumped at too low a price.

But in the meantime, our children are unprotected from linguistic pollution. What we need, comrades, is a brutal trade commissar in charge of imported language. Especially for toy instructions.

Such a commissar would make hurt by dropping heavy things upon an importer whose instructions teach my child to talk funny. It's true, that by dropping heavy things upon an importer some bubbles can be occurred. But that constitutes a legitimate entrepreneurial risk. That's what capitalism and importing is all about: risk.

Don't laugh. This cause is serious. It's not only that my daughter will start saying things like, "Daddy, don't occur a spanking to make hurt." There is a potential monopoly thing here. What happens when all children start talking Import-English? And talk it when they grow up? Then American manufacturers will have to follow suit in order to communicate with customers. Otherwise they will lose their share of the market. Procter & Gamble will advertise, "Avail you Soap of Ivory." Coca-Cola, it's the real thing, will have commercials saying, "Authentic Item This." Before you know it, politicians will say "revenue enhancement" instead of "taxes."

I must digress. There is yet one more instruction from the game:

> If the screen is destructed
> and liquid is flew on h-
> and, although the liquid
> is nonpoisonous, clean h-
> and with soap.

My friends, the question is not whether the liquid that flew is nonpoisonous. Is the language non-poisonous? Can it be spoke fluently? The answer to you, reader, he or she as the case may be, is that such language is not non-poisonous. Yes, he or she as the case may be, it is poisonous.

Is that the way to beat the trade war? By making woe bubbles on importer's head? Maybe she is. If we have language barrier to drop hurt on their trade barrier, we make trade war deterred. Also have good English pristine, how he meant to be in first place.

April 2, 1987

Business-bopping

Both political parties are chattering about how they are "going to make America competitive again."

The Democrats will propose a trade bill to make us competitive. Republicans maintain that the bill will undoubtedly be protectionist, boosting the price of imports, making goods more expensive for consumers.

But the Republicans also know the bill will be politically sexy because it will be said to "save jobs," and, moreover, it has villains to beat up on. Who? "Unfair foreigners" who take advantage of Uncle Sugar.

Indicators: *Deficits*

A. The budget deficit is shrinking . . .

1. The Federal Deficit as a Percentage of GNP

Year	Percentage of GNP
1945	22.4%
1950	1.2%
1955	0.8%
1960	+0.1%
1965	0.2%
1970	0.3%
1975	3.5%
1980	2.8%
1985	5.4%
1989	2.9%
1990 (July)	2.9% (est.)

A. (cont.) . . . as are federal expenditures as a percentage of GNP.

2. U.S. Federal Government Expenditures as a Percentage of GNP

Year	Percentage of GNP
1945	43.6%
1950	16.0%
1955	17.7%
1960	18.2%
1965	17.6%
1970	19.8%
1975	21.8%
1980	22.1%
1985	23.9%
1989	22.2%
1990	21.8% (est.)

B. U.S. productivity continues to climb, but at a slower rate than earlier.

U.S. Worker Productivity, 1950–88 (Index: 1977 = 100)

Year	Output per Hour
1950	40
1955	51
1960	53
1965	72
1970	79
1975	85
1977	100
1980	103
1985	122
1988	138

C. Although the U.S. has become more reliant on trade over time, it remains one of the two most autarkic nations.

Autarky Index: Trade as a Function of Gross Domestic Product

1988			U.S.
Country	Total	Year	Total
Japan	15.9%	1950	6.9%
U.S.	16.1%	1960	7.2%
Italy	32.2%	1970	8.5%
France	36.4%	1975	13.5%
W. Ger.	47.7%	1980	17.8%
U.K.	40.6%	1985	14.5%
Canada	47.3%	1989	16.5%

D. Most major industrialized countries carry budget deficits.

The Big Seven and Their Central Government Deficits

Country	1983	1985	1987	1989	1990 (est.)
Japan	4.9%	3.7%	1.9%	0.8%	0.6%
Germany	1.9%	1.2%	1.4%	0.4%	1.0%
France	3.0%	2.9%	2.3%	1.7%	1.4%
United Kingdom	2.7%	2.3%	1.1%	+1.3%	+0.7%
Italy	11.7%	13.6%	11.5%	11.0%	10.9%
Canada	6.2%	6.6%	4.3%	3.6%	2.9%
United States	5.2%	4.9%	3.6%	2.8%	2.1%
(excluding Social Security Surplus)	5.2%	5.2%	4.1%	3.9%	3.4%

Source notes are on page 399.

So the Republicans have to have a way to "save jobs" too, and they also need a villain. They have found both in a place surprising for Republicans: the corporate suite.

Republican business-bashing was started by Deputy Secretary of the Treasury Richard Darman. He says we're not competitive because our corporate executives leave the office early to play golf and after 4 P.M. can only be reached in their car phones. (Doesn't Darman know Japanese businessmen play golf?) Anyway, says Darman, America is developing a "corpocracy," much like a government bureaucracy, that is "bloated, risk-averse, inefficient and unimaginative."

Secretary of Commerce Malcolm Baldridge also asked, "Why can't we compete?" Because our car manufacturers went for style instead of quality, he says, and our electronic manufacturers let the Japanese beat us with our own inventions: transistors, color TV, VCRs and robotics.

Baldridge says it happened because our corporations grew fat. There are too many "middle managers," and "our best graduates head for the ivory tower of planning, finance or consulting, instead of production."

Fine. Foreigner-fragging and business-bopping keep both groups nervous, which is a healthy state for them.

But, if it's all right to aggravate them, we ought not necessarily aggravate ourselves. There is a central fact about the competitiveness argument that is too often ignored. The root of our problem is success.

Why are our farmers less competitive than before? Because American agricultural technology—seeds, irrigation, fertilizer—has succeeded. India, which once needed American grain, now exports their own. But it is in our interest that India succeeds. It's the world's largest democracy.

What about dumb business decisions on cars, color TV, VCRs, robotics? What about foreigners being unfair?

There is some truth to both charges, although it is also true that the number of U.S. manufacturing jobs has held constant while the value of our manufactured goods has gone up. Still, foreign competitors beat us to the punch in many instances.

But is this bad? Do we want a world where America dominates every commercial field? Is it so terrible to get VCRs from Japan?

It might be if there were a net loss of American jobs or a declining standard of living in America. But we have increased both the numbers and rate of people at work. Real income in America has gone up.

Some Americans have lost jobs due to exports. That can yield a personal tragedy. But the data tells us that, overall, they find other jobs and, overall, make more money.

Meanwhile, other countries prosper. They use a free enterprise model to compete with us. Sometime they win.

That's good, not bad. Our goal has been to create a prosperous, democratic community of trading nations. That makes for a world where American values are secure and spreading. We have succeeded beyond our dreams. Maybe we ought to thank unfair foreigners and slothful American executives. Something's worked out right.

December 11, 1986

Quickie Recession

What would happen if we had a recession and no one came? What would happen if it's already happened?

The offering of such metaphysical economic questions requires little courage these days. Even an economic illiterate like me can speculate. After all, look at the record of the experts: How many learned economic analysts told us in advance about Black Monday?

Consider recessions. Over the years, conservative economists have indicated that recessions are good for you, or for us, or for America; that is, they are necessary. Recessions, they've said, are nature's way of saying take it easy. Recessions, it's been maintained, "purge" the economic system of excesses.

For one example, here is what allegedly happens if the economy gets "overheated": Unemployment goes down substantially. Wages are bid up. Inflation ensues or is feared. Investors, accordingly, want more rent for their money, and interest rates go up. Loans for houses and consumer and capital goods become more costly. People and companies then slow down their buying. There is less demand for goods and services. Companies produce less, sell less and earn less. The value of their stock diminishes. The Dow Jones industrial average goes down.

About then everyone gets scared and upset. A recession commences. There is less demand for labor. Unemployment goes up. Wages stop rising. Inflation is less of a threat. Interest rates go down. Buying commences. The economy re-ignites without its earlier excesses. We march forward to the future with a new bounce in our step.

The trouble with this purging process is that it can take a year or two and that lots of people get hurt in the process. Some people lose their jobs. Some people can't buy a house. At best, it's not pleasant. At worst, it's tragic.

Consider now Black Monday—a 508-point drop in the Dow, 22 percent of its value, an all-time one-day record decline. Is it possible that on Black Monday and during the subsequent volatility we actually had a "quickie recession," the functional equivalent of a real recession?

After all, it scared the hell out of people, just what a recession is supposed to do. It might even have scared the Democrats into cutting spending. It might even have scared Ronald Reagan into raising taxes. Those, recall, are the two major responses that have been called for by both economists and pundits who believe that the budget deficit is surely the square root of all evil.

After all, what happened? The market investors who normally would have spent a miserable year watching the Dow drop 500 points, took their medicine in a particularly compressed and brutal form. But the rest of the country suffered little. (So far, anyway.) The system was scared, and it may have purged itself. Interest rates fell. Now the economy can keep on growing.

Under this theory, then, some of the usual beneficial effects of recession have already been realized without most of the long-term difficulty we usually get. We got the gain without the pain. We had our recession and no one came.

October 29, 1987

Share the Freedom Dividend

Buy.

If you can, if you're cautious about it, buy. Because the stock market is more than it seems to be, buy.

As this column is closed on Monday morning, Oct. 16, 1989, the last we know about the stock market is that it plummeted 190 points on Friday.

Buy. Why? For some small reasons.

Buy because the market shakeout will make it more difficult to do leveraged buyouts, which will add some rationality to stock prices, which will reduce market volatility in the long term, which is probably quite good for stock prices.

Buy because while everyone has been snickering about "accounting tricks," the deficit has gone down from 6 percent of the GNP is 1985 to 3 percent today. It is still shrinking. It is a manageable, if unfortunate, situation. Apparently, when no one was looking, the dumped-upon Gramm-Rudman-Hollings legislation has put something of a sloppy brake on the big deficits.

Buy because the GRH budget "sequestration," which has just gone into effect, will probably further cut federal spending. Talk about sloppy. But it can do with a cleaver what ought to have been done with a scalpel.

Buy. Why? For some bigger reasons.

Buy because the idea that it is bad news that "foreigners are buying up America" is a crock. Foreigners are investing in America because the economy and the nation are very healthy. This is the only large, stable, democratic, growing, capitalist market in the world. There are profits to be made here. West Europeans and Japanese are also investing here because

Indicators: *Investment*

A. Foreign investment in the U.S. has risen steadily over time. The composition of foreign investment has shifted away from Canada and toward Japan.

Total Value of U.S. Investment Abroad and Foreign Investment in the U.S. (in Millions of 1988 Dollars)

Year	U.S. Investment Abroad	Foreign Investment in U.S.	Percentage of Total from: Canada	Europe	Japan
1970	$ 217,993	$ 38,225	23.5%	72.0%	1.7%
1975	$ 253,748	$ 56,583	19.3%	67.2%	2.1%
1980	$ 304,842	$117,544	14.6%	65.9%	4.2%
1985	$ 251,842	$201,928	9.3%	65.8%	10.5%
1988	$ 326,900	$328,850	8.3%	65.8%	16.2%
1989	$ 393,436	$400,817	7.9%	65.4%	17.4%
1989	$1,460,600*	$842,800*			

* Estimated current market value of investment.
Note: 1989 figures are in 1989 dollars.

B. The U.S. spends the most money on research and development but, counting only non-defense spending, Japanese and Germans spend higher proportions of their GNP.

1. *Gross Domestic Expenditures on Research and Development, in Billions of Current Pruchasing Power Parity Dollars.*

Year	Japan	W. Germany	U.S.
1982	$27.9	na	$ 81.1
1983	$33.2	$16.6	$ 89.1
1985	$40.1	$20.0	$110.1
1987	$46.1	$22.9	$120.3
1988	na	$24.2	$127.7

2. *Nondefense Research and Development Spending as a Share of GNP*

Year	Percentage of GNP Japan	W. Germany	U.S.
1981	2.3%	2.4%	1.8%
1984	2.5%	2.5%	1.8%
1987	2.8%	2.6%	1.8%

Source notes are on page 399.

3. *U.S. Government Expenditures on Research and Development*

Year	Percentage of GNP Nondefense	Total
1950	0.1%	0.4%
1960	0.3%	1.4%
1970	0.7%	1.5%
1980	0.6%	1.1%
1985	0.4%	1.2%
1990 (est.)	0.4%	1.1%

C. Although the six largest banks in the world are Japanese, the United States dominates the list of the most profitable banks.

Top 10 Banks in the World

By Assets	By Profitability
1. Dai-Ichi	1. Wells Fargo
2. Sumimoto	2. BankAmerica
3. Fuji	3. Banco Bilbao
4. Mitsubishi	Viscaya (Sp.)
5. Sanwa	4. Skandinaviska
6. Industrial	Banken (Swe.)
Bank/Japan	5. NCNB (U.S.)
7. Credit Agri-	6. National Aust.
cole (Fr.)	7. Security Pacific
8. National	8. First Chicago
Bank, Paris	9. Paribas (Fr.)
9. Citicorp	10. Abbey
10. Tokai	National (U.K.)

the U.S. market will grow by 20 million people in the 1990s while their domestic markets will mostly remain stagnant or shrink.

Buy because the idea that America won't be able to compete due to our dumb kids is also a crock. The best universities in the world are in America.

Buy because the idea that we're mortgaging the future of our children is also malarkey. The health research, roads, airports, education and medical care bought by the government will accrue to the benefit of our kids even if those goods and services are bought on credit. Anyway, the standard of living keeps going up, and by any standard of human prosperity, those kids will likely be rich.

Buy. Why? Because of a very big reason.

Money managers too often talk about the stock market in terms of interest rates, dividends and buyouts.

That is monetary myopia. From the point of view of a non-speculating investor, the market is better seen as being about America, and the world, and the future. It is about the sum total of capitalist commercial activity at a time when commerce reflects health, art, transportation, leisure and the state of global politics.

By such criteria, the world is only at the beginning of a great boom.

That boom, in this half-century, has been fueled by surging technology. That surge continues.

The boom has been fed by capitalism, which has expanded enormously, and is now spreading further at the speed of a sell order on a Friday afternoon.

That boom may now reach critical mass because of a new factor: victory. The non-free, non-technological and non-capitalist nations of the world have probably been vanquished. That tends to be reported on the news pages under the heading "Gorbachev" instead of on the business pages under the heading "Growth." But the economic impact of freedom cannot be understated.

We are probably in for a turbulent but potent freedom boom that can make the recent markets look tame.

Freedom yields democratic capitalism and a market economy. A market economy yields wealth. These days, wealth spreads everywhere; that's what "interdependence" and "globalization" mean. We will share in the freedom dividend.

So, if you can, if you're careful, buy. It's the beginning, not the end.
October 18, 1989

And that was before the bullish news about rising fertility in the United States, and the likelihood of more legal immigration, also bullish.

Japanese Buy-out No Sell-out

The Mitsubishi Estate Co. of Japan has purchased the controlling interest in Rockefeller Center in Manhattan. In an earlier incarnation, Mitsubishi Corporation produced airplanes that shot at Americans.

The Sony Corporation, also Japanese, has purchased Columbia Pictures. Columbia owns the patriotic, flag-waving American classic "Mr. Smith Goes to Washington," starring Jimmy Stewart-san.

The Japanese are the publicized lightning rods, but enormous investments are also coming in from Germany, England, and Holland.

It's a clammy feeling. Suppose a latter-day Rip Van Winkle fell asleep on December 8, 1941, and woke up in the fall of 1989. His first hazy thought might well be, "Japan won the war." It's enough to boil the blood of any red-blooded American, isn't it?

Perhaps not. Are foreigners—Japanese and others—really "buying up America"? Is what's happening bad for us? Here are some ideas and facts to consider as the debate gets screechy:

Americans have greater direct investments in Japan than Japanese have in America. (The trend, however, is moving in a pro-Japanese direction.)

It was not very long ago that the buying-up complaints were going the other way. American corporations were being pounded for investing overseas. That was said to be terrible because America needed capital. Now we're getting it.

Real estate is a particularly passive investment. Suppose Mitsubishi buys the office building you work in. As Dorothy Parker asked after the death of Calvin Coolidge, "How can you tell?" What are the Mitzis going to do, ship it to Yokohama? Might they raise your rent? Might they sell the building? Are those things ever done by sweet American landlords?

The same week that Mitz bought Rock, the second richest man in the world, Taikichiro Mori, bought Four Oaks Place, an office-building complex in Houston.

Interesting, New York City has just taken a big commercial hit; Exxon announced that it would move its headquarters to Dallas. And Houston is vastly overbuilt, with much unrented office space. So what are foreign investors saying? That the American economy, even in its problem areas, is still so comparatively healthy that they want to put their money here.

The real estate purchases do not create wealth or jobs. But follow the money. What happens to the $846 million that goes to the Rockefeller heirs? What will they do with the money? Perhaps invest it in American businesses that do create jobs and wealth. Alternatively, they will put the money in banks, and the banks will loan money to domestic investors.

The Sony purchase of Columbia is also a compliment. What have they bought? The right to use their capital to sell the wildly popular American entertainment culture around the world.

And, by the way, America is still doing some buying itself. Ford has just purchased Jaguar, Britain's last independent auto manufacturer.

Perhaps Americans ought to calm down about the buying-up threat and about Japan. By American superpower standards. Japan is still a minor league player—Triple A to be sure, but minor league nonetheless. Japan is a country with half our population, aging rapidly, with a lower standard of living, with archaic agricultural and retail sectors, militarily defenseless, with crowded and exorbitantly expensive housing. But they do have a lot of money.

Follow the foreign money. There is an aspect of this situation that is rarely considered. Historically, no one buys up America. Investors usually only sink in.

Foreigners put their money here. Then they come over here to oversee their investments, or send their sons, or their managers, to do it. Then the investors, or their sons, or their managers, or the wives thereof, become entranced with the barbarian Yankee customs. And some of them settle here. (The son of the founder of Sony is a big investor in Colorado real estate.)

So we get the original capital. Then we get the talent. Then we get the inheritance.

We don't nationalize the investments. We nationalize the investors. Terrible, huh?

November 8, 1989

All the world is a marketplace. Our commerce reflects and influences our culture, demography, attitudes, politics and foreign policy, indeed, all the topics in this volume.

Thus, our immigration policy, discussed earlier, has a potent impact on business: the skill level of our labor force, wage rates, and the size of our domestic market come most quickly to mind. But, when you think of it, immigration policy also shapes our abilities to deal with the booming economies of Asia. Consider again how many Asians have come here recently—from China, Taiwan, Japan, Korea, the Philippines, India, Thailand and Hong Kong. Perhaps Americans will fit right in to the commerce of those booming rim-lands of the Orient. We may end up as the best common denominator of that diverse area. Do not forget: The United States is one of those Pacific rim-lands.

As the world business community globalizes, picture the following

split-screen scenes. An American and a German corporation are each
seeking to expand into Korea. The German corporation engages in
an extensive search for an executive who speaks German and Korean
and knows both cultures. It is a long search and, at its end, not
entirely successful. As the American firm engages in a similar search,
looking for someone who speaks Korean and the corporate home
office language, a young man walks in seeking a job. He has graduated
from a prestigous American university with top grades, has shown
himself to be diligent worker, loves golf, speaks perfect English, can
tell you why the Redskins are really the best team in the NFL, has
Korean parents, and speaks perfect Korean. Demographics influence
commerce.

And commerce influences culture. In late 1989 the United States
and Japan signed an agreement to increase greatly the number of
flights between the two nations. (The new flights will begin in October
1990.) Accordingly, travel to and from Japan and America should
become more convenient and cheaper.

It is a commercial transaction, to be sure. Yet, all the Japanese
pilots will speak English, the international language of aviation. A
majority of the passengers will be Japanese coming to America, rather
than the other way around. There are several reasons for this. The
Japanese government, protectionist in so many other ways, is actively
encouraging overseas tourism, in part to reduce trade surpluses.
America is still the number one tourist draw in all the world. Something
is still going on here that everyone else wants to see, and it's not
just Disneyland on cheap dollars.

What are those additional Japanese tourists going to think when
they get the impact of America firsthand? Particularly, Japanese
women? American women have good jobs. They are first-class citizens.
How long will it take for that idea to flood over Japan? (About two-
thirds of Japanese immigrants to the United States are women.)
At the end of the day, might we not be talking about the even-
greater Americanization of Japan? Can that do anything but help
American business? Commerce influencing culture, influencing
commerce.

Everything influencing everything. That's always true, but rarely
so powerfully apparent as when Saddam Hussein invaded Kuwait in
August of 1990. That was an economic, business, political,
geopolitical, military and cultural story all rolled up into one.

The American role should have reminded everyone who the omni-
power is.

Thanks, Saddam, We Needed That

Some years ago, there was a television commercial for an after-shave lotion that showed a drowsy man slapping himself. Suddenly alert, the slapped man says, "Thanks, I needed that."

If America acts firmly on the Iraqi invasion of Kuwait, then we, and the West, and the world, can soon send that message to Iraqi dictator Saddam Hussein: "Thanks, Saddam, we needed that."

American presidents always want to create what geopoliticians call "a new world order." Few get the opportunity. George Bush has it, because, in the post-Cold War era, the global community needs and wants a new order. We all didn't win the Cold War only to return to Saddam-style gangsterism.

The new order involves peace and stability, unthreatened by thugs. As the Iraq situation shows, only a world led by America can offer this.

A first step on a long path would be to use Hussein as an object lesson. He is being compared to Hitler, an aggressor no one would stop. Wrong. The real analogy should be that dictators do go too far, and they do end up dead.

Ignore the piffle about U.S. military weakness. We don't need American ground troops for this one. Iraq is essentially a land-locked nation with a one-crop economy. An American-organized blockade, with symbolic co-participants, is the way to go.

It can be done. If the Turkish and Saudi oil pipelines are shut down, and the few Iraqi and Kuwaiti ports are sealed, little oil will leave Iraq. By cutting roads and rails, little food will get in. (If necessary, Iraqi airfields and Saddam's palace can be rubble-ized.)

Only America has the military and political ability to put such a blockade in effect. It should go forward unless Saddam gets completely out of Kuwait—pronto. No new-world-order lesson is taught by letting him retain influence in Kuwait and saying aren't we wonderful, we kept him out of Saudi Arabia. That is appeasement.

It's said blockades don't often work. But a big reason they haven't has been obstruction by the Soviet Union. A year ago, we would have properly fretted about a blockade. Would the Soviets react militarily? Would they veto a United Nations plan?

But in Year One of a potential new global order the Soviets are either out of play, or on our side. Accordingly, the legitimizing force of the U.N. Security Council can also be with us.

It can be done. There is a changed domestic political equation. Bush's options are broad. Even liberals are whooping for action.

The public is tough-minded: A CNN call-in survey shows that, by 81 percent to 19 percent, Americans say use military force, if necessary.

It can be done. The petro-crunching 1970s are long gone. Due to conservation and substitutes, oil makes up a lesser share of both our energy budget and our GNP. Huge supplies in our strategic reserves were designed for use in situations like this one.

Will oil turmoil yield recession? It might. No one knows.

We do know that we've had recessions before. We do know that we've survived them all. We do know that sooner or later we'll have one again.

And we should know that a new world order, where bandits can't break the windows, is, long-term, the most bullish news there is. It's worth paying for.

We should also thank Saddam for getting Congress worried enough to stop cutting the defense budget. If our lawmakers stay worried, perhaps we'll thank Saddam for a new American energy policy, including renewed attention to nuclear power and offshore drilling, the oil exploration of the Arctic National Wildlife Refuge, and more energy conservation.

Finally, let's thank Saddam for ending that stuff about America not being No. 1. Is this worldwide crisis going to be solved by energetic Japanese or unified Germans?

It's pretty clear what the global community needs: probably a top cop, but surely a powerful global organizer. Somebody's got to do it. We're the only ones who can.

So for all that, Saddy baby, thanks. We needed this.

August 7, 1990

In the early fall of 1990, talk of recession is in the air. The tumult in the Middle East is only a part of it; after all, we've had eight years of economic growth, which, as they say, has been the longest peace-time economic expansion in American history.

I cannot tell you whether the "looming" recession will materialize, nor can I tell you whether, if it does, it will be mild or severe. I can predict with certainty that if there is even a minuscule downward wiggle in the economy, the television news will be full of sorry scenes in unemployment offices and on food lines.

There is something else I can tell you: In 1990, all facets considered, we are a damn sight better off than we were in 1980 or in 1989. We are more prosperous, and the world is more peaceful than it has been in a very long time. Freedom is in flower.

Things have been going so remarkably well, it is unnerving and unnatural. Where is the operative aspect of the law of nature that demands that people always screw things up? I'm superstitious. Maybe a recession, a mild one, would take the jinx off. It would be a cheap price for the distance we've travelled.

Epilogue: Bet Your Bottom Dollar on It

In 1963, after the assassination of President John Kennedy, the English poet John Masefield wrote a verse in honor of the slain leader. In it he called Americans "a wondrous race."

If Americans were already that then, what are we now—now that we come from every spot in the world, intermarrying, creating a new stock, and somehow making it work as the global omni-power?

Going back further, and looking ahead, my sense of the matter is to be found on the back of the dollar bill. There, on the Great Seal of the United States, are three sayings which spell out the past and the future.

Consider first "Annuit coeptis"; that is, "He has looked with favor upon our beginning." The first two hundred years have indeed been remarkable.

Consider "E pluribus unum"—that is, "One from many." We are surely ahead of where we were in the "many" aspect. We do come from everywhere. Whether we will remain "one," a unified wondrous people remains to be seen, but the evidence cited in this volume seems to me to argue in the positive.

And consider "Novus ordo seclorum." It means, "The new order of the ages."

How arrogant! Less than 4 million people on a sliver of land far from everywhere that mattered, telling the world that they would show the world how it ought to be done.

Who did they think they were? Who did they think Americans would be? What gall!

Did Franklin and Adams and Jefferson (they were the original committee that worked on the Great Seal) know about a global communications grid peddling Americana? Did they know that the United States would become the most powerful military force on earth, and involved all over the earth—back when oceanic isolationism was, and was to be, the wise policy of a fledgling nation for another century and a half? Did they sense that English would become the universal language, even though the world would first see German as the language of science and French as the language of the arts?

Did they know that Americans would come from each continent, back when Franklin was still complaining that German-Americans were too "clannish" and didn't want to speak English? Did they know that Americans would one day write the rock music and win the Nobel prizes? Could they have known that American pluralism would one day become the inevitable global model, and that even the grudging mother nations in Europe would one day come to understand that "one from many" may be the only way the world can work?

Could they have known that if Americans felt that they were, as Lincoln would say, "an almost chosen people," they would have to learn that such a feeling yields not only the fun of grandeur, but the burden of stark responsibility. Could they have even sensed the problems: race, education, crime, values, and politics? Could they perhaps have sensed the unique way we deal with our problems—exaggerating, denouncing, demagoguing—and simultaneously, sometimes causally sometimes not, responding, always imperfectly, frequently successfully?

Perhaps they did, because there it is, right on the dollar bill, and still on the dollar bill—after the traumas of Vietnam and Watergate, after the greening of America, after greed, after stagflation, after not-competitive, after over-stretch, after the poisoning of the planet—after all that and more, there it is: "The new order of the ages."

Half a millennium of American history is ending. And the story of the wondrous race is only reaching the nicest part, a people apart, always complaining, entering now the broad sunlit uplands, fine terrain indeed, and leading the world there.

Notes to Indicators

Ethnicity, p. 47.

A: U.S. Bureau of the Census.

B: Survey by the Roper Organization, March 20–27, 1982.

C: U.S. Bureau of the Census, *Current Population Survey*, Series P-20, 1988; "Star-Crossed," Fran Schumer, *New York Magazine*, April 2, 1990; Dr. Egon Mayer, City University of New York; *From Many Strands: Ethnic and Racial Groups in Contemporary America*, Stanley Lieberson and Mary C. Waters, Russell Sage Foundation, New York, 1988.

D: U.S. National Center for Health Statistics; U.S. Census Bureau; Population Reference Bureau; Brigham Young University; Professor Steven Cohen of Queens College.

Total Fertility Rate (TFR)—Number of children born per woman, aged 15–44, over the course of her fertile years.

All figures are based on data from the 1980 Census except for Jews and Mormons.

Note: Total U.S. TFR in 1989 is 2.00.

Hispanics, p. 60.

A: U.S. Bureau of the Census; Population Reference Bureau.

B: National Assessment of Educational Progress, 1985.

C: Population Reference Bureau.

D-1: U.S. Bureau of the Census, *Current Population Reports*, Series P-60.

D-2: U.S. Bureau of the Census, *Current Population Surveys*; U.S. Department of Labor, unpublished data.

Blacks, p. 67.

A: U.S. Bureau of the Census, *Current Population Surveys.*
See also Education Indicator B for 25–29 year olds (p. 91).

B: U.S. Bureau of the Census, U.S. Census of the Population, *Current Population Reports.*

C: U.S. Bureau of the Census, U.S. Census of the Population, *Current Population Reports.*

D: U.S. Bureau of the Census, *Current Population Reports*, Series P-60.

E: Gallup Polls October 1977, December 1980, January 1984, and December 1989. (Other Indicators with race breakouts appear in Indicators for Ethnicity, Health, and Crime and Drugs.)

Immigration, p. 74.

A1: U.S. Immigration and Naturalization Service (INS), Statistical Yearbooks; *A Count of the Uncountable*, Robert Warren and Jeffrey Passel, *Demography*, August 1987.

Illegal Immigrant Estimates: 2 million were estimated by the Census Bureau to have been living in the U.S. prior to 1980. The Census Bureau estimates that a net additional 200,000 have been entering annually since then.

A2: U.S. INS, Statistical Yearbook; *A Count of the Uncountable*, Robert Warren and Jeffrey Passel, *Demography*, August 1987.

*To prevent double-counting, does not include an estimated 1.9 million former illegal aliens who claimed amnesty under the 1986 Immigration Reform and Control Act. In theory, they are included as earlier illegal aliens.

B: CBS/New York Times Poll, June 1986.

C: INS, Statistical Yearbooks.

Note: The number of immigrants admitted by occupational and skill preferences and their families is limited to 54,000 annually.

D: INS.

E: U.S. Bureau of the Census, *Projections of the Population of the United States, by Age, Sex, and Race: 1988 to 2080* (1989). Current estimates derived from the same projections.

Note: Previous immigration assumes 500,000 net annual immigrants, while new estimates assume 800,000. Previous total fertility rate assumes 1.8 children per woman, while new estimates assume 2.0 children per woman.

Health, p. 82.

A: U.S. National Center for Health Statistics.

B: U.S. National Center for Health Statistics.

C: U.S. Health Care Financing Organization.

D: The World Bank, *World Development Report*; U.N. Food and Agricultural Organization.

E: U.S. National Center for Health Statistics.

F: U.S. National Center for Health Statistics.

Family, p. 85.

A, B, C-1, C-2: U.S. National Center for Health Statistics.

D: Surveys by the Roper Organization for Virginia Slims.

Education, p. 91.

A: Institute of International Education, *Open Doors*, annual issues. Survey is limited to accredited American universities and colleges.

B: U.S. Bureau of the Census, Census of Population, *Current Population Reports*, series P-20.

See also Blacks, Chart A (p. 67).

C: U.S. National Center for Education Statistics; American Federation of Teachers.

D: U.S. Department of Education, National Center for Health Statistics, *Statistics of Public Elementary and Secondary Day Schools*. Rates are for Public Schools.

E: College Entrance Exam Board, *National College Bound Seniors*, annual. Before 1967 the averages included all test takers. Since 1967 only college bound seniors are included.

F: U.S. Department of Education, National Center for Education Statistics, International Assessment of Educational Progress, A *World of Differences*, by Educational Testing Service. Note: Math and science scores range from 0 to 1,000, with a mean of 500 and a standard deviation of 100.

Crime and Drugs, p. 102.

A: U.S. Department of Justice, Bureau of Justice Statistics, *Historical Statistics on Prisoners in State and Federal Institutions, 1955–86.*

B1: Federal Bureau of Investigation, *Uniform Crime Reports,* 1988.

B2: Federal Bureau of Investigation, *Uniform Crime Reports,* 1980–88.

C: U.S. Department of Justice, Bureau of Justice Statistics, *National Crime Surveys,* 1973–88.

Notes: "Personal"—Rape, robbery, assault, personal larceny.

"Violent"—Rape, robbery, or assault.

"Home"—Household crime: Burglary or larceny of a residence or motor vehicle theft.

D: Institute for Social Research, University of Michigan.

Values, p. 116.

A: Gallup Cross-National Values Surveys, 1981.

B: *Fundamental Values: A Global Perspective,* Gallup International Research Institute, 1981–2.

C: *The Gallup Report,* Number 249, 1986.
Question in its Entirety: How proud are you to be an American—very proud, quite proud, not very proud, or not at all proud?

D: Surveys by the National Opinion Research Center, *General Social Surveys,* latest that of February–April, 1989.

E: Surveys by the Gallup Organization for Phi Delta Kappan, latest that of May 5–June 11, 1989; as compiled in *The American Enterprise,* May/June, 1989.

F: Surveys by the Gallup Organization, latest that of January 1, 1990.

Income/Programs, p. 121.

A1: U.S. Bureau of the Census, *Current Population Reports.*

A2: U.S. Bureau of the Census, *Current Population Reports.*

B1: Department of Commerce; Department of the Treasury; compiled in the *Social Security Bulletin,* Annual Statistical Supplement, 1988.

B2: Social Security Administration, *Social Security Bulletin,* February, 1990.

C: Freedom House, *Table of Social and Economic Comparisons,* 1989–90.

*PPP—Estimated Purchasing Power Parities, in constant dollars, based on price comparisons of individual items covering over 150 categories of expenditure.

Poverty/Pensions, p. 127.

A: U.S. Bureau of the Census, *Current Population Reports*. Notes: The Census Bureau changed its definitions of non-cash income after 1986. CPI-U-X1 is a Census Bureau experimental Consumer Price Index for historical comparisons. "Non-cash"-recipient value, institutional benefits not included. Before 1970 noncash benefits were minimal and it can be assumed that the poverty rate was very similar to "cash only" under each calculation.

B: U.S. Bureau of the Census, *Current Population Reports*.

Notes: CPI-U-X1 is an experimental Consumer Price Index for historical comparisons.

"Non-cash"-Recipient value, institutional benefits not included. Before 1970 noncash benefits were minimal.

C: *Social Security and Private Pensions: Providing for Retirement in the Twenty-first Century; Income of the Population 55 or Older*, 1976–1988, U.S. Department of Health and Human Services; as compiled in the Employee Benefit Research Institute Issue Brief. Notes: Pensions are in addition to Social Security; 2010–20 projections are for persons aged 35–44 in 1989.

D: Employment Benefit Research Institute.

*Includes Government pensions but not Social Security.

E: U.S. Bureau of the Census.

Spending, p. 132.

See also Communications Indicator, VCR Ownership.

A1: Bureau of Economic Analysis, *National Income and Product Accounts; Survey of Current Business*, July issues.

Note: Recreation consists of entertainment, reading material, sporting equipment, toys, club membership, and a fairly wide range of "Other" activities.

A2: Look Magazine, *National Auto and Tire Survey*, 1964; Federal Highway Administration, *Nationwide Transportation Survey*, 1984; U.S. Department of Energy, Household Vehicle Energy Consumption, 1989.

A3: U.S. Bureau of the Census, *American Housing Survey, Current Housing Reports*, H–150–87.

A4: Department of Commerce, U.S. Travel and Tourism Agency.

A5: Major League Baseball; National Football League; National Basketball Association.

A6: Electronic Industries Association; Nielsen Media Research.

Housing/Infrastructure, p. 137.

A1: U.S. Bureau of the Census, *Annual Housing Survey*, 1974 and *Current Population Surveys*, to 1987.

A2: U.S. Bureau of the Census, *Annual Housing Survey*, 1974 and *Current Population Surveys*, to 1987.

B: U.S. Bureau of Economic Analysis, *National Income and Product Accounts; Survey of Current Business*, July issues.

Note: Housing Costs include rent, mortgages, taxes, utilities and all other direct costs, but not indirect costs such as home furnishings.

C: Office of Management and Budget, *1991 Budget of the United States Government, Historical Tables*.

Environment, p. 146.

A: U.S. Environmental Protection Agency, *National Air Quality and Emissions Trends Report*.

B: Office of Management and Budget, *1991 Budget of the U.S. Government*, Historical Tables.

C: U.S. Bureau of Economic Analysis, *Survey of Current Business*; Data Resources Institute, Lexington, Mass.

D. U.S. Agency for International Development, *Users Guide to the Office of Population*; Population Crisis Committee.

Demographics, p. 159.

A1: Population Reference Bureau; *U.N. World Population Prospects*, "medium variant"; Maryland Institute for Resource Development.

Total Fertility Rate—lifetime children per woman.

A2: *World Population Prospects*, 1988, United Nations; Population Reference Bureau, *World Population Data Sheet, 1990*.

Eastern Europe—includes Albania, Bulgaria, Czechoslovakia, E. Germany, Hungary, Poland, Romania, Yugoslavia.

Western Europe—includes Austria, Belgium, Denmark, Finland, France, W. Germany, Greece, Iceland, Ireland, Italy, Luxembourg, Netherlands, Norway, Portugal, Spain, Sweden, Switzerland, and the United Kingdom.

B: Population Reference Bureau.

C: *World Population Prospects*, 1988; Population Reference Bureau, *1989 World Data Sheet*.

Communications, p. 207.

A: BIS Mackintosh Limited, London; Television Bureau of Advertising, *Trends in Television*, annual; Electronic Industries Association.

B: "English, English Everywhere," *Newsweek*, November 15, 1982; Robert McCrum, *The Story of English*; *Oxford English Dictionary*.

Note: English speakers outside Great Britain and her ex-colonies (which include Australia, Canada, Hong Kong, New Zealand, South Africa, and the United States).

C: National Football League.

D: Cable News Network.

E: *Variety*. MPAA—Motion Picture Association of America.

USSR, p. 218.

A: ABC News/Washington Post Poll, November 18–23, 1989.

B: Surveys by the Roper Organization, latest that of 1988–9 combined, as compiled by *The American Enterprise*, January/February, 1990.

C: Surveys by CBS/New York Times, latest that of November 26–28, 1989, as compiled in *The American Enterprise*, January/February, 1990. Note: Wording of question varied slightly.

D: Surveys by the Roper Organization, latest that of February, 1990.

Defense, p. 246.

A: Office of Management and Budget, *Historical Tables*; Norman Ornstein, American Enterprise Institute.

B: Gallup News Poll, January 8, 1990.

C: Surveys by the Gallup Organization. Latest that of January 8, 1990.

D: U.S. Agency for International Development, *U.S. Overseas Loans and Grants and Assistance from International Organizations*, annual.

Freedom, p. 278.

A: Freedom House, *Comparative Survey of Freedom*.

B: Freedom House, *Comparative Survey of Freedom*.

C: Surveys by the Roper Organization, latest that of July 15–22, 1989, as compiled in *The American Enterprise*, January/February 1990.

American Politics, p. 297.

A: Times-Mirror & Gallup Study, *The People, Press & Politics*, September 1987.

B: Federal Election Commission, *Reports on Financial Activity*, as compiled in *Vital Statistics on Congress, 1989–90*, American Enterprise Institute.

C1: *Vital Statistics on Congress 1989–90.*

C2: *Congressional Directory; Congressional Quarterly Weekly Report*, as compiled in *Vital Statistics on Congress, 1989–90.*

D: Federal Election Commission, PAC Count press release, issued annually.

Party Politics, p. 311.

A1: Surveys by CBS News/New York Times, latest that of September 12–20, 1989, as compiled in *The American Enterprise*, January/February 1990.

A2: Surveys by CBS News/New York Times, latest that of September 12–20, 1989, as compiled in *The American Enterprise*, January/February 1990.

B1: Statistics of the Presidential and Congressional Elections of November 4, 1980; *Congressional Directory* (1983, 1985); *Congressional Quarterly Weekly Reports*; as compiled in *Vital Statistics on Congress 1989–90*, American Enterprise Institute.

B2: Statistics of the Presidential and Congressional Elections of November 4, 1980; *Congressional Directory* (1983, 1985); *Congressional Quarterly Weekly Reports*; as compiled in *Vital Statistics on Congress 1989–90.*

C: *Congressional Quarterly Weekly Reports*, as compiled in *Vital Statistics on Congress 1989–90.*

D: *Congressional Quarterly; ABC News Elections Systems, 1984–88*; as compiled in The '88 Vote, ABC News. Note: In 1968 and 1980 a third party candidate took more than 5% of the vote.

American Exceptionalism, p. 368.

A1: Gallup International Research Institutes, National Opinion Research Center, International Social Survey Program, 1987–8.

A2: Gallup International Research Institutes, International Research Associates. National Opinion Research Center, International Social Survey Program, 1987–8.

A3: National Opinion Research Center, April 1989.

A4: Zentralarchiv für Empirische Sozialforschung, as compiled in *The American Enterprise*, March/April 1990.

A5: International Social Survey Program, 1986.

A6: National Opinion Research Center, April 1989.

Competitiveness, p. 370.

A: Central Intelligence Agency, *Handbook of Economic Statistics*, 1989.

B: International Monetary Fund, *International Financial Statistics*, as compiled in *The Myth of America's Decline*, by Henry Nau.

C: U.S. National Science Foundation.

D: Organization for Economic Cooperation and Development.

E: Gallup Poll, May 21, 1982.

F: Organization for Economic Cooperation and Development.

Deficits, p. 378.

A1: Office of Management and Budget, *1991 Budget of the U.S. Government*, Historical Tables.

A2: Office of Management and Budget, *1991 Budget of the U.S. Government*, Historical Tables.

B: U.S. Department of Labor, Bureau of Labor Statistics, November 1989.

C: International Monetary Fund, *International Financial Statistics*.

D: Organization for Economic Cooperation and Development, *Economic Outlook*, December 1989.

Note: OECD numbers may vary slightly from OMB numbers due to different methods of calculation. In 1990, OMB updated their estimates in July while OECD did not.

Investment, p. 382.

A: U.S. Bureau of Economic Analysis, *Survey of Current Business*; U.S. Department of State, Planning and Economic Analysis Staff.

B1: Organization for Economic Cooperation and Development.

B2: U.S. Department of Labor, Bureau of Labor Statistics.

B3: Office of Management and Budget, *1991 Budget of the U.S. Government*, Historical Tables.

C: IBCA, Ltd., as compiled in *Business Week*, July 2, 1990.

Acknowledgments

A broad book that takes a swing at a great many topics sooner or later becomes, in addition to being a book, an enterprise.

In the present case, for example, we deal with Scoop Jackson and Jesse Jackson, marriage and intermarriage, fertility and infertility, Supply-side demography and Voodoo demography, the environment and environmentalists, polls and Poles, Israel and Iraq, Japan and Japan-bashing, business and business-bashing, and why baseball is boring, among other things.

Most of these topics have their experts, and sub-experts on sub-topics. Armies of scholars are always trying to figure out ways to measure what they have found difficulty measuring, which is plenty. If you are going to write about these topics, you'd better talk to lots of experts.

And so, acknowledging help for a book that also becomes an enterprise could become an enterprise in itself. That's not going to happen now. Here is a lean and mean cut at it.

The organization that deals with the enterprises in my life is the American Enterprise Institute. For me, it's a great place. I do what I want to do, with access to learned colleagues, and support from skilled staff. I have started and finished three books in the last nine years. I don't think I could have done that without my association with AEI.

AEI went through a very difficult financial time in the early 1980s. It was saved by a dedicated Board of Trustees, by foundation, corporate and individual funders who cared, and by Chris DeMuth, AEI's President since 1986, who has set into motion activity that has reinvigorated AEI. In thanking Chris for his help, I mean, too, to salute the whole idea of the place.

Rather than thanking the whole AEI roster, which deserves it, let me note here those with whom I have the most contact. That list begins with Karlyn Keene, the editor of The American Enterprise (TAE) magazine. She is a peach. Her dedicated gang on TAE includes my friend Kay Smith, the managing editor, who has helped me immeasurably, Jennifer Baggette, who, with Kay, computerized me, Paula Duggan, a brilliant art director, and Mikel Morton, the very capable young woman who is my (shared) assistant/secretary.

The colleagues at AEI with whom I deal most directly and frequently include: Norman Ornstein, Michael Novak, Tony Dolan, Bill Schneider (who often see drafts of my columns and comment upon them, sometimes favorably), and John Makin, Bob Goldwyn, Herb Stein, Irving Kristol, Jeane Kirkpatrick, Walter Berns, Bob Bork, Suzanne Garment, Marvin Kosters, Michael Ledeen, Richard Perle, Josh Muravchik, Allan Gerson, Karl Zinsmeister and Richard Scammon.

There are also substantial thanks due to those who make up the AEI infrastructure. Among these are Executive Vice President David Gerson, Isabelle Davidoff, Evelyn Caldwell, Paul Vizza and Tom Skladony. A special note of thanks goes to Cecil Moore, Louise Wiggins, Fanny Ellison, and Sharrief Tate, who have helped so much to make life pleasant at AEI.

Also: David Drembus, Chris Bryan, Brad Jones, Mark Schmitt, David Zlowe, Christine Carroll and Ellen Corbin.

My research assistant Tevi Troy is a very able, persevering, personable and promising young man. He has labored above and beyond the call of duty.

Over the years I have done a great deal of work with the U.S. Bureau of the Census. The scholars there have been of enormous help to me. They include: Gordon Green, Barbara Boyle Torrey, Godfrey Baldwin, Gregory Spencer, Gregory Robinson, Fred Hollman, Enrique Lamas, Arthur Norton, Campbell Gibson, Signe Wetrogan, Ward Kingkade, Martin O'Connell, Roger Herriot, Nampeo McKinney, Paul Siegel, Mark Littman and Glen King.

Many people from other organizations helped, either generally, or for specific pieces. This is a very partial list, typically excluding those who are cited in the text: Carl Haub and Art Haupt, Population Reference Bureau; Ann Bixby, Social Security Administration; Stephanie Ventura and Robert Heuser, National Center for Health Statistics; Robert Warren and Christine Davidson, Immigration and Naturalization Service; W. Vance Grant, National Center for Education Statistics; Dr. John Ryan, Freedom

House; Jennifer Davis, Dallas Salisbury, Employee Benefit Research Institute; Jonathan Schaffel, DYG (Daniel Yankelovich Group); John Stimson, Wayne Hal, Arlene Easley, and Art Neef, Bureau of Labor Statistics; Michael Ulan, State Department Projections and Economic Analysis Section; Professor Jim Lynch, American University; Joan Johnson and Mike Rand, Bureau of Justice Statistics; Dave Ryan, Environmental Protection Agency; Bonnie Maguire and Gene Puglese, House Immigration Subcommittee; Gary Turner, Federation for American Immigration Reform; Fritz Attaway and Matt Gerson at the Motion Picture Association of America; Kristin Moore of Child Trends, Inc., David Harris, Gary Rubin, and Michelle Anish at the American Jewish Committee; Roland Eggleston and Walter Wisniewski of Radio Free Europe/Radio Liberty; Frank Bean of the University of Texas.

It is often hard, in a work of this breadth, to single out people who helped the author. Some help is specific, for a single article, but much of it happens, by seepage, over the years. Among those who deserve thanks are: Everett Ladd, Seymour Martin Lipset, David Ifshin, Mark Siegel, Tom Kahn, Jack Kemp, Lane Kirkland, Steve Klaidman, Peter Rosenblatt, Harry Middleton, Sar Levitan, Tom Foley, Michael Pack, Pat Moynihan, Peter Bernstein, Lee Rainie, Jerry Buckley, Elizabeth Gross, Roger Rosenblatt, Norman Sherman, Gene Pell, Meyer Rashish, Jerrold Schechter, Michael Schneider, Victoria Sackett, Martin Schramm, Gerald Slater, John Wallach, Jim Woolsey, David Gutmann, Polly Kosko, Eric Breindel, Mary Lou Forbes, Arnaud de Borchgrave, Jim Rosenthal, Herb Moskovitz, Marilyn and Hal Weiner, Tom Mann, Eliot Abrams, Bernie Aronson, Jack Valenti, Hy Bookbinder, Hal Sonnenfeldt, Jerry Jasinowski, Sandy Trowbridge, Harry McPherson, Bruce Porter, Mark Pomar, Norman Podhoretz, Midge Decter, Stephen Hess, David Kusnet, Monica Powell, Josh Darsa, Al From, Will Marshall, Roy Dexheimer, Sonny Dogole, Ervin Duggan, Mel Elfin, Jonathan Schull, Betsy Wood-Schull, Steve Forbes, Carl Gershman, Victor Gilinsky, Norman Abelman, Ed and Jackie Cohen, Steve and Dinah Abelman, Helen and Dorothy Saks, Jim Schmidt, Gene Schull, Elinor Schull, Max Kampelman, David Gergen, James Q. Wilson, John McLaughlin, Richard Schifter, Linda Chavez, Max Greene, Leonard Zax, Joel Swerdlow, Deborah Schull, Mary Louise Caravatti, Al Shanker, Steve Miller, Yona and Hal Rothwax, Peter Hart, Vicki Thomas, Allen Weinstein, Les Lenkowsky, and particularly Penn Kemble.

Particular thanks, for obvious reasons, are tendered to David Hendin, Senior Vice President for United Media, and editors Robert Levy and Gail Robinson for all their help regarding my weekly syndicated column.

The publishers of this book, The Free Press, did remarkable work. The role of Erwin Glikes, President and Publisher of The Free Press, is described in the text. Assistant Editor Noreen O'Connor skillfully stayed on top of the project from day to day. Managing Editor Eileen DeWald provided the push to get this complicated volume on the rails and out of the station.

My immediate family, ranging in age from 90½ to 6½, is not only the well-spring of my life, but a source of never-ending professional help. My father, Judah Wattenberg, who was born in late 1899, offers constructive critiques of my columns and television work. My sister, the actress Rebecca Schull, has been a steady source of support.

My older children, Sarah, Ruth, and Daniel, are great adults now. Ruth and Daniel are also in the public affairs trade and we have vigorous discussions that other people may think are arguments. (Ruth is with the American Federation of Teachers, and knows what I'm up to. She arranged a meeting with some Eastern European teachers' union leaders, one of whom said, "Our young people score better on math than yours. Everybody scores better on math than Americans. But Americans make everything happen and get everything done.") Sarah is a psychiatric social worker and is teaching me about a whole other facet of life.

My youngest child, Rachel, aged 6½, is also quite a teacher. We periodically consider the idea of writing a children's book together.

My wife, Diane, not only presides over our enterprise, but is my most regular, most important critic, and my best friend.

We all seem to be flourishing in our own way in this first universal nation. God willing, that will continue.

Washington, D.C.
August 1990

Index